LABOR AND EMPLOYMENT
RELATIONS ASSOCIATION SERIES

Employment and Disability: Issues, Innovations, and Opportunities

Edited By

Susanne M. Bruyère

First Edition
ISBN 978-0-913447-18-5
Price: $34.95

LABOR AND EMPLOYMENT RELATIONS ASSOCIATION SERIES

LERA *Proceedings of the Annual Meeting* (published online annually, in the fall)

LERA *Annual Research Volume* (published annually, in the summer/fall)

LERA Online Membership Directory (updated daily, member/subscriber access only)

LERA *Labor and Employment Law News* (published online each quarter)

LERA *Perspectives on Work* (published annually, in the fall)

Information regarding membership, subscriptions, meetings, publications, and general affairs of the LERA can be found at the Association website at www.leraweb.org. Members can make changes to their member records, including contact information, affiliations, and preferences, by accessing the online directory at the website or by contacting the LERA national office.

LABOR AND EMPLOYMENT RELATIONS ASSOCIATION
University of Illinois at Urbana-Champaign
School of Labor and Employment Relations
121 Labor and Employment Relations Building
504 East Armory Ave., MC-504
Champaign, IL 61820
Telephone: 217/333-0072 Fax: 217/265-5130
Website: www.leraweb.org
E-mail: LERAoffice@illinois.edu

Acknowledgments

I would like to thank the many people who have contributed to make this volume possible. First and foremost, a sincere thanks to Ariel Avgar, associate professor and associate dean of outreach in the Cornell University ILR School, who in his role as editor of the LERA annual research series first proposed to me the idea of a volume with a focus on employment and disability. A sincere thanks as well to Peggy Currid, whose editorial assistance has added immeasurably to the final product in clarity and editorial accuracy!

This volume is the collective contribution of the approximately two dozen individual authors who have generously given their effort and expertise to the 12 chapters included here. The transdisciplinary focus both within and across chapters has offered a richness of perspectives that we believe markedly enhances the value of this volume. I am very grateful to each of you for your willingness to share your significant insights and your valuable time in writing each of these chapters. A thanks as well to my colleague and friend, Harry Katz, former ILR School dean and LERA president, for his willingness to write the foreword.

Our author team was afforded the added advantage to further inform and curate our respective chapters through the generosity of many individuals who provided us the benefit of their review and feedback. Although these reviewers are named in each chapter, I would like to personally acknowledge each of them for their contribution to the quality of this volume. Sincere thanks to

- Ruth Allison, senior research associate, TransCen
- Marjorie Baldwin, professor of economics, Arizona State University
- Linda Batiste, principal consultant/legislative specialist, Job Accommodation Network
- Melissa Bjelland, research associate, Cornell University
- Ruth Brannon, (retired) director, Office of Research Sciences, National Institute on Disability, Independent Living, and Rehabilitation Research
- Dexter Brooks, associate director, Office of Federal Operations, US Equal Employment Opportunity Commission
- Alex Bryson, professor of quantitative social science, University College London
- John Budd, professor of work and organizations, University of Minnesota
- Adrienne Colella, James W. McFarland Distinguished Chair of Business, Tulane University
- Sherrill Curtis, Curtis Consulting Group
- Andrew Eddy, Untapped Group

- Hank Farber, Hughes-Rogers Professor of Economics, Princeton University
- Michael Fieldhouse, DXC Technology
- Bill Fowler, veterans employment representative, New York State Department of Labor
- Tim Goldstein, neurodiverse communication specialist
- Jim Gross, professor of labor relations, law, and history, Cornell University
- Barry Hirsch, professor and W.J. Usery Chair of the America Workplace, Georgia State University
- Anne Hirsh, co-director, Job Accommodation Network
- Jacqueline Hyatt, senior research associate, TransCen
- Edgar Johnson, staffing consultant, Workforce Recruitment and Retention, Cornell University
- David Jones, workforce analyst, US Department of Labor Employment and Training Administration
- Melanie Jones, professor of economics, Cardiff University
- Kari Kelly, founder and CEO, Atypical Workplace
- Wilma Liebman, former chair, National Labor Relations Board
- Adam Litwin, associate professor of industrial and labor relations, Cornell University ILR School
- Sophie Mitra, professor of economics, Fordham University
- Daniel Mont, co-president and co-founder, Center for Inclusive Policy
- Barbara Murray, (retired) senior disability consultant, International Labour Organisation
- Lou Orslene, co-director, Job Accommodation Network
- Julia Pollack, doctoral fellow, RAND Corporation
- Marcia Scheiner, president, Integrate Advisors
- Marie Strahan, independent consultant, former federal career executive and member of the Kansas Bar
- Natalie Veeney, diversity program manager, US Office of Personnel Management
- Jose Velasco, vice president of products and innovation, SAP
- Paula Voos, professor of labor studies and employment relations, Rutgers University
- Tina Williams, deputy director, Office of Federal Contract Compliance Programs, US Department of Labor
- Angela Winfield, associate vice president for inclusion and workforce diversity, Cornell University

In addition, we are grateful to James McCaffrey, BTL Investments, for his support of Cornell efforts contributing to the completion of the veterans' chapter. We want to also acknowledge Moriah Willow, social scientist and statistician, US Equal Employment Opportunity Commission, for his assistance in obtaining and working with data used in the research described in two of these chapters.

Finally, I want to acknowledge the significant contribution of Sara VanLooy, publications specialist with the Yang–Tan Institute at Cornell, for significant efforts in helping us manage the time line for moving this publication through the writing and editing process, for proofing and editing all of the chapters before they went to the publisher, and in contributing to several chapters as a co-author. Your partnership in this process has been invaluable!

A sincere thanks to all of you, for your efforts that enabled us to bring together a collection of expertise and information that will hopefully inform and inspire future readers to join in needed action to improve employment outcomes for individuals with disabilities, both nationally and around the world.

Contents

Foreword

Harry C. Katz
Cornell University

Few would quarrel with the view that social and private policies should strive to improve economic outcomes and promote more inclusive practices for the more than 15% of the world's population that has a disability. The real challenge is identifying how to achieve those objectives. This volume goes a long way in doing so.

This new research volume from the Labor and Employment Relations Association (LERA) offers a rich collection of papers providing both new research and thorough assessment of what has been learned from prior research and organizational practices. In doing so, this volume provides a sorely needed update to *New Approaches to Disability in the Workplace*, the LERA volume on related issues published 20 years ago, edited by Terry Thomason, John F. Burton Jr., and Douglas Hyatt.

There has been much progress over those 20 years in the economic status of individuals with disabilities and with efforts to more fully eliminate the discrimination and harassment they often face. But as this new volume shows, there is much room for further improvement. For example, people with disabilities are half as likely to be in the labor force and earn on average only 63% as much as others (in the United States). More hopeful are the recent efforts of organizations to make use of digital technology to create more opportunities for people with disabilities.

As with many economic and social outcomes in today's world, there is a wide diversity of experience. On the positive side, this volume includes helpful lessons from a number of public and private organizations that have adopted creative approaches. At the same time, the enforcement of well-meaning public policies is often shown to be deficient, and new approaches regularly fail to reach individuals who have limited means.

Let's hope that the next LERA volume covering the work experiences of people who have disabilities will reveal that the many helpful insights provided in this volume were taken seriously.

Harry C. Katz is Jack Sheinkman Professor and director of the Scheinman Institute on Conflict Resolution at the Cornell University ILR School. He is also president-elect of the International Labor and Employment Relations Association and a past president of the Labor and Employment Relations Association.

Introduction

Susanne M. Bruyère
Cornell University

IMPORTANCE OF THE ISSUE

It is timely to have a research volume of the Labor and Employment Relations Association (LERA) focusing on the challenges and opportunities around employment and individuals with disabilities in the United States and globally. It has been 20 years since the 1998 LERA volume titled *New Approaches to Disability in the Workplace*, edited by Terry Thomason, John Burton Jr., and Douglas Hyatt. was published. That work provided an excellent overview of the importance of a focus on disability and the workplace; myths about the ability of people with disabilities to work; and the role of government, unions, and workplace supports that can assist in supporting individuals—when disability does occur—to facilitate timely return to work.

A great deal has occurred in both the field of disability and the world of work since that volume was published. Countries have begun to collect information about disability in their census surveys, improving our understanding of the sheer size of this population. Around the world, nations are implementing legislation and regulations that provide individuals with disabilities improved access to education, employment, and public services, as well as to civil society as a whole. The world of work is changing as well: Talent is being drawn from new places, and the delivery of products and services increasingly relies on technology.

This chapter presents a preliminary overview of some of the trends that make this topic important, as well as a brief description of how this volume as a whole is designed. It is our hope that the contents will further inform readers about both the challenges that these changes present and how in the United States and other countries, businesses are responding proactively to move the needle on employment disparities for individuals with disabilities.

Prevalence and Continuing Employment Disparities

A 2011 report issued by the World Health Organization and the World Bank estimated that people with disabilities make up 15% of the world's population—or one billion people (World Health Organization and World Bank 2011). While that may already seem like a large number, these figures are thought to be significant *underestimates* of the actual proportion of the global population that people with disabilities represent. This is because national census surveys often do not have good ways to identify individuals with disabilities, and people with disabilities predominantly reside in rural areas where census data collection might not reach, particularly in low- and middle-income countries (World Health Organization and World Bank 2011).

A global focus on disability continues to be important not only because of the sheer size of the population but also because employment continues to be a critical area of inequality for people with disabilities around the world. In many countries, data on the workforce participation rates of people with disabilities are not available (World Health Organization and World Bank 2011). However, in countries where such data are available, surveys show that, on average, people with disabilities are half as likely as their nondisabled peers to be in the labor force. For example, in the United States in 2017, 37% of working-age people with disabilities were in the labor force compared with 79% of people without disabilities (Erickson, Lee, and von Schrader 2017). These labor force participation disparities lead to lower median household income rates and a higher proportion of individuals with disabilities living in poverty. In 2017, the median household income for individuals with disabilities in the United States was $45,500 compared with $71,000 for households that have no working-age members with disabilities (Erickson, Lee, and von Schrader 2017). As a result, a significantly higher proportion of people with disabilities are living in poverty: 26%, compared with 10% of those without disabilities (Erickson, Lee, and von Schrader 2017).

These disparities illustrate the continued importance of a focus on disability, particularly as it relates to employment participation. In this volume, we will talk about the myriad ways that governments and employers are focusing on these issues both domestically and globally, and the assessments to date of the effectiveness of these approaches.

Regulatory Frameworks Addressing Employment Disparities

Improved documentation of the status of people with disabilities and increased global awareness led to the 2008 passage of the United Nations Convention on the Rights of Individuals with Disabilities (UNCRPD) (United Nations, no date). The UNCRPD was the first binding international human rights treaty to codify the rights of people with disabilities on a global scale. Adopted by the General Assembly in December 2006, the UNCRPD currently has 161 signatories and 177 ratifying parties (UN Enable 2019). The Convention covers a broad array of human rights topics, including an explicit right to work and related rights pertaining to nondiscrimination, awareness raising, education and training, rehabilitation, accessibility, and quality of life. While many countries such as the United States were already at the forefront of implementing inclusive disability policies, for people with disabilities in many of the other 177 countries ratifying to date, the impact has been a resulting revision of laws, policies, programs, and services that are incrementally bringing about needed changes in line with the Convention's principles and requirements. The UNCRPD is also a powerful international legal instrument that contains specific mandates for states parties to facilitate increased responsibilities and buy-in by business, such as increasing employer awareness, building incentives into regulations, and mandating labor market–driven skills development policies and practices (Saleh and Bruyère 2018).

In the United States, an example of recent regulations to improve employment outcomes for individuals with disabilities is the Office of Federal Contract Compliance Programs (OFCCP) final rule, changing the regulations implementing Section 503 of the Rehabilitation Act of 1973 (as amended). The regulations went into effect in March 2014, setting new nondiscrimination and affirmative action requirements for federal contractors and subcontractors related to the employment of qualified individuals with disabilities. For example, contractors now are required to offer applicants and employees the opportunity to self-identify as a person with a disability and to use the data collected to understand their progress toward a 7% utilization goal for employment of individuals with disabilities (US Department of Labor, no date). There is limited information available on how organizations are implementing the recent regulations and what successes or challenges they are encountering, but in this volume we provide some preliminary information about research done to date to assess the impact of these new regulations.

Changing Nature of Work and the Workplace

People with disabilities are an important group to include when considering the changing nature of work. Digital innovation is touching every aspect of our lives and every sector of the economy. It provides previously unavailable access to knowledge, products, services, talent, and organizational relationships. Technology enables improved matching between available labor and labor markets around the world. Digital talent platforms can further improve matchmaking between workers and jobs, ultimately raising labor participation rates by previously marginalized groups such as individuals with disabilities (Manyika 2017).

The "gig economy" is significant and growing fast, as evidenced by the number of new companies (Hathaway and Muro 2016). In principle, the gig economy might offer increased access to the labor market for people in rural areas, people with transportation issues, or people with mobility disabilities. Flexible working arrangements and digital platforms enable organizations to meet current and anticipated challenges by giving employees choices in how and where they work; this often also accommodates previously marginalized workers, widens the labor pool, and creates needed business agility (Future of Work Institute 2012). Although, in theory, the flexibility offered by flex place and flex time may be a boon, perhaps increasing employment opportunities for people with disabilities, the possibility of new inequities being created will also need to be vigilantly monitored. In addition, more than half of the world's population is still offline, limiting the potential for those most needing improved access to employment opportunities (Manyika 2017).

For people with disabilities, the digital divide has been historically significant and is still very real. The cost and accessibility of digital products and services have been long-standing issues for people with disabilities. However, decreases in the cost of technology and increasing awareness of the need for inclusive design suggest that the benefits of the revolution in information and communications technology may be becoming accessible to people with disabilities (Raja 2016).

In addition, while remote work offers new employment opportunities, there are inherent risks as well (Hodgson 2016). It is often presumed that stamina, travel issues, and physical access concerns mean that individuals with disabilities will be better served by working at home, perhaps as independent contractors or entrepreneurs. While certainly some individuals may be advantaged by the opportunity for remote work and fewer or flexible work hours, routinely relegating these type of arrangements to people with disabilities may lead to longer-term inequities in pay and advancement opportunities, as well as limiting their opportunities for community participation and social inclusion (Baker, Moon, and Ward 2006). Proactive economic development and workplace policies can use new technologies to create opportunities for training and work while being mindful of unintended inequities.

CONTENTS OF THIS VOLUME

In light of the continuing employment disparities and the rapidly changing workplace resulting from globalization and technology intensification, we have selected topics for this volume to illuminate continuing and emerging issues and opportunities for improving employment outcomes for individuals with disabilities. The remainder of this introductory chapter provides an overview of the contents of this volume, which further explores facets of some of these trends by detailing results from a variety of related studies. The 12 chapters focus on a wide variety of employment and disability-related topics such as private and federal sector employer response to regulatory requirements for affirmative hiring of people with disabilities, and specific issues needing attention to facilitate individuals with the experience of specific conditions, such as behavioral disorders and autism. Brief highlights of the work to come follow.

In Chapter 1, "US Employment and Disability Policy Framework: Competing Legislative Priorities, Challenges, and Strategies," Matthew Saleh, Thomas Golden, and Ellice Switzer provide an overview of the evolution of US employment and disability policy over the past century. US employment and disability legislation evolved from early policies that supported and protected war veterans and civil servants with disabilities. This legislative framework subsequently grew to include workers compensation and protections, social insurance and means-tested entitlements, a state–federal partnership for vocational rehabilitation, workforce development and other community-based services and supports, civil rights employment protections, and more. However, these policies came out of many different contexts, and they reflect divergent perspectives on and about disability. The authors discuss the relationship between various laws and the competing legislative priorities that emerged during different eras of US policy development. Three areas where these competing priorities are most evident are reviewed: (1) medical versus social model definitions of disability under different policy agendas; (2) discontinuities in Social Security eligibility, disability determinations, and return-to-work initiatives; and (3) the persistence of sheltered employment in the wake of competitive integrated employment reforms and Employment First initiatives. The authors introduce these competing priorities with a brief historical overview of relevant laws and the policy contexts within which they arose. They then turn to contemporary US employment and disability policy, lingering contradictions, and the efforts needed going forward to navigate policy contradictions to reduce employment disparities for people with disabilities.

Employer policies and practices that reduce discrimination and improve inclusion are essential pathways to the full employment of individuals with disabilities. In Chapter 2, "Minimizing Discrimination and Maximizing Inclusion: Lessons from the Federal Workforce and Federal Subcontractors," Hassan Enayati, Sarah von Schrader, William Erickson, and Susanne Bruyère focus on the evidence of employer best practices from two sectors: the federal government and federal subcontractors. These employers' relative share of the total US workforce, their diversity in occupational representation, the disability employment regulatory requirements that apply to them, and the data reporting standards they are required to meet all afford an opportunity to carefully examine the relationship between the employment of individuals with disabilities and employer policies and practices. The authors provide an overview of the key employment policies and regulations that affect the federal workforce and federal subcontractors. This chapter then describes the level, trends, and types of employment observed for employees with disabilities in these sectors and draws from a range of sources to identify lessons learned from the federal workforce and subcontractors. An analysis of the Federal Employee Viewpoint Survey summarizes where disparities exist in federal workplace experiences and perspectives by disability status. The researchers discuss how agency practices may moderate these disparities, as well as how specific practices relate to observed employment outcomes for individuals with disabilities. Using federal contractor compliance reviews and United States Equal Employment Opportunity Commission charge data, Enayati et al. highlight the characteristics of employers who are able to comply with equal employment opportunity law, predictors of discrimination violations, and predictors of a charge. Finally, they discuss the implications of these best practices for labor relations, mediation/arbitration professionals, and conflict resolution specialists.

The employment of people with disabilities has received significant attention, but little is known about how unions affect their employment experiences. To address this, in Chapter 3, "Disability and the Unionized Workplace," Mason Ameri, Mohammed Ali, Lisa Schur, and Douglas Kruse analyze monthly Current Population Survey data from 2009 through 2017 and find that the unionization rate declined more rapidly among employees with disabilities. The authors report that the results are not due to demographic or occupational factors but to the lower rate at which people with disabilities are hired into unionized jobs. The results suggest that the lower hiring rate more than offsets the greater job retention of unionized workers with disabilities. Given that employers generally control hiring, the authors report that it therefore appears employers are particularly reluctant to hire people with disabilities into jobs with union protections. Overall, in the union context, workers with disabilities appear more likely to be "last hired" but less likely to be "first fired." The authors also find that the union wage premium for workers with disabilities is greater than the premium for workers without disabilities, and it more than offsets the disability pay gap among non-union workers. The disability pay gap remains but is only half as large among union workers. The exploratory data presented in this chapter reveal that both union membership and disability status increase the likelihood of requesting accommodations, supporting the voice model of unions. Overall, the results indicate that unions raise wages, decrease pay disparities, and increase job retention for workers with disabilities, but unionized positions are becoming less available to workers with disabilities.

Reasonable accommodation is a legal obligation for most employers and it is good business practice to offer needed supports. However, employers struggle with this, as evidenced by the high rate of discrimination charges that cite reasonable accommodation as an issue. Chapter 4, "Creating an Accommodating Workplace: Encouraging Disability Disclosure and Managing Reasonable Accommodation Requests," by Sarah von Schrader, LaWanda Cook, and Wendy Strobel Gower, provides an overview of the legal requirements and the potential pitfalls in the practical implementation of accommodation in the workplace. From the perspective of the employee with a disability, perhaps the greatest barrier to accommodation is the need to disclose a disability to the employer. von Schrader et al. summarize some of the key factors in making that decision and the risks involved. Then, using data from the 2012 Current Population Survey Disability Supplement, the authors describe both the prevalence and correlates of accommodation requests reported and how those may inform practice around accommodation. To better understand where conflicts may arise in the accommodation process, they review a summary of disability discrimination charges that cite failure to accommodate as an issue. The chapter ends by highlighting how employers can develop policy and practice to support accommodation in the process and limit the employee relations issues that all too commonly arise.

Chapter 5, "Unwelcoming Workplaces: Bullying and Harassment of Employees with Disabilities," by LaWanda Cook, Sarah von Schrader, Valerie Malzer, and Jennifer Mimno, examines workplace bullying and harassment issues and their resultant impact on people with disabilities. There is growing awareness of ways that bullying moves beyond the schoolyard to regularly impact people at work—especially those who are members of historically marginalized groups. As Americans live and work longer, more people will develop or acquire a disability during their working years. In addition, as baby boomers leave the workforce, employers will need to rely on available workers, including individuals with disabilities, to replace them. Understanding the workplace bullying experienced by individuals with disabilities will be essential as the US workforce becomes increasingly diverse and as workplace expectations become increasingly demanding. This chapter features findings from two Cornell University workplace studies—one about work–life balance among people with disabilities and another that examines discrimination charges that cite harassment under the Americans with Disabilities Act. The authors highlight the lived experience of bullying targets, including bullying that centered on identities other than, or in intersection with, disability. Cook et al. explain how and when anti-harassment law applies to disability-related bullying, discuss the rights of targeted people with disabilities, and consider the role of organizational leadership in supporting employee wellness and discouraging and appropriately addressing bullying. They conclude with specific suggestions for creating healthier, more welcoming and inclusive workplaces.

We turn our focus on two groups that employers are increasingly considering as sources of new labor force talent in Chapters 6 and 7. In Chapter 6, "Welcoming (All) Veterans into Our Workplaces: The Employment of Veterans with Disabilities," Hannah Rudstam, James Whitcomb, and Lorin Obler focus on employment opportunities and remaining challenges for veterans, especially those with disabilities. Over the past two decades, employers have been eager to welcome veterans into their workforce, making special efforts to hire and retain veteran employees. Veterans bring a lot to a workplace: skills, discipline, loyalty, and teamwork. This is as true for veterans with service-connected disabilities as it is for others. Unfortunately, for the roughly one quarter of veterans with a service-connected disability, the "Veterans Are Welcome" banners are not applicable. The authors discuss how employment relations practitioners are positioned to play a key role in mediating employment outcomes for veterans with disabilities. Being effective in this role involves understanding the broad range of employment issues facing veterans with disabilities, and this chapter provides information that will equip labor and employment relations (LER) practitioners with the human, legal, and practical knowledge they need. Human issues focus on the daily struggles faced by veterans with disabilities and the implications of these struggles for workplace policies. Legal issues revolve around the laws and programs for veterans with disabilities. Finally, practical considerations focus on creating workplace cultures and sustainable practices that truly welcome all veterans, including those with disabilities.

Youth represent a significant portion of the population of individuals with disabilities. In Chapter 7, "Youth with Disabilities: A Human Resource for the 21st-Century Workforce," Thomas Golden, Kelly Clark, and Catherine Fowler discuss how tapping into this population has been a fruitful strategy for many employers. Companies have successfully trained, hired, and/or placed young people to achieve significant success in adding to their much-needed labor pool. Employers need to understand the context that impacts employment-related training and engagement in work for this young population in order to effectively tailor their programs and approach to this talented workforce. This chapter provides a broad overview of factors related to positive employment outcomes for youth with disabilities. The authors present case examples from US and international firms that have successfully trained, recruited, and hired youth with disabilities, with perspectives on their contributions to company profitability and the overall work environment. The authors also discuss efforts by the US government to promote an environment to support employment outcomes for youth with disabilities that reinforce and complement employer efforts toward improving employment of youth with disabilities.

Mental illness is one of the largest categories of disability in workplaces both within the United States and globally. In Chapter 8, "Mental Illness and Employment: Understanding a Major Disability Population in the US Workforce," Hannah Rudstam, Hsiao-Ying (Vicki) Chang, and Hassan Enayati discuss employment issues specific to this population and how LER professionals can assist in improving employment outcomes. Despite some improvements over the past two decades, people with mental illness continue to face significant discrimination at work and are confronted by a unique set of diversity/inclusion challenges in the workplace. People with mental illnesses are more likely than people with other disabilities to be blamed for their condition. Employers continue to hold many misperceptions that fuel workplace discrimination, such as a fear of increased workplace violence, disruptions in productivity, and negative interactions with customers. Employers also struggle with understanding how to accommodate workers with mental illness. Bringing evidence to counteract these misperceptions can be challenging. Much research has been based on individuals with serious mental illness. The wide range of diagnoses and symptom severity among people in the workplace makes it difficult to draw conclusions from these studies. Prior literature has tended to focus narrowly on how to prevent mental illness in the workplace by, for example, managing job stress or avoiding hiring applicants who disclose mental illnesses. This article highlights the role that LER professionals can play to address and alleviate this discrimination. It provides information to enhance LER practitioners' understanding of mental illness from a diversity/inclusion perspective, focusing on mental illness as a source of employment discrimination. The authors identify key points for LER practitioners regarding workplace discrimination faced by applicants and workers with mental illness. For each point, they discuss relevant research and recommend actions that LER practitioners can take to be more effective in addressing workplace discrimination faced by this very large group of people with disabilities in the workplace.

The technology industry comprises employers who offer a high concentration of positions in science, technology, engineering, and mathematics, or STEM, fields. In Chapter 9, "Employment in High-Tech Industries: What Does It Mean for People with Disabilities?," William Erickson, Sara VanLooy, and Wendy Strobel Gower describe the challenges of improving employment outcomes for individvuals with disabilities in these sectors. The authors examine the state of employment for people with disabilities within and outside the tech industry. Following a discussion of existing definitions and approaches, Erickson et al. classify industries as core high-tech, health high-tech, and non-high-tech industries. Using data from the United States Census Bureau's American Community Survey, the authors explore the employment of persons with disabilities in high-tech sectors relative to other industries. Given the importance of the education pipeline that moves individuals toward STEM employment, they also examine the role that postsecondary education has in careers within high-tech industries, focusing on young, recent college graduates in STEM and non-STEM fields. They discuss the implications of these results for the education, hiring, and employment of persons with disabilities. The chapter further highlights the challenges that people with disabilities face in pursuing careers in high-tech/STEM fields and the implications for LER professionals.

One of the most significant barriers to positive employment outcomes for individuals with disabilities has been stigma and stereotypes about their capabilities. In Chapter 10, "Autism at Work: Targeted Hiring Initiatives and What We Can Learn for Other Groups," Susanne Bruyère discusses the challenges for neurodiverse individuals, particularly those with autism, in equitable access to employment opportunities and emerging employer initiatives. Recently, employers in technology-intensive sectors have initiated targeted hiring initiatives for autistic people that offer a different perspective. These companies are trying to understand how to use the unique characteristics of this group to contribute to particular industry job needs. The chapter provides background information on autism, examples of specific programs and company efforts, considerations around such specialized hiring programs, and implications for future affirmative hiring initiatives for targeted populations with specific disabilities. Employment statistics about autistic people are used to illustrate and confirm past employment disparities and the early evolution of interest in targeting this group for special hiring initiatives. The authors conclude with an overview of the lessons that have been learned to date and their implications for these types of programs and similar future proactive hiring initiatives for other disability populations.

Disability is a global phenomenon, and many individuals with disabilities live on the margins of society worldwide, especially with regard to access to employment, education, healthcare, and other services. In Chapter 11, "Global Perspectives on Employment for People with Disabilities," Matthew Saleh talks about how disability intersects with other demographic factors to contribute to social exclusion. Globally, 88% of individuals with disabilities live in the world's poorest countries, while 90% live in rural areas. Meanwhile, lesser access to employment opportunities leads to higher prevalence of poverty and a lower standard of living. Because cultural attitudes toward disability differ significantly across nations and regions (often compounded by complex gender, ethnic, geographic, and other sociodemographic identities), Saleh discusses "thematic barriers" to employment globally, with reference to specific nation-level examples. The author begins with an overview of the global perspective, including worldwide prevalence rates, employment rates, economic statuses, educational opportunities and disparities, and the global regulatory environment. He then discusses global disability policy generally in the 2008 UN Convention on the Rights of Persons with Disabilities, Article 27 (Work and Employment) and additional relevant international treaties, case law, and initiatives. Saleh also explores specific thematic barriers and impediments to employment and promising trends, practices, and approaches to addressing these issues.

Many low- and middle-income countries do not provide additional benefits for people with disabilities, relying instead on traditional means-testing assessment, with an income-based poverty line for eligibility. In Chapter 12, "Impact of Cash Transfers on Access to Employment of People with Disabilities," Ola Abu Alghaib discusses the limitations of current approaches across country boundaries. Allocating fixed benefits to all beneficiaries may not reflect the real levels of people with disabilities' needs, particularly since most face additional disability-related costs. As a result, these programs do not encourage or enable people with disabilities to gain economic independence by participating in the workforce. Even in high-income countries that offer pro-employment cash transfer schemes for disability, challenges to economic empowerment remain, such as overwhelming administrative paperwork and (in)accessibility of the physical environment. This chapter discusses how existing cash transfer programs and practices in high- and low-/middle-income countries also allow people with disabilities to participate in gainful employment. Over the past decade, high-income countries have increasingly embraced social protection schemes such as cash transfer programs as a pro-employment mechanism for people with disabilities, in part due to research and evidence reported in the influential 2015 UN Special Rapporteur on the Rights of Persons with Disabilities. The author presents different modalities of disability benefits being operated in Europe and various low- and middle-income countries. For example, the UK schemes illustrate the range of benefits and services that can be provided to people with disabilities within a twin-track social protection framework that addresses social vulnerability while also offering economic protection. By contrast, many low- and middle-income countries retain a narrow safety-net conception of social protection for addressing disability. Though a few countries are moving toward a more comprehensive approach that looks beyond poverty alleviation, disability benefits are mostly still restricted to people with disabilities who are assessed as being unable to work. The chapter closes with suggestions on how LER professionals globally can help to alleviate administrative and accessibility costs for people with disabilities.

In the volume's conclusion, "The Way Forward: Implications for Labor and Employment Professionals and the Future Workplace," Susanne Bruyère, draws together the conclusions across the volume to offer a multi-layered distillation of implications for public policy, employers, employment and disability community service supports, human resources practice, and workplace professionals in LER and other fields. Developing a strong future labor force will require concerted efforts to enhance vocational preparation for youth, as well as the development of strategies for reskilling the current workforce. Grassroots-level efforts can be supported in a larger framework that includes public policies such as vocational training and workforce development initiatives, as well as social welfare safety nets.

Multinationals need to increase awareness of new regulations emerging globally and their implications for workplace practice. In the United States, reinvigorated disability-focused regulations in both the federal workforce and the federal contractor community are requiring organizations to create better metrics and analytics to document disability equity in their practices. Affirmative hiring initiatives for neurodiverse individuals, as well as increasing awareness of the employer's role around workforce mental health and returning veterans, heighten the need for education and enhanced awareness of the employer's role in creating and implementing policies and practices that protect individual privacy while encouraging access to needed accommodations. Policy makers, educational institutions, employers, community workforce development organizations, and individual workplace professionals each have a role to play in addressing the employment inequities for individuals with disabilities that have been sustained for far too long.

IN CONCLUSION

It is our hope that the information provided in these chapters, and collectively across this LERA volume, will contribute to raising awareness of the issues confronting equitable access to full workforce participation for people with disabilities. Regulatory changes occurring both in the United States and globally, as well as emerging corporate initiatives to facilitate inclusion of diverse groups not previously included in the labor force, offer potential cause for optimism that change is occurring. Labor and employment relations professionals have a significant role that they can play in making this happen.

The authors would like to thank the many individuals who afforded us the benefit of their expertise and time in reviewing this work, who are acknowledged separately in each chapter.

REFERENCES

Baker, P., N. Moon, and A. Ward. 2006. "Virtual Exclusion and Telework: Barriers and Opportunities of Technocentric Workplace Accommodation Policy." *Work: Journal of Prevention, Assessment & Rehabilitation* 27 (4): 421–430.

Erickson, W., C. Lee, and S. von Schrader. 2017. "Disability Statistics from the American Community Survey (ACS)." Ithaca, NY: Cornell University Yang-Tan Institute on Employment and Disability. http://www.disabilitystatistics.org

Future of Work Institute. 2012. "The Benefits of Flexible Working Arrangements: A Future of Work Report." London, UK: Hot Spots Movement. http://bit.ly/2W3NAsK

Hathaway, I., and M. Muro. 2016. "Tracking the Gig Economy: New Numbers." Washington, DC: Brookings Institute. https://brook.gs/2W40E1q

Hodgson, G. 2016. "The Future of Work in the Twenty-First Century." *Journal of Economic Issues* 50 (1): 197–216. doi:10.1080/00213624.2016.1148469

Manyika, J. 2017 (May). "Technology, Jobs, and the Future of Work: Executive Briefing." San Francisco, CA: McKinsey & Company. https://mck.co/2W6SQMk

Raja, D.S. 2016. "Bridging the Disability Divide Through Digital Technologies." Background Paper for the "World Development Report: Digital Dividends." Geneva, Switzerland: World Bank. http://bit.ly/2W30RBT

Saleh, M., and S. Bruyère. 2018. "Leveraging Employer Practices in Global Regulatory Frameworks to Improve Employment Outcomes for People with Disabilities." *Journal of Social Inclusion* 6 (1): 18–28. doi:10.17645/si.v6i1.12

Thomason, T., J.F. Burton, Jr., and D.E. Hyatt, eds. 1998. "New Approaches to Disability in the Workplace." *Proceedings of the Annual Meeting, Volumes 1 and 2.* Madison, WI: Industrial Relations Research Association.

United Nations. No date. Convention on the Rights of Persons with Disabilities (CRPD). Geneva, Switzerland: United Nations Department of Economic and Social Affairs. http://bit.ly/2W8NeBd

United Nations. 2015. "Special Rapporteur on the Rights of Persons with Disabilities, No. A/70/297. Geneva, Switzerland: United Nations Human Rights Office of the High Commissioner. http://bit.ly/2HZIolB

United Nations. 2019. "CRPD and Optional Protocol Signatures and Ratifications." Geneva, Switzerland: United Nations Department of Economic and Social Affairs: Disability. http://bit.ly/2W8NeBd

US Department of Labor. No date. "Regulations Implementing Section 503 of the Rehabilitation Act." Washington, DC: Office of Federal Contract Compliance Programs. http://bit.ly/2ME4DxQ

World Health Organization and World Bank. 2011. "The World Report on Disability." Geneva, Switzerland: World Health Organization and World Bank.

Chapter 1

US Employment and Disability Policy Framework: Competing Legislative Priorities, Challenges, and Strategies

Matthew C. Saleh
Thomas P. Golden
Ellice Switzer
Cornell University

INTRODUCTION: WHY COMPETING LEGISLATIVE PRIORITIES MATTER

Employment and disability legislation in the United States evolved from early policies providing support and protection to war veterans and civil servants with disabilities. In subsequent years, legislative frameworks grew dramatically, to include (1) workers compensation and protections, (2) social insurance and means-tested entitlements, (3) a state–federal partnership for vocational rehabilitation, (4) workforce development and other community-based services and supports, (5) civil rights employment protections, and more. However, many of these policies emerged during different periods, and they reflect divergent perspectives of and about disability. Despite the promulgation of an extensive federal policy landscape, people with disabilities continue to experience disparities in economic and employment outcomes. For example, as of 2017, the employment rate of noninstitutionalized people with disabilities (ages 21–64) in the United States was approximately 37.3%, compared with 71.4% of people without disabilities (Erickson, Lee, and von Schrader 2017). For specific disability types, this gap is even larger: The estimated employment rate of people with cognitive disabilities was 27.9%, and 17.8% for people with "independent living disabilities" (resulting from a physical, mental, or emotional condition) (Erickson, Lee, and von Schrader 2017).

Focus often falls on individual prescriptive measures and legislative efforts, but in this chapter we discuss the relationship between different laws and the competing legislative priorities that emerged during different eras of US policy development. We also discuss how these competing priorities might be partly responsible for incomplete efforts to end employment gaps and segregatory/exclusionary employment practices. In some cases, coexisting legislative aims contradict rather than reinforce important policy objectives, with real-world implications. In this chapter, we discuss three areas where these competing priorities are most evident: (1) medical versus social model definitions of disability under different policy agendas; (2) discontinuities in Social Security eligibility, disability determinations, and return-to-work initiatives; and (3) the persistence of sheltered employment in the wake of competitive integrated employment reforms and Employment First initiatives. To illustrate these competing priorities, we first provide a brief historical overview of relevant laws and the policy contexts within which they arose. We then look at the trajectory of US employment and disability policy into contemporary times, along with the efforts needed to navigate policy contradictions to reduce employment disparities for people with disabilities.

EVOLUTION OF THE US EMPLOYMENT AND DISABILITY POLICY FRAMEWORK

The First 100 Years of US Disability Policy

To understand the policy contradictions that developed over time in the United States, it is important to present an account of the history from which contemporary disability employment policy emerged. Baynton (2017: 8) notes that, for much of US history, policy makers deemed it justifiable to discriminate against people with disabilities, and moreover "the *concept* of disability [was] used to justify discrimination against other groups by attributing disability to them." For example, policy debates about citizenship and rights for women, ethnic/racial minorities, and immigrants often hinged on attributing higher rates of disability—and lower mental, emotional, and physical capacities—to marginalized populations in order to "clarify and define who deserved, and who was deservedly excluded from, citizenship" (Baynton 2017: 18). Discourses such as these demarcated disability as an unacceptable deviation and a sign of genetic weakness, placing the experience of disability within the lower rungs of societal acceptance (Davis 1995). In the late 19th century, these discourses began to manifest as municipal laws—known historically and colloquially as "ugly laws"—focused on physical or mental deviations from the norm as publicly offensive attributes, galvanized by the Social Darwinist view and openly calling for the segregation and removal of people with disabilities from society (Schweik 2009).

These calls for eugenic exclusion often resulted in extreme measures, including institutionalization and sterilization. Monumental human rights violations resulted, as mental institutions experienced severe overcrowding, "making attempts at moral treatment impossible ... as the custodial functions of the asylums became primary" (Braddock and Parish 2001: 33). Advances in science, medicine, and technology coincided with the growing custodial function, and a "medical model" of disability became pre-eminent. Policies and practices disregarded natural human diversity in favor of an obsession with treatment and cures, conceiving of disability as "a functional loss" or deficit and reflecting the belief that "when the interventions of medical science cannot resolve the problem and enable the individual to function within the norm, the person is considered to be permanently flawed" (Rothman 2018: 15).

The Rise of Social Insurance, Workers Compensation, and Vocational Rehabilitation

Some notable exceptions to the custodial approach could be found in early statutory provisions of relief for injured military veterans and civil servants, especially after the Civil War. For example, from 1861 to 1885, a number of laws, while vague in defining and rating disability, offered compensation for conditions obtained in military service that resulted in disability (Prechtel-Kluskens 2010; see also 13 Stat. 387, 1864; 17 Stat. 566, 1873). Standards for applying and claiming benefits usually centered on a veteran's incapacity "for procuring a subsistence by manual labor" (12 Stat. 566, 1862; 2 Stat. 376, 1806). As we will see, this focus on the ability or inability to work would come to predominate disability employment policy.

The first workers compensation law for federal employees was enacted in 1882 (2 Stat. 55), providing up to two years' salary to any member of the federal US Life Saving Service who attained a disability in the line of duty, or to their survivors in case of death (Szymendera 2017). By the start of the 20th century, further disability policies intended to provide income and work security to individuals with disabilities began to emerge. The proliferation of state workers compensation laws was one important development during this period, with the first state program passing in 1911 and every state having a workers compensation law by 1948 (Bruyère and Saleh 2017).

The federal government also enacted a series of related laws such as the Federal Employers Liability Act of 1908 (45 U.S.C. §51 et seq.), which protected and provided compensation for railroad workers with job-related injuries in instances where the employer was partially negligent, and the Federal Employees' Compensation Act of 1916 (Public Law 64-267), which provided compensation for lost wages to federal civil service employees who experienced work-related injuries.

The Smith–Hughes Act of 1917 (Pub. L. No. 64-347) established vocational education for veterans injured in service to their country to facilitate their return to work. This was quickly followed by the Smith–Sears Veterans Rehabilitation Act of 1918 (Pub. L. No. 65-178), initiating a program of vocational rehabilitation and return to civil employment for veterans with disabilities after World War I. The successes realized under the Smith–Sears Act contributed to the passage of the Smith–Fess Act of 1920 (Civilian Rehabilitation Act, Pub. L. No. 66-236), which made the rehabilitation program available to the civilian population of people with physical disabilities. These early laws reinforced the policy aim of supporting individuals whose disabilities were derived from normatively valued societal contributions but did so at the exclusion of the broader population of people with developmental, intellectual, and mental health disabilities, many of whom were still being institutionalized at the time (Dumont and Dumont 2008). The Smith–Fess Act's federal rehabilitation program was not extended to other disability populations until it was amended in 1943 by the Barden–La Follette Act (Pub. L. No. 78-113).

Another important development during this period was the Fair Labor Standards Act of 1938 (Fair Labor Standards Act [FLSA], 29 U.S.C. §203), federal legislation which, among other objectives, established a minimum wage, child labor standards, and overtime pay eligibility. Importantly, the FLSA also allowed employers to obtain certificates allowing them to compensate individuals "whose earning or productive capacity is impaired by age, physical or mental deficiency, or injury" at below minimum wage (29 U.S.C. §214(c)). This provision still exists, with significant implications for policy and is something we return to later in the chapter.

The original Social Security Act of 1935 (42 U.S.C. §§301-1305) included several provisions for general welfare, as well as a social insurance program designed to pay retired workers ages 65 and up. In 1956, the act was amended to provide benefits to workers with disabilities 50 through 64 years old and children with disabilities. In 1960, it was again expanded to provide benefits payments to workers with disabilities of any age and their dependents. Medicare and Medicaid health coverage followed in 1965 (42 U.S.C. §1395 et seq.). Social insurance entitlements were further expanded in 1972 with the creation of the Supplemental Security Income (SSI) program to ensure a minimal level of income for aged, low-income individuals and people with disabilities. These social insurance programs provided income maintenance and healthcare for the large population meeting the eligibility criteria. During the 1980s and 1990s, both Social Security programs for people with disabilities experienced a shift in focus toward return-to-work programming. This new emphasis was in addition to, and sometimes at odds with, the pre-existing focus on income maintenance priorities and cash benefits claims processing (Svihula and Estes 2007). The Social Security Act's social insurance program for former workers who cannot work because of a disability (Social Security Disability Insurance [SSDI]) and its means-tested welfare program (SSI) continue to rely on a quasi-judicial disability determination process for claiming benefits, hinging on the inability to "engage in Substantial Gainful Activity … by a reason of any medically determinable physical or mental impairment" (Social Security Act 2000, §423(d)(1)(A)). As we will see, this determination process is occasionally at odds with return-to-work efforts, in spite of continued legislative efforts to retrofit Social Security to prioritize and encourage employment outcomes.

Paradigm Shift: De-Institutionalization and Community-Based Services/Supports

The 1970s ushered in a new paradigm for domestic disability policy, with a focus on civil rights and employment protections. New laws emerged that afforded people with disabilities more opportunities to live and work in their own communities, including increased options for community living and employment for all people with disabilities and efforts to end institutionalization practices for people with disabilities affecting independent living. In 1972, an attempt by Senator Hubert Humphrey to amend the Civil Rights Act of 1964 (42 U.S.C. §1983) to add disability as a protected class (alongside race, color, religion, sex, and national origin) met with little support (Colker and Grossman 2013). However, during the following year, Congress passed the Rehabilitation Act of 1973 (29 U.S.C. §701 et seq.), one of the most important disability employment laws in US history. The Rehabilitation Act covered a range of objectives, including (1) expanding the state–federal partnership for the public vocational rehabilitation program; (2) authorizing the formula grant programs for vocational rehabilitation, supported employment, independent living services, and client assistance; and (3) establishing the first disability nondiscrimination provisions in employment by prohibiting disability discrimination in the federal sector (29 U.S.C. §794). The act's nondiscrimination provisions included a duty to accommodate, an important step toward embracing a de-medicalized, inclusive view of disability employment policy by requiring federal employers to mitigate existing environmental barriers and considering an employee's qualifications in light of potential accommodations.

The policy shift during this period brought about what Bradley (1994) refers to as the "community development era," with new laws investing heavily in building infrastructure through community living options, sheltered workshops, special education programs, and issues of community access to transportation, housing, telecommunications, and other domains (Blessing, Golden, and Bruyère 2009). Some laws seeking to enhance community participation across multiple domains included the Education for All Handicapped Children Act of 1975 (89 Stat. 773); the Developmentally Disabled Assistance and Bill of Rights Act of 1975 (Pub. L. No. 94-103), which made state grant funding conditional on the creation of protection and advocacy programs and services; and the 1978 amendments to the Rehabilitation Act providing for consumer-controlled centers for independent living. Despite this array of new legislation, efforts to disentangle community services from medical models of care experienced challenges. These community rehabilitation efforts often maintained a focus on "fixing" or managing an impairment to bring individuals within acceptable societal norms, and employment gaps remained large.

During that period, a different type of exclusion also emerged in which many people with disabilities were effectively re-institutionalized within smaller, segregated, and congregated community settings (Whitehead 1986). The sustained emphasis on treatment continued to overwhelm the objectives of community integration and providing supports to help mitigate environmental barriers in the community. Scholars have also noted that, with regard to the de-institutionalization movement, the "community development of the required array of social and psychiatric services did not keep pace with the rate of reduction of hospitalization," resulting in continued "financial, geographic, psychological, and societal barriers" to receiving services, difficulties obtaining employment and a livable wage, and in some cases reabsorption into other systems, such as correctional facilities (Bachrach 1987: 75; Steadman et al. 1984). As such, advocacy efforts shifted from focusing on state hospitals to focusing more broadly on segregated residential and work settings (Cremin 2012). Many of the challenges that emerged during this period remain pertinent in contemporary policy considerations.

COMPETING PRIORITIES IN CONTEMPORARY EMPLOYMENT AND DISABILITY POLICY

Nondiscrimination and a Social Model of Disability

Modern disability employment policy is a tale of competing paradigms: initiatives that align with the civil rights movement and modern notions of substantive equality (e.g., full community integration and integrated employment at competitive wages) and the persistence of more segregated models and systems of care that grew out of previous policy regimes (Lok and de Rond 2013). In recent decades, policy has shifted yet again toward efforts to supplant the medical model and segregatory practices in a substantive manner leading to equal *outcomes*. These policies typically utilize variations of a "social model" of disability, which recognize that disability is not inherent to the individual but rather exists in the interaction of impairment and environment (Oliver 1990). As Samaha (2007: 1256) puts it, this can be viewed as a reframing of the "causation account" of disability, defining disability "as disadvantage caused by the confluence of (1) personal impairment and (2) a social setting comprising architecture, economics, politics, culture, social norms, aesthetic values, and assumptions about ability." Part of this reframing involved taking a critical historical lens to the "sick role" in Western society (Parsons 1975: 257), which "critics of the medical model associate … with belittling norms that relieve impaired persons from social obligations yet demand they abide by professional medical judgment" (Samaha 2007: 1256–1257).

Many of the Rehabilitation Act's conceptual and semantic frameworks served as the basis for the landmark Americans with Disabilities Act (ADA) of 1990, a federal law extending Section 504's prohibition of discrimination on the basis of disability to private employers (Title I) and state and local governments (Title II), as well as implementing accessibility requirements for places of public accommodation (Title III). Title I of the ADA prohibits covered employers from discriminating against qualified individuals on the basis of disability, with respect to applications, hiring, firing, advancement, compensation, training, or the privileges and benefits of employment. The three-pronged ADA definition of disability mirrors the Rehabilitation Act and includes (1) any physical or mental impairment that substantially limits one or more major life activities, (2) a record of such an impairment, or (3) being regarded as having such an impairment (42 U.S.C. §12102(1)). Prong one, or "actual" disability, requires that the individual have a substantial limitation to a major life activity, meaning they are substantially limited in the ability to perform the function compared with "most people in the general population" (29 CFR §1630.2(j)(1)(v)). For ADA protections to apply, an individual must be "qualified" for the position, meaning they are able to perform the essential job functions, with or without reasonable accommodation.

In 2008, Congress responded to Supreme Court rulings that limited the ADA definition of disability by passing the ADA Amendments Act (ADAAA, Public Law 110-325), which increased coverage by (1) adding a "major bodily functions" category of coverage, (2) providing a nonexhaustive list of major life activities and bodily functions, (3) clarifying that "substantial limitation" is not meant to be a demanding standard and that duration of impairment is not dispositive, and (4) prohibiting consideration of the ameliorative effects of mitigating measures (e.g., medication, assistive technologies) (29 CFR §1630.2(j)). The necessity of clarifying and broadening ADA coverage stemmed from a tendency by courts to resort to medical models of disability, narrowing coverage to apply only to those individuals significantly limited in their capacity to work rather than focusing on the broader protections needed to prevent discrimination and ensure that disability is accommodated in the workplace.

COMPETING DEFINITIONS OF DISABILITY IN MODERN FEDERAL LAW

Discontinuities and competing legal frameworks are perhaps most easily observed in how "disability" is defined. Anti-discrimination laws such as the ADA, Rehabilitation Act, and Fair Housing Act consider the role of the environment as a disabler and acknowledge that alterations can reduce the degree or occurrence of disability. The ADA definition, described above, was initially problematic and illustrated the difficulties inherent in moving policy away from the medical model. The Supreme Court issued legal opinions that dramatically narrowed the definition of disability intended by the legislature, curtailing ADA coverage. In doing so, the court created a "Goldilocks dilemma," where claimants were "either 'not disabled enough' to warrant the protections of the ADA, or 'too disabled' to be a 'qualified individual' for the respective job" (Areheart 2008: 184). Congress disagreed with these narrowing constructions and passed the ADAAA to undo the court's restriction on coverage. An analysis of post-ADAAA litigation found a significant decrease in summary judgments for employers owing to a lack of disability status but an increase in rulings that an individual is not "qualified for" employment (Befort 2013), further evidencing Areheart's (2008) Goldilocks dilemma.

While anti-discrimination laws tend to focus on substantial limitations to any "major life activity," the Social Security system still defines disability as an inability to work. For disability benefits eligibility, a person must have a "severe" disability, or combination of disabilities, that has lasted, or is expected to last, at least 12 months or result in death and which prevents working at a level of "substantial gainful activity" (42 U.S.C. §423(d)(1)). Qualitative research by Dorfman (2017), investigating the role that identity politics play in the relationship between institutions and beneficiaries, found evidence that beneficiaries who identified with the social model of disability (rather than the medical model) held more critical views of the procedure for retaining benefits, felt less control over the process, had to "present an image" of their disability that was not necessarily true, and felt that the process discouraged them from participating fully in the labor market. The tension between current and prior policy regimes, and disability paradigms, is evident in these contradictions, and US courts have at times become entangled in determining whether "total disability" under social insurance claims and ADA protections for "qualified" individuals with disabilities were compatible frameworks (*Cleveland v. Policy Management Systems*, 526 U.S. 795 1999; *Molina v. Pocono Medical Center*, 2013 WL 4520458, M.D. Pa. 2013).

Similarly, in eligibility determinations for vocational rehabilitation services, state offices define disability based on whether an individual has a physical or mental impairment that constitutes or results in a "substantial impediment" to employment. By comparison, the ability to work is just one possible major life activity under the ADA. This type of definitional discontinuity exists in other contexts as well. For instance, state-level workers compensation is partially at odds with disability anti-discrimination law because, while the ADA and other laws focus on the steps an employer must take to remove barriers by providing accommodations and modifying workplace environment and culture, workers compensation laws operate from the perspective that impairments cause work limitations, requiring employees to emphasize limitations caused by their disability to demonstrate benefits eligibility but do so in a manner that may undermine ADA accommodations requests (Bruyère and Saleh 2017; Geaney 2004).

Social Security Innovations Focused on Returning to Work

Despite contemporary law and policy targeted at increasing employment outcomes and substantive equality in the workplace for people with disabilities, the employment and economic outlook for people with significant disabilities has remained relatively unchanged. Significant increases in the receipt of SSDI and SSI benefits among people with disabilities during the late 20th and early 21st centuries led to concerns that the Social Security system was de-incentivizing benefits recipients from returning to work because of the impact on benefits eligibility, creating "poverty traps" founded on a tenuous dependence on income or healthcare maintenance and leading to further exclusion from the labor market (see, e.g., Autor and Duggan 2006; Eide and Ingstad 2011). The Ticket to Work and Work Incentives Improvement Act of 1999 (TWWIIA, Pub. L. No. 106-170) sought to address this issue by modifying benefits retention frameworks, providing employment preparation and job placement services to reduce reliance on cash benefit programs, and expanding healthcare eligibility (through state-administered Medicaid buy-in programs and allowing beneficiaries to retain Medicare coverage while working).

The act established the Ticket to Work and Self-Sufficiency Program, which provided a method for delivery of services and supports needed to obtain employment. These new return-to-work supports were intended to support the movement of beneficiaries toward employment and greater economic self-sufficiency by means such as removing work-triggered continuing disability reviews that might impede a beneficiary's path to work. For example, the Expedited Reinstatement of Benefits incentive allowed beneficiaries who became ineligible for benefits when they began gainful work to return to cash benefit status if they subsequently lost that income within five years. The act provided two options to expand healthcare: extending Medicare for 93 months once a beneficiary begins work and allowing states to establish Medicaid buy-in programs for working people with disabilities who meet the disability standard but have earnings above regular Medicaid limits. Most states now have a Medicaid buy-in program. The Work Incentives Planning and Assistance (WIPA) under Ticket to Work provides counseling about benefits and the effects of work on benefits, and conducts outreach to SSI/SSDI beneficiaries and families about federal and state work incentives programs. Livermore, Prenovitz, and Schimmel (2011) found that receipt of WIPA services and encouragement to use work incentives led to improved employment outcomes and decreased dependence on disability benefits.

Competing Disability and Return-to-Work Agendas in Social Insurance

Despite innovations and hard-won incremental changes to the Social Security Act, all of the social insurance programs under the act have retained a medical standard of disability that recognizes only permanent disability that limits ability to work at substantial levels (Martin and Weaver 2005). However, the promulgation of work-incentive programs under both the SSDI and SSI programs, along with the passage of TWWIIA, recognized that a portion of the population of beneficiaries under both programs could work and should be provided opportunity through various incentives, services, and supports to move toward increased self-sufficiency (Golden, Zeitzer, and Bruyère 2014). An unfortunate tension still exists between the objectives of social insurance/income security and returning to work. Individuals spend and invest considerable energy to become entitled to benefits. Shortly thereafter, the Social Security Administration tries to encourage them to work, despite the fact that to meet the initial eligibility criteria they had to verify an inability to work. This presents considerable challenges to those who may be attempting to develop plans toward greater self-sufficiency—navigating the return-to-work process while ensuring they have critical economic and health-care safety nets to ensure their health and well-being.

Focus on Competitive Integrated Employment and Equal Outcomes

The Workforce Investment Act of 1998 (WIA) served as a continuation and improvement of the vocational rehabilitation services portion of the Rehabilitation Act, with the goal of requiring states to coordinate federally funded employment and training services into a single comprehensive one-stop system (US General Accounting Office 2003). In an effort to streamline the previous system, in which parties sought services from a variety of sources in what was often a costly and confusing process (Hager and Sheldon 2006), WIA designated 17 categories of programs as mandatory partners with the one-stop system. These categories included veterans' employment and training services, adult literacy programs, US Department of Housing and Urban Development–administered employment and training, and US Department of Labor–administered employment training for migrant workers, Native Americans, youths, and dislocated workers. Any person who could demonstrate a physical, mental, or learning disability resulting in a substantial impediment to his or her ability to work was eligible for WIA services (Pub. L. No. 105–220, §6(9)(A)). The program presumed eligibility for people qualified to receive SSI or SSDI, provided that they sought WIA services for the purpose of finding work (Pub. L. No. 105–220, §102(3)(A)(ii)). Similar to requirements under the Rehabilitation Act, if vocational rehabilitation agency resources were inadequate to serve every individual seeking employment, agencies were required to provide services according to an order of selection, with more severe disability types given priority (Pub. L. No. 105–220, §101(a)(5)(A); 29 U.S.C. §721).

The Workforce Innovation and Opportunity Act (WIOA) of 2014 superseded the WIA, aiming to further align state vocational rehabilitation programs with other core programs of the workforce development system. To accomplish this, it set out requirements for unified strategic planning, common performance accountability measures, one-stop delivery, and increased services to youth with disabilities in the areas of workplace skills, exercising self-determination in career interests, and obtaining work-based experiences (29 U.S.C. §3101 et seq.). Under the WIOA amendments to the Rehabilitation Act, the role of the vocational rehabilitation agency is to assist individuals with disabilities in making informed choices with respect to their desired employment outcomes and the services necessary to achieve that goal, including assisting eligible individuals in the development of a written individualized plan for employment (34 CFR §361.45). Lawmakers enacted WIOA "against the backdrop of a proliferation of state Employment First initiatives" (Novak 2015: 101), which shifted the focus to integrated, community-based work at or above the minimum wage. Under

WIOA, sheltered employment and nonwork-day activities do not constitute acceptable work outcomes, and the law places significant limitations on subminimum wage work (29 U.S.C. §794g; 34 CFR §361.5(c)(9)). WIOA supports access to real-world education and workforce development opportunities for job seekers in the system, such as work-based learning, customized training, and pay-for-performance contracts (29 U.S.C. §3123(b)(4)(B)). WIOA's job-driven programs emphasize engaging employers and matching them with skilled individuals, including through a wider array of work-based learning opportunities under the vocational rehabilitation program (e.g., apprenticeships and internships) (29 U.S.C. §3112-3198). New final regulations in 2016 updated the definition of vocational rehabilitation outcomes in WIOA Title IV (programs authorized by the Rehabilitation Act), finalizing a shift from "gainful employment" to "competitive integrated employment" for people with disabilities and specifying that "customized employment" constitutes a valid employment outcome. This new terminology reflects a shift toward emphasizing integrated employment opportunities and pay commensurate with that of workers without disabilities in similar occupations, with similar training, experience, and skills (29 U.S.C. §705(5)).

Competitive Integrated Employment and FLSA Subminimum Wage Certificates

Facility-based work programs—also known as "sheltered workshops"—were once considered a progressive, modern approach to community integration. However, they grew controversial because of their segregated settings and the existence of special certificates, granted by the Department of Labor under Section 14c of the Fair Labor Standards Act of 1938 (29 U.S.C. §214(c)), allowing employers—usually community-based nonprofit organizations—to compensate workers with significant disabilities at subminimum wage. Sheltered workshops have evolved over the years to encompass a complex array of funding mechanisms and pre-vocational services. They remain, in most states, an integral service for people with significant disabilities, ideally providing an opportunity to contribute to society with their labor, earn a paycheck, and be in a supervised, safe environment throughout the day. It is this last fact, perhaps more than any other, that makes sheltered employment a hot-button issue for many family members and advocates for people with disabilities who oppose the elimination of this service option—as nationwide Employment First policy agendas, emphasizing competitive integrated employment for all, take hold (Dague 2012).

Historically, this framework creates disincentives for organizations that operate sheltered workshops to transition people out of facility-based settings into integrated community employment; the transition rate out of sheltered employment is quite low (between 1% and 5%) (Migliore 2010). Moreover, the work performed in sheltered settings is often reliant on the productivity of the most skilled workers, who may otherwise be able to pursue community-based employment at much higher rates of pay. Sheltered work is also often reimbursed to provider agencies at higher rates than services supporting competitive integrated employment (Cimera 2012). Despite the recent federal policy action designed to promote competitive integrated employment over segregated facility-based options, a growing backlash to the movement away from facility-based settings manifested in a call to reopen the rules and definitions in WIOA regarding competitive integrated employment in favor of policies that embrace "choice" in vocational programming, and the Department of Education announced its intent to reopen the regulations (US Department of Education Office of Special Education and Rehabilitation Services 2018).

The multiple policy agendas converging on the issue of pre-vocational services and subminimum wage jobs in sheltered settings contribute to the policy narrative surrounding pre-vocational and work activities for those individuals least likely to be employed in competitive jobs, primarily those with intellectual and developmental disabilities. Opposition to facility-based segregated employment has been bolstered by a national movement toward adoption of an Employment First agenda and the first ever codified definition of "competitive integrated employment" in WIOA. However, care must be taken to recognize the potential pitfalls of the transition away from sheltered employment, including the possibility that the shift may result in less vocational activity for people with significant disabilities in the absence of comprehensive planning and new service models. In fact, one state-level study found that, in the absence of such forethought on the part of policy makers, more than half of individuals who were working in sheltered workshops are now unemployed, and those who were employed in the community were working fewer hours and instead receiving more services such as day habilitation (Phoenix and Bysshe 2015). Commentators note, however, that this analysis may have limited generalizability, and the lack of long-term, longitudinal data on the impacts of a shift to Employment First frameworks contributes to confusion and limitations in policy makers' ability to make data-driven decisions about policies that encourage or discourage sheltered employment (Conroy, McCaffrey, and Liacopoulos 2016).

The result is a patchwork of policies and supports designed to improve employment outcomes for people with disabilities, based on differing eligibility criteria aimed at multiple subpopulations. Current funding mechanisms are neither reflective of the policy trend to improve the lives of people with disabilities by increasing competitive integrated employment nor of the desire of fiscal conservatives to limit costs associated with such services. Butterworth et al. (2011: 10) provide quantitative evidence to substantiate that observation, noting that the number of people being served by state-funded developmental disabilities services grew by 22% in the first decade of the 21st century, but the number of people in competitive integrated employment only grew by 4.7%. Analysis of expenditures in 40 states shows that facility-based programs and services continue to be funded at a rate that far exceeds the rate of funding for competitive integrated employment programs: 86.4% versus 13.6% of total dollars spent. This may in part explain the growth in the number of individuals being served in facility-based nonwork programs, even as policies designed to end segregated employment roll out (Winsor et al. 2017).

NAVIGATING THE POLICY ARENA

In reading some of the preceding commentary, one reaction might be exasperation, as the development of this metaphorical patchwork of legislation has developed not only out of competing necessities but also out of legitimate and diverse policy objectives, both in service of, and sometimes only tangentially related to, the contemporary objective of ensuring substantive equality. The disability policy arena is complex and frequently misunderstood by stakeholders in the employment arena—employers, individuals with disabilities and their families, and providers of employment services. Ad hoc executive orders, new rules under federal laws, changes to the social safety net, and advocacy by special interest groups combine to create a multifaceted policy environment that is deeply understood by only a relative few. In navigating this policy landscape, it is the responsibility of policy makers, advocates, scholars, and practitioners to hold evidence in high regard when considering the successes and shortcomings of current policies and when setting new priorities for improving the employment of people with disabilities.

Resolving Policy-Level Contradictions

In a final report, the Ticket to Work and Work Incentives Advisory Panel (2007) emphasized the need for Congress to create a new paradigm to support economic self-sufficiency for people with significant disabilities, including investment in disability program modernization that redefines the disability standard, establishment of a large-scale demonstration to evaluate a transition to economic self-sufficiency program targeting youth and young adults, better coordination of disability programs at the federal level, and promotion of workforce connection and retention strategies.

These proposed actions on the part of the federal government are contradicted by the lack of legislative action to create better opportunities for people with significant disabilities to obtain integrated employment at a competitive wage. In 2014, Congress directed the federal Advisory Committee on Increasing Competitive Integrated Employment for Individuals with Disabilities (ACICIEID) to examine the policy landscape of disability employment programs and to recommend necessary changes toward improved outcomes and strategies for increased oversight over the use of subminimum wage certificates under Section 14(c) of the FLSA. In its final report to Congress, the committee recognized the need to align state and federal policies (including those implemented by states under the Medicaid authorities) and prioritize funding for initiatives that result in competitive integrated employment. The committee also recommended that "Congress amend the FLSA to allow for a multi-year, well-planned phase out of Section 14(c)" (ACICIEID 2016: 2). Though there have been several legislative attempts to date, so far the goals of the committee regarding the FLSA have been unrealized. Recent attempts include provisions within the 2019 Raise the Wage Act, which (if passed) would eliminate payment of subminimum wages to people with disabilities over a period of five years by amending Subparagraph (A) of Section 14(c)(1) of the FLSA (H.R. 582 2019).

Activists within the disability community hold contradictory viewpoints on the issue of sheltered employment and subminimum wages, which clouds the issue in the minds of legislators who often lack enough knowledge of the complex policy landscape to make informed decisions independently. At this point in the process, the role of advocacy and activism bears primary importance in terms of influence over both setting policy agendas and implementation of state initiatives under Employment First priorities, to emphasize unification of policies and systems alignment.

Empowering Individuals to Exercise Self-Determination in Navigating Multiple Systems

Decades of research have shown that the best outcomes for people are often generated by programs that are also the greatest value to taxpayers: lower-cost, community-based services designed to facilitate economic and social inclusion, financial self-sufficiency, and reduced reliance on public benefits. One powerful example involves the demonstrated effectiveness of work incentives and benefits planning services for SSI/SSDI beneficiaries and families, suggesting that empowering individuals with knowledge about their benefits can improve their employment outcomes and decrease dependence on benefits (Livermore, Prenovitz, and Schimmel 2011). Benefits planning services can be offered as a vocational rehabilitation agency–funded service and can encourage self-determination in benefits planning goals and address concerns among SSI/SSDI recipients about the potential loss of cash or healthcare benefits (e.g., Medicaid or Medicare) (Sheldon 2018). Presently, state vocational rehabilitation agencies implement diverse strategies to fund and deliver benefits planning services, including (1) participating in SSA's competitive WIPA grant process, (2) combining WIPA funding and another state source (e.g., vocational rehabilitation agency funding) to provide benefits planning through vocational rehabilitation staff, and (3) funding benefits planners through a fee-for-service model (Sheldon 2018). One common theme in the literature involves the struggles for procedural justice in disability determination processes (for example, in social insurance and vocational rehabilitation services) (Dorfman 2017) and the discontinuities in that process with other policy agendas, such as return-to-work programs and services and civil rights employment protections under the ADA. Empowering individuals and families to better understand the process, the rules, and their rights can have important impacts.

Our national history of segregation of people with disabilities in school, work, and residential settings has led to a variety of legislative initiatives intended to increase the oversight and accountability of disability service systems. Among those are the network of disability rights organizations that provide protection and advocacy and client assistance services (which arose from the Developmental Disabilities Assistance and Bill of Rights Act of 1975) and the national network of independent living centers (authorized under Title VII of the Rehabilitation Act of 1973). The mandates of these organizations require both individual and systems-level advocacy, providing a powerful platform for self-advocates, families, and allies. Disability rights networks play an active role in legal advocacy related to due process monitoring, integrated settings enforcement, and other issues surrounding the competitive integrated employment of people with disabilities (Bates-Harris 2012). The flexible design and peer-to-peer model of independent living centers allow for responsive action within communities to increase inclusion and self-agency of people with disabilities, which frequently includes programs and services to promote economic self-sufficiency through benefits counseling and employment supports.

Considerations for Employers and Labor Relations Professionals

Setting policy aside, it is important to also remember that individuals with disabilities represent one side of the equation, but employer buy-in and a focus on convergent interests is necessary to achieve positive outcomes. Policy mediates this relationship, and laws and policies can be similarly confusing to employers, who often act against their own self-interest in excluding people with disabilities from their talent pools and often operationalize false assumptions about the rules that US disability employment policy does and does not impose. In the federal sector, new regulations for Section 503 of the Rehabilitation Act reflect potential strategies for encouraging employer buy-in, reflecting the notion that federal agencies and contractors should be "model employers." In 2013, the US Office of Federal Contract Compliance Programs published new final regulations for Section 503 (41 CFR Part 60–741), establishing a nationwide "aspirational goal" of 7% for federal contractors and subcontractors hiring people with disabilities (41 CFR §60-741.45). Although not a quota, the new goal requires appropriate outreach and recruitment activities, along with data collection, reporting, and accountability measures for demonstrating effective outreach activities, and it requires contractors to invite applicants to self-identify as having a disability during the pre- and post-offer phases (41 CFR §60-741.42).

Disability self-identification, and disability disclosure more generally, remains a complex issue for employers and employees alike. Known barriers to employee self-identification include a perceived risk of termination or loss of healthcare benefits, limitations on promotion opportunities, unsupportive management, and differential treatment by co-workers and supervisors (von Schrader, Malzer, and Bruyère 2013). In 2017, the US Equal Employment Opportunity Commission issued new regulations amending the implementation of Section 501 of the Rehabilitation Act and clarifying the meaning of "affirmative action," requiring federal agencies to adopt employment goals and take "specific steps reasonably designed" to gradually increase their numbers of employees with disabilities, set subgoals for individuals with "targeted disabilities," and provide personal assistance services (e.g., dressing, eating, using the restroom) to employees with targeted disabilities where needed to work or participate in work-related travel (29 CFR §1614.203; 82 Federal Register 654).

Public and private employers alike can take a more proactive role in better understanding their own responsibilities under the array of potentially applicable pieces of federal legislation. The ADA, for instance, interacts in interesting and unexpected ways with laws such as the Family Medical Leave Act of 1993 (Family and Medical Leave Act [FMLA], 29 U.S.C. §2601) and the National Labor Relations Act of 1935 (NLRA, 29 U.S.C. §151–169). For example, while FMLA "serious health conditions" and ADA disabilities are not mutually exclusive categories, the two laws have different employer expectations pertaining to the provision of leave. Leave can be an ADA reasonable accommodation but isn't required if it would impose an undue burden; the FMLA offers no such exception. Similarly, time spent on a light-duty option may be an ADA accommodation but doesn't count against an FMLA leave entitlement. To provide another example, private sector employers with unionized employees are subject to the NLRA, which prohibits them from dealing directly with employees about employment terms and conditions; at the same time, the ADA prohibits employers from entering into collective bargaining agreements that discriminate against individuals covered by the ADA (42 U.S.C. §12112(b)(2)). One way this conflict has played out in the courts has involved issues with reassignment as an accommodation and potential conflict with seniority systems (*U.S. Airways, Inc. v. Barnett*, 535 U.S. 391 2002).

While the scope of responsibilities can be confusing and derives from a range of different federal legislation complicated by other federal rule making and state law, employers can benefit from considering policies for hiring, retaining, and promoting employees with an eye for diversity and inclusion. The provision of reasonable accommodations by employers is a strong example of this. Despite a traditional tendency among employers to fall back on stereotypes about the expense of accommodations and the effect on business margins, employers who do provide accommodations report that they tend to be inexpensive or even free (Job Accommodation Network 2018). Fifty-nine percent of employers reported that accommodations resulted in no expense, while 36% experienced a one-time cost. Employers also reported a high return on investment (Unger et al. 2002) and improved retention rates, organizational culture, and productivity (Kaye, Jans, and Jones 2011).

Organizational diversity more generally has been shown to have indirect or collateral benefits, including reductions in liability, stronger appeal to a diverse customer base, and a greater innovation/organizational problem-solving capacity (Yap and Konrad 2009). Assertions such as these amount to the "business case" for hiring people with disabilities and, importantly in our present discussion, for going beyond simple legal compliance. While the existence of competing legislative priorities has very real implications for individuals, practitioners, and employers, the existing frameworks are navigable where their shortcomings are recognized and addressed. The work of individual stakeholders is to consider the implications of different laws, standards, definitions, and requirements in light of their relationship to one another and to identify solutions that reflect modern prerogatives—not only of equal opportunity but also of equal results.

ACKNOWLEDGMENTS

The authors would like to thank Ariel Avgar, associate professor of labor relations, law, and history, Cornell University; Ruth Brannon, (retired) director, Office of Research Sciences, National Institute on Disability, Independent Living, and Rehabilitation Research; and Marie Strahan, independent consultant, former federal career executive, and member of the Kansas Bar, for their reviews, feedback, and thoughtful commentary.

REFERENCES

Advisory Committee on Increasing Competitive Integrated Employment for Individuals with Disabilities (ACICIEID). 2016 (Sep. 15). "Final Report." http://bit.ly/2UNqb1x

Areheart, Bradley A. 2008. "When Disability Isn't Just Right: The Entrenchment of the Medical Model of Disability and the Goldilocks Dilemma." *Indiana Law Journal* 83 (1): 181–232. http://bit.ly/2UWnk6n

Autor, David H., and Mark G. Duggan. 2006. "The Growth in the Social Security Disability Rolls: A Fiscal Crisis Unfolding." *Journal of Economic Perspectives* 20 (3): 71–96. doi:10.1257/jep.20.3.71

Bachrach, Leona L. 1987. "Deinstitutionalization in the United States: Promises and Prospects." *New Directions for Mental Health Services* 1987 (35): 75–90. doi:10.1002/(ISSN)1558-445310.1002/yd.v1987:3510.1002/yd.23319873508

Bates-Harris, Cheryl. 2012. "Segregated and Exploited: The Failure of the Disability Service System to Provide Quality Work." *Journal of Vocational Rehabilitation* 36 (1): 39–64. doi:10.3233/JVR-2012-0581

Baynton, Douglas C. 2017. "Disability and the Justification of Inequality in American History." In *The Disability Studies Reader*, edited by Lennard J. Davis, pp. 17–34. New York, NY: New York University Press.

Befort, Stephen F. 2013. "An Empirical Analysis of Case Outcomes Under the ADA Amendments Act." *Washington and Lee Law Review* 70 (4): 2027–2071.

Blessing, Carol J., Thomas P. Golden, and Susanne M. Bruyère. 2009. "Evolution of Disability Policies and Practices in the United States: Implications for Global Implementation of Person-Centered Planning. In *Disabilities: Insights from Across Fields and Around the Work, Practice, Legal, and Political Frameworks*, edited by Catherine A. Marshall, Elizabeth Kendall, Martha E. Banks, and Reva Mariah S. Gover, pp. 1–16. Santa Barbara, CA: Praeger/ABC-CLIO.

Braddock, David L., and Susan L. Parish. 2001. "An Institutional History of Disability." *Handbook of Disability Studies*, edited by Gary L. Albrecht, Katherine Seelman, and Michael Bury, pp. 11–68. Thousand Oaks, CA: Sage. doi:10.4135/9781412976251.n2

Bradley, Valerie J. 1994. "Evolution of a New Service Paradigm." In *Creating Individual Supports for People with Developmental Disabilities*, edited by Valerie J. Bradley, John W. Ashbaugh, and Bruce C. Blaney. Baltimore, MD: Paul H. Brookes.

Bruyère, Susanne M., and Matthew C. Saleh. 2017. "Disability Policy and Law." In *The Professional Practice of Rehabilitation Counseling*, edited by Vilia M. Tarvydas and Michael T. Hartley, pp. 95–119. New York, NY: Springer.

Butterworth, J., A.C. Hall, F. Smith, A. Migliore, and J. Winsor. 2011. "StateData: The National Report on Employment Services and Outcomes." Boston MA: Institute for Community Inclusion. http://bit.ly/2QA7cD5

Cimera, Robert E. 2012. "The Economics of Supported Employment: What New Data Tell Us." *Journal of Vocational Rehabilitation 37* (2): 109–117. doi:10.3233/JVR-2012-0604

Colker, Ruth, and Paul D. Grossman. 2013. *The Law of Disability Discrimination* (8th ed.). New York, NY: LexisNexis.

Conroy, James W., Robert McCaffrey, and George Liacopoulos. 2016 (Feb.). "Closing Sheltered Employment Settings: Report on a Pilot Test of a National Opinion Leader Survey." Haverton, PA: Center for Outcome Analysis. http://bit.ly/2KDScoe

Cremin, Kevin M. 2012. "Challenges to Institutionalization: The Definition of Institution and the Future of Olmstead Litigation." *Texas Journal on Civil Liberties & Civil Rights* 17 (2): 143–180.

Dague, Bryan. 2012. "Sheltered Employment, Sheltered Lives: Family Perspectives of Conversion to Community-Based Employment." *Journal of Vocational Rehabilitation* 37 (1): 1–11. doi:10.3233/JVR-2012-0595

Davis, Lennard. 1995. *Enforcing Normalcy: Disability, Deafness and the Body*. London, UK: Verso.

Dorfman, Doron. 2017. "Re-Claiming Disability: Identity, Procedural Justice, and the Disability Determination Process." *Law & Social Inquiry* 42 (1): 195–231. doi:10.1111/lsi.12176

Dumont, Matthew P., and Dora M. Dumont. 2008. "Deinstitutionalization in the United States and Italy: A Historical Survey." *International Journal of Mental Health* 37 (4): 61–70. doi:10.2753/IMH0020-7411370405

Eide, Arne H., and Benedicte Ingstad. 2011. *Disability and Poverty: A Global Challenge*. Bristol, UK: Policy Press.

Erickson, William, Camille Lee, and Sarah von Schrader. 2017. "Disability Statistics from the American Community Survey (ACS)." Ithaca, NY: Cornell University Yang-Tan Institute on Employment and Disability. www.disabilitystatistics.org

Geaney, John H. 2004. "The Relationship of Workers' Compensation to the Americans with Disabilities Act and Family and Medical Leave Act." *Clinics in Occupational and Environmental Medicine* 4 (2): 273–293. doi:10.1016/j.coem.2004.02.001

Golden, Thomas P., Ilene Zeitzer, and Susanne M. Bruyère. 2014. "New Approaches to Disability in Social Policy: The Case of the United States. In *Labor and Employment Relations in a Globalized World: New Perspectives on Work, Social Policy, and Labor Market Implications*, edited by Toker Dereli, Y. Pinar Soykut-Sarica, and Asli Şen-Taşbaşi, pp. 73–114. New York, NY: Springer.

Hager, Ronald M., and James R. Sheldon. 2006. "State and Federal Vocational Rehabilitation Programs: Services and Supports to Assist Individuals with Disabilities in Preparing for, Attaching to, and Advancing in Employment." Policy and Practice Brief. Ithaca, NY: Work Incentives Support Center, Cornell University. http://bit.ly/2KCDWfm

Job Accommodation Network. 2018. "Accommodation and Compliance: Low Cost, High Impact." http://bit.ly/2KJctsK

Kaye, H. Stephen, Lita H. Jans, and Erica C. Jones. 2011. "Why Don't Employers Hire and Retain Workers with Disabilities?" *Journal of Occupational Rehabilitation* 21 (4): 526–536. doi:10.1007/s10926-011-9302-8

Livermore, Gina, Sarah Prenovitz, and Jody Schimmel. 2011 (Sep. 19). "Employment-Related Outcomes of an Early Cohort of Work Incentives Planning and Assistance (WIPA) Program Enrollees." *Mathematica Policy Research*. http://bit.ly/2OucKBE

Lok, Jaco, and Mark de Rond. 2013. "On the Plasticity of Institutions: Containing and Restoring Practice Breakdowns at the Cambridge University Boat Club." *Academy of Management Review* 56 (1): 185–207. doi:10.5465/amj.2010.0688

Martin, Patricia P., and David A. Weaver. 2005. "Social Security: A Program and Policy History." *Social Security Bulletin* 66 (1): 1–15. http://bit.ly/2KAz2j8

Migliore, Alberto. 2010. "Sheltered Workshops." In *International Encyclopedia of Rehabilitation*, edited by John H. Stone and Michael Blouin. Buffalo, NY: Center for International Rehabilitation Research Information and Exchange.

Novak, Jeanne. 2015. "Raising Expectations for U.S. Youth with Disabilities: Federal Disability Policy Advances Integrated Employment." *Center for Educational Policy Studies Journal* 5 (1): 91–110.

Oliver, Michael. 1990. *The Politics of Disablement: A Sociological Approach*. New York, NY: St. Martin's Press.

Parsons, Talcott. 1975. "The Sick Role and the Role of the Physician Reconsidered." *The Milbank Memorial Fund Quarterly. Health & Society* 53 (3): 257–278. doi:10.2307/3349493

Phoenix, Janet A., and Tyler Bysshe. 2015. "Transitions: A Case Study of the Conversion from Sheltered Workshops to Integrated Employment in Maine." Washington, DC: Milken Institute School of Public Health Department of Health Policy and Management, George Washington University.

Prechtel-Kluskens, Claire. 2010. "'A Reasonable Degree of Promptitude': Civil War Pension Application Processing, 1861–1885." *Prologue: Quarterly of the National Archives and Records Administration* 41 (1). http://bit.ly/2KB3Znr

Rothman, Juliet. 2018. *Social Work Practice Across Disability*. New York, NY: Routledge.

Samaha, Adam M. 2007. "What Good Is the Social Model of Disability?" *University of Chicago Law Review* 74 (4): 1251–1308.

Schweik, Susan M. 2009. *The Ugly Laws: Disability in Public*. New York: New York University Press.

Sheldon, James R. 2018 (Dec.). "Building State Vocational Rehabilitation Agency Benefits Planning Capacities." Washington, DC: Vocational Rehabilitation Youth Technical Assistance Center, Institute for Educational Leadership.

Steadman, Henry J., John Monahan, Barbara Duffee, Eliot Hartstone, and Pamela C. Robbins. 1984. "The Impact of State Mental Hospital Deinstitutionalization on United States Prison Populations, 1968–1978." *The Journal of Criminal Law & Criminology* 75 (2): 474–490. doi:10.2307/1143164

Svihula, Judie, and Carroll L. Estes. 2007. "Social Security Politics: Ideology and Reform." *Journal of Gerontology* 62 (2): 579–589. doi:10.1093/geronb/62.2.S79

Szymendera, Scott D. 2017. "The Federal Employees' Compensation Act (FECA): Workers' Compensation for Federal Employees." Washington, DC: Congressional Research Service. http://bit.ly/2KAVVmA

Ticket to Work and Work Incentives Advisory Panel. 2007. "Building on the Ticket: A New Paradigm for Investing in Economic Self-Sufficiency for People with Significant Disabilities." Washington, DC: Ticket to Work and Work Incentives Advisory Panel, Social Security Administration.

Unger, Darlene D., Paul Wehman, Satoko Yasuda, Leanne Campbell, and Howard Green. 2002. "Human Resource Professionals and the Employment of People with Disabilities: A Business Perspective." In *Employers' Views of Workplace Supports: Virginia Commonwealth University Charter Business Roundtable's National Study of Employers' Experiences with Workers with Disabilities*, edited by Darlene D. Unger, John Kregel, Paul Wehman, and Valerie Brooke. Richmond, VA: Virginia Commonwealth University.

US Department of Education, Office of Special Education and Rehabilitative Services. 2018 (May 9). "The Secretary Plans to Issue a Notice of Proposed Rulemaking to Amend Regulatory Definitions in 34 CFR Part 361 Implementing Programs Under the Rehabilitation Act of 1973, as Amended, Made by the Workforce Innovation and Opportunity Act." Washington, DC: US Department of Education. http://bit.ly/2KDkAqv

US General Accounting Office. 2003. "Workforce Investment Act: One-Stop Centers Implemented Strategies to Strengthen Services and Partnerships, but More Research and Information Sharing Is Needed." Washington, DC: US General Accounting Office. http://bit.ly/2KCJS88

von Schrader, Sarah, Valerie Malzer, and Susanne Bruyère. 2013. "Perspectives on Disability Disclosure: The Importance of Employer Practices and Workplace Climate." *Employee Responsibilities and Rights Journal* 26 (4): 237–255. doi:10.1007/s10672-013-9227-9

Whitehead, Claude W. 1986. "The Sheltered Workshop Dilemma: Reform, or Replacement." *Remedial and Special Education* 7 (6): 18–24. doi:10.1177/074193258600700607

Winsor, Jean, Jaimie Timmons, John Butterworth, John Shepard, Cady Landa, Frank Smith, Daria Domin, Alberto Migliore, Jennifer Bose, and Lydia Landim. 2017. "StateData: The National Report on Employment Services and Outcomes, 2016." Boston, MA: Institute for Community Inclusion, University of Massachusetts Boston. http://bit.ly/2KKpRfQ

Yap, Margaret, and Alison M. Konrad. 2009. "Gender and Racial Differentials in Promotions: Is There a Sticky Floor, a Midlevel Bottleneck, or a Glass Ceiling? *Industrial Relations* 64 (4): 593–619. doi:10.7202/038875ar

Chapter 2

Minimizing Discrimination and Maximizing Inclusion: Lessons from the Federal Workforce and Federal Subcontractors

Hassan Enayati
Sarah von Schrader
William Erickson
Susanne M. Bruyère
Cornell University

INTRODUCTION

Improving the labor market outcomes of individuals with disabilities requires a clear understanding of the employer policies and practices that increase inclusion and decrease discrimination. This chapter leverages the availability of disability employment measures in the federal workforce and among federal subcontractors to identify these lessons on inclusion and nondiscrimination. We demonstrate later in the chapter the wide range of sectors and occupations covered by these two groups of employers. Moreover, these employers are relevant to a large section of the American workforce, with roughly a quarter of all working Americans employed by a federal subcontractor or in the federal workforce. According to estimates from the Office of Federal Contract Compliance Programs (OFCCP), based on the 2016 EEO-1 data, there are approximately 25,000 federal contractors employing approximately 33 million workers. Additionally, 2.7 million executive-branch civilian employees work in the federal workforce (US Office of Personnel Management 2014).

The intent of Sections 501 and 503 of the Rehabilitation Act of 1973, and later Title I of the Americans with Disabilities Act of 1990 (ADA), was the improvement of employment outcomes and the elimination of employment discrimination against individuals with disabilities. These groundbreaking laws led to important changes in employer practices around disability (Bruyère, Golden, and VanLooy 2011), yet individuals with disabilities continue to be significantly unemployed and underemployed compared with their nondisabled peers. In 2017, 37.3% of individuals with disabilities of working age (21–64) were in the workforce, compared with 79.4% of people without disabilities (Erickson, Lee, and von Schrader 2019). People with disabilities who are employed still experience lower pay, less job security, fewer opportunities for advancement and training, and less participation in workplace decision making than do nondisabled employees (Schur, Kruse, Blasi, and Blanck 2009). Post-hire engagement and employment success are critical factors in continued employment and the ability of individuals with disabilities to be economically self-sufficient.

Workplace diversity and inclusion practices have the potential to level the playing field and improve the employment outcomes of individuals with disabilities. These practices can mitigate workplace discrimination, as the workplace environment mediates the cognitive processes that result in discrimination by individuals (Baron and Pfeffer 1994). However, much of the empirical research to date focuses on employer attitudes toward applicants and employees with disabilities and toward disability itself, finding that attitudes of supervisors and co-workers have a strong effect on the experiences of employees with disabilities (Bruyère, Erickson, and Ferrentino 2003; Colella 1996, 2001; Colella, DeNisi, and Varma 1998; Florey and Harrison 2000; Hernandez, Keys, and Balcazar 2000). While important, this is not sufficient to identify the proactive practices that might mitigate biases and stereotypes and create powerful proactive changes in the workplace experience of people with disabilities.

Even within the broader area of diversity management, little research connects formal organizational practices either to employee-level outcomes such as job satisfaction, engagement, or to macro-level organizational outcomes such as diversity representation and turnover (Kulik 2014). While a few studies focus on women and minority groups (e.g., Dobbin and Kalev 2013; Kalev, Dobbin, and Kelley 2006 in the private sector; Naff and Kellough 2003 in the federal sector), almost no research has directly addressed the question of how organizational policies and practices affect the employment of people with disabilities (DCSRC 2008; Pitts and Wise 2009). It is understood that organizational characteristics such as policies and practices do impact the employment experiences and outcomes of individuals with disabilities (Stone and Colella 1996), but gathering empirical data that directly connect to outcomes is difficult. Studies of employer practices around diversity and disability have frequently examined organizational perceptions of the effectiveness of a practice rather than actually measuring the difference it made (Erickson, von Schrader, Bruyère, and VanLooy 2013; Kulik 2014). Other studies use self-reported employee data, such as the perceived fairness and responsiveness of the organization to employee needs, levels of job satisfaction, and turnover intention (Schur, Kruse, Blasi, and Blanck 2009) but do not study the impact of specific policies or practices.

Part of the problem in the United States has been the historical lack of data collection regarding disability within private organizations because employers perceived it to be prohibited under the ADA. A recent study in the Canadian context found a "meaningful association" between strong, proactive diversity practices and the overall representation of people with disabilities in an organization (Konrad, Yang, and Maurer 2016). The US EEOC has collected data on disability in federal agencies since 1981 and has collected detailed disability data through the MD-715 since 2004. These data can be instrumental in filling the current knowledge gap, moving beyond identifying "meaningful associations" to understand how employer practices actually *impact* the hiring, retention, advancement, and inclusion of individuals with disabilities.

In this chapter, we argue that two essential features of the federal and federal contractor workforce allow us to draw important lessons on improving the labor market outcomes for people with disabilities. First, a key set of policies applies to these employers that is intended to increase the representation of people with disabilities. Second, those policies require regular data collection, which makes studying workplace outcomes possible.

In the remainder of the chapter, we present the findings from the federal workforce and then move on to the federal contractors. In our discussion of the federal workforce, we document legislation and policy that has guided federal disability employment practice and then compare the disability representation in the federal sector and private sector over the past ten years. We then present new evidence of the differences by disability status in workplace experiences and perceptions among federal government employees, the workforce representation across federal pay categories, and relationships between agency practices and agency workforce representation of disability. We then transition our focus to federal contractors by starting with a summary of the legislation and policy that has guided federal contractor disability employment practice. Next, new findings comparing employers with and without compliance violations are shared before highlighting established practices associated with higher disability employment among contractors. The chapter concludes with a discussion of the implications of our findings for labor relations, mediation/arbitration professionals, and conflict resolution specialists.

FEDERAL WORKFORCE

Key Policies and Regulations Affecting the Employment of Individuals with Disabilities

The US federal government is one of the world's largest employers, with 2.7 million executive branch civilian employees (US Office of Personnel Management 2014), accounting for nearly 1.8% of all US civilian workers (author calculation based on US Census Bureau estimates). The federal government has been subject to disability nondiscrimination legislation since 1973. The Rehabilitation Act of 1973 was intended to "empower individuals with disabilities to maximize employment, economic self-sufficiency, independence, and inclusion and integration into society, through ... research ... to ensure that the Federal Government plays a leadership role in promoting the employment of individuals with disabilities" (US EEOC, no date). Section 501 of the Rehabilitation Act prohibits employment discrimination against people with disabilities in the federal sector. Section

501 requires that each covered federal department and agency file with the EEOC an affirmative action program plan for the hiring, placement, and advancement of individuals with disabilities. The plan must include a description of the extent to which and methods the department or agency will use to address the needs of employees with disabilities. The regulations require that these plans be updated and reviewed annually, and approved by the EEOC (US EEOC 2017).

On July 26, 2010, President Barack Obama signed Executive Order 13548 (Executive Order No. 13548, 2010) "to establish the Federal government as a model employer of individuals with disabilities." Federal agencies must also comply with Executive Order 13163 (Executive Order No. 13163, 2000), which called for 100,000 people with disabilities to be hired over the next five years. Employees are encouraged to self-identify as having a disability on form SF 256; from 2011 through 2014, 71,967 nonseasonal, full-time permanent employees with disabilities were hired (US Office of Personnel Management 2015b). The representation of individuals who self-identified as having any disability increased from 7% of the federal workforce in 2010 to 9% in 2014, while the percentage of individuals with a "targeted" disability rose from 0.90% to 1.07% (US Office of Personnel Management 2015b). "Targeted disabilities" are those that the federal government has identified for special emphasis, and include deafness, blindness, missing extremities, partial paralysis, complete paralysis, convulsive disorders, intellectual disability (previously called mental retardation), mental illness, and distortion of limb and/or spine.[1] These rates, while lower than recently updated federal goals of 12% disability and 2% targeted disability representation (AAIDFE 2017), are higher than typically seen in the private sector. Some federal agencies have been more successful than others in increasing the hiring and retention of individuals with disabilities, leading to the question, What practices influence these and other key employment outcomes? Given the nature of diversity practices, a better understanding of what works in the federal sector can provide insights to the private sector.

We argue that despite differences between the federal sector and private sector, the diversity of employee characteristics and occupations in the federal sector (Falk 2012) and similarities in practice/policy implementation across these sectors (Bruyère 2000) make the lessons learned in the federal sector relevant to the private sector. It is true that employees in these two sectors differ in terms of average education, tenure with employer, and distribution of occupations (Falk 2012). That said, the distribution of occupations within the federal sector covers the same categories as the private sector, with a difference of less than three percentage points in half of the occupational groupings—for example, comparing federal to private workforces, administrative or office support is 15% versus 14%, and service is 14% versus 12% (Falk 2012). Thus, both sectors include a range of occupations, and this diversity of characteristics supports the claim to generalizability. Moreover, federal subcontractors are looking to the federal sector for guidance as they strive to comply with updated Section 503 regulations, and federal employers have historically provided a standard for equity in employment (O'Leary 2009). In research working groups conducted by Cornell University as a part of an Employer Practices Rehabilitation Research and Training Center program funded by the National Institute on Disability, Independent Living, and Rehabilitation Research, private sector employers and federal sector representatives had productive dialogs about affirmative recruitment and facilitating disability disclosure among employees (Barrington 2016).

Disability Employment in the Federal Sector Relative to the Private Sector

Comparing the federal workforce's disability representation with that in the private sector is a reasonable first step in assessing the federal government's goal of being a model employer of individuals with disabilities. Using American Community Survey (ACS) 2008–2016 data, Table 1 (next page) summarizes the proportion of federal versus private sector employees with a disability using different measures of disability. The ACS disability measure identifies respondents who answer affirmatively to having a cognitive, ambulatory, independent living, self-care, vision, or hearing disability and is the current standard measure of disability in many large surveys in the United States, including the Current Population Study and the Behavioral Risk Factor Surveillance System.

The first two columns of Table 1 reveal two interesting patterns. First, the federal workforce has consistently had a higher percentage of employees with disabilities (ACS disability). Over the time period shown, the gap between federal and private sectors (columns 1 and 2) ranged between 1.6 and 2.5 percentage points, which represents a third to over a half of the private sector's rate. Second, disability representation dipped in the middle of this time window for both sectors, with the federal workforce showing a faster and stronger post-recession recovery.

The next three clusters of columns (columns 3 through 8) highlight the important role that veterans with a service-connected disability of 30% or more play in the overall disability representation in the sector. Since 2011, at least 10% of federal employees identify as having a disability (both veterans and nonveterans), whereas private sector employees with disabilities have remained steadily at roughly 5% of the private sector workforce since 2008. It becomes clear from the final two columns of Table 1 that the large growth in the employment of individuals with disabilities in the federal workforce is driven by the rapid expansion of the share of veterans with service-connected disabilities. Overall, the federal government has outperformed the private sector in the employment of individuals with disabilities, specifically veterans with service-connected disabilities.

While the federal government has historically employed many people with disabilities, recent inroads in disability representation have been affected by

TABLE 1
Proportion of Federal and Private Sector Employment of People with Disabilities (2008–2016)

	ACS* Disability		ACS Disability or Veterans with Service-Connected Disability**		ACS Disability, Excluding Veterans with Service-Connected Disability		Veterans with Service-Connected Disability	
	1	2	3	4	5	6	7	8
Year	Federal	Private	Federal	Private	Federal	Private	Federal	Private
2008	6.4	4.8	9.3	5.0	5.5	4.7	3.8	0.3
2009	6.3	4.4	9.7	4.7	5.4	4.4	4.3	0.3
2010	5.8	4.2	9.1	4.5	5.0	4.2	4.1	0.3
2011	6.1	4.2	10.1	4.5	5.0	4.2	5.0	0.3
2012	6.3	4.2	10.6	4.5	5.0	4.1	5.6	0.4
2013	6.6	4.5	11.4	4.8	5.2	4.4	6.1	0.4
2014	6.8	4.5	11.6	4.8	5.4	4.4	6.2	0.4
2015	6.5	4.5	11.7	4.8	5.0	4.4	6.6	0.4
2016	7.2	4.7	13.0	5.0	5.4	4.6	7.7	0.5

Note: Based on author's calculations from an analysis of ACS 2008–2016 Public Use Microdata Samples (PUMS). Sample includes all full-time, full-year workers in the United States, regardless of age. Private employers include for-profit and not-for-profit employers only.
*American Community Survey.
**Veterans with a service-connected disability are limited to those reporting a 30% or higher service-connected disability rating. The sample excludes postal office, state, and local government employees as well as self-employed workers.

increasing representation of veterans with disabilities. A number of veteran hiring authorities and initiatives exist that may explain the significantly greater representation of veterans with disabilities in the federal sector. Current hiring authorities, such as the Veteran Recruitment Appointment and the 30% or More Disabled Veteran authority, allow agencies to noncompetitively hire qualified veterans with disabilities. Examining the role of these programs and initiatives could be fertile ground for future research in understanding employer practices that could reduce the under-representation of individuals with disabilities in the workplace.

Group Differences in Self-Reported Experiences and Perceptions in the Federal Sector

While there has been research in the management and public administration literature on the differential experiences of women and racial/ethnic minorities, there is relatively little information about the workplace experiences of individuals with disabilities. In a Canadian study, women with disabilities were noted as much less satisfied with many aspects of their work experiences than women without disabilities, but the data did not allow for studying the interaction of gender with disability status (Burke 1999). Disability employment rates in the federal sector are high relative to the private sector, as evidenced by the ACS data and reports by the Office of Personnel Management (OPM). While the federal government has been successful in increasing the number of employees with disabilities, a long-standing concern exists that there is a limited career path once hired (Lewis and Allee 1992). It is of interest to better understand the experiences of these federal employees with disabilities. In 2012, the federal government added a disability question to the Federal Employee Viewpoint Survey (FEVS), a survey conducted by the OPM designed to understand employees' perceptions of agency management. In 2015, 14% of respondents self-identified as individuals with disabilities on the FEVS. Further information about the FEVS is available in annual technical and data reports available at https://www.opm.gov/fevs/reports.

Reports prepared by the OPM generally demonstrate that employees with disabilities rate their experiences in the federal workforce lower than their peers without disabilities (US Office of Personnel Management 2015a). In this section, we will look more deeply at group differences, and in particular, we will examine whether there are "double jeopardy" effects—that is, does being a female with a disability differentially disadvantage an individual in terms of her experience in working in the federal government as reported on the FEVS?

The analyses that follow shed light on how federal employees perceive their work experiences and provide insight into perceptions about opportunities for advancement as well as overall job satisfaction. In particular, we examine differences in composite job satisfaction, opportunities for professional development and training, quality of supervisor relationship, procedural fairness, and fairness in rewards/recognition by disability status.

The items that make up these scales are presented in Table 2 (next page). Using OPM reports and previous studies of the FEVS as sources to inform item selection for each construct of interest, we examined item polychoric correlation matrices, used exploratory factor analysis to identify items that clustered statistically, conducted a confirmatory factor analysis with all eight scales, and then examined measurement invariance by disability status.[2] Our analysis supported the development of the eight scales (five of which are presented here) and indicated strong factorial invariance by disability supporting the appropriateness of group comparisons (Putnick and Bornstein 2016).[3]

The statistics presented in Table 3 (page 41) indicate that employees with disabilities in the federal government are more likely to be minorities, be male, have military experience, be less educated, be older, and have less tenure. Perhaps the most striking finding is that even after excluding military agencies, 67% of the federal workforce with disabilities has military service experience compared with 22% of those without disabilities.

TABLE 2
Scale Reliability and Items from the 2015 Federal Employee Viewpoint Survey (FEVS)

Quality of supervisor relationship (standard coefficient α = 0.95)
42. My supervisor supports my need to balance work and other life issues.
48. My supervisor listens to what I have to say.
49. My supervisor treats me with respect.
51. I have trust and confidence in my supervisor.
52. Overall, how good a job do you feel is being done by your immediate supervisor?
Professional development and training (standard coefficient α = 0.85)
1. I am given a real opportunity to improve my skills in my organization.
18. My training needs are assessed.
68. How satisfied are you with the training you receive for your present job?
Fairness (standard coefficient α = 0.91)
22. Promotions in my work unit are based on merit.
23. In my work unit, steps are taken to deal with a poor performer who cannot or will not improve.
24. In my work unit, differences in performance are recognized in a meaningful way.
25. Awards in my work unit depend on how well employees perform their jobs.
33. Pay raises depend on how well employees perform their jobs.
Organizational fairness/procedural justice (standard coefficient α = 0.86)
17. I can disclose a suspected violation of any law, rule or regulation without fear of reprisal.
37. Arbitrary action, personal favoritism and coercion for partisan political purposes are not tolerated.
38. Prohibited personnel practices (for example, illegally discriminating for or against any employee/applicant, obstructing a person's right to compete for employment, knowingly violating veterans' preference requirements) are not tolerated.
Job satisfaction (standard coefficient α = 0.90)
40. I recommend my organization as a good place to work.
65. How satisfied are you with the recognition you receive for doing a good job?
67. How satisfied are you with your opportunity to get a better job in your organization?
69. Considering everything, how satisfied are you with your job?
70. Considering everything, how satisfied are you with your pay?
71. Considering everything, how satisfied are you with your organization?

Note: Data source: 2015 FEVS. The table lists the FEVS items included in each of five scales described in this chapter.

TABLE 3
Respondent Characteristics by Disability Status Among Federal Employee Viewpoint Survey (FEVS) Sample (Weighted)

Variable	Percentage of Employees with Disabilities	Percentage of Employees Without Disabilities	p-value
Minority	45.0	38.5	< 0.0001
Female	34.9	49.0	< 0.0001
US military service experience*	67.3	21.8	< 0.0001
Supervisor/manager/senior leader	14.3	19.7	< 0.0001
Less than bachelor's degree	44.7	33.7	< 0.0001
Bachelor's degree	30.4	34.6	
Post-bachelor's degree	24.9	31.7	
Under 40 years old	20.2	28.5	< 0.0001
40–49	26.4	27.3	
50–59	36.2	30.6	
60 or older	17.2	13.6	
5 or fewer years of federal tenure	29.0	21.2	< 0.0001
6–14 years	37.7	38.7	
15 or more years	33.4	40.1	

Note: Estimates presented are based on the 2015 FEVS survey, with sample limited to non-military agencies and complete responses to demographic variables and scales score. The analysis uses the weight variable recommended in the FEVS documentation.

*Military service experience means the respondent indicated that she or he is either currently in National Guard or Reserves or is retired, separated, or discharged from US military service.

Table 4 (next page) presents means, standard deviations, and effect sizes for the differences between groups of interest. As found in OPM reports, federal employees with disabilities consistently rate their experiences lower than those without a disability, and this is generally the case for other groups of interest (female vs. male, minority vs. nonminority, and military experience vs. no military experience), although there are a few exceptions (for example, females report slightly higher job satisfaction than males). Because of the large sample size, group differences are nearly all significant; therefore, we present effect sizes to understand the magnitude of the differences. The takeaway from this table is that, while the effect sizes are small by traditional criteria, the effect sizes for disability are typically more than twice the size of other group differences. As noted above, the next question is whether people with disabilities who are also members of other groups differ on these constructs. To examine adjusted group differences, we conducted unweighted multiple linear regression analyses for each of the five separate scales as dependent variables. We included two-way interactions of

TABLE 4
Disability Group Differences and Effect Size by Demographic Groups on Federal Employee Viewpoint Survey (FEVS) Constructs (Weighted)

	Mean (SD) Employees with Disabilities	Mean (SD) Employees Without Disabilities	Difference (Standard Error of Difference)	Disability Effect Size	Minority Effect Size	Female Effect Size	Military Effect Size
Supervisor_Rel. (quality of relationship with supervisor)	3.75 (2.32)	3.96 (1.86)	–0.218 (0.005)	–0.114	–0.071	–0.032	–0.039
Professional_dev. (professional development opportunity)	3.21 (2.24)	3.42 (1.85)	–0.205 (0.005)	–0.108	–0.009	0.012	–0.048
Fairness (fairness in rewards/ recognition)	2.62 (2.18)	2.79 (1.90)	–0.169 (0.006)	–0.087	0.019	–0.003	–0.050
Org_Fair (procedural fairness)	3.20 (2.45)	3.49 (1.96)	–0.298 (0.006)	–0.147	–0.083	–0.039	–0.051
Job_satComp (composite job satisfaction)	3.18 (2.06)	3.39 (1.73)	–0.212 (0.005)	–0.119	–0.015	0.013	–0.044

Note: Scale scores range from 1 to 5, with 5 being more positive. Only respondents who completed at least half of the items on a scale have a scale score and were included in the sample. The effect size was calculated by dividing the mean difference by pooled SD. The analysis uses the weight variable recommended in the FEVS documentation.

disability and other groups of interest (minority status, female, and military experience) in the models.

The results are interesting and suggest that there are consistent disparities between individuals with and without disabilities, with individuals with disabilities having lower adjusted scores on all scales. In general, there were no meaningful interactions between minority status and disability in the models. The interaction between military experience and disability was consistent across scales, with employees with military service experience and a disability having higher ratings than those without military experience and a disability. The gap between employees with military experience with disabilities and those without disabilities was much smaller than the parallel gap for employees without military experience with and without disabilities. This is illustrated in the adjusted means by group presented in Figure 1 for the professional development opportunity scale.

Also interesting are the observed interactions between gender and disability status (controlling for military experience and other variables). Being a female with a disability is associated with significantly lower scores on each scale compared with males with disabilities and with females without a disability. On professional development and job satisfaction scales, females without disabilities score slightly higher or at the same level as males without disabilities, but females with disabilities are significantly disadvantaged compared with their male coun-

FIGURE 1
Professional Development: Interaction Between Disability Status and Military Experience

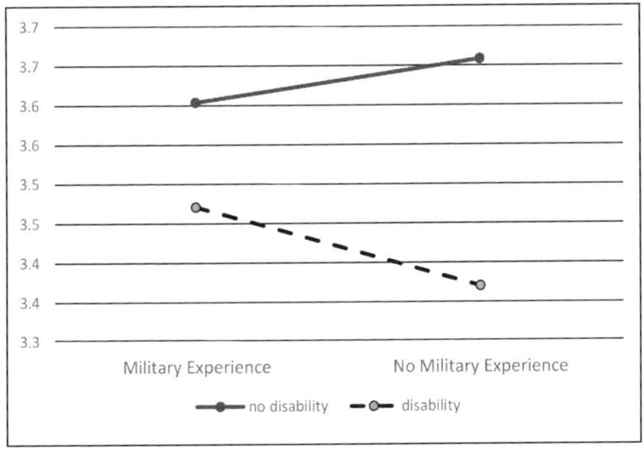

Note: The figure presents the interaction between disability status and military experience in a regression with the dependent variable of professional development. The values presented are the least square means for each group. The model adjusts for sex, minority status, supervisor status (nonsupervisor/team leader vs. supervisor/manager/senior leader), education level (bachelor's degree, less than bachelor's, post-bachelor's), age group (under 40, 40–49, 50–59, 60 and older), and federal tenure (5 or fewer years, 6–14 years, 15 or more years). The model also includes fixed effects for agency.

terparts. This is illustrated in the adjusted means by group presented in Figure 2 (next page) for professional development.

Key Takeaways

In this analysis of the FEVS, while the effect sizes are small, people with disabilities have consistently lower scale scores—that is, people with disabilities rate their job satisfaction, opportunities for professional development, supervisor relationship, procedural fairness, and fairness in rewards/recognition lower than their peers without disabilities. Other groups varying by minority status, sex, and military experience tend to have much smaller group differences than those observed by disability status. However, that does not tell the whole story, and examining the intersection of groups paints a richer picture. With so many people with military experience among federal employees with disabilities, it is noteworthy that military experience is associated with higher ratings for employees with disabilities, while military experience is typically not associated with higher scores among those without disabilities. It will be important to understand why military experience is associated with higher scores among people with disabilities but not those without disability—perhaps veterans with a disability hold a higher status in agencies? Meanwhile, being a female with a disability seems to lead to being

FIGURE 2
Professional Development: Interaction Between Disability Status and Gender

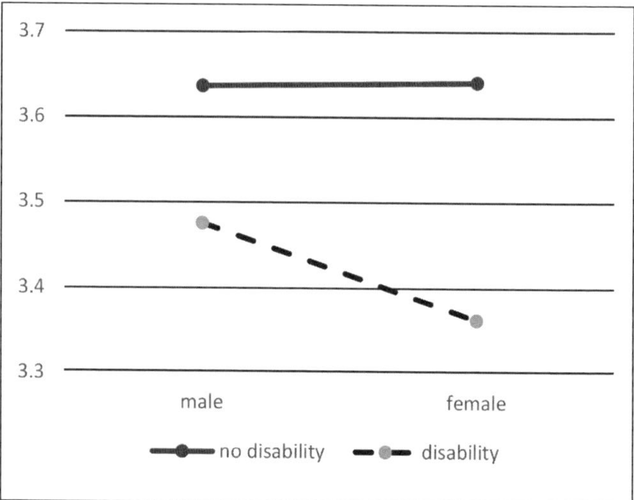

Note: The figure presents the interaction between disability status and military experience in a regression with the dependent variable of professional development. The values presented are the least square means for each group. The model adjusts for sex, minority status, supervisor status (nonsupervisor/team leader vs. supervisor/manager/senior leader), education level (bachelor's degree, less than bachelor's, post-bachelor's), age group (under 40, 40–49, 50–59, 60 and older), and federal tenure (5 or fewer years, 6–14 years, 15 or more years). The model also includes fixed effects for agency.

doubly disadvantaged: Females with disabilities have lower scores than males with disabilities as well as females without disabilities. Gathering more qualitative information about what might drive these groups' differences will be important in both understanding and addressing these disparities. Further research linking these data with information presented in the next section on agency practices and agency demographics may help to understand whether changes in policy or practice affect the experiences and perceptions of federal employees with disabilities.

Disability Policies and Practices Within Federal Agencies

The set of federal agency policies and practices and their relationship to disability employment in the agency provides another opportunity through which the federal workforce can be a useful guide on the employment of individuals with disabilities. In this section, we present an analysis of novel data examining the relationship between agency-level disability-related policies and practices and the realized percentage of the workforce with a disability. The federal government's long-term commitment to data collection on disability representation as well as policies and practices allows for analysis that would be otherwise challenging in the private sector.

The data for this analysis come from Management Directive 715 (MD-715), collected by the EEOC. The MD-715 reporting tracks workforce and applicant flow data over time by disability status as well as by targeted disability type for all federal units with at least 100 employees. The MD-715 contains two data components used in this analysis: Part G and B tables. Part G data capture an annual agency self-assessment indicating the presence of 123 diversity practices; these have been developed to guide agencies to adopt what are believed to be model diversity practices. The B tables focus on disability and present workforce counts in 14 groups: total, those with no disability, those not identified, those with a disability, and those with a targeted disability, which is further subdivided by disability type. For each group, the number of employees by appointment, occupational category, position in the General Schedule and wage grades, and other breakdowns are included.

Table 5 describes the sample of agencies used in this analysis.[4] There is reasonable variation in the size of the agencies, with 46% falling into the small employer size category (under 1,000 employees), 31% medium sized (between 1,000 and 9,999 employees), and 24% large (over 9,999 employees). One fifth of the sample are cabinet-level agencies, which fall into one of the medium or large size categories. Across these agencies, the average percentage of the workforce with disabilities is 7.5%, with representation ranging from 1.6% to 15.3%.

A significant advantage of studying workforce patterns across employers in the federal context is the ability to leverage the predominant method for determining compensation, based on the General Schedule. The pay method puts employees within 1 of 15 grades, and within each grade are ten steps. Compensation increases as grade or step increases. In our analysis, the outcome of interest is workforce representation, and as noted earlier, there is a perception that employees with

TABLE 5
Agency Characteristics from Analysis of MD-715 Data

	Mean	Standard Deviation	Minimum	Maximum	Count
Percentage of workforce with disabilities	7.53	3.01	1.63	15.25	59
Workforce size					
Small (≤ 999)	45.76	50.25	0	100	59
Medium (1000–9999)	30.51	46.44	0	100	59
Large (≥ 10,000)	23.73	42.91	0	100	59
Percentage of workforce in highest-grade positions	51.66	18.90	16.26	81.83	59
Cabinet agency	20.34	40.60	0	100	59

Note: Agency characteristics of the 59 parent agencies used in the MD-715 analysis.

disabilities have a limited career path once hired. Reports from OPM highlight that disability representation has increased but that employees with disabilities continue to be more highly represented in lower pay grades (US Office of Personnel Management 2016). Our analysis of the disability representation across grade-level groups, as seen in Figure 3, is consistent with these findings and highlights two key observations. First, the share of the workforce with a disability decreases as the grade level increases. Second, disability representation has increased for all grade groups since 2012. While the federal government has made strides to show that it can be a model employer for individuals with disabilities by increasing the representation, there remains room for improvement in the distribution of individuals with disabilities across the employment and compensation structure.

To examine the relationship between disability workforce representation and agency policy/practices, we focus on 13 policies and practices that specifically mention workers with disabilities or accommodations (Table 6). These data come from the Agency Self-Assessment Checklist Measuring Essential Elements described in Part G of the MD-715 and cover the areas of demonstrated commitment from agency leadership, integration of EEO into the agency's strategic mission, management and program accountability, proactive prevention, and efficiency. Table 6 describes the prevalence of these policies and their relationship

FIGURE 3
Share of the Federal Workforce with Disabilities over Time by Grade-Level Grouping

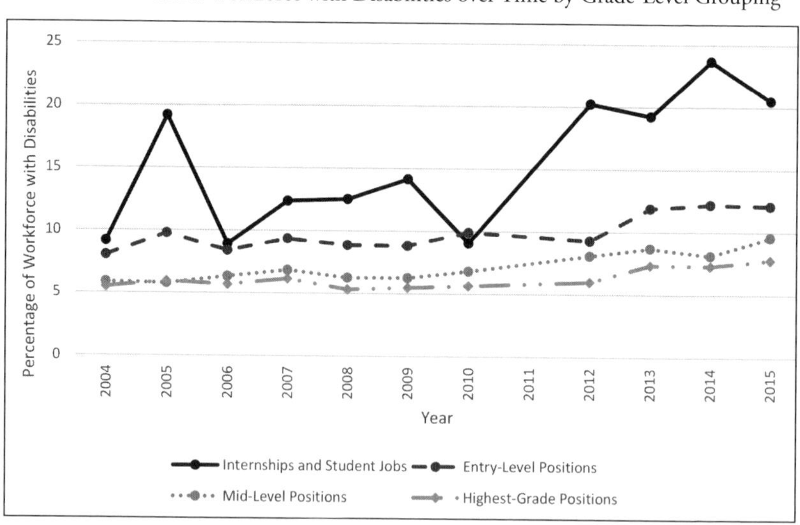

Note: Trend analysis of the share of federal workforce with disabilities by grade-level grouping. This analysis mapped General Schedule (GS) levels 3 through 15 into four categories following the Partnership for Public Service's (2018) methodology. Internships and student jobs correspond to GS-3 and GS-4. Entry-level positions are GS-5 to GS-7. Mid-level positions map to GS-8 to GS-12, and highest-grade positions are GS-13 through GS-15.

TABLE 6
Prevalence and Odds Ratios for the Probability That an Agency Has a Specific Policy or Practice in Place

		Odds Ratios, Workforce Size		Odds Ratios, Highest-Grade Position					
	Percentage, All	Medium	Large	Moderate	High	Cabinet	Years	Years Sq.	N
Managers evaluated on provision of accommodations	95.5 (267)	0.316 (0.309)	4.410 (5.683)	0.201 (0.221)	— —	0.221+ (0.199)	0.339 (0.238)	1.091+ (0.0565)	203
Accommodation procedures available	95.1 (304)	0.802 (0.696)	1.726 (1.753)	0.893 (0.593)	1.363 (1.240)	0.409 (0.268)	1.211 (0.512)	1.007 (0.0335)	304
Managers trained on accommodation responsibilities	88.1 (302)	1.652 (0.809)	2.703+ (1.545)	0.659 (0.318)	1.279 (0.744)	0.654 (0.303)	0.907 (0.240)	1.015 (0.0197)	302
Disability programs sufficiently staffed	87.5 (295)	4.120** (2.203)	1.656 (1.117)	0.993 (0.485)	1.836 (1.069)	0.908 (0.593)	1.350 (0.345)	0.988 (0.0178)	295
Centralized accommodations provision	93.7 (302)	1.458 (1.463)	0.203 (0.230)	3.261+ (2.090)	0.454 (0.377)	0.212 (0.215)	0.673 (0.235)	1.027 (0.0244)	302
Sufficient funds to train/update managers on accommodation	92.6 (298)	3.057 (2.361)	0.565 (0.444)	0.707 (0.451)	0.488 (0.381)	0.726 (0.583)	1.006 (0.303)	1.002 (0.0194)	298
Accommodation decisions are reviewed	93.6 (296)	0.918 (0.704)	2.138 (2.345)	0.601 (0.450)	0.814 (0.615)	0.161+ (0.150)	0.685 (0.325)	1.023 (0.0323)	296
Trends in workforce profiles are analyzed	88.6 (297)	5.589** (2.962)	7.791** (5.500)	4.329** (1.969)	33.94*** (34.87)	0.451 (0.258)	0.948 (0.277)	1.014 (0.0218)	297
Trends in occupations are analyzed	86.5 (296)	3.518** (1.670)	4.383* (3.295)	2.821* (1.208)	9.375*** (5.912)	0.526 (0.332)	0.889 (0.240)	1.015 (0.0196)	296
Trends in grade levels are analyzed	87.3 (299)	3.506** (1.675)	2.518 (1.741)	2.486* (1.060)	12.07*** (9.088)	0.669 (0.378)	0.878 (0.232)	1.017 (0.0193)	299
Trends in compensation are analyzed	81.5 (298)	2.808* (1.161)	2.650+ (1.402)	2.987** (1.155)	3.264** (1.483)	0.641 (0.288)	0.941 (0.211)	1.015 (0.0166)	298
Trends of the effects of management are analyzed	80.9 (299)	2.556* (1.080)	3.106* (1.691)	2.960** (1.125)	3.939** (1.822)	0.872 (0.397)	0.940 (0.212)	1.015 (0.0166)	299
Designated accommodation official	98.3 (300)	5.957 (10.27)	3.160 (4.826)	0.903 (1.140)	0.884 (1.215)	0.502 (0.627)	1.976 (1.320)	0.967 (0.0523)	300

with agency characteristics. All the policies and practices were commonly used; the least prevalent practice was "analysis of trends of the effects of management," which was in place for 81% of "agency years" (i.e., the level of observation in the analysis). As a set, the practices of analyzing trends in the human resources data have relatively lower prevalence than the other items. The most prevalent policy was having a designated accommodation official, with over 98% of agencies reporting that policy.

Columns 2 through 8 of Table 6 present odds ratios from logistic regression analysis of each of the 13 policies and practices on agency characteristics. Relative to small agencies, medium-sized agencies are over four times as likely to have disability programs considered to be sufficiently staffed. Medium- and large-sized agencies are more likely to analyze workplace trends, with medium-sized 5.6 times and large-sized agencies 7.8 times as likely to analyze workforce profiles than small agencies.

Now we consider the proportion of all employees within an agency at the highest grade levels of GS 13 through 15. The concentration of employees in the highest grades of the General Schedule likely corresponds to differences in the underlying tasks and demands an agency requires because the grades themselves are based on job difficulty, responsibilities, and required qualifications (US Office of Personnel Management, no date). Table 5 showed that the percentage of the workforce in the highest grades ranged from 16% to 82%. Splitting the proportion of the agency workforce in the highest-grade positions into three groups—low, moderate, and high—highlights another employer characteristic predictive of these policies and practices.[5] Again, the set of trends in human resources items are more common among agencies with more employees at GS 13 or above. While agencies in the moderate concentration group are 4.3 times as likely to analyze trends in workforce profiles compared with low agencies, agencies with high a concentration of the workforce in highest-grade positions are nearly 34 times as likely to engage in this practice. Table 6 demonstrates that the implementation of these policies and practices is fairly standard across federal agencies; however, instances where certain items are not implemented are correlated with key characteristics of the agencies.

Building on this understanding of the relationship between agency characteristics and implementation, we then modeled the predictive role of each policy and practice on the representation of individuals with disabilities within an agency. Fractional logit regressions were conducted separately for each policy and practice, modeling the percentage of the workforce with a disability on the existence of the policy or practice, agency characteristics, and a quadratic of time. Following Wooldridge (2010), Table 7 provides the robust average partial (noncausal) effects from these models.[6] Only 3 of the 13 items were statistically significant at the conventional threshold of 0.05, while a fourth item is included when considering p-values under 0.1. Centralized provision of accommodations predicts an agency with higher disability representation by 1.1 percentage points. Similarly, analyzing trends in compensation and the effects of management are separately associated with workforces with a 1.2 percentage point higher representation of individuals with disabilities.

Key Takeaways

While most agencies have many of these policies and practices, there remains room for increased use. Three of the policies examined here are tied with significantly higher levels of disability representation. Individuals with disabilities have a higher level of representation in the federal workforce compared with the private sector. That said, they are disproportionately in low-grade, and thus low-paying, positions. Improving labor market outcomes of individuals with disabilities cannot stop at getting them in the door at lower levels within the organization; they need to be hired across the organization's structure and be given opportunities for advancement.

TABLE 7
Predictive Role of Policies and Practices on the Percentage of Workforce with a Disability

	Percentage of Workforce with a Disability
Managers evaluated on provision of accommodations	–0.00517 (0.00485)
Accommodation procedures available	–0.00957* (0.00566)
Managers trained on accommodation responsibilities	–0.000595 (0.00519)
Disability programs sufficiently staffed	0.00638 (0.00579)
Centralized accommodations provision	0.0113** (0.00521)
Sufficient funds to train/update managers on accommodation	0.00133 (0.00543)
Accommodation decisions are reviewed	–0.00561 (0.00422)
Trends in workforce profiles are analyzed	0.00567 (0.00356)
Trends in occupations are analyzed	0.00444 (0.00321)
Trends in grade levels are analyzed	0.00506 (0.00325)
Trends in compensation are analyzed	0.0115*** (0.00355)
Trends of the effects of management are analyzed	0.0115*** (0.00351)
Designated accommodation official	0.00504 (0.00902)

Note: Robust partial averages effects of the predictive, noncausal role of the policies and practices on the percentage of the workforce with a disability. Standard errors are reported in parentheses and clustered at the district level.
Significance levels: * $p < 0.1$, * $p < 0.05$, ** $p < 0.01$, *** $p < 0.001$.

FEDERAL SUBCONTRACTORS

Key Policies and Regulations

Federal subcontractors serve as another interesting employer group when considering best practices of minimizing discrimination and maximizing inclusion for employers more broadly. They provide a valuable comparison with the federal government in that they are required to follow a specific set of employment regulations and record certain workforce metrics, all while being part of the private sector. Federal subcontractors are subject to affirmative action requirements under Section 503 of the Rehabilitation Act of 1973. This regulation prohibits federal contractors and subcontractors from discriminating in employment against individuals with disabilities and requires these employers to take affirmative action to recruit, hire, promote, and retain these individuals. As revised, the regulations strengthen the affirmative action provisions to aid contractors in their efforts to recruit and hire individuals with disabilities and improve job opportunities for those individuals. The regulations also include changes to the nondiscrimination provisions to bring them into compliance with the ADA Amendments Act (ADAAA) of 2008 (US Department of Labor 2014).

In March 2014, new regulations went into effect related to implementation of Section 503 of the Rehabilitation Act of 1973, as amended), setting new requirements for federal contractors and subcontractors (both groups called contractors henceforth) and related to nondiscrimination and affirmative action in the employment of qualified individuals with disabilities. For example, contractors with $15,000 or more in federal contracts are now required to offer applicants and employees the opportunity to self-identify as a person with a disability and further to use the data collected to understand their progress toward a 7% utilization goal for employment of individuals with disabilities.[7] Contractors must apply the goal to each of their job groups, or to their entire workforce if the contractor has 100 or fewer employees. To be able to identify individuals with disabilities to measure progress in reaching this goal, the regulations require that contractors invite applicants to self-identify as having a disability at both the pre-offer and post-offer phases of the application process, using language prescribed by the OFCCP. The regulations also require that contractors invite all their employees to self-identify every five years as individuals with disabilities, using the prescribed language.

The current regulations also have personnel data analysis obligations. Each year, contractors must perform utilization analysis and assess known problem areas. For continued problem areas, contractors have to develop action-oriented plans to address these areas. Additional annual documentation requirements include a report comparing the number of applicants with disabilities relative to the number hired. The regulations move beyond within-year analysis by requiring the data be retained for three years to support trend analysis.

Comparing Employers with and Without Compliance Violations

Past research has shown that federal contractors experience charges citing Title I of the ADA at a higher rate than private employers without federal contracts (von Schrader and Nazarov 2015). This may in part be due to the additional responsibilities of federal contractors to educate their workforces about nondiscrimination laws (e.g., posting notices in public areas). Further, smaller federal contractor establishments have higher charge rates than larger contractors, perhaps related to more limited HR and employee relations infrastructure in smaller federal contractors (von Schrader and Nazarov 2015). In the EEOC data upon which these analyses were done, it is not possible to observe the practices and policies of the firms that may be related to charge rates. However, these data do provide an opportunity to identify employer groups—for example, smaller organizations, which are more likely to receive charges, may struggle with implementing the nondiscrimination requirements of the ADA. In this section, we use another dataset to understand federal contractors' compliance with EEO laws.

The following analysis examines the characteristics that distinguish a firm in compliance with EEO laws from one not in compliance.[8] We use audit reviews performed by the OFCCP, which provides information on firms with and without evidence of a disability violation under EEO laws. As part of its effort to enforce EEO laws, the OFCCP reviews the policies of contractors under one of two audit mechanisms: scheduled compliance evaluations and complaint-based investigations.

The OFCCP data cover 43,246 reviews, with 39,311 unique contractor establishments between 2004 and 2018. Figure 4 (next page) illustrates the trends in the number of closed reviews and the percentage of those reviews that were complaint-based investigations. During the study period, the number of closed reviews fell by 90%, from 7,316 reviews in 2004 to 770 in 2018. The percentage of reviews that were complaint-based investigations has fluctuated substantially over time, with highs of over 20% and lows below 4%. Since the drop in 2013 to 2014, the percentage of complaint-based investigations has steady increased over time.

Seeing the advantage of these data in understanding employer characteristics associated with a violation requires a comprehension of the potential outcomes of a review. An OFCCP review can close with the determination that the establishment complied with EEO laws and OFCCP regulations, or the OFCCP can determine that the establishment has one of two types of violations, discrimination or technical. A *discrimination violation* means that the contractor violated EEO laws by engaging in discrimination against applicants or employees. A *technical violation* occurs when the contractor either fails or refuses to comply with OFCCP regulations. In this analysis, a review that finds both technical and discriminatory violations is classified as a discrimination violation.

FIGURE 4
Trends in the Closure and Type of Reviews

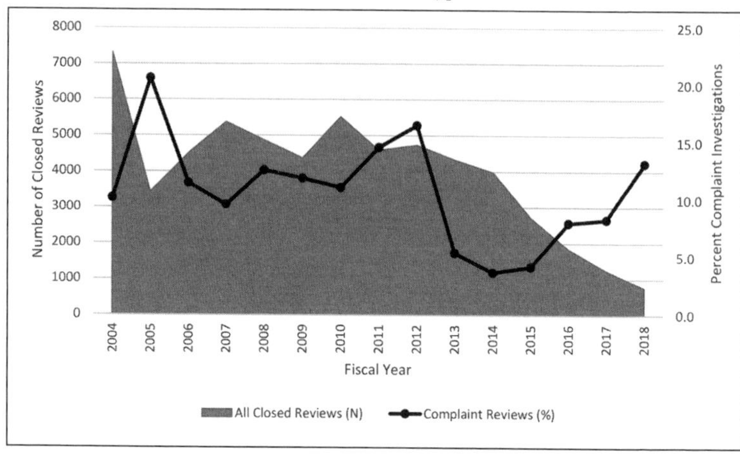

Note: Authors' calculation of time trend in the number of closed reviews and the percentage of complaint investigations using OFCCP data.

Table 8 presents the summary statistics of the key employer characteristics and review outcomes in the data. Of the 43,266 reviews, just over 17% were found to be in violation, with 14.5% having a technical violation and 3% having a discrimination violation. Establishments varied in their key characteristics: size, existence of a parent company, sector, county-level unemployment rate, and region.

Key Takeaways

Table 9 (page 54) presents the estimates of the relationship between establishment characteristics of federal contractors and violations of EEO laws or OFCCP regulations.[9] The findings broadly uphold prior research examining the ADA charge rates. Establishment size is negatively associated with having either any violation or a technical violation, with a 1% increase in size associated with a 0.03 percentage point reduction in the likelihood of any violation. Interestingly, that relationship breaks down when considering only discrimination violations (the far less common type of violation), where an increase in size predicts an increase in the risk of a violation. Having a parent company reduces the likelihood of all violation groups. Unsurprisingly, there is a positive concave relationship between local unemployment levels and the risk of all violation groups. When we look collectively at size and parent company status, the estimates from Table 9 match with the idea that larger employers, either directly or as part of a parent company, are less likely to receive a violation during the review process. One possible

TABLE 8
Descriptive Statistics of Review Outcomes and Establishment Characteristics

Variables	Mean	Standard Deviation	Minimum	Maximum
Violation type				
Any violation	17.4	37.93	0	100
Discrimination violation	3.01	17.08	0	100
Technical violation	14.5	35.23	0	100
Establishment characteristics				
Number of employees	375.8	1,675	1	272,653
Has parent	82.0	0.384	0	1
Industry: Manufacturing	31.3	0.464	0	1
Industry: Professional	12.8	0.334	0	1
Industry: Health	6.92	0.254	0	1
Industry: Administrative support	8.56	0.280	0	1
Industry: Other sector	4.04	0.491	0	1
County unemployment rate	6.11	2.081	1.200	10
County unemployment rate (squared)	41.7	27.82	1.440	100
Northeast	12.3	0.329	0	1
Mid-Atlantic	14.9	0.356	0	1
Southeast	20.4	0.403	0	1
Midwest	19.4	0.395	0	1
Southwest	15.2	0.359	0	1
Pacific	17.8	0.382	0	1

Note: Descriptive statistics of the OFCCP data used in analysis of 43,246 reviews. The mean values for parent company status, industry, and region variables are presented as percentages for ease of interpretation.

explanation may be that larger employers are more likely to have more heavily staffed and better-equipped human resources departments, which would be more able to remain current with EEO laws, OFCCP regulations, and other good employer practices. If this rationale holds, there is an argument supporting policies that equip smaller companies with the most current information on compliance and best practices.

Practices and Policies Associated with Higher Disability Employment

In this section, we shift the focus from employer characteristics predicting noncompliance with EEO laws or OFCCP regulations to a discussion of specific

TABLE 9
Estimates of the Probability of a Review Ending in a Violation on Establishment Characteristics

	Any Violation	Discrimination Violation	Technical Violation
Log size	−3.130***	0.332***	-3.548***
Has parent	−15.72***	−1.287***	−14.46***
Professional	−0.634	−1.566***	0.917
Health	5.498***	0.209	5.209***
Administrative support	5.201***	-1.094***	6.229***
Other	2.332***	-0.189	2.504***
County unemployment rate	3.773***	0.733**	3.077***
County unemployment rate (squared)	−0.282***	−0.0431*	−0.241***
Mid-Atlantic	−4.420***	0.873**	−5.213***
Southeast	0.887	0.375	0.506
Midwest	−1.307	−0.433	−0.870
Southwest	−11.69***	−0.281	−11.47***
Pacific	0.833	0.531	0.430
Observations	43,236	43,236	43,236
Adjusted R^2	0.085	0.025	0.087

Note: Each specification contains year indicator variables. The excluded categorical groups are manufacturing for sector and the Northeast for region. Standard errors are reported in parentheses and clustered at the district level.
Significance levels: * $p < 0.05$, ** $p < 0.01$, *** $p < 0.001$.

employer practices and policies most strongly associated with higher employment levels of people with a disability. We move beyond employer characteristics onto practices and policies that employers can implement to potentially increase the likelihood of employing persons with disabilities. In 2005, the US Government Accountability Office submitted a report to Congress that summarized leading diversity management practices and agency examples identified by experts in the field (US Government Accountability Office 2005). The report highlighted nine practices and policies: top leadership commitment, diversity included in the strategic plan, linking diversity to performance, quantitative and qualitative measures of impact of diversity programs, leadership accountability, succession planning, recruitment, involvement of employees, and diversity training.

The role of organizational commitment to disability diversity is essential. Visible top leadership commitment to diversity has been repeatedly demonstrated as a predictor of successful disability recruiting (Bruyère 2000; Domzal, Houtenville, and Sharma 2008; Gilbride, Stensrud, Vandergoot, and Golden 2003). Bruyère

(2000) found that employers reported visible top management commitment as the most effective means of reducing barriers to employment for people with disabilities. Employers have expressed that the inclusion of disability in diversity policy within an organization and as part of the strategic plan serves as a leading way to convey leadership commitment (DCSRC 2008). While an active recruitment plan is a widely agreed-upon practice to increase the employment of individuals with disabilities, it is not universally implemented—with large variation, depending on the size of the employer (Bruyère, Erickson, and VanLooy 2006; Domzal, Houtenville, and Sharma 2008).

In a 2011 survey of human resource professionals, Erickson and co-authors (2014) examined the relationship between a set of employer policies and practices and the hiring of individuals with disabilities. Federal contractors comprised just over a quarter of their sample.

Key Takeaways

Table 10 (next page) summarizes key findings regarding federal contractors from the Erickson and co-authors' (2014) study. Columns 1 and 2 report the prevalence of each practice separately for contractors and noncontractors after controlling for a set of employer characteristics such as size, sector, and profit/nonprofit status. Federal contractors were more likely to report having each practice. The gap in prevalence rates is striking for nearly all the practices—for example, 60% of contractors reported actively recruiting individuals with disabilities compared with only 32% of noncontractors. In only three of the ten practices was the difference not statistically significant: internships for individuals with disabilities, advanced notice regarding reasonable accommodations, and evaluation of pre-employment screenings. The study went on to demonstrate that these practices lead to positive employment outcomes, with all but the tenth practice predicting an increase in the probability that the organization hires an individual with a disability. The affirmative action requirements faced by federal contractors may be partially responsible for these outcomes.

IMPLICATIONS

Employment disparities for Americans with disabilities are still a significant reality. Collection of more precise data about employer characteristics and workplace policies and practices that contribute to improved employment outcomes is a critical initial step in addressing these disparities. The federal government's long-term commitment to data collection on disability representation and related policies and practices allows for an analysis that would be otherwise challenging in the private sector. In addition, the OFCCP's more recent regulation updates introduce enhanced precision in targets and reporting to increase disability representation in the federal contractor workforce, and similarly allows for observation of the impact of the regulations on employer behaviors. Analyzing these

TABLE 10
Prevalence of Practices and the Estimate of an Employer Hiring a Person with a Disability by Each Practice

	Federal Contractor		
	(1)	(2)	(3)
Hiring/Recruiting Practices	No	Yes	Odds Ratio
N	245	94	339
Actively recruiting people with disabilities	32%	60%	3.2†
Relationships with community organizations	45%	75%	2.7†
People with disabilities in diversity and inclusion plan	47%	72%	3.2†
Explicit organizational goals for people with disabilities	16%	48%	4.1†
People with disabilities considered in management performance	9%	26%	3.1†
Internships for people with disabilities	16%	29%	5.7†
Strong senior management commitment	29%	46%	4.8†
Reviews online job application accessibility	19%	41%	2.1†
Advance notice to applicants regarding reasonable accommodations in job application process	57%	62%	2.7†
Evaluates pre-employment screenings to ensure they are unbiased	61%	67%	1.2

Note: Columns 1 and 2 were excerpted from Table 3 in Erickson et al. (2014). Column 3 is from Table 4 in Erickson et al. (2014).
† Odds ratio significant at the $p < 0.5$ level.

data and identifying implications for good practice has been the focus of this chapter. In this final section, we identify lessons from the findings presented above related to federal and federal contractor employers that may inform employers more broadly.

Data Collection Is Essential

To understand disability in the workplace, disability self-identification data must be collected from the workforce. These data make it possible to understand disability representation (across job and pay categories) and to establish a baseline upon which to assess progress. Further, integrating data collection on disability into engagement surveys can help to assess progress not only in representation but also in the experiences and perceptions of this group in the workplace.

Affirmative Recruitment Strategies Can Make a Difference

Results from the federal sector study suggest that having targets and affirmative recruitment policies (as well as ways to collect data to measure this progress) are associated with improved disability representation in the workforce. The documented representation of people with disabilities in the federal workforce is well above the rates in the private sector, with nearly 9% of individuals self-identifying as a person with a disability (US Office of Personnel Management 2015a). Further, the federal focus on hiring veterans with disabilities seems to be positively related to increased disability representation in the federal government, with large increases over the past decade.

Recruitment Is Not Enough: Inclusion and Advancement Opportunity Should Be Managed

Simply increasing the diversity of the workplace in terms of disability representation is not a sufficient goal or outcome. Rather, true workplace disability inclusion needs to be managed and monitored across the entire employment process, as documented by prior race and gender diversity studies (Prieto, Phipps, and Osiri 2011).

As previously pointed out, OPM reports have generally determined that employees with disabilities rate their experiences in the federal workforce lower than their peers without disabilities (US Office of Personnel Management 2015a). These results suggest that individuals with disabilities are less satisfied with their federal work experience than individuals without disabilities. The further analysis presented in this chapter demonstrates that certain groups of individuals with disabilities, once in the federal workforce, might indeed be differentially disadvantaged, leading to perceived if not validated inequities. For example, on professional development opportunity and job satisfaction scales in the surveys conducted in the federal workforce, females without disabilities score slightly higher or at the same level as males without disability, but the females with disabilities are significantly disadvantaged compared with their male counterparts. The intersection of identities and the differential experiences of certain groups are important to consider so that any issues can be investigated and addressed.

In addition, as further established in the federal sector analyses described here, the share of the workforce with a disability decreases as the grade level increases, which is validation of a long-standing concern that there is a limited career path for employees with disabilities, once they have been hired. Employers such as the federal government can use data on representation and advancement to gain an improved understanding where disparities (and therefore their policy and practices vulnerabilities) exist to be proactive in trying to mitigate such concerns by engaging in documented good practices.

Some Organizations/Agencies May Need More Support in Implementing EEO Laws and Regulations

Studying the characteristics of differentially disadvantaged individuals in the workforce is one way of better understanding how to improve outcomes in equitable access to employment. Examining the characteristics of the organizations that are having difficulty in pursuing known good practices is another approach. In examining the federal sectors, for example, results established that relative to small agencies, medium-sized agencies are over four times as likely to have disability programs considered to be sufficiently staffed. Another example from these data is the finding of how a larger concentration of highest-grade employees in the workforce positively predicts the likelihood of an organization using its data to analyze trends in workforce profiles. In the federal contractor study presented here, results provide information on how characteristics such as establishment size and having a parent company are associated with lower rates of violations in the OFCCP audit data. Having the internal expertise to manage EEO laws and regulations can help to increase compliance and ideally work toward the larger goal of the contractor regulations—disability inclusion in the workplace.

CONCLUSION

Hopefully, the overarching message that comes through in the examples provided here from the federal and federal contractor data is that pursuing good policies and practices, as well as having targets and the ability to measure outcomes relative to the goals set, is advantageous both to the organization and to individual employees. This is especially true in moving the needle for groups who have been historically under-represented in the workforce, such as individuals with disabilities. The federal government and federal contractors are more likely to have disability-inclusive policies and practices in place, such as top leadership commitment to an affirmative outreach for candidates, deliberate recruitment strategies, and centralized provision of accommodations. However, data must be consistently used for effective policies and practices to be strategically pursued, and for those policies and practices that are not effective to be discarded or tweaked to improve outcomes. Having these data allows employers to measure the effectiveness of their outreach and recruitment efforts, and annual reporting provides accountability to the commitment that the organization has embraced. Without such information, labor and employment relations professionals have little documented evidence to go on to address individual grievances when they occur. In the broader picture, we will be also far less well equipped to advise organizations on how to proactively put good policies and practices in place that will mitigate such issues before they occur.

ACKNOWLEDGMENTS

The research presented in this chapter was supported in part by funding as follows:

- From the US Department of Labor under cooperative agreement number IL-EO-30273-17-60-5-36. This material does not necessarily reflect the views or policies of the US Department of Labor, nor does mention of trade names, commercial products, or organizations imply endorsement by the US government. One hundred percent of the total costs of the project or program is financed with federal funds, for a total of $249,999.

- Under a grant to Cornell University for Connecting Practices to Outcomes: Lessons from the Federal Sector Workplace from the National Institute on Disability, Independent Living, and Rehabilitation Research, Administration for Community Living, US Department of Health and Human Services (NIDILRR grant number 90IFRE0014). NIDILRR is a center within the Administration for Community Living (ACL), Department of Health and Human Services (HHS). The contents of this publication do not necessarily represent the policy of NIDILRR, ACL, or HHS, and endorsement by the federal government should not be assumed.
- The ILR School Solicitation of Cornell Expertise Related to Innovations in Employment, Workplace Productivity, and Employee Engagement.

We would also like to thank the US Equal Employment Opportunity Commission Office of Federal Operations, Office of Personnel Management, and Department of Labor's Office of Federal Contract Compliance Programs for their partnerships and support in accessing and interpreting data. The contents of this publication do not necessarily represent the policy of the EEEOC, OPM, or OFCCP, and endorsement by the federal government should not be assumed.

Several individuals were kind enough to provide feedback on an earlier version of the chapter including Dexter Brooks, associate director, Office of Federal Operations, US Equal Employment Opportunity Commission; Natalie Veeney, diversity program manager, US Office of Personnel Management; Tina Williams, deputy director, Office of Federal Contract Compliance Programs, US Department of Labor; and Adrienne Colella, James W. McFarland Distinguished Chair of Business, Tulane University.

ENDNOTES

[1] The targeted disability categories listed are those used for the MD-715 data presented in this chapter (2004 to 2015). The SF 256 was updated in October 2016, and the new form is available at http://bit.ly/2YBPDFa.

[2] The scale development process was iterative and used information from several sources. We examined reports produced by OPM and studies by other researchers using the FEVS and examining similar constructs (Fernandez, Resh, Moldogaziev, and Oberfield 2015). Further, we had the benefit of industrial–organizational psychologists Lisa Nishii from Cornell University and Adrienne Colella from Tulane University, who grouped items based on content into different possible scales of interest.

[3] In our analyses below, we restricted the full 2015 FEVS sample by excluding military agencies (because those agencies have a unique workforce composition) as well as individuals with missing scale scores, disability status (some smaller agencies do not have disability data available in the public use file), or demographic information. An individual must have given responses to more than half of the items on a scale to get a scale score. The overall 2015 sample decreased from 421,748 to 364,078 with the elimination of military agencies and to 284,266 with the exclusion of those missing scale score data or demographic information. There were 33,523 respondents with disabilities and 250,743 without disabilities in the unweighted sample used in the analysis.

[4] The MD-715 data were restricted to 59 parent agencies (i.e., agencies that are not subagencies), between 2004 and 2015. An additional ten agencies were removed from the sample because of small workforce size (fewer than 50 employees).

[5] The distribution of the percentage of workforce in highest-grade positions was separated at the 25th and 75th percentiles. Agencies under the 25th percentile are considered low, while those between the 25th and 75th are considered moderate. High agencies are in the highest quartile of the distribution.

[6] While the average partial effect calculation was used to interpret the point estimates from the fractional logit models, the authors do not claim that these estimates are causal. Rather, the estimates highlight the predictive role of the policies and practices in question.

[7] See http://bit.ly/2ME4DxQ for more description.

[8] Funding is provided by the US Department of Labor under cooperative agreement number IL-EO-30273-17-60-5-36. The findings and comments reflected here do not necessarily reflect the views or policies of the US Department of Labor.

[9] A linear probability model tests the relationship between employer characteristics and the probability of violating EEO laws or OFCCP regulations. The outcomes of any violation, discrimination violation, and technical violation are converted to binary measures. The independent variables of interest are the natural logarithm of establishment size, an indicator for having a parent company, sector, a quadratic in the county-level unemployment rate, and region. Year fixed effects are included in the model as well as standard errors made robust to heteroscedasticity.

REFERENCES

Affirmative Action for Individuals with Disabilities in Employment (AAIDFE). Final Rule. 82 Fed. Reg. 654 (2017) (to be codified at 29 CFR Part 1614). http://bit.ly/2MGOcUZ

Baron, J.N., and J. Pfeffer. 1994. "The Social Psychology of Organizations and Inequality." *Social Psychology Quarterly* 57(3): 190–209. http://bit.ly/2MF6EgO

Barrington, Linda. 2016. "Engaging Employers as Stakeholders." In *Disability and Employer Practices: Research Across the Disciplines*, edited by Susanne M. Bruyère, pp. 27–56. Ithaca, NY: Cornell University Press.

Bruyère, S.M. 2000. "Disability Employment Policies and Practices in Private and Federal Sector Organizations." Ithaca, NY: Cornell University Yang-Tan Institute on Employment and Disability. http://bit.ly/2YLYaWp

Bruyère, S., W.A. Erickson, and J. Ferrentino. 2003. "Identity and Disability in the Workplace." *William and Mary Law Review* 44 (3): 1173–1196.

Bruyère, S.M., W.A. Erickson, and S.A. VanLooy. 2006. "The Impact of Business Size on Employer ADA Response." *Rehabilitation Counseling Bulletin* 49 (4): 194–206.

Bruyère, S.M., T. Golden, and S. VanLooy. 2011. "Legislation and Rehabilitation Professionals." In *Medical Aspects of Disability*, 4th ed., edited by S. Flanagan, H. Zaretsky, and A. Moroz, pp. 669–686. New York, NY: Springer.

Burke, R. 1999. "Disability and Women's Work Experiences: An Explanatory Study." *International Journal of Sociology and Social Policy* 19 (12): 21–33.

Colella, A. 1996. "The Organizational Socialization of Employees with Disabilities: Theory and Research." *Research in Personnel and Human Resources Management* 14: 351–417.

Colella, A. 2001. "Coworker Distributive Fairness Judgments of the Workplace Accommodation of Employees with Disabilities." *Academy of Management Review* 26: 100–116.

Colella, A., A.S. DeNisi, and A. Varma. 1998. "The Impact of Ratee's Disability on Performance Judgments and Choice of Partner: The Role of Disability–Job Fit Stereotypes and Interdependence of Rewards." *Journal of Applied Psychology* 83: 102–11.

Disability Case Study Research Consortium (DCSRC). 2008. *Conducting and Benchmarking Inclusive Employment Policies, Practices, and Culture*. Washington, DC: Disability Case Study Research Consortium.

Dobbin, F., and A. Kalev. 2013. "The Origins and Effects of Corporate Diversity Programs." In *Oxford Handbook of Diversity and Work*, edited by Q. Roberson, pp. 253–281. New York, NY: Oxford University Press. doi:10.1017/CBO9781107415324.004

Domzal, C., A. Houtenville, and R. Sharma. 2008. "Survey of Employer Perspectives on the Employment of People with Disabilities: Technical Report." (Prepared under contract to the Office of Disability and Employment Policy, US Department of Labor). McLean, VA: Cherry Engineering Support Services.

Erickson, W., C. Lee, and S. von Schrader. 2019. "2017 Disability Status Report: United States." Ithaca, NY: Cornell University Yang-Tan Institute on Employment and Disability.

Erickson, W., S. von Schrader, S. Bruyère, and S. VanLooy. 2013. "The Employment Environment: Employer Perspectives, Policies, and Practices Regarding the Employment of Persons with Disabilities." *Rehabilitation Counseling Bulletin* 57 (4): 195–208. doi:10.1177/0034355213509841

Erickson, W., S. von Schrader, S. Bruyère, S. VanLooy, and D.S. Matteson. 2014. "Disability-Inclusive Employer Practices and Hiring of Individuals with Disabilities." *Rehabilitation Research, Policy, and Education* 28 (4): 309–328.

Executive Order No. 13163, 3 CFR 46563 (2000).

Executive Order No. 13548, 3 CFR 45039 (2010).

Falk, J. 2012. "Comparing the Compensation of Federal and Private-Sector Employees, 2011 to 2015." Washington, DC: Congressional Budget Office. http://bit.ly/2MFErGv

Fernandez, S., W.G. Resh, T. Moldogaziev, and Z.W. Oberfield. 2015. "Assessing the Past and Promise of the Federal Employee Viewpoint Survey for Public Management Research: A Research Synthesis." *Public Administration Review* 75 (3): 382–394.

Florey, A.T., and D.A. Harrison. 2000. "Responses to Informal Accommodation Requests from Employees with Disabilities: Multistudy Evidence on Willingness to Comply." *Academy of Management Journal* 43: 224–233.

Gilbride, D., R. Stensrud, D. Vandergoot, and K. Golden. 2003. "Identification of the Characteristics of Work Environments and Employers Open to Hiring and Accommodating People with Disabilities." *Rehabilitation Counseling Bulletin* 46 (3): 130–137.

Hernandez, B., C. Keys, and F. Balcazar. 2000. "Employer Attitudes Toward Workers with Disabilities and Their ADA Employment Rights: A Literature Review." *Journal of Rehabilitation* 66: 4–16.

Kalev, A., F. Dobbin, and E. Kelly. 2006. "Best Practices or Best Guesses? Assessing the Efficacy of Corporate Affirmative Action and Diversity Policies." *American Sociological Review* 71 (4): 589–617. doi:10.1177/000312240607100404

Konrad, A.M., Y. Yang, and C.C. Maurer. 2016. "Antecedents and Outcomes of Diversity and Equality Management Systems: An Integrated Institutional Agency and Strategic Human

Resource Management Approach." *Human Resource Management* 55 (1): 83–107. doi:10.1002/hrm.21713

Kulik, C.T. 2014. "Working Below and Above the Line: The Research–Practice Gap in Diversity Management." *Human Resource Management Journal* 24 (2): 129–144. doi:10.1111/17488583.12038

Lewis, G.B., and C.L. Allee. 1992. "The Impact of Disabilities on Federal Career Success." *Public Administration Review* 52 (4): 389–397.

Naff, K.C., and J.E. Kellough. 2003. "Ensuring Employment Equity: Are Federal Diversity Programs Making a Difference?" *International Journal of Public Administration* 26 (12): 1307–1336. doi:10.1081/PAD-120024399

O'Leary, A. 2009. "Making Government Work for Families: The Federal Government's Role as Employer and Contractor in Improving Family-Friendly Policies." Washington, DC: Center for American Progress. https://ampr.gs/2MEWTPw

Partnership for Public Service. 2018. "Pay and the General Schedule (GS)." *Go Government*. http://bit.ly/2VGTCi7

Pitts, D.W., and L. Wise. 2009. "Workforce Diversity in the New Millennium: Prospects for Research." *Review of Public Personnel Administration* 30 (1): 44–69. doi:10.1177/0734371X 09351823

Prieto, L., S. Phipps, and J. Osiri. 2011. "Linking Workplace Diversity to Organizational Performance: A Conceptual Framework. *Journal of Diversity Management* 4 (4): 13–22.

Putnick, D.L., and M.H. Bornstein. 2016. "Measurement Invariance Conventions and Reporting: The State of the Art and Future Directions for Psychological Research. *Developmental Review* 41: 71–90.

Schur, L., D. Kruse, J. Blasi, and P. Blanck. 2009. "Is Disability Disabling in All Workplaces? Workplace Disparities and Corporate Culture." *Industrial Relations: A Journal of Economy and Society* 48 (3): 381–410.

Stone, D.L., and A. Colella. 1996. "A Model of Factors Affecting the Treatment of Disabled Individuals in Organizations." *Academy of Management Review* 21 (2): 352–401.

US Department of Labor. 2014. Office of Federal Contract Compliance Programs (OFCCP): "Frequently Asked Questions: New Section 503 Regulations." Washington, DC: US Department of Labor. http://bit.ly/2MEwRIs

US Equal Employment Opportunity Commission (US EEOC). No date. "The Rehabilitation Act of 1973: Sections 501 and 505." Washington, DC: US Equal Employment Opportunity Commission. http://bit.ly/2VEIr9J

US Equal Employment Opportunity Commission (US EEOC). 2017. "Affirmative Action for Individuals with Disabilities in Federal Employment." Washington, DC: US Equal Employment Opportunity Commission. http://bit.ly/2VCcTkM

US Government Accountability Office. 2005. *Diversity Management: Expert-Identified Leading Practices and Agency Examples.* Washington, DC: US Government Accountability Office.

US Office of Personnel Management. No date. "Pay And Leave: Pay Systems." Washington, DC: US Office of Personnel Management. http://bit.ly/2VEMnqM

US Office of Personnel Management. 2014. "Federal Employee Viewpoint Survey Results: Employees Influencing Change." Technical Report. Washington, DC: US Office of Personnel Management. http://bit.ly/2Khv2TR

US Office of Personnel Management. 2015a. "2015 Federal Employee Viewpoint Survey Results: Report by Demographics." Washington, DC: US Office of Personnel Management. http://bit.ly/2VGKav4

US Office of Personnel Management. 2015b. "Report on the Employment of Individuals with Disabilities in the Federal Executive Branch: Fiscal Year 2014." Washington, DC: US Office of Personnel Management. http://bit.ly/2VCd9QM

US Office of Personnel Management. 2016. "Report on the Employment of Individuals with Disabilities in the Federal Executive Branch: Fiscal Year 2015." Washington, DC: US Office of Personnel Management. http://bit.ly/2VBoMYd

von Schrader, S., and Z. Nazarov. 2015. "Employer Characteristics Associated with Discrimination Charges Under the Americans with Disabilities Act." *Journal of Disability Policy Studies* 26 (3): 153–163. doi:10.1177/1044207314533385

Wooldridge, J.M. 2010. *Econometric Analysis of Cross Section and Panel Data.* Cambridge, MA: MIT Press.

Chapter 3

Disability and the Unionized Workplace

Mason Ameri
Rutgers University

Mohammad Ali
Pennsylvania State University–Harrisburg

Lisa Schur
Douglas Kruse
Rutgers University

INTRODUCTION

Expanding employment opportunities for people with disabilities is one of the primary goals of the 1990 Americans with Disabilities Act (ADA), the 2008 ADA Amendments Act (ADAAA), and the 2006 United Nations Convention on the Rights of Persons with Disabilities. People with disabilities still face low employment rates, however, nearly three decades after the passage of the ADA. In fact, only 35.9% of working-age people with disabilities were employed in the United States in 2016, compared with 76.8% of those without disabilities (Lauer and Houtenville 2018). People with disabilities represent one tenth (10.6%) of the US working-age population (Lauer and Houtenville 2018). Owing to their low employment levels, however, they represent only 5.2% of employed individuals (Lauer and Houtenville 2018). Their low employment levels are in part due to employer reluctance to hire them (Ameri et al. 2018). People with disabilities who are employed face a variety of disparities including lower earnings, less job security, and lower job satisfaction than co-workers without disabilities, both in the United States and in other countries (Jones 2008; Jones, Latreille, and Stone 2006; Jones and Sloane 2010; Kruse, Schur, Rogers, and Ameri 2018; Mitra and Kruse 2016; Schur, Kruse, and Blanck 2013; Schur et al. 2017).

Unions are recognized as providing many benefits for workers. These benefits include higher wages, better benefits, just-cause dismissal protections, grievance procedures, and a collective voice for workers to negotiate pay and working conditions (Farber 1986; Freeman and Medoff 1984; Hirsch 2004). At a societal level, unions have been found to reduce economic inequality (Farber, Herbst, Kuziemko, and Naidu 2018). The wage and inequality effects appear to transcend country boundaries (Rios-Avila and Hirsch 2014). Despite these advantages of unions for workers, unionization has been declining in the United States—over the past three decades the percentage of workers in unions has halved from 20.1% of the workforce in 1983 to 10.7% in 2017 (US Bureau of Labor Statistics, no date). However, the union wage premium has stayed roughly constant as the level of unionization has changed (Farber, Herbst, Kuziemko, and Naidu 2018).

Despite the large amount of scholarly literature on unions, little is known about the effects of unions on workplace outcomes for people with disabilities, or even about the basic question of how likely it is for workers with disabilities to be affiliated with unions. Given the benefits that unions generally provide, and the projected increase in disability prevalence as baby boomers age and medical technologies improve, this is an important area of inquiry. Union-established worker protections may benefit workers with disabilities by reducing the disparities they face in the workplace, but union policies may also limit the ability of workers with disabilities to gain access to jobs appropriate to their abilities. We argue that the study of unions and disability can further reveal barriers and facilitators to employment for workers with disabilities.

This paper examines three basic questions about the relationship between disability and unions:

- How likely are employees with disabilities to be in jobs covered by union contracts, and has this been changing in recent years?
- How do unions affect the disability pay gap?
- How likely are unionized workers to request and receive workplace accommodations?

The answers to these questions shed light on policies—in both union and non-union contexts—that can enhance employment opportunities for workers with disabilities.

We address the first two questions using representative data from the Current Population Survey (CPS) between the period 2009 through 2017, relying on union and wage data in the out-going rotation groups combined with six disability measures introduced in the CPS in late 2008. The third question is addressed using a special CPS supplement in May 2012 focused on disability issues. The question of what policies may help or hurt workers with disabilities is discussed in the literature review and conclusion.

LITERATURE REVIEW

Several theoretical models shape perspectives about people who live with disabilities (Mitra 2018; Schur, Kruse, and Blanck 2013; World Health Organization 2001). We describe three common models—the medical, social, and universal models. The medical model views disability as an impairment within an individual, with little or no relation to the environment. According to the the medical model, the focus is on curing impairments rather than on changing the environment. The social model views disability as caused by an interaction between an individual's impairments and his or her environment, with the result that certain environments may "create" disability that would not exist in other contexts—for example, a flight of steps that enter the workplace can "disable" a wheelchair user who is otherwise highly capable of working. The social model was developed and used by the disability rights movement to empower people with disabilities and helped drive the push for legislation such as the ADA. The universal model also views disability as dependent on the environment but has a more fluid view of disability as existing on a continuum both across humans and across time, with almostevery person experiencing disability at some point in life. The universal model emphasizes that disabilities may be temporary, permanent, or episodic. The ultimate goal is to achieve a more accommodating system for workers with disabilities and society in general. It could be argued that unions, as intermediary bodies that represents workers' interests before management, may be a good institutional vehicle to help achieve this goal. However, as discussed below, evidence in this area is inadequate and needs more attention.

While many union contracts address disability issues (Basas 2013), systematic information on the relation of disability to unionization levels and union policies is not available. One example of a program that seeks to assist union employees is the Accommodating DisAbled People in Transition (ADAPT) program negotiated by the United Auto Workers with General Motors (Joint Activity System 2019). This program lays out options for union employees to be retained at work, or return from work, after sickness or workers compensation leave, including options for workers to obtain alternative jobs if they can no longer perform their original jobs.

Looking more broadly, Basas (2013) identifies two tensions in union policies regarding disability. The first tension is between treating disability as a civil rights issue (consistent with the social model) and protecting the employment of union workers who experience disability. In examining collective bargaining agreements of the American Federation of State, County and Municipal Employees (AFSCME), Basas concludes that policies enacted in contracts reflect the medical model of disability, which views disability exclusively as a health or medical problem to be cured. Basas observes that these agreements address only sick leave, workers compensation, and injuries, which are factors that relate mostly to the onset of disability at work. Their emphasis does not seem to be on inclusion and changing the workplace environment in line with the ADA's principal objective of equal access and opportunity (Basas 2013). Moreover, according to Basas, another tension exists between individual interests that are protected by the ADA and "the collective good position of union representation where individual interests are submitted to the needs of the whole" (2013: 75)—that is, workers with disabilities risk disrupting the status quo regarding seniority, job reassignment, job restructuring, and flexible scheduling to which unions have historically adhered.

As a result, some claim that collective bargaining agreements may often hurt workers with disabilities because they lack provisions demonstrating true inclusion, which may reflect resistance by some unions and employers to the ADA and lack of understanding about disability as a social category (Basas 2013; Williams-Whitt 2007). For example, no public sector collective bargaining agreements in the sample examined by Basas (2013) included technology-based provisions to accommodate workers with disabilities, despite many technology-based accommodation requests from workers with disabilities.

On the basis of these tensions, Basas (2013) raises questions about whether unions improve the labor market status of workers with disabilities and notes that they may mainly benefit workers whose onset of disability happens at work. Even for current workers, however, there is room for more support (Basas 2013). Her review of public sector collective bargaining agreements shows that most contracts lack procedures for raising disability-related matters, soliciting accommodations, and ensuring that ADA requirements are followed (Basas 2013).

While Basas claims that most union contracts are based on the medical model of disability and do not explicitly use the social model, it should be noted that the social model's focus on the importance of the environment is reflected in union policies that sometimes provide reassignment or other accommodations to enable members to work and remain productive.

The potential for unions to play a positive role is supported by Williams-Whitt (2007), who examined 72 arbitration cases using semi-structured interviews of managers, union representatives, employees with disabilities, and occupational health workers in multiple industries. The respondents narrated episodes of successful and unsuccessful attempts to accommodate workers with disabilities. This analysis found that "unions may have a particularly influential role to play by nudging collective beliefs and norms about accommodation" (2007: 419). Unions can also assist with workers compensation claims, offer emotional support, uphold contact with workers who are away and rehabilitating, offer guidance to employers about the ADA, and take other actions to lessen employer animosity created by disruptions to the existing state of affairs (Williams-Whitt 2007). The potential for unions to play a positive role obviously depends on the nature of the labor–management relationship—many employers would resist union efforts to be more involved in these areas.

The union voice may be particularly important for workers with disabilities. Studies have indicated that workers with disabilities fare better in workplaces where employers pay more attention to individual needs and where accommodations are more common, as accommodations for workers with disabilities do not stand out as "special treatment" and engender resentment or jealousy (Schur, Kruse, Blasi, and Blanck 2009; Stone and Colella 1996). To the extent that unions facilitate more accommodation requests, they make accommodations more common and less stigmatizing.

Some disability accommodations conflict with seniority rights bargained in the contract (Schur 1998), and the Supreme Court ruled in *US Airways v. Barnett* that the ADA does not require an employer to assign a disabled employee to a particular position when the assignment would violate the employer's established seniority system.[1] Unions are covered entities under the ADA, and as such they are entitled to medical information used in making an accommodation and required to keep such information confidential.[2]

While employers have a duty to bargain over disability accommodations and other policies affecting current employees, they typically do not have to bargain with the union over hiring of workers with disabilities in the United States because hiring policies and practices are not a mandatory subject of bargaining.[3] The exception is that a hiring practice is a mandatory subject of bargaining when there is an objective basis for believing it to be discriminatory because such discrimination affects the terms and conditions of employment for current employees. In addition, before making a bargaining demand, the union is entitled to information relevant to the issue of discrimination if it has a rational basis for believing that the practice may discriminate. The National Labor Relations Board (NLRB) quoted the Supreme Court saying that "the elimination of discrimination and its vestiges is an appropriate subject of bargaining." Although prior cases on this topic were based on race and sex discrimination, the principles would presumably apply to disability discrimination.

Disability organizations can play an important role in how unions deal with disability issues. As described by Bagenstos (2016), the relationship between the disability rights movement and labor is complicated (as has been true regarding the civil rights movement and labor). Sometimes unions have supported disability rights efforts, such as in recent struggles to challenge Medicaid budget cuts under the ADA and the push by the Service Employees International Union for increased wages and benefits for direct care workers who provide home- and community-based service. At other times, unions and disability rights advocates have been in conflict, such as in the 1970s and 1980s when AFSCME fought de-institutionalization of people with mental disabilities. More recently, state Medicaid cuts led many disability advocates to fear unions' efforts would lead to re-institutionalization of many people with disabilities.

Another example of the conflict is the US Department of Labor's 2013 rules that expanded Fair Labor Standards Act (FLSA) protections for home care workers. This was supported by some disability rights groups but opposed by others that feared increased FLSA coverage would lead to re-institutionalization of people with disabilities and less control by consumers over how care workers do their jobs—especially if the workers were unionized. Bagenstos (2016) argues that disability rights groups need to support efforts of unions for decent wages and FLSA protections for home care workers for both moral and practical reasons. The moral argument is that all workers deserve fair pay and FLSA is the main way our society ensures this.[4] The practical argument from Bagenstos (2016) is that better quality of home care and less turnover occur when homecare workers receive better pay.

The UK experience can provide insights into disability and unions. Echoing the tension identified by Basas (2013), Foster and Fosh (2010) argue that the UK's Disability Discrimination Act (DDA) follows a medical model of disability in which the law requires employers to provide reasonable accommodation to employees with disabilities, but the requests for such accommodations are to be made by individual employees with disabilities, and reasonable accommodations are individually negotiated with management. Hence, the British model conflicts with the collective approach supported by unions. The authors delve into the antecedents of the DDA and argue that in the United Kingdom, the movement to pass the DDA was built on the assumption that disability is an individual issue. Therefore, the resulting law did not focus on social aspects of discrimination and established a legal system that relied more on experts than on giving voice to employees with disabilities. In doing so, it avoided encouraging organizations to create conducive organizational cultures and policies for employees with disability.

Foster and Fosh (2010) claim that for the UK system to work, proactive representation of employees with disabilities in the workplace is necessary to avoid discrimination. Drawing on interviews with employees with disabilities, trade union officials, disability-related voluntary organizations, and government organizations, they find that disability organizations play a positive role in the workplace for employees with disabilities. They argue, however, that unions are the only workplace actors that can reconfigure the organizational strategies to integrate and institutionalize disability concerns. They note that while unions address discrimination in job retention, discrimination against people with disabilities is not addressed at the point of recruitment, and one way to overcome this issue is to develop links between unions and groups that support individuals with disabilities. They argue that full-time union officers may play an especially positive role in disability accommodations when employees with disabilities are reluctant to reveal their disabilities and where the broader policy to mitigate discrimination does not exist.

A recent UK innovation is the creation by unions of "disability champions," as described by Bacon and Hoque (2012, 2015). The position of disability champions was created to bridge the gap among unions, employees with disabilities, and management. These individuals receive a five-day training to become "lay workplace union activists." Their job includes offering advice to employees with disabilities and employers on disability issues, including informing employees with disabilities about their rights, supporting these rights before management, facilitating policy and practice change, and improving grievance procedures. The authors find that disability champions improve the ability of unions to represent individuals with disabilities and enhance the voice of employees with disabilities, which has a positive impact on employer efforts to make reasonable accommodations. They argue that this is consistent with Freeman and Medoff's (1984) model in which unions can have a positive impact by providing "direct voice channels," which can be formal (e.g., collective bargaining) or informal (e.g., dialogs with management). Additionally, they note that disability champions may have an impact through the "facilitation effect" (Budd and Mumford 2004) as they inform the employees with disabilities about their rights and help facilitate representation and grievance procedures. The potential for positive union effects is indicated by the finding that unions can positively influence the adoption of a range of equal opportunity practices (Hoque and Bacon 2014).

The role of disability champions is also described by Richards and Sang (2016) based on interviews with disability champions, neurologically impaired employees, and union officials. This innovation illustrates an important way in which unions can provide a voice to employees with disabilities and institutionalize disability concerns in organizational strategy and culture.

In sum, there are conflicting perspectives on how well unions address the concerns of workers with disabilities. There is remarkably little evidence on either the prevalence or effects of unions for workers with disabilities. One study found that in 1984, union coverage was slightly higher among men with more-stigmatized disabilities and slightly lower among men with less-stigmatized disabilities than among men without disabilities (Baldwin and Johnson 1994). Regarding outcomes, data from a 1992 survey show that union status was associated with an increased likelihood of women's employment following onset of a health impairment, although this did not happen for men (Daly and Bound 1996). The potential for unions to reduce the disability pay gap is supported by a study that finds that unions reduce the wage penalty associated with obesity (Debeaumont and Nsiah 2016), although evidence from 1984 finds that union premiums were just slightly higher among workers with disabilities than among nondisabled workers (Baldwin and Johnson 1994).

The conflicting perspectives highlight the need for new evidence to shed light on the experiences of workers with disabilities with respect to unions. Given the sparseness and age of prior evidence, we analyze more recent evidence on prevalence, trends, pay, and accommodations for workers with disabilities in unions.

HOW LIKELY ARE WORKERS WITH DISABILITIES TO BE IN UNIONS?

Unionized workers may be more likely than non-union workers to have disabilities because (1) union workers are older on average (US Bureau of Labor Statistics 2018), and age is associated with an increased likelihood of disability (Erickson, Lee, and von Schrader 2018), (2) they tend to be over-represented in blue-collar jobs where the risk of disabling injuries is higher, and (3) union contracts often have provisions facilitating return to work and accommodations for workers with disabilities.

The opposite relation may hold, however, to the extent that union contracts give preference for light-duty positions or preferable schedules to workers with more seniority over workers who experience disabling injuries (Schur 1998). In addition, unions may negotiate provisions for disability income in collective bargaining agreements for injured workers, and such income may facilitate their withdrawal from the workforce.

We examine the levels and trends in union coverage using CPS out-going rotation groups over every month in the period 2009 through 2017, comprising a total of 1,497,721 individual employee observations (including all employees 16 or older, and excluding self-employed). The out-going rotation groups contain information on union status and wage levels, which is combined with the six disability measures introduced in the CPS in late 2008. These six measures consist of questions on four basic types of disabilities (hearing, visual, cognitive, and ambulatory) and two types of activity limitations (self-care and navigating independently outside the home). While the activity limitations generally indicate more severe disabilities, the yes/no nature of the questions does not allow a better measure of severity (as explored in Miller et al. 2011). The questions are shown in the appendix to this chapter. We follow the convention of the US Bureau of Labor Statistics that a "yes" answer to any question qualifies one as having a disability, although we also break out the measures by type of disability for some analyses. There are 54,950 observations of employees who are recorded with a disability, representing a weighted 3.37% of all employee observations.[5] Among those recorded with a disability, 33.6% report a hearing disability, 15.5% report a vision disability, 25.5% report a cognitive disability, 39.1% report an ambulatory disability, 6.2% report a self-care disability, and 12.7% report an independent living disability. All of our estimates use CPS weights to reflect population averages more accurately. Note that we also did all analyses for union membership rather than union coverage, with very similar findings.

We recognize two potentially tricky issues with this sample. The first is that union status may influence the reporting of disability. The reporting of disability appears to be sensitive to employment conditions: It has been found that nonemployed people are more likely than employed people to over-report medical conditions (Baker, Stabile, and Deri 2004). While the issue of "justification bias" (leading nonemployed workers to report a disability to justify their lack of employment) would not appear to be relevant in comparing union and non-union workers, it is possible that union workers may be more aware of their legal rights and consequently less afraid to report a disability. In addition, the greater health care access of union workers may affect the reporting of disability because health care can reduce the likelihood of developing a disability. While these issues may affect the overall level of reporting of disability, they are unlikely to affect the trends on which we focus. A second issue is that the period 2009 through 2017 may be different from earlier periods, given that it was subsequent to the financial crisis and recession of 2008, and it followed the passage of the 2008 ADAAA that expanded coverage of the ADA. We return to the timing issue in the discussion.

Levels of Unionization

Workers with disabilities were more likely than nondisabled workers to be covered by unions across the 2009 through 2017 period, as shown in Table 1 (next page). The difference is slight (13% compared with 12.5%) but strong enough to be statistically significant. The gap varies by a number of demographic and job characteristics. The gap is similar in the private sector, although among public sector workers, those with disabilities have a lower unionization rate. The type of disability matters, too. While workers with hearing impairments are significantly more likely than workers without disabilities to be covered by unions, those with cognitive or independent living disabilities are significantly less likely to be covered. Only a small difference in the disability union gap exists between women and men, but age is an important factor because workers with disabilities are less likely to be covered by unions in the youngest (18–34) and oldest (65 or higher) age groups.

Part of the overall union gap may be due to the disproportionate representation of employees with disabilities in blue-collar occupations that have generally higher unionization rates. In Table 1, the breakdown by occupation shows that employees with disabilities have higher unionization rates than employees without disabilities in six of the ten major occupations, including significant positive gaps in management-related and office-administrative support occupations.

The higher union rate among workers with disabilities is preserved when controlling for detailed occupation but not when controlling for demographic variables. Table 2 (page 75) reports linear probability models predicting the likelihood of union coverage, first without controls (column 1), then with detailed occupational controls using 564 dummies (column 2), and then adding demographic controls (column 3).[6] The positive disability effect disappears from columns 1 to 3, indicating that workers with disabilities are no more or less likely to be covered by unions after controlling for demographic variables. Additional unreported tests show that this switch is driven by controlling for age (using both linear and squared terms), indicating that the positive disability effect in column 1 is due to the higher average age of workers with disabilities.

Table 2 also shows that the relative likelihood of union coverage varies by type of disability. The likelihood is highest among those with hearing and ambulatory impairments and lowest among those with cognitive impairments. The hearing and ambulatory coefficients decrease substantially when controlling for occupation and demographic variables in column 6, which indicates they are primarily responsible for the flipping of the overall disability coefficient from column 1 to column 3. These two disabilities are also the most positively correlated with age.

TABLE 1
Union Coverage by Disability Status

	Unionization Rate			Sample Sizes	
	No Disability	Disability	Difference	No Disability	Disability
Overall	12.5%	13.0%	–0.5%**	1,442,771	54,950
Private sector	7.5%	7.9%	0.5%**	1,198,369	45,024
Government	39.4%	37.0%	–2.4%**	244,402	9,926
Disability type					
Hearing		14.9%	1.9%**		19,232
Visual		11.8%	–1.2%		8,216
Cognitive		9.5%	–3.5%**		13,765
Ambulatory		13.5%	0.5%**		21,313
Self-care		13.0%	0.0%		3,274
Independent living		10.6%	–2.4%**		6,825
Gender					
Men	13.1%	13.5%	0.5%*	727,446	28,615
Women	11.9%	12.4%	0.5%*	715,325	26,335
Age					
18–34	8.8%	7.5%	–1.2%**	503,196	10,884
35–49	14.2%	14.3%	0.0%	477,978	13,183
50–64	16.0%	16.4%	0.4%	396,990	22,455
65+	10.8%	9.7%	–1.2%**	64,607	8,428
Occupation					
Management, business, and financial	5.5%	7.8%	2.3%**	210,879	5,861
Professional and related	19.1%	19.8%	0.7%	341,906	10,143
Service	11.6%	10.9%	–0.7%	250,699	11,648
Sales and related	3.6%	4.1%	0.5%	145,649	5,365
Office and administrative support	10.5%	12.7%	2.2%**	194,377	8,164
Farming, fishing, and forestry	3.4%	3.3%	–0.1%	11,183	494
Construction and extraction	19.8%	20.9%	1.1%	65,679	2,291
Installation, maintenance, and repair	16.7%	16.0%	–0.7%	49,660	2,050
Production	14.2%	15.0%	0.8%	85,273	4,391
Transportation and material moving	17.8%	14.9%	–2.9%**	87,466	4,543

**$p < 0.01$, *$p < 0.05$.

The fact that older people are more likely to have hearing and ambulatory disabilities helps explain why the coefficients on these variables have the largest declines from column 4 to column 6 when age and age squared are added as controls.

TABLE 2
Predicting Union Membership
(Dependent variable: union coverage [dummy]; based on linear probability models)

	(1)	(2)	(3)	(4)	(5)	(6)
Disability	0.0047** (2.79)	0.0041** (2.58)	–0.0025 (–1.55)			
Type of disability						
Hearing				0.0261** (8.52)	0.0144** (5.01)	0.0066* (2.29)
Visual				–0.0090* (–2.16)	–0.0045 (–1.13)	–0.0080* (–2.02)
Cognitive				–0.0318** (–9.99)	–0.0212** (–7.07)	–0.0158** (–5.29)
Ambulatory				0.0129** (4.40)	0.0133** (4.79)	0.0019 (0.70)
Self-care				0.0125 (1.66)	0.0094 (1.32)	0.0105 (1.49)
Independent living				–0.0166** (–3.32)	–0.0168** (–3.58)	–0.0143** (–3.06)
Demographics						
Female			–0.0114** (–17.11)			–0.0114** (–17.05)
Age			0.0075** (65.69)			0.0075** (65.76)
Age squared			–0.0001** (–53.02)			–0.0001** (–53.14)
Hispanic			–0.0030** (–3.45)			–0.0031** (–3.53)
Black			0.0168** (15.95)			0.0168** (15.95)
Other race			0.0098** (9.27)			0.0098** (9.26)
High school			0.0341** (33.03)			0.0341** (32.98)
Some college, no degree			0.0459** (40.72)			0.0458** (40.64)
Associate's degree			0.0494** (36.65)			0.0493** (36.57)
Bachelor's degree			0.0395** (32.78)			0.0394** (32.70)
Graduate degree			0.0711** (47.04)			0.0710** (46.98)
Year dummies	Yes	Yes	Yes	Yes	Yes	Yes
564 occupation dummies	No	Yes	Yes	No	Yes	Yes
Observations	1,497,721	1,497,721	1,497,721	1,497,721	1,497,721	1,497,721
R-squared	0.000	0.157	0.165	0.000	0.157	0.165

** $p < 0.01$, * $p < 0.05$; robust t-statistics in parentheses.

Trends in Unionization

While the average rate of unionism across all years from 2009 through 2017 was slightly higher among workers with disabilities, Figure 1 shows the trend was more negative for workers with disabilities over this period. Unionization decreased from 13.5% to 11.9% among workers without disabilities, whereas it decreased from 14.9% to 11.3% among workers with disabilities. The latter drop of 3.6 points was over twice the drop of 1.6 points for workers without disabilities.

The trend is broken out by type of disability in Figure 2, which shows roughly similar declines among workers with each of the disabilities.

This differential decline is not explained by occupational or demographic factors, as evidenced by regressions in Table 3. The disability interaction with the time trend shows a yearly decline that is 0.24 greater among workers with disabilities (column 1), which narrows to only 0.21 points when controlling for

FIGURE 1
Trend in Disability Union Coverage

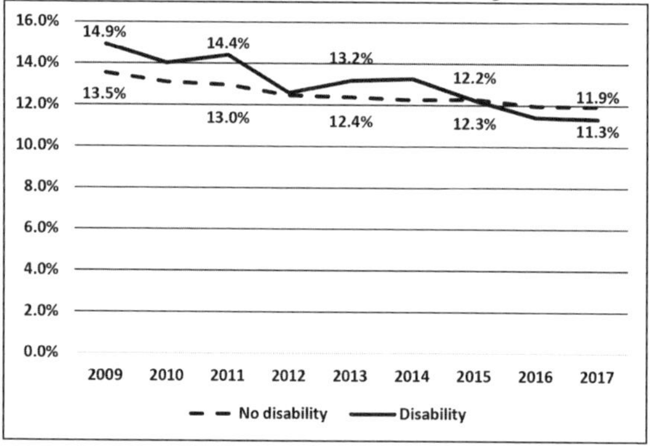

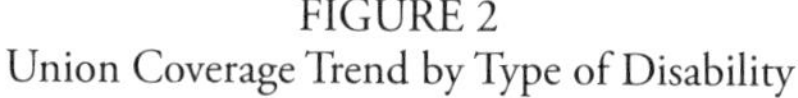

FIGURE 2
Union Coverage Trend by Type of Disability

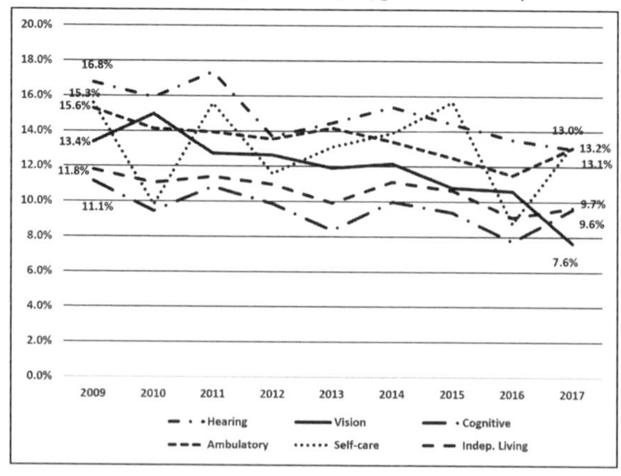

TABLE 3
Predicting Trends in Union Coverage
(Dependent variable: union coverage [dummy]; based on linear probability models)

	(1)	(2)	(3)	(4)	(5)	(6)
Main effects						
Any disability	0.0147** (4.63)	0.0128** (4.27)	0.0057 (1.91)			
Hearing disability				0.0343** (5.98)	0.0223** (4.13)	0.0140** (2.59)
Vision disability				0.0093 (1.16)	0.0131 (1.76)	0.0097 (1.32)
Cognitive disability				–0.0325** (–5.27)	–0.0201** (–3.46)	–0.0149* (-2.56)
Ambulatory disability				0.0174** (3.18)	0.0174** (3.35)	0.0061 (1.18)
Self-care disability				0.0032 (0.23)	–0.0025 (–0.19)	0.0006 (0.05)
Independent living disability				–0.0165 (–1.74)	–0.0219* (–2.48)	–0.0199* (–2.26)
Linear year	–0.0019** (-15.39)			–0.0019** (–15.61)		
564 occupation dummies	No	Yes	Yes	No	Yes	Yes
Interactions of linear year with						
Any disability	–0.0024** (–3.77)	–0.0021** (–3.49)	–0.0020** (–3.30)			
Hearing disability				–0.0020 (–1.74)	–0.0019 (–1.76)	–0.0018 (–1.64)
Vision disability				–0.0045** (–2.88)	–0.0043** (–2.93)	–0.0043** (–2.97)
Cognitive disability				0.0002 (0.17)	–0.0002 (–0.22)	–0.0002 (–0.20)
Ambulatory disability				–0.0011 (–0.97)	–0.0010 (–0.91)	–0.0010 (–0.92)
Self-care disability				0.0022 (0.77)	0.0028 (1.02)	0.0023 (0.85)
Independent living disability				–0.0000 (–0.01)	0.0012 (0.67)	0.0013 (0.74)
564 occupation dummies	No	Yes	Yes	No	Yes	Yes
Demographic controls	Yes	Yes	Yes	Yes	Yes	Yes
Observations	1,497,721	1,497,721	1,497,721	1,497,721	1,497,721	1,497,721
R-squared	0.000	0.158	0.166	0.000	0.158	0.166

** $p < 0.01$, * $p < 0.05$.
Robust t-statistics in parentheses

occupation (column 4) and 0.20 points when also controlling for demographics (column 3). As shown in column 4, when broken out by type of disability, the largest relative declines in unionization were among people with vision impairments, while the time trend interactions could not be distinguished from zero for the other disability types. There is very little change in time trend interactions from column 4 to column 6 for any of the disability types when controlling for occupational trends and demographic variables. In addition, we tested separate models for public and private sector workers and found similar declines in union coverage over time in both sectors.

Changes in Disability Status and Union Coverage

What might explain the more significant decline in unionization for employees with disabilities? We attempt to shed more light on this puzzle by tracking individual CPS respondents over a 12-month period. Half of the respondents in an out-going rotation month were interviewed 12 months earlier, and half were interviewed 12 months later. We followed the procedure used by Madrian and Lefgren (1999) to match respondents across time, based not just on household and respondent number but also on gender, age, race, and educational status. We track the movements of each respondent among six categories created by the permutations of disability status with nonemployed, non-union employed, and union employed.[7] Unlike Tables 1 and 2 that include only current employees, the transition matrix includes all out-going rotation group members age 16 or older, so that it includes both labor market participants and non-participants. The total number of matched observations is 910,541 from 2009 through 2017. The resulting matrix of transitions is shown in Table A.1 in the appendix.

We recognize some difficulties in tracking the union status of workers over time. The first is that a one-year comparison does not provide much time to capture disability and union transitions. The Family and Medical Leave Act (FMLA), for example, provides a guarantee of 60 days of unpaid leave for a medical issue, and it is possible that union workers who acquired disabilities were especially likely to remain "employed" without working because of the FMLA or union-negotiated income with extended leave (Johnson and Ondrich 1990). A second methodological issue is that disability and union status may be misreported, and it is well known that misreports exacerbate the downward bias of estimated effects when using longitudinal data (owing to the large number of misidentified "changers" in the independent variable who have little change in the dependent variable). This is less of a problem for us because we are not using the longitudinal data to estimate the effects of disability on wages or other outcomes. Instead, we are using longitudinal data to track general changes in union coverage. We do not have a good way to estimate the magnitude of errors in reporting of union and disability status. We recognize that many of the "transitions" reported in Table A.1 may reflect misreporting in one period, but such misreporting should be equally likely in the first and second periods (after adjusting for differences in interview mode as we do) so that the misreporting balances out, and the net changes are still informative in decomposing the *changes* in union coverage.

With these cautions, we configure the data from the transition matrix by dividing all individuals into four categories by changes in disability status:

1. those who did not report a disability in either the first or second period
2. those who had the onset of a disability (reporting one in the second but not first period)
3. those who recovered from a disability (reporting one in the first but not second period)
4. those who had a disability in both periods

Table 4 (next page) shows that union workers in period 1 were more likely than non-union workers to stay employed in period 2, among all of the disability transition categories. For example, among those who had a disability in both periods, 83.4% of union workers in period 1 remained employed in period 2 (row 4), compared with 76.9% of non-union workers (row 8). The ratio of these two numbers is 1.084, and the difference from 1.00 (which would indicate an equal likelihood of remaining employed) is statistically significant (row 16).

While unions appear to help the retention of workers with disabilities, these workers are less likely to become newly covered in union jobs (probably because employers are less likely to hire them in union positions). Column 2 shows the union coverage percentage broken out by change in disability status. Continuance of union coverage was higher for those who had a disability in both periods (74.9%) than for those without a disability in either period (68.6%) (rows 1 and 4). The difference is statistically significant. The opposite story holds, however, for those with a disability in both periods who began as non-union workers in period 1. In fact, only 3.5% became union workers in period 2, compared with 4.6% of workers without disabilities in either period (column 2, rows 5 and 8). (Note that these comparisons refer to whether the person remained a union employee, although they may not necessarily have remained in the same job.)

Table 5 (page 81) confirms that these two differences are maintained in multinomial logit regressions that control for demographic factors and year. Regressions were run separately for three groups based on their status in period 1 of being union employees, non-union employed, or nonemployed. Within each of these three groups, the multinomial regressions predicted their status in period 2 as a union employee, non-union employed, or nonemployed. The disability transitions are used as predictors of the employment transitions. The relative risk ratio of 1.307 in column 1 indicates that unions were especially likely to retain workers with disabilities—that is, people who started as union workers and had a disability in both periods were more likely to remain union covered in period 2 than were those without a disability in either period, relative to their likelihoods of becoming non-union employed workers.

TABLE 4
Changes in Disability Status, Employment, and Union Coverage
(Figures based on CPS respondents matched across 12 months, 2009–2017, from transition matrix in Table A.1)

		Outcome: Employed in Period 2	Outcome: Union Coverage Among Employed in Period 2	Ratio of Union Coverage in (2) Relative to Those with No Disability in Either Period
		(1)	(2)	(3)
Union employee in period 1				
1	No disability either period	93.8%	68.6%	—
2	Onset of disability in second period	79.1%	68.0%	0.991
3	Recovered from disability in second period	88.0%	68.6%	1.000
4	Disability in both periods	83.4%	74.9%	1.092**
Non-union employed in period 1				
5	No disability either period	91.4%	4.6%	—
6	Onset of disability in second period	74.6%	4.1%	0.899
7	Recovered from disability in second period	85.1%	4.8%	1.044
8	Disability in both periods	76.9%	3.5%	0.773**
Not employed in period 1				
9	No disability either period	17.6%	6.8%	—
10	Onset of disability in second period	4.2%	7.8%	1.146
11	Recovered from disability in second period	6.2%	7.4%	1.089
12	Disability in both periods	2.2%	6.7%	0.997
Union/non-union ratio				
13	No disability either period	1.026**		
14	Onset of disability in second period	1.061**		
15	Recovered from disability in second period	1.035**		
16	Disability in both periods	1.084**		

*p < 0.05 **p < 0.01.

In contrast, the 0.829 ratio in column 3 shows that workers with disabilities were especially unlikely to be hired into unionized positions. That is, people who started as non-union workers and had a disability in both periods were less likely to become union workers in period 2 than those without a disability in either period. The 0.805 ratio in column 5 indicates that nonemployed people with disabilities were less likely to become union employees than non-union employed in period 2, but this difference is not statistically significant. These patterns are maintained in unreported estimates that separate self-employed workers from other non-union workers. While having a disability in both periods appears to affect the likelihood of either becoming or remaining a union employee in period 2,

TABLE 5
Predicting Union Coverage with Disability Transitions
(Based on multinomial logit regressions predicting union employee, non-union employed, or nonemployed in period 2. Figures are relative risk ratios, representing likelihood of entering category in period 2 relative to likelihood of becoming non-union employed worker)

	Regression 1, Including All Union Employees in Period 1		Regression 2, Including All Non-Union Employed in Period 1		Regression 3, Including All Non-employed in Period 1	
	Relative Likelihood in Period 2 of Becoming		Relative Likelihood in Period 2 of Becoming		Relative Likelihood in Period 2 of Becoming	
	Union employee	Non-employed	Union employee	Non-employed	Union employee	Non-employed
	(1)	(2)	(3)	(4)	(5)	(6)
Disability transitions						
No disability either period (base)						
Onset of disability in second period	0.942 (–0.81)	3.069** (11.32)	0.933 (–1.04)	3.166** (38.50)	0.966 (–0.25)	2.864** (27.43)
Recovered from disability in second period	0.984 (–0.25)	1.576** (4.46)	1.092 (1.64)	1.560** (14.05)	0.942 (–0.57)	2.006** (23.17)
Disability in both periods	1.307** (2.82)	2.757** (7.93)	0.829* (–2.30)	2.520** (25.51)	0.805 (–1.59)	5.721** (48.94)
Demographics						
Female	1.037 (0.90)	0.939** (–2.96)	1.405** (28.40)	1.005 (0.29)	1.549** (33.70)	0.641** (–10.09)
Age	0.890** (–13.06)	1.098** (16.20)	0.847** (–82.45)	1.039** (9.54)	0.918** (–39.01)	1.120** (13.44)
Age squared	1.002** (16.49)	0.999** (–14.49)	1.002** (85.07)	1.000** (–9.54)	1.001** (58.89)	0.999** (–12.74)
Hispanic	0.946 (–0.89)	0.813** (–6.42)	1.091** (4.80)	1.202** (6.79)	0.939** (–3.58)	1.120 (1.84)
Black	1.030 (0.50)	0.673** (–12.63)	1.520** (21.71)	1.911** (25.42)	1.115** (5.49)	1.151* (2.15)
Other race	0.897 (–1.44)	0.744** (–7.59)	1.264** (10.38)	1.114** (3.37)	1.218** (8.46)	0.870 (–1.63)
High school	0.918 (–1.00)	1.485** (7.47)	0.686** (–18.59)	1.420** (8.52)	0.711** (–17.40)	1.437** (4.91)
Some college, no degree	0.904 (–1.13)	1.635** (8.99)	0.650** (–20.13)	1.367** (7.27)	0.611** (–24.60)	1.198* (2.31)
Associate's degree	0.788* (–2.44)	1.715** (9.41)	0.518** (–25.14)	1.481** (8.57)	0.545** (–21.68)	1.666** (5.40)
Bachelor's degree	0.656** (–4.64)	1.607** (8.77)	0.455** (–34.60)	1.416** (8.21)	0.573** (–22.94)	1.506** (4.75)
Graduate degree	0.694** (–3.90)	2.023** (12.66)	0.390** (–34.67)	1.872** (14.21)	0.521** (–21.08)	2.289** (8.67)
Year dummies	Yes		Yes		Yes	
Observations	66,005		479,798		361,804	

Robust z-statistics in parentheses. $^{**}p < 0.01$, $^{*}p < 0.05$. Demographic predictors are based on values in first year. Based on CPS longitudinal matches, 2009–2017.

there was no significant effect from the onset of, or recovery from, a disability between the two periods (though again we caution that many of these apparent changes may reflect measurement error in disability status).

The decline in union coverage from 2009 through 2017, thus, does not appear to be due to demographic or occupational factors but instead results from a disproportionately low intake of workers with disabilities among those who started out as non-union workers. This is only partially counterbalanced by unions' greater retention of workers with disabilities once they have union coverage, so the net effect is a faster decline in the overall union rate for workers with disabilities.

As mentioned earlier, these results may reflect a special period following the 2008 financial crisis and the enactment of the 2008 ADAAA. Prior research shows that workers with disabilities are more likely than those without disabilities to be laid off in times of distress (Kaye 2010; Mitra and Kruse 2016). Our results, in contrast, indicate that union workers with disabilities were more likely to be kept on during this period. The 2008 ADAAA, however, may have played a role if employers became less likely to hire union workers with disabilities owing to the increased coverage provided by that act, based on the perception that it had become more difficult to fire workers with disabilities. In addition, while employers may have been reluctant to hire workers in general after the 2008–2010 crisis given that the recovery was still uncertain, they may have been particularly reluctant to hire people with disabilities.

HOW DO UNIONS AFFECT THE DISABILITY PAY GAP?

Disability is linked to lower pay for workers with disabilities, and at least part of the pay gap appears to reflect discrimination (Baldwin and Choe 2014a, 2014b; Baldwin and Johnson 2006; Kruse, Schur, Rogers, and Ameri 2018). Unions may reduce this pay gap, both because unions raise wages in general and because union contracts may reduce wage dispersion and discriminatory wage gaps, as indicated by evidence that unions narrow the black/white pay differential (Freeman and Medoff 1984; McGregory 2013; Peoples 1994). While the union wage premium is higher for men than for women (Gabriel and Schmitz 2014), unions tend to narrow the overall gender pay gap because they raise the relative pay of women, who tend to be at the bottom of the wage distribution (Blau and Kahn 2003). As noted earlier, unions appear to reduce the wage penalty associated with obesity (Debeaumont and Nsiah 2016), while evidence from 1984 finds slightly higher union premiums among workers with disabilities than among nondisabled workers (Baldwin and Johnson 1994).

Using the 2009 to 2017 CPS data for all employees, we find that the union wage effect is larger for employees with disabilities than for those without disabilities.[8] Based on the standard wage equations presented in Table 6 (next pages), the union wage premium for workers without disabilities is 0.214 log points, or 23.9% higher pay. The disability main effect is –0.106, indicating 10.1% lower pay for non-union workers with disabilities (consistent with the results from Kruse, Schur, Rogers, and Ameri 2018), while the positive disability interaction of 0.047 indicates that unions are linked to a wage premium of 0.214 + 0.047 = 0.261 log points, or 29.8% higher pay for unionized workers with disabilities compared with non-union workers with disabilities.[9]

Figure 3 illustrates the joint effects of unions and disability on pay rates. The disability pay gap among non-union employees is –10.1%. Union employees with disabilities earn 16.8% more than non-union employees without disabilities and 29.8% more than non-union employees with disabilities. There is nonetheless a –5.7% pay gap between union employees with and without disabilities, which is a bit more than half of the –10.1% disability pay gap among non-union employees. In other words, unions clearly reduce but do not eliminate the disability pay gap.

The difference in the union wage premium holds up when running separate regressions for employees with and without disabilities (Table 6, next pages; columns 2 and 3), and the union premium is fairly consistent across disability types (columns 4 to 9), with estimated premiums from 28.4% to 37.2%.[10]

The union premium estimated here is larger than the simple differences found by Hirsch and Macpherson (2018: 21), which range between 0.138 and 0.151 log points over the 2009 through 2017 period. Further testing shows that this difference is due to controlling for occupation because our coefficient for the base union premium is 0.147 before controlling for occupation, 0.169 when controlling for ten major occupations, and 0.214 when controlling for 564 detailed occupations. We also found similar union premiums for workers with and without disabilities in the private and public sectors, with only a slightly lower union premium and disability wage gap in the public sector.[11]

FIGURE 3
Disability and the Union Wage Effect

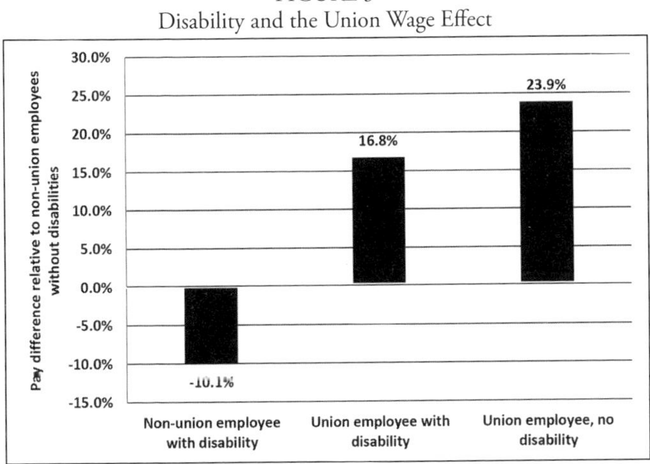

TABLE 6
Disability and the Union Wage Effect (Dependent variable = ln(hourly pay))

	Sample		
	All	No Disability	Disability
	(1)	(2)	(3)
Union coverage	0.214** (132.68)	0.214** (132.40)	0.247** (29.29)
Disability	–0.106** (–33.64)		
Disability interacted with union coverage	0.047** (6.06)		
Female	–0.109** (–85.49)	–0.110** (–85.30)	–0.076** (–10.66)
Potential labor market experience	0.021** (153.70)	0.022** (154.21)	0.013** (17.96)
Potential labor market experience squared	–0.000** (–107.19)	–0.000** (–108.20)	–0.000** (–11.56)
Hispanic	–0.065** (–42.65)	–0.067** (–43.42)	–0.003 (–0.27)
Black	–0.074** (–42.02)	–0.076** (–42.32)	–0.033** (–3.22)
Other race	–0.011** (–5.46)	–0.011** (–5.38)	–0.019 (–1.66)
High school	0.104** (54.09)	0.104** (53.53)	0.103** (10.00)
Some college, no degree	0.165** (78.97)	0.165** (77.83)	0.167** (14.81)
Associate's degree	0.204** (84.83)	0.205** (83.92)	0.183** (14.22)
Bachelor's degree	0.364** (151.77)	0.366** (150.40)	0.307** (22.65)
Graduate degree	0.554** (186.24)	0.556** (184.56)	0.488** (27.13)
Part-time	–0.115** (–70.32)	–0.109** (–65.08)	–0.215** (–27.89)
Year dummies	Yes	Yes	Yes
564 occupation dummies	Yes	Yes	Yes
Observations	929,234	893,734	35,500
R-squared	0.529	0.530	0.489

Sample					
Hearing Disability	Vision Disability	Cognitive Disability	Ambulatory Disability	Self-Care Disability	Independent Living Disability
(4)	(5)	(6)	(7)	(8)	(9)
0.255** (18.35)	0.250** (11.33)	0.260** (12.71)	0.254** (18.79)	0.281** (6.64)	0.302** (10.04)
−0.112** (−8.47)	−0.104** (−5.28)	−0.025 (−1.87)	−0.066** (−5.29)	−0.031 (−0.93)	−0.033 (−1.54)
0.015** (11.23)	0.012** (6.21)	0.009** (6.91)	0.012** (8.79)	0.013** (3.62)	0.004 (1.65)
−0.000** (−8.84)	−0.000** (−3.95)	−0.000** (−4.77)	−0.000** (−6.06)	−0.000* (−2.57)	−0.000 (−0.19)
−0.022 (−1.13)	−0.013 (−0.63)	0.032 (1.64)	−0.016 (−0.99)	−0.036 (−0.83)	−0.028 (−0.88)
−0.018 (−0.74)	−0.036 (−1.51)	−0.018 (−0.84)	−0.037* (−2.54)	−0.007 (−0.19)	−0.046 (−1.49)
−0.007 (−0.36)	−0.025 (−0.95)	−0.041 (−1.84)	−0.003 (−0.17)	0.023 (0.50)	0.041 (1.23)
0.097** (5.07)	0.065* (2.53)	0.086** (4.60)	0.115** (6.69)	0.156** (3.59)	0.138** (4.95)
0.134** (6.47)	0.107** (3.61)	0.168** (8.18)	0.169** (8.83)	0.187** (3.67)	0.211** (6.10)
0.142** (6.26)	0.144** (4.09)	0.186** (7.65)	0.180** (8.38)	0.309** (4.94)	0.263** (6.13)
0.267** (11.31)	0.232** (6.25)	0.297** (11.46)	0.298** (13.01)	0.338** (5.57)	0.376** (8.58)
0.439** (13.97)	0.379** (7.78)	0.556** (14.03)	0.478** (16.87)	0.456** (6.14)	0.569** (9.53)
−0.164** (−11.03)	−0.213** (−10.56)	−0.206** (−15.02)	−0.226** (−17.97)	−0.285** (−8.15)	−0.270** (−11.98)
Yes	Yes	Yes	Yes	Yes	Yes
Yes	Yes	Yes	Yes	Yes	Yes
12,291	5,340	9,142	13,463	1,929	4,108
0.488	0.513	0.513	0.470	0.658	0.608

Robust t-statistics in parentheses.

**$p < 0.01$, *$p < 0.05$.

Based on CPS cross-sectional data, 2009–2017.

ARE UNIONIZED WORKERS MORE LIKELY TO REQUEST ACCOMMODATIONS?

Generally, unions provide workers with an increased voice on the job (Freeman and Medoff 1984), which may help workers with disabilities in asking employers for accommodations. Union contracts often spell out procedures for accommodating workers who develop disabilities, including providing grievance procedures for employees who feel that they have been treated unfairly. The contract language may, however, also restrict the availability of accommodations. For example, unless specified otherwise, the right of senior workers to be assigned to vacant light-duty positions outweighs the right of injured workers to be reassigned there (Schur 1998).

Consistent with the voice perspective, we find that union-covered workers, in general, are more likely than non-union employees to request accommodations, regardless of disability status (Table 7). These results are based on a special CPS supplement on disability issues conducted in May 2012. Employees were first asked, "Have you ever requested any change in your current workplace to help you do your job better? For example, changes in work policies, equipment, or schedules (yes/no)." If employees selected yes, they were then asked, "Were the changes granted? (yes/no/partially)." It should be noted that the accommodation would not have to be disability related.

Accommodation requests were highest among union workers with disabilities (17.9% in column 4), next highest among non-union workers with disabilities (13.6% in column 2), next highest among union workers without disabilities (11.5% in column 3), and lowest among non-union workers without disabilities (9.0% in column 1). There appears to be a positive effect both of unions and of having a disability, on the likelihood of requesting an accommodation. The likelihood of having a request partially or fully granted appears higher among people with disabilities (11.2% compared with 7.3% among non-union employees, and 12.0% compared with 9.0% among union employees, although the latter difference is not statistically significant).

Both unionization and disability continue to exert positive effects on the likelihood of an accommodation request when controlling for demographic and occupation variables, as shown in logit results in column 1 of Table 8 (page 88). The odds ratios show that disability creates a 72% increase, and union coverage creates a 30% increase, in the odds of requesting an accommodation. The interaction coefficient, however, is not significant, indicating that the effects of unionization and disability are additive rather than interactive. The outcomes of these requests, in columns 2 through 4 of Table 8 show that unionized workers in general were significantly more likely to make requests that were denied, only partially granted, or fully granted, while workers with disabilities were almost twice as likely as those without disabilities to make requests that were fully granted (column 4). There is again no significant interaction effect between unionization and disability in predicting the results of requests.

TABLE 7
Unions and Accommodation Requests

	Non-union employees		Union employees	
	No disability	Disability	No disability	Disability
	(1)	(2)	(3)	(4)
Requested accommodations in current job	9.0%*	13.6%	11.5%	17.9%**
Granted accommodations in current job, as % of all employees				
Any granted	7.3%	11.2%	9.0%**	12.0%
Partially granted	1.6%	1.7%	2.8%**	3.1%
Fully granted	5.7%	9.6%	6.2%	9.0%
Requested accommodations (n)	31, 955	1,190	4,827	157

*Difference between employees with and without disabilities is significant at p <.0 05.
**Difference between union and non-union employees is significant at p < 0.05.
Based on CPS supplement, May 2012.

These results support the idea that unions provide a voice mechanism encouraging employees to ask for accommodations and that the mechanism has similar effects for workers with and without disabilities. Unionized workers with disabilities are the most likely to request accommodations and have them fully granted, but the combination of unionization and disability is additive rather than interactive. In other words, unions may increase the likelihood of accommodations in general but appear to do so as much for workers without disabilities as for those with disabilities. It should be noted that while there are a respectable 38,129 workers with union data in the CPS supplement, this sample contains only 157 unionized workers with disabilities. These numbers should therefore be considered exploratory.

LIMITATIONS

As in all studies, there are limitations and qualifications to our analysis. The standard disclaimers about causality apply: There may be selection effects, so we cannot be certain that having a disability increases the likelihood of remaining a union employee or raises the union wage premium. Our use of longitudinal data for employment changes that control for pre-existing differences, and testing of selection effects for the wage premium, helps alleviate such concerns.

As described earlier, context may be very important. Our results pertain to the period following the passage of the 2008 ADAAA and the 2008–2010 recession, both of which could influence the results. Employers may have become less likely to hire union workers with disabilities as a result of the increased coverage

TABLE 8
Predicting Accommodation Requests and Results (based on logit regressions predicting accommodation requests and results. Figures are odds ratios in column 1, and relative risk ratios in columns 2 to 4 representing likelihood of accommodation outcome relative to likelihood of not making any request [excluded category])

	Regression 1 logit	Regression 2 multinomial logit: Likelihood of outcome relative to likelihood of no accommodation request		
	Requested accommodation	Accommodation requested but not granted	Accommodation requested and partially granted	Accommodation requested and fully granted
	(1)	(2)	(3)	(4)
Union coverage	1.3025** (4.48)	1.3469* (2.43)	1.6049** (4.05)	1.1872* (2.22)
Disability	1.7187** (5.31)	1.4339 (1.58)	1.2379 (0.74)	1.9464** (5.60)
Union coverage* disability interaction	1.0339 (0.13)	1.7029 (1.19)	1.0832 (0.13)	0.8554 (–0.46)
Demographics				
Female	1.1172* (2.44)	1.0653 (0.63)	1.0079 (0.08)	1.1670** (2.75)
Age	1.0651** (6.17)	1.0710** (2.97)	1.1133** (4.21)	1.0512** (4.07)
Age squared	0.9993** (–5.98)	0.9993** (–2.66)	0.9987** (–4.21)	0.9994** (–3.99)
Hispanic	0.7184** (–4.38)	0.7491 (–1.74)	0.6749*(–2.23)	0.7238** (–3.47)
Black	0.7322** (–4.04)	1.0108 (0.07)	0.7982 (–1.32)	0.6278** (–4.55)
Other race	0.7403** (–3.42)	0.9598 (–0.22)	0.6808 (–1.77)	0.6999** (–3.34)
High school	1.5698** (3.93)	1.7629* (2.56)	1.9854* (2.38)	1.3997* (2.29)
Some college, no degree	2.1176**(6.36)	1.8852** (2.73)	2.9543** (3.72)	2.0130** (4.63)
Associate's degree	2.0584** (5.78)	1.5949 (1.87)	2.4454** (2.88)	2.1351** (4.80)
Bachelor's degree	2.2907** (6.94)	1.8361* (2.57)	3.2494** (3.99)	2.2279** (5.26)
Graduate degree	2.4837** (7.19)	1.5893 (1.75)	4.0207** (4.61)	2.4361** (5.53)
23 occupation dummies	Yes		Yes	
Observations	38,129		38,129	

Robust z-statistics in parentheses; *p < 0.01, **p < 0.05; based on CPS supplement, May 2012.

provided by the 2008 act, based on the perception that it would be more difficult to fire workers with disabilities. Also, employers may have been particularly reluctant to hire people with disabilities after the 2008–2010 financial crisis, given that the recovery was still uncertain in the early years.

Sample sizes are always an important consideration. We are fortunate to have very large sample sizes of close to 1.5 million for the cross-sectional analyses of union coverage, over 900,000 for the longitudinal changes in union coverage, and over 900,000 for analyses of the union wage premium. The analyses of union accommodations, however, rely on samples of 38,000 workers overall and only 157 unionized workers with disabilities. The latter results should therefore be considered exploratory.

As in most studies, we raise more questions than we can answer. We do not know the full experiences of workers with disabilities in unions and unionized workplaces, so we cannot examine the full range of union effects. We also cannot measure union policies regarding disability, and therefore can suggest, but not definitively assess, their role in explaining our results.

SUMMARY AND CONCLUSION

Despite the substantial literature documenting labor market disparities facing workers with disabilities, and the advantages that unions can provide to workers in general, there is almost no existing evidence on the prevalence and effects of unions among workers with disabilities. This chapter uses new data to examine trends in unionization, union wage effects, and accommodation requests by disability status to explore how unionized workplaces may facilitate and/or impede employment of workers with disabilities.

Our key findings are as follows:

- The union rate for employees with disabilities in the United States declined more rapidly than for employees without disabilities over the period 2009 through 2017.
- This faster decline is not explained by other demographic or occupational factors or by workers with disabilities disproportionately leaving union jobs (in fact, they are more likely to be retained in union jobs than in non-union jobs). It is instead tied to a lower likelihood of workers with disabilities being hired into union jobs than into non-union jobs. Relative to the common complaint that workers with disabilities are "last hired, first fired," in the union context they appear more likely to be "last hired" but less likely to be "first fired."
- The union wage premium is 29.8% for workers with disabilities, relative to non-union workers with disabilities. This is greater than the 23.9% union premium for workers without disabilities, and it more than offsets the –10.1% disability pay gap among non-union workers, but union

workers with disabilities still earn 5.7% less than union workers without disabilities.

- Union workers both with and without disabilities are more likely than their non-union counterparts to request workplace accommodations, which reflects a positive additive effect of both union coverage and disability status. By providing greater voice in general, unions may benefit workers with disabilities by decreasing employer resistance and potential stigma and co-worker resentment associated with accommodation requests. Our exploratory results indicate, however, that accommodation requests made by workers with disabilities are about equally likely to be granted in union and non-union settings.

While we do not have systematic data on union contracts, the literature indicates that contract provisions on disability are generally concerned with helping existing employees who are injured or otherwise develop impairments while they are employed. This fits with our findings that unions increase the job retention of workers who have a disability lasting at least 12 months. It appears that most union contracts do not include provisions for accommodating new hires with disabilities, probably because workplace accommodations are seen as employer obligations and outside the union role. We find a lower likelihood that non-union workers with disabilities will enter a union job, relative to their counterparts without disabilities.

It should be recognized that employers are responsible for hiring in most unionized settings, so the lower rate of hiring people with disabilities in union settings may reflect employer reluctance to hire people with disabilities into positions with union protections where they will be more difficult to lay off. It should also be noted that our period of study (2009–2017) immediately followed the passage of the 2008 ADA Amendments Act, which was designed to increase coverage by clearing up and expanding legal interpretations of the ADA; consequently, the increased coverage may have made employers even more reluctant than they were before to hire workers with disabilities into union jobs. This period also followed the 2008–2010 recession, which may have made employers particularly anxious about hiring workers with disabilities in the early stages of the recovery because they may have perceived these workers as riskier.

Unions in the United Kingdom have developed a strategy of creating "disability champions" who are resources for employees with disabilities, employers, and unions on disability issues, and advocate for workers with disabilities. Two studies find that the disability champions have improved outcomes both for workers with disabilities and for employers, helping workers preserve employment and employers retain valuable human capital and avoid costly turnover.

Several authors suggest that unions could also enhance outcomes for workers with disabilities by working more closely with outside disability organizations. Many employers have successfully worked with nonprofit and government organizations in identifying, recruiting, and training qualified individuals with disabilities for employment positions (National Council on Disability 2007). Unions may similarly find it useful to work with employers and outside organizations to identify, recruit, and help train people with disabilities for unionized jobs. This could involve creating a permanent union office to represent employees with disabilities that coordinates with voluntary disability organizations and, in essence, institutes a proactive union approach to disability within and outside the organizations. In cases where unions are more involved in hiring, such as by providing hiring halls, they could pursue a more active role with outside organizations to create pipelines of workers with disabilities (e.g., through apprenticeship programs). Finally, it would be good for unions and employers to ensure that collective bargaining agreements contain clear policies not only for existing workers but for new hires as well (though hiring policies and practices are not a mandatory subject of bargaining in the United States, as noted earlier). While collective bargaining contracts have been criticized for using the medical model of disability, some union policies, such as on job reassignment and scheduling, focus on adapting the environment to accommodate the needs of workers with disabilities. This is in line with the social model's view that the environment is a crucial factor in whether an impairment limits employment and productivity and thereby becomes a disability.

Our results raise interesting research questions about the employment of people with disabilities. The higher union wage premium among workers with disabilities suggests either that unions help decrease discriminatory wage differentials as they appear to do for black workers, and/or unions help raise the relative productivity of workers with disabilities, possibly through increased stay-at-work and return-to-work policies that provide accommodations for workers who develop disabilities while employed. It would be valuable to explore which of these (or other) explanations is responsible for the differential in the union wage premium. Given the higher wage premium and job retention of workers with disabilities in unionized jobs, unions appear to provide significant benefits to workers with disabilities. They may not have the opportunity to do so because hiring decisions for unionized jobs are driven by employers. Some of the value of unions for workers with disabilities may be the result of establishing written policies in collective bargaining agreements governing the treatment of disability; one study in a non-union context found that written policies were more important than expressed intentions in subsequent hiring of people with disabilities (Araten-Bergman 2016). The reasons behind the low hiring rate of workers with disabilities into unionized jobs is another excellent question for investigation. It would be valuable to explore whether this is due to employer reluctance to hire people with disabilities into unionized jobs, reluctance by unions to encourage applicants with disabilities, an unwelcome environment for new workers with disabilities in unionized jobs, or other factors. Further research could also explore any differences in employment experiences in unionized workplaces between workers with visible and invisible disabilities, which we could not do with our measures.

People with disabilities have historically faced many employment barriers, and it appears that working in a unionized setting can improve their workforce participation and help them achieve greater economic equality. As the population ages, there will be more workers with disabilities in the coming decades. The decline in union coverage among people with disabilities is sobering. Nevertheless, in some respects, unionized workplaces may serve as models for how to increase retention and pay equity for workers with disabilities. It would be valuable for unions, employers, workers with disabilities, disability advocacy groups, and policy makers to work together to ensure greater job opportunities and more positive employment outcomes for people with disabilities.

ACKNOWLEDGMENTS

We appreciate useful comments and advice from Ariel Avgar, associate professor of labor relations, Cornell University ILR School; Melissa Bjelland, research associate, Cornell University; Alex Bryson, professor of quantitative social science, University College London; John Budd, professor of work and organizations, University of Minnesota; Hank Farber, Hughes–Rogers Professor of Economics, Princeton University; Barry Hirsch, professor and W.J. Usery Chair of the America Workplace, Georgia State University; Melanie Jones, professor of economics, Cardiff University; Wilma Liebman, former chair, National Labor Relations Board; Sophie Mitra, professor of economics, Fordham University; and Paula Voos, professor of labor studies and employment relations, Rutgers University.

APPENDIX

Questions used by the Census Bureau to identify disability status on the American Community Survey (http://bit.ly/2Yoi1eu):

- Is this person deaf or does he/she have serious difficulty hearing?
- Is this person blind or does he/she have serious difficulty seeing even when wearing glasses?
- Because of a physical, mental, or emotional condition, does this person have serious difficulty concentrating, remembering, or making decisions?
- Does this person have serious difficulty walking or climbing stairs?
- Does this person have difficulty dressing or bathing?
- Because of a physical, mental, or emotional condition, does this person have difficulty doing errands alone such as visiting a doctor's office or shopping?

TABLE A.1
Transition Matrix for Union and Disability Status
(figures represent cell percentages among all respondents matched over any 12 months in 2009–2017)

	Transition to						
	Nonemployed, no disability	Nonemployed, disability	Non-union employee, no disability	Union employee, no disability	Non-union employee with disability	Union employee with disability	Totals
Transition from	1	2	3	4	5	6	
1 Nonemployed, no disability	22.72%	2.87%	4.56%	0.29%	0.12%	0.01%	30.57%
2 Nonemployed, disability	3.15%	6.50%	0.19%	0.01%	0.14%	0.01%	9.99%
3 Non-union employee, no disability	4.25%	0.28%	43.59%	1.81%	0.81%	0.03%	50.77%
4 Union employee, no disability	0.38%	0.03%	1.76%	3.99%	0.03%	0.07%	6.26%
5 Non-union employee with disability	0.20%	0.19%	1.07%	0.04%	0.63%	0.02%	2.15%
6 Union employee with disability	0.02%	0.02%	0.04%	0.10%	0.02%	0.06%	0.26%
Totals	30.70%	9.89%	51.22%	6.24%	1.74%	0.20%	100.00%

N = 910,541. Figures weighted using CPS weights with adjustment for differential reporting of disability by interview type.

ENDNOTES

[1] *US Airways v. Barnett*, 535 US 391 (2002). The National Labor Relations Board (NLRB) later used this ruling to declare that an employer violated the duty to bargain by unilaterally providing an accommodation in conflict with the collective bargaining agreement (*Industria Lechera de Puerto Rico*, 344 NLRB 1075 (2005)).

[2] Roseburg Forest Products, 331 NLRB 999 (2000).

[3] Star Tribune, 295 NLRB 543 (1989). See also US Postal Service, 308 NLRB 1305 (1992), enf. denied 18 F3d 1089 (3d Cir 1994) (board did not err in "concluding that a hiring practice is a mandatory subject of collective bargaining where there is an objective basis for believing it to be discriminatory").

[4] Exceptions include when workers do not need these protections (e.g., for well-paid salaried employees), or the moral argument is outweighed by the economic unsustainability of giving full FLSA protections to necessary workers (e.g., firefighters in very small departments), but neither exemption applies in the case of homecare workers.

[5] This figure is lower than the figure derived from the American Community Survey (Lauer and Houtenville 2018), even though the disability questions were the same. The difference probably reflects differences in survey mode, question placement, and other factors discussed in Schur, Kruse, and Blanck (2013: 14–20).

[6] The results are similar using probit models in place of linear probability models.

[7] Note that to keep the number of categories manageable, we combined non-union employees with self-employed, though we also tested models that separate self-employed from non-union employees with little difference in the pattern of results. We made adjustments in the weights to

account for the greater likelihood of telephone interviews in the second year because the data clearly show that people are less likely to report disability in a telephone interview than in a personal interview.

[8] The regressions are based only on employees and use the natural logarithm of hourly pay as the dependent variable, adjusted for inflation using the monthly Consumer Price Index. Allocated values, which are imputed in the CPS for people who did not report earnings, are excluded because their inclusion will bias union and disability estimates toward zero (Bollinger and Hirsch 2006; Hirsch and Schumacher 2004). Nonresponse is highest in the left and right tails of the earnings distribution, indicating that estimates of earnings differentials are most likely to be biased in the tails rather than the middle of the distribution as we estimate here (Bollinger, Hirsch, Hokayem, and Ziliak 2018). After the allocated values were excluded, the sample was reweighted to reflect the likelihood of nonresponse using code kindly provided by Barry Hirsch. We also tested employment selection equations using the Heckman correction with the number of household members under age 6, ages 6–15, ages 16+ nonemployed, and ages 16+ employed excluding respondent, as additional variables determining selection into employment. The results were very similar between regressions corrected and not corrected for selection.

[9] While Budd and Na (2000) find differences in the union premium between members and nonmembers in union-covered jobs, our estimates using union membership instead of coverage produce very similar results.

[10] Wald tests show that the nondisability union coefficient in column 3 is significantly different from the union coefficients for any disability in column 2 (p = 0.0001), hearing disability in column 4 (p = 0.0027), cognitive disability in column 6 (p = 0.0199), ambulatory disability in column 7 (p = 0.0027), and independent living disability in column 9 (p = 0.0021). The significance levels are lower when comparing the nondisability union coefficients with the union coefficients for vision disability in column 5 (p = 0.0890) and self-care disability in column 8 (p = 0.0803).

[11] When regression 1 in Table 6 is run just for private (public) workers, the coefficient is 0.222 (0.195) on union coverage, –0.107 (–0.094) on disability, and 0.048 (0.034) on the union–disability interaction. All coefficients remain significant at the 0.01 level in both sectors. The coefficients are significantly different at the 0.01 level between the public and private sectors for union coverage but not for disability or the disability–union interaction. These figures imply a union premium for workers with (without) disabilities of 30.9% (24.9%) in the private sector and 25.7% (21.5%) in the public sector.

REFERENCES

Ameri, Mason, Lisa Schur, Meera Adya, Scott Bentley, Patrick McKay, and Douglas Kruse. 2018. "The Disability Employment Puzzle: A Field Experiment on Employer Hiring Behavior." *ILR Review* 71 (2): 329–364.

Araten-Bergman, T. 2016. "Managers' Hiring Intentions and the Actual Hiring of Qualified Workers with Disabilities." *International Journal of Human Resource Management* 27 (14): 1510–1530.

Bacon, Nick, and Kim Hoque. 2012. "The Role and Impact of Trade Union Equality Representatives in Britain." *British Journal of Industrial Relations* 50 (2): 239–262.

Bacon, Nick, and Kim Hoque. 2015. "The Influence of Trade Union Disability Champions on Employer Disability Policy and Practice." *Human Resource Management Journal* 25 (2): 233–249.

Bagenstos, Samuel R. 2016. "Disability Rights and Labor: Is This Conflict Really Necessary?" *Indiana Law Journal* 92: 277–298.

Baker, Michael, Mark Stabile, and Catherine Deri. 2004. "What Do Self-Reported, Objective, Measures of Health Measure?" *Journal of Human Resources* 39 (4): 1067–1093.

Baldwin, Marjorie, and Chung Choe. 2014a. "Re-Examining the Models Used to Estimate Disability-Related Wage Discrimination." *Applied Economics* 46 (12): 1393–1408.

Baldwin, Marjorie, and Chung Choe. 2014b. "Wage Discrimination Against Workers with Sensory Disabilities." *Industrial Relations* 53 (1): 101–124.

Baldwin, Marjorie, and William Johnson. 1994. "Labor Market Discrimination Against Men with Disabilities." *Journal of Human Resources* 29 (1): 1–19.

Baldwin, Marjorie, and William Johnson. 2006. "A Critical Review of Studies of Discrimination Against Workers with Disabilities." In *Handbook on the Economics of Discrimination*, edited by William Rodgers, pp. 119–160. Northampton, MA: Edgar Elgar.

Basas, Carrie G. 2013. "Universally Designing the Public Sector Workplace: Technology as Disability Access." *WorkingUSA* 16 (1): 69–86.

Blau, Francine, and Lawrence Kahn. 2003. "Understanding International Differences in the Gender Pay Gap." *Journal of Labor Economics* 21 (1): 106–144.

Bollinger, C.R., and B.T. Hirsch. 2006. "Match Bias from Earnings Imputation in the Current Population Survey: The Case of Imperfect Matching." *Journal of Labor Economics* 24 (3): 483–519.

Bollinger, C.R., B.T. Hirsch, C.M. Hokayem, and J.P. Ziliak. 2018 (July). "Trouble in the Tails: What We Know About Earnings Nonresponse Thirty Years After Lillard, Smith, and Welch." IZA Discussion Paper 11710. Bonn, Germany: IZA Institute of Labor Economics.

Budd, J.W., and K. Mumford. 2004. "Trade Unions and Family-Friendly Policies in Britain." *ILR Review* 57 (2): 204–222.

Budd, John W., and In-Gang Na. 2000. "The Union Membership Wage Premium for Employees Covered by Collective Bargaining Agreements." *Journal of Labor Economics* 18 (4): 783–807.

Daly, M.C., and J. Bound. 1996. "Worker Adaptation and Employer Accommodation Following the Onset of a Health Impairment." *The Journals of Gerontology Series B: Psychological Sciences and Social Sciences* 51 (2): S53–S60.

Debeaumont, Ron, and Christian Nsiah. 2016. "Do Unions Reduce the Wage Penalty Experienced by Obese Women?" *Economics Bulletin* 36 (1): 281–290.

Erickson, W., C. Lee, and S. von Schrader. 2018. "2016 Disability Status Report: United States." Ithaca, NY: Cornell University Yang-Tan Institute on Employment and Disability.

Farber, Henry S. 1986. "The Analysis of Union Behavior." *Handbook of Labor Economics*, Vol. 2, edited by Orley Ashenfelter and Richard Layard. Amsterdam, Netherlands: North Holland Publishing.

Farber, Henry S., Daniel Herbst, Ilyana Kuziemko, and Suresh Naidu. 2018. "Unions and Inequality over the Twentieth Century: New Evidence from Survey Data" Working Paper No. 24587. Cambridge, MA: National Bureau of Economic Research.

Foster, Deborah, and Patricia Fosh. 2010. "Negotiating 'Difference': Representing Disabled Employees in the British Workplace." *British Journal of Industrial Relations* 48 (3): 560–582.

Freeman, Richard, and James Medoff. 1984. *What Do Unions Do?* New York, NY: Basic Books.

Gabriel, P.E., and S. Schmitz. 2014. "A Longitudinal Analysis of the Union Wage Premium for US Workers." *Applied Economics Letters* 21 (7–9): 487–489.

Hirsch, Barry T. 2004. "Reconsidering Union Wage Effects: Surveying New Evidence on an Old Topic." *Journal of Labor Research* 25 (2): 233–266.

Hirsch, B.T., and D.A. Macpherson. 2018. "Union Membership and Earnings Data Book: Compilations from the Current Population Survey." Washington, DC: US Bureau of National Affairs.

Hirsch, B.T., and E.J. Schumacher. 2004. "Match Bias in Wage Gap Estimates Due to Earnings Imputation." *Journal of Labor Economics* 22 (3): 689–722.

Hoque, K., and N. Bacon. 2014. "Unions, Joint Regulation and Workplace Equality Policy and Practice in Britain: Evidence from the 2004 Workplace Employment Relations Survey." *Work, Employment and Society* 28 (2): 265–284.

Johnson, W.G., and J. Ondrich. 1990. "The Duration of Post-Injury Absences from Work." *Review of Economics and Statistics* 72 (4): 578–586.

Joint Activity System. 2019. "ADAPT (Accommodating DisAbled People in Transition)." Program description of the UAW-GM Center for Human Resources. http://bit.ly/2uAWt0F

Jones, Melanie K. 2008. "Disability and the Labour Market: A Review of the Empirical Evidence." *Journal of Economic Studies* 35 (5): 405–424.

Jones, Melanie K., Paul L. Latreille, and Peter J. Sloane. 2006. "Disability, Gender, and the British Labour Market." *Oxford Economic Papers* 58 (3): 407–449.

Jones, Melanie K., and Peter J. Sloane. 2010. "Disability and Skill Mismatch." *Economic Record* 86: 101–114.

Kaye, H. Stephen. 2010. "The Impact of the 2007–09 Recession on Workers with Disabilities." *Monthly Labor Review* 133 (10): 19–30.

Kruse, D., L. Schur, S. Rogers, and M. Ameri. 2018. "Why Do Workers with Disabilities Earn Less? Occupational Job Requirements and Disability Discrimination." *British Journal of Industrial Relations* 56 (4): 798–834.

Lauer, E.A., and A.J. Houtenville. 2018. "Annual Disability Statistics Compendium: 2017." Durham, NH: University of New Hampshire, Institute on Disability.

Madrian, Brigitte C., and Lars John Lefgren. 1999. "A Note on Longitudinally Matching Current Population Survey (CPS) Respondents." Technical Working Paper No. 247. Cambridge, MA: National Bureau of Economic Research.

McGregory, Richard. 2013. "An Analysis of Black–White Wage Differences in Nursing: Wage Gap or Wage Premium?" *Review of Black Political Economy* 40 (1): 31–37.

Miller, K., D. Mont, A. Maitland, B. Altman, and J. Madans. 2011. "Results of a Cross-National Structured Cognitive Interviewing Protocol to Test Measures of Disability." *Quality & Quantity* 45 (4): 801–815.

Mitra, S. 2018. *Disability, Health and Human Development.* New York, NY: Palgrave MacMillan.

Mitra, Sophie, and Douglas Kruse. 2016. "Are Workers with Disabilities More Likely to Be Displaced?" *International Journal of Human Resource Management* 27 (14): 1550–1579.

National Council on Disability. 2007. "Empowerment for Americans with Disabilities: Breaking Barriers to Careers and Full Employment." Washington, DC: National Council on Disability. http://bit.ly/2HW7ZMb

Peoples, James. 1994. "Monopolistic Market Structure, Unionization, and Racial Wage Differentials." *Review of Economics and Statistics* 76 (1): 207–211.

Richards, James, and Kate Sang. 2016. "Trade Unions as Employment Facilitators for Disabled Employees." *International Journal of Human Resource Management* 27 (14): 1642–1661.

Rios-Avila, Fernando, and Barry T. Hirsch. 2014. "Unions, Wage Gaps, and Wage Dispersion: New Evidence from the Americas." *Industrial Relations* 53(1): 1–27.

Schur, Lisa. 1998. "Do Seniority Systems 'Trump' the ADA? Conflicts Between Collective Bargaining Agreements and the Duty to Accommodate Disabled Workers." *Journal of Individual Employment Rights* 7 (2): 167–186.

Schur, Lisa, Kyongji Han, Andrea Kim, Mason Ameri, Meera Adya, Peter Blanck, and Douglas Kruse. 2017. "Disability at Work: A Look Back and Forward." *Journal of Occupational Rehabilitation* 27 (4): 482–497.

Schur, Lisa, Douglas Kruse, and Peter Blanck. 2013. *People with Disabilities: Sidelined or Mainstreamed?* Cambridge, UK: Cambridge University Press.

Schur, Lisa, Douglas Kruse, Joseph Blasi, and Peter Blanck. 2009. "Is Disability Disabling in All Workplaces? Workplace Disparities and Corporate Culture." *Industrial Relations* 48 (3): 381–410.

Stone, Dianna, and Adrienne Colella. 1996. "A Model of Factors Affecting the Treatment of Disabled Individuals in Organizations." *Academy of Management Review* 21: 352–401.

US Bureau of Labor Statistics. No date. "Data Retrieval: Labor Force Statistics." Data Retrieval Tool. Washington, DC: US Bureau of Labor Statistics. http://bit.ly/2uwrp2s

US Bureau of Labor Statistics. 2018 (Jan. 19). "Union Members–2017." News Release, USDL-18-0080. Washington, DC: US Bureau of Labor Statistics. http://bit.ly/2HW9UAn

Williams-Whitt, Kelly. 2007. "Impediments to Disability Accommodation." *Relations industrielles/Industrial Relations* 62 (3): 405–432.

World Health Organization. 2001. "The International Classification of Functioning, Disability and Health." Geneva, Switzerland: World Health Organization.

Chapter 4

Creating an Accommodating Workplace: Encouraging Disability Disclosure and Managing Reasonable Accommodation Requests

Sarah von Schrader
LaWanda Cook
Wendy Strobel Gower
Cornell University

Accommodating employees and applicants is a potentially powerful way to increase performance, productivity, and satisfaction in the workplace. The focus of this chapter is on the reasonable accommodation process for individuals with disabilities, with special attention given to relevant laws and regulations to which employers must adhere. We also offer insight into the perspectives of applicants and employees, many of whom are concerned about disclosing a disability and requesting an accommodation. Further, we present data that describe where conflicts arise in the reasonable accommodation process from the perspective of the employee with a disability. On the basis of a review across literature and examination of secondary data, we offer recommendations for employers, providing practical suggestions for encouraging disclosure and implementing a fair and transparent process for accommodations.

To set the stage for this chapter, we briefly introduce two employees with disabilities who are valued members of their organizations:

> Tracy, a young woman with bipolar disorder, is a well-liked childcare provider working in a daycare center. She has been employed for over six years but is currently in a difficult situation with her manager. She occasionally misses a few days when adjusting to changes in her medications and making related visits to her doctor. Her new manager is frustrated by Tracy's absences because her late notice often leaves him without adequate coverage. Tracy, meanwhile, worries that disclosing a highly stigmatized disability will lead her manager and others at the organization to treat her differently and feel differently about her, not to mention the concern some parents of the children she cares may have if she discloses.

> Roberto's vision is deteriorating faster than he would like to admit. He works in a medical facility handling scheduling and insurance claims filing. He is no longer able to see the computer screen well, and this contributes to errors and a slower work pace. The thought of telling his employer worries him; his deteriorating vision is related to another health condition but also to the natural aging process.

He has never needed to ask for help at work and does not want to start now.

To be eligible for the employment-related protections of the Americans with Disabilities Act (ADA), a worker must be a qualified individual with a disability and must disclose that disability. When a disability is disclosed to an employer, the ADA offers protections against discrimination and an opportunity for dialog about what type of an accommodation may enable the individual to effectively do his or her job. Both Tracy and Roberto have a disability under the ADA and would likely benefit from a workplace accommodation, but their hesitation to disclose those disabilities could prevent them from getting the supports they need. Without understanding that these workers have disabilities, to their managers, Tracy's absence and Roberto's slow, inaccurate work simply look like performance issues. However, in both cases, an inexpensive accommodation would likely allow them to perform better.

While the ADA offers protections for individuals with disabilities, accommodation is not just a disability issue: About 8.6% of workers without disabilities and 12.7% workers with disabilities have asked for some sort of accommodation to do their job better (von Schrader, Xu, and Bruyère 2014). Such requests include flexibility in scheduling, new equipment, or a change in workplace policy. In fact, according to Current Population Survey data, over 95% of accommodation requests come from people without disabilities. Employers who proactively accommodate all members of the workforce may limit the need for individuals with disabilities to disclose. This sort of accommodating workplace culture has been shown to be particularly beneficial for employees with disabilities (Schur, Kruse, Blasi, and Blanck 2009). Significant benefits have also been noted for the organization. For example, a study conducted by Loy (2017) on behalf of the Job Accommodation Network cited direct benefits such as retaining valued employees, increased employee productivity, increased attendance among workers with and without disabilities, enhanced workplace diversity, and savings in workers compensation or insurance cost, and improved overall company safety. While the benefits of accommodation are great, it is common for organizations to struggle with the accommodation process; in fact, accommodation represents the second most common issue (behind discharge) in discrimination charges filed under the ADA (Bruyère, von Schrader, Coduti, and Bjelland 2010).

The remainder of this chapter considers various aspects of disability disclosure and the accommodation process, first defining these concepts and then drawing from related literature and recent work by our team of authors. We begin with the issue of disability disclosure as it initiates the reasonable accommodation process. We describe the potential challenges and benefits of sharing disability-related information, and we consider how employers can create an environment that may encourage disclosure. Next, we provide an overview of the accommodation request and response process, providing the perspective of the different parties involved and highlighting the need for education, policy, and process to guide this ongoing dialog. Finally, we examine data on discrimination charges under the ADA that cite reasonable accommodation; these data offer insight on both the patterns of these charges and, through analysis of case notes, illustrate ways that conflict around reasonable accommodation manifests. Taken together, the findings presented in this chapter inform a discussion of employer practices that support effectively accommodating employees with disabilities.

DEFINING DISCLOSURE AND REASONABLE ACCOMMODATION UNDER THE ADA

Protections offered by Title I of the ADA (or, for federal sector employers, Section 501 of the Rehabilitation Act) are essential to creating an opportunity for some workers with disabilities to access needed accommodations. A step back to define some terms may be helpful. According to the US Equal Employment Opportunity Commission (2002), "reasonable accommodation" is any change in the work environment or in the customary approach to performing a job task that enables an individual with a disability to enjoy equal employment opportunities. In other words, accommodations allow people with disabilities to approach their work differently in order to overcome barriers presented by the functional limitations of a disability.

Employers must provide accommodations in the application process, in performing the essential functions of a position, and in the enjoyment of equal benefits and privileges of employment (US EEOC 2002). In the private sector and at the state and local government levels, the ADA requires employers to provide reasonable accommodations to employees and applicants who are qualified individuals with disabilities, unless doing so would cause an undue hardship. Whether an accommodation creates an undue hardship is a factual issue based on factors such as the type of accommodation, its cost, and the size and nature of the employer's business (US EEOC 2002). Typically, accommodations are low in cost (Loy 2017). In cases where the employer claims an undue financial hardship or administrative burden, they must consider all of the resources at their disposal before deciding against an accommodation. For example, if one location of a national company were to claim providing an accommodation was an undue financial burden, it is the national company that would have to prove it could not bear the cost. The financial status of the one location would not be sufficient to demonstrate undue burden.

The process of deciding on accommodations is meant to be an interactive one between the employer and employee, with the employer having the final say as to what is "reasonable." (US EEOC 2002). The ADA does not require the employer to provide the specific accommodation an employee may request, but the provided accommodation must be effective in enabling the employee to perform her or his essential job functions (US EEOC 2002). Gutman (2015) holds that when defining marginal and essential job functions, an employer must be sure that these labels will stand up to analysis. The goal of workplace accommodations is to level the playing field—not to equip the employee to outperform others—although managers are likely to have excellent performers with and without disabilities within their workforce.

Employers are required only to accommodate known disabilities (US EEOC 2002; "The ADA," US EEOC, no date). This means that the person with a disability must disclose the disability to her or his employer and let them know that she or he has to do the work differently because of a disability in order to complete the essential functions of the job. In the context of the ADA, disability disclosure means directly sharing information about a disability with an employer. This might include sharing a diagnosis or specific information about limitations caused by a disability. In the workplace, sharing information about a disability is required under the ADA if an employee requests a reasonable accommodation (US EEOC 2002). However, individuals are under no obligation to disclose a disability at work, unless they are seeking an accommodation.

DISABILITY DISCLOSURE AND SELF-IDENTIFICATION IN THE WORKPLACE

In the past, employers were often hesitant to encourage disability disclosure because awareness of a disability means that employer responsibilities under the ADA, including nondiscrimination and accommodation, are in effect. However, encouraging employees to share information about disability, often as part of an accommodation request, can benefit the employer by allowing an interactive dialog about accommodation that may improve productivity and retention, such as in the cases of Tracy and Roberto presented at the beginning of this chapter.

An employer may also benefit if employees are willing to self-identify as a person with a disability for an employer's equal employment opportunity (EEO) data collection purposes because then the employer can measure progress toward diversifying their workforce to include individuals with disabilities. When employees self-identify as having disabilities, the employer is able to understand effective recruitment and outreach strategies by measuring changes in applicant and hiring rates and how people with disabilities are represented across job categories.

Two large groups of public and private employers—federal employers and federal contractors—are required to affirmatively recruit, hire, and retain individuals with disabilities under Section 501 and Section 503, respectively, of the Rehabilitation Act of 1973. Under Section 503 regulations that went into effect in March 2014, federal contractors and subcontractors must offer applicants and employees an opportunity to self-identify as a person with a disability (the US Department of Labor's Office of Federal Contract Compliance Programs [OFCCP] has developed a form for collecting these data). The recent 503 regulations recommend a workforce utilization goal of 7% of employees with disabilities across job categories. While the number of people with disabilities covered by the ADA is unknown, the 7% utilization goal is based on an analysis of American Community Survey (ACS) data that estimated 5.7% of the civilian labor force has a disability. The utilization goal was increased from that number to account for the effects of discrimination in keeping individuals out of the labor force, and the definition of disability used on the ACS that likely does not include many people with disabilities or chronic medical conditions that are covered under the broader definition of the 2008 ADA Amendments Act ("Frequently Asked Questions," US OFCCP, no date).

While self-identification also involves making an employer aware of a disability, the term differs from disclosure with regard to whom the information needs to be shared with, why the information is shared, and what specific information is needed. Disability disclosure is a required first step in requesting a reasonable accommodation, often made to a supervisor or human resources professional, and ideally will begin a dialog about accommodation needs. However, self-identification is voluntarily reporting a disability for the purpose of helping an organization gauge its success at diversifying its workforce to include more people with disabilities, for example, as the recent Section 503 regulations require ("Regulations," US OFCCP, no date). Under Section 503, an individual is given an opportunity to report whether he or she has a disability, but the individual does not report any information about what the disability is. If a person self-identifies as having a disability for the purpose of helping the organization document disability representation within its workforce, that employee would still need to disclose whether she or he wanted to request a disability-related workplace accommodation. Not surprisingly, employees are much more likely to disclose a disability to a manager or co-worker than to self-identify on an EEO form (Nishii and Bruyère 2014). Employers such as the federal government also have greater self-identification on anonymous surveys, like the Federal Employee Viewpoint survey, than on their SF-256 self-identification form (Murray and von Schrader 2014). The way the information is used (and how it is conveyed to the employee/applicant) can be an important factor in whether an individual decides to share information related to a disability.

A 2017 study of the short-term impacts of the March 2014 updates to Section 503 regulations found that many contractors are struggling to get employees to self-identify. Only about 15% of survey respondents indicated that they had met the 7% utilization goal, and more than 50% had a self-identification rate of 2% or less (von Schrader and Bruyère 2018). These federal contractors pointed out a number of reasons for low rates of self-identification, including logistical challenges of collecting this information to the challenge of building trust among applicants and employees that would make them comfortable in disclosing this type of information. According to the ACS, approximately 11% of working age adults have a disability (Erickson, Lee, and von Schrader 2017), but many companies are getting only 2% to self-identify. Clearly, individuals are hesitant to share this information.

Barriers to Disclosure from the Perspective of Individuals with Disabilities

Decisions about disclosure are very personal. Employers may be surprised to learn that even in situations when a reasonable accommodation could help a person perform essential job functions, he or she may not choose to disclose a disability. Workers with nonvisible disabilities may choose to "pass" as nondisabled in an attempt to avoid disability-related stigma (Campbell 2008; Santuzzi and Waltz 2016), and they are less likely than people with visible disabilities to disclose a disability during the hiring phase, opting to disclose later in the employment process (von Schrader, Malzer, and Bruyère 2014). Individuals with readily apparent disabilities face the possibility that others will view disability as their defining characteristic (Lutz and Bowers 2005; Watson 2002) and may be particularly reluctant to share details about their disabilities in a work setting (Cook and Shinew 2014).

von Schrader, Malzer, and Bruyère (2014) found that the number-one reason workers with disabilities gave for not disclosing a disability was the perceived risk of being fired or of not being hired (73%). Other "very important" factors in deciding not to disclose a disability included concern that the employer might focus on disability (62%), possible loss of healthcare benefits (61.5%), fear that disclosure would limit opportunities (61.1%), an unsupportive supervisor (60.1%), and concern about being treated differently (57.8%) and/or being viewed differently in the workplace (53.8%). Still, others choose not to disclose because their disability does not affect their job performance (44%), and some wish to keep their disability private (27.9%).

The primary reason for the reluctance to disclose is that it will result in some type of workplace mistreatment from colleagues and supervisors (von Schrader, Malzer, and Bruyère 2014). The belief that disclosure could result in negative consequences is not unfounded. Rather, it is based on long-standing, limiting beliefs about people with disabilities and their potential to work and contribute to society. Although there has been a positive shift in how we think about disability over the past few decades, disparities in education, hiring rate, pay, and promotional opportunities between people with and without disabilities continue to exist (Schur et al. 2017). Misperceptions about the capabilities of people with disabilities still influence hiring decisions (Ameri et al. 2015) and the workplace experiences of individuals on the job (Smith and Andrews 2015). After all, in a literal sense, to be disabled means that one is "impaired or limited by a physical, mental, cognitive, or developmental condition" (Merriam-Webster, no date).

Thus, it is a challenge for some to consider people with disabilities as suited for the workplace, where ability and productivity are paramount. People with disabilities themselves may also subscribe to limiting paradigms about disability and may find it difficult to reconcile a disability identity with the perception of a "capable" person (Campbell 2008; Cook and Shinew 2014; Jammaers, Zanoni, and Hardonk 2016).

Employees with disabilities may experience different reactions to disclosure even within the same workplace (Reed et al. 2017). Additionally, they may find themselves needing to make impromptu disclosure decisions throughout the day, possibly jeopardizing their employment and relationships with workplace colleagues (Oldfield, MacEachen, Kirsh, and MacNeill 2016). In a recent study of employed adults with disabilities, 97% had disclosed to at least one person (i.e., colleague, supervisor, and/or HR representative), with a mostly positive or neutral response (Cook 2017). Carefully planning when and how much to share about one's disability is a strategy employees use to increase the likelihood of a positive response (Santuzzi, Waltz, Finkelstein, and Rupp 2014; von Schrader, Malzer, and Bruyère 2014). This is understandable because the consequences of disability disclosure are significant and varied.

Response of Manager/Co-Workers

Having an apparent disability and/or disclosing a disability has been found to disadvantage both job applicants (Brohan et al. 2012) and existing employees (Balser 2000; Schur, Kruse, Blasi, and Blanck 2009). In von Schrader, Malzer, and Bruyère's (2014) study of disability disclosure in the workplace, less than 10% of those who disclosed rated their immediate disclosure experience as negative; however, 24% rated the longer-term consequences of their disclosure as negative. Some differences were noted, based on whether the disability was readily apparent. Employees with nonapparent or somewhat apparent disabilities reported experiencing negative immediate and long-term consequences more often than did employees with very apparent disabilities.

Research indicates that employees with disabilities are concerned that disclosing a disability may lead to consequences such as lowered expectations, isolation from co-workers, or increased likelihood of termination (Brohan et al. 2012; Dalgin and Bellini 2008; Dalgin and Gilbride 2003; Madaus, McGuire, and Ruban 2002). In a recent study of work–life balance among employees with disabilities by Cook, von Schrader, Malzer, and Mimno (this volume), 23% of participants reportedly experienced harassment/discrimination within the past 12 months. Specifically, they reported that they were paid less for work equal to that of their colleagues, denied professional development and advancement opportunities, denied reasonable accommodations, excluded from workplace socializing and employee recognition activities, and mocked and verbally abused, often in front of others.

How Employers Can Reduce These Barriers

Despite these potentially detrimental consequences, disclosure can be beneficial for individuals and organizations. In an inclusive workplace climate, disclosing a disability may enable an employee to be more authentic because they do not have to hide or downplay an identity that they may view as salient (Nishii 2013; von Schrader, Malzer, and Bruyère 2014). Disclosure may also lead to establishing meaningful co-worker relationships and greater support within the workplace community. Additionally, as previously mentioned, disclosure initiates the interactive process when an employee is seeking a workplace accommodation.

von Schrader, Malzer, and Bruyère 2014 suggest several actions that employers can take in order to increase the likelihood of disability disclosure among employees:

- Encourage positive supervisor–employee relationships by helping managers and supervisors build skills in listening, conflict resolution, and the reasonable accommodation process.
- Demonstrate a commitment to disability inclusiveness by including disability in the organization's diversity statement, including employees with apparent disabilities (alongside those who may or may not have disabilities) in promotional materials, and encourage applications from individuals with disabilities in the company's recruitment initiatives.
- Make it clear to applicants and employees with disabilities that the company offers opportunities for professional development and advancement.

As noted, certain employers, such as federal contractors, are particularly motivated to encourage self-identification of disability. While self-identification has a different process and purpose than disclosure, they both involve sharing personal information about disability status. In a recent survey of federal contractors, employer representatives reported taking several actions to encourage self-identification (von Schrader and Bruyère 2018). Practices included offering more opportunities and reminders to self-disclose, clearly stating the purpose of self-disclosure, implementing a formal self-identification campaign, and highlighting successful employees who had self-disclosed. Each of these practices was deemed at least moderately effective by employers, with the latter two approaches being rated slightly higher. Many employers noted that the greatest barrier to self-identification was trust. One survey respondent commented that the greatest barrier is "the challenge of overcoming perceptions, despite appropriate communication, that disability status will be shared or known by others such as a manager." Another respondent shared, "No matter how much you tell them, it doesn't matter; it's hard to break that belief that they will be judged." Addressing the barrier of trust is difficult. Open communication and a genuine demonstration of a commitment to disability inclusion are critical to creating a workplace where employees feel comfortable self-identifying and/or disclosing that they have a disability.

THE PROCESS OF PROVIDING A REASONABLE ACCOMMODATION

When employers are aware of workers' disabilities and willing to provide needed accommodations, the individual, his or her colleagues, and the organization as a whole tend to benefit (Loy 2017; Solovieva, Dowler, and Walls 2011). Ongoing research by the Job Accommodation Network (JAN) demonstrates numerous direct and indirect benefits of providing workplace accommodation, including increased individual and overall company attendance and productivity, improved co-worker and customer interactions, and increased customer base and profitability.

Concern about disclosure is not the only barrier to employees seeking accommodations. Baldridge and Veiga (2001) outline a model for the likelihood that a person will request a workplace accommodation. The model incorporates various factors that are taken into account by the employee, including workplace attributes, the magnitude of the accommodation, and the employee's personal assessment of usefulness and fairness of the request, as well as a normative assessment of how this request will be perceived by others. Related studies have explored more deeply some aspects of this model, and this literature is summarized in Kulkarni and Lengnick-Hall (2013). Barriers that may limit accommodation requests include discomfort with help-seeking where independence is valued within workplace norms (Kulkarni 2012), concerns that co-workers will interpret the accommodation as unfair (Colella 2001; Colella, Paetzold, and Belliveau 2004), and the need for requesting an accommodation repeatedly (e.g., sign language interpreter) (Baldridge and Veiga 2006).

As illustrated by the examples of Tracy and Roberto, disclosing a disability involves a certain amount of risk to the applicant or employee with a disability. Tracy worries that her manager and co-workers will treat her differently and that parents will not want her to care for their children because of an assumed risk. Roberto worries that others will view him as less capable. However, in the absence of disclosure and resultant access to needed accommodations, these employees have performance issues that can lead to discipline and eventually to termination. When an employer has a well-documented reasonable accommodation policy, it creates clear guideposts for both employees and managers. All parties become aware of the organization's philosophy on accommodation and understand what will happen and whom to contact when an applicant or employee requests an accommodation. In fact, experiences of disability-related bias are directly influenced by the manager's awareness of clear policies for accommodation, a designated office to address accommodation questions, and a formal decision-making process for the provision of accommodation (Nishii and Bruyère 2014). Further, when everyone has to go through the same process to receive an accommodation, it reduces the likelihood that those who are members of other marginalized groups (e.g., racially diverse employees) will experience disparate treatment when they request an accommodation.

Role of Managers

Research illustrates that managers are critical players in implementing an organization's reasonable accommodation policies. Employees with disabilities are at least 60% more likely to disclose their disability to their supervisor rather than to human resources or on an EEO form (Nishii and Bruyère 2014). It is not always easy for managers to recognize disability disclosure. A good rule of thumb is that any time an applicant or employee says, "because of X medical condition or disability, I'm having trouble with Y job task," it is a disability disclosure. For example, this statement likely constitutes disclosure: "I'm sorry I arrived late to the meeting. My psychiatrist switched my medication, and it is taking some time for me to adjust," while "I feel really tired today; I think my allergies are kicking in" may not constitute disclosure because the employee has not indicated specific difficulty with essential job functions or expected workplace behaviors. When in doubt, managers should be encouraged to reach out to human resources. After an employee discloses a disability, the manager can ask whether the employee needs a reasonable accommodation to address the issue. The manager should then implement whatever reasonable accommodation policy the organization has in place. It should be noted that, without a disclosure, it would be unwise for the employer to make assumptions about why the employee is not meeting attendance or performance expectations. Assuming that someone has a disability and providing accommodations without understanding the individual's particular needs is problematic. Whether or not an employee has a disability, when job performance is a concern, a manager needs to ask if there is anything she or he can do to help the employee meet expectations.

Performance Concerns and Disclosure

Timing of disclosure is important. Ideally, an applicant or an employee will feel safe enough to disclose a disability as soon as he or she is aware of the need for an accommodation. Unfortunately, this is not always the case. If performance issues arise from an undisclosed disability, a manager must open the door to a discussion about the cause of a performance issue. In any performance dialog, managers should focus on concrete events and ask whether there is anything the employee can tell the manager that will help the manager understand the possible reason for the performance issue. This question gives the employee an opportunity to describe the reasons he or she is struggling, and it creates an opportunity for the employee to disclose. The manager can then ask how he or she can support the employee to improve performance. If an employee fails to disclose until a disciplinary action or termination occurs, the employer is under no obligation to rescind the discipline (US EEOC 2002). Up until the point of termination, the employer should initiate the reasonable accommodation process as soon as disclosure occurs.

The Reasonable Accommodation Process

Initiating the Interactive Process

After an applicant or employee discloses a disability, the employer must initiate the interactive process. The interactive process requires the participation of both the employer and the employee, and it should occur in a timely manner. There is no standard definition of "timely manner"; the EEOC, which has primary responsibility for enforcing Title I of the ADA, states that an employer should respond "expeditiously" to a request for reasonable accommodation (US EEOC 2002). It is entirely reasonable for an employer to follow up an accommodation request with a request for an employee to provide written information that clarifies the request. Critical questions include

- What part of your job are you having difficulty with because of your disability, medical, or pregnancy-related health condition?
- Why are these tasks difficult for you? Or stated another way, what is the functional limitation that makes this task difficult for you?
- Do you have any recommendations for potential solutions?

Documenting Disability

When the need for an accommodation is not obvious, the employer can seek limited medical information from a healthcare professional to verify the need for accommodation. The two primary questions to ask a health professional are the following:

- Does the patient experience a disability as defined by the ADA? (Providing a short definition of the ADA's definition of disability may be helpful to medical providers.)
- Based on the employee's job description and in your medical opinion, is the employee able to perform the essential functions of the job with or without reasonable accommodation?

Health professionals can provide information on the functional limitations associated with the disability that interfere with the employee's ability to perform essential functions of the job. They can also describe how functional limitations affect performance. Health professionals may also be able to recommend potential accommodations that would help to address the functional limitations. While the EEOC allows employers to seek a medical diagnosis, that information is not necessary to verify the need for an accommodation. In determining accommodations, a diagnosis can be deceiving because it does not provide information as to why the disability or medical condition makes performing the essential functions of the job difficult. In some cases, it will only serve to feed the assumptions that managers may make about the applicant or employee's ability to perform at work.

Identifying an Accommodation

The next phase in the process requires the employer to identify potential accommodations. Employers must weigh possible solutions in light of the work environment, the job tasks, and potential effectiveness to resolve the issue the employee is experiencing because of the disability. A solution that would work very well for one job or employee may not work for another. For example, consider a person who is having difficulty holding a telephone receiver because of pain in her or his hands. If the person has a private office, a speakerphone may be an ideal solution. If she or he works in a shared space, a headset may be much more appropriate to ensure clarity and privacy for callers. Small employers report that the search for possibilities is difficult—they report being overwhelmed with information and not knowing when to stop looking (Chang, von Schrader, and Strobel Gower 2018). The ADA National Network or JAN can be useful resources to identify and narrow the options. Both the manager and the employee should be active participants in deciding what will work. Ultimately, it is up to the employer to identify which accommodation will be implemented, but it must be effective. An employer may have to try more than one accommodation before identifying something that works.

Implementing the Accommodation

Putting the identified accommodation into place in a reasonable amount of time is important. When implementing the accommodation, the employer should ensure that it is set up appropriately and that the employee understands how to access and use the accommodation to complete job tasks. In some cases, such as implementation of new software, additional training may be necessary. Give the employee a reasonable period to grow accustomed to the accommodation before holding him or her to production standards.

Ensuring the Accommodation Is Effective

An evaluation of the effectiveness of the accommodation is a critical component of the accommodation process. The employer should monitor the employee's production and ability to do the work in a timely manner. Also, it should be ensured that the employee can meet established performance expectations. If one accommodation is not effective, it is often necessary to implement and evaluate an alternative before assuming the employee is not qualified for their job. Finally, the employer should work with the employee and her or his manager to monitor the accommodation to make sure that it continues to address the issue satisfactorily. In some cases, the disability will evolve over time, resulting in new or changing accommodation needs.

Role of Labor Unions in the Reasonable Accommodation Process

Labor unions can create an added layer of complexity to the provision of reasonable accommodation because employers must comply with both the ADA and the National Labor Relations Act (NLRA). Unfortunately, very little guidance is available on the impact of collective bargaining agreements on an employer's implementation of the ADA (Barnard 2009). The American Bar Association (no date) states that provisions in the NLRA prohibit an employer from the following:

1. changing the working conditions of union-represented employees without first affording the union notice of the proposed changes and an opportunity to bargain,
2. unilaterally altering the provisions of a negotiated collective agreement, or
3. engaging in direct dealing with employees represented by a labor organization.

The ADA clearly "prohibits employers and unions from entering into collective bargaining agreements that discriminate against covered applicants and employees" (Johnston, Bruyère, and Reiter 2011). Under the NLRA, a union has obligations for fair representation of its members, which require that unions act reasonably, represent their members in good faith, and do not discriminate (NLRA; 29 U.S.C. §§ 151–169). This duty may require the union to assist an employee in requesting an accommodation and working with an employer to identify a reasonable accommodation for the employee they represent (Johnston, Bruyère, and Reiter 2011). That being said, if requested accommodations do not affect terms and conditions of employment (e.g., providing an interpreter or a piece of assistive technology to perform job duties), the employer is free to make accommodations for union-represented employees. However, when the terms or conditions of employment are impacted (e.g., light duty is requested or a preferential schedule is requested), the union will need to work with the employer to identify a solution (Johnston, Bruyère, and Reiter 2011).

The complexity of the interaction between the NLRA and the ADA resulted in a memorandum of understanding between the EEOC and the National Labor Relations Board, which enforces NLRA, to work together to resolve complaints filed that involve union-represented employees (US EEOC 1993). Under the NLRA, the union "is the exclusive representative of the employees" in working with the employer to identify effective accommodation options. Employers are "prohibited from implementing any change in the terms and conditions of employment without offering the union an opportunity to bargain over the proposed changes" (Johnston, Bruyère, and Reiter 2011).

In the face of this requirement, employers must afford the union the opportunity to represent its members in reasonable accommodation discussions. The EEOC states that when a union-represented employee requests a reasonable accommodation, the employer must seek to accommodate the individual without violating the collective bargaining agreement. If that is not possible, the employer and the union should attempt to negotiate a variance to the collective bargaining agreement. Unless the union can demonstrate that the reasonable accommodation has an adverse effect on other employees in the bargaining unit, an employer cannot use the existence of the collective bargaining agreement to deny a reasonable accommodation. The courts generally protect seniority rights because many accommodations that would affect seniority rights are not found to be reasonable (Gutman 2015; Johnston, Bruyère, and Reiter 2011). Of course, any time an employer denies a reasonable accommodation, the employer is required to engage in a good faith effort to identify an alternative accommodation to meet the needs of its employees.

WHERE EMPLOYERS STRUGGLE WITH ACCOMMODATION

When an individual perceives that he or she has been discriminated against based on disability, he or she can file a charge under the ADA with the EEOC or a state or local Fair Employment Practices Agency (FEPA). Failure to provide a reasonable accommodation is the second most common issue on ADA charges from 1993 to 2007, cited on about 25% of charges; the first most common issue (63%) is discharge (Bruyère et al. 2010). Bruyère et al. (2010) highlight several disability types that more commonly cite reasonable accommodation on discrimination charges under the ADA. During those years, 35% of charges filed by people with the following conditions cited reasonable accommodation: anxiety disorder, post-traumatic stress disorder, pulmonary/respiratory impairment, multiple sclerosis, asthma, allergies, chemical sensitivity, nonparalytic orthopedic impairment, and cumulative trauma disorder. In several of those cases, the disability is likely not apparent and would require a disclosure to access a needed accommodation.

Other research on the ADA charge data has highlighted that larger employers are more likely to face allegations on issues of reasonable accommodation compared with other issues. Further, industries such as manufacturing, public administration, educational services, transportation and warehousing, information, and utilities have more reasonable accommodation allegations compared with non-accommodation allegations (West et al. 2008). The number of charges under the ADA filed has been increasing annually, but those numbers have been leveling out in more recent years (von Schrader and Erickson 2017; US EEOC

2018). As demonstrated in Figure 1, the percentage of charges citing reasonable accommodation has increased over time, with over 36% of charges in 2014 citing failure to provide reasonable accommodation.

Understanding where in the accommodation process the charging party perceives that the process broke down may help other employers to avoid similar mistakes. We conducted a qualitative analysis of case notes from verified charges. Verified charges are those with a merit outcome for the charging party; that is, charges that were withdrawn with benefits for the charging party, settled with benefits, or where the charge went to conciliation after an EEOC merit decision. Our analysis focused on case notes that described the particulars of the perceived discriminatory act as reported by the charging party and collected using the EEOC's Form 5 "Charge of Discrimination" form. There were approximately 70,000 closed ADA charges in 2013 and 2014, with 21.4% having a merit outcome. Among ADA charges that cited reasonable accommodation, the merit rate was slightly higher than charges overall, at 23.9%. It should be noted that these numbers do not match those reported by the EEOC because they also include charges received by state and local FEPAs, which typically account for 30% to 40% of charges filed annually. Table 1 (next page) presents more information about the population of charges from which we drew our sample, presenting characteristics of all verified ADA charges, verified reasonable accommodation

FIGURE 1
Percentage of ADA Charges Citing Reasonable Accommodation as an Issue, 1993–2014

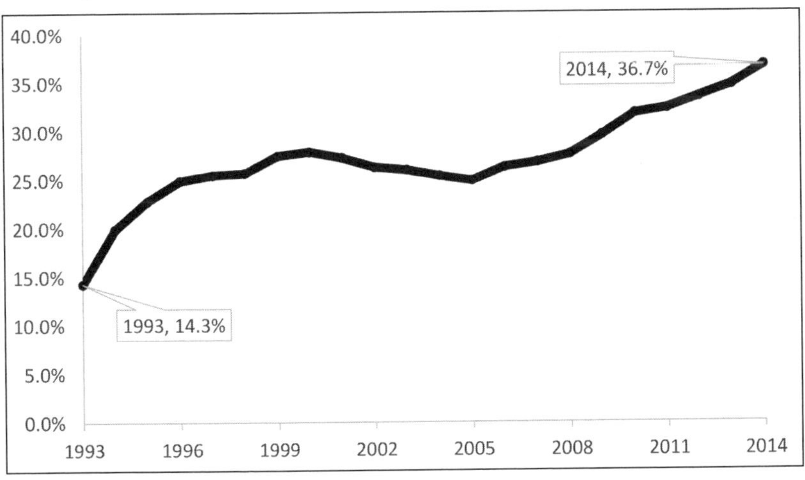

Source: Calculation by Sarah von Schrader, Cornell University Yang-Tan Institute on Employment and Disability, using data from EEOC's Integrated Mission System. Both EEOC and FEPA charges are included in aggregations. Summaries of data are based on our aggregations and do not represent the EEOC's official aggregation of the data.

TABLE 1
Reasonable Accommodation–Related Case Note Analysis, Sample Characteristics

	Sampled charges with Form 5 data (N = 78)	Sampled charges (N = 100)	All verified reasonable accommodation charges (N = 5,810)	All verified ADA charges (N = 14,832)
Most common issues cited (a single charge can cite one or more)				
Discharge	50.0%	54.0%	57.4%	59.8%
Reasonable accommodation	100%	100%	100%	39.2%
Terms and conditions	24.4%	22.0%	22.6%	21.1%
Harassment	21.8%	23.0%	14.4%	15.9%
Type of disability* cited on charge (a single charge can cite one or more)*				
Nonspecific	39.7%	42.0%	39.2%	42.6%
Orthopedic	24.4%	21.0%	21.1%	15.4%
Behavioral	12.8%	15.0%	16.9%	16.3%
Medical	23.1%	23.0%	19.7%	17.8%
Sensory	5.1%	4.0%	5.5%	5.0%
Neurological	9.0%	8.0%	7.5%	5.9%
Other statutes cited (a single charge can cite one or more)				
% citing Age Discrimination in Employment Act	11.5%	9.0%	11.5%	16.0%
% citing Title VII of the Civil Rights Act	21.8%	24.0%	23.1%	27.0%
Charging party characteristics				
% male	42.9%	47.5%	41.9%	44.2%
Respondent characteristic				
Large employer (500+ employees)	51.4% (N = 70)	48.4% (N = 91)	43.0% (N = 4,807)	37.3% (N = 12,305)
Office receiving charge				
FEPA receiving office	1.2%	1.0%	32.5%	38.8%

*Type of disability categories are defined in Feuerstein, Luff, Harrington, and Olsen (2007).

Note: Verified reasonable accommodation charges are also included in the all verified number ADA charge numbers presented.

Source: Calculations by Sarah von Schrader, Cornell University Yang-Tan Institute on Employment and Disability, using data from EEOC's Integrated Mission System from fiscal years 2013 and 2014. Both EEOC and FEPA charges are included in aggregations. Summaries of data are based on our aggregations and do not represent the EEOC's official aggregation of the data.

charges, our sample of verified reasonable accommodation charges with case notes, and our sample verified reasonable accommodation charges with Form 5 data (some case notes in the sample did not include Form 5 information).

An ADA charge can (and often does) cite multiple issues (e.g., discharge, reasonable accommodation, harassment), multiple bases (e.g., disabilities such as depression and diabetes), and even multiple statutes (age discrimination under the Age Discrimination in Employment Act and disability discrimination under the ADA). The population of verified reasonable accommodation charges is similar to the overall population of verified charges in terms of the percentage that cite the common issues of discharge, terms and conditions, and harassment. For example, 57% of verified reasonable accommodation charges also cite discharge and, based on a reading the case notes, it is a common outcome when there is a failure to accommodate.

Using a conventional content analysis approach, as described in Hsieh and Shannon (2005), we analyzed a total sample of 78 charges from fiscal years 2013 and 2014 that met the criteria described above. In terms of the sample used for the content analysis (N = 78), one major difference is the proportion of charges that were filed with FEPAs. In general, the completeness rates for variables in the EEOC's Integrated Mission System (the database that houses the charge data) are lower for FEPAs, and documentation of Form 5 data in the FEPA case notes is quite rare; therefore, the sample for analysis does not include the expected number of FEPA charges based on the population.

Our analysis of the case notes included documenting, where available, the occupation of the charging party, the specific condition, and type of accommodation requested, as well as coding and developing themes across case notes. While the perspective is from the charging party, not the employer, these descriptions offer important lessons for employees and employers alike. A summary of findings in four key areas is presented below.

Occupations of Charging Party and Type of Accommodations

In the sample of charges, the occupational categories of the charging parties were grouped into four broad categories as follows: management, business, science, and arts occupations (11%); sales and office occupations (35%); service occupations (19%); and natural resources, construction, and maintenance occupations; and production, transportation, and material moving occupations (35%). Nationally, about 27% of the civilian employed population with disabilities work in management, business, science, and arts occupations (US Census Bureau 2018). When comparing the 11% representation among our sample of reasonable accommodation charges, this suggests that individuals in these relatively higher education/skill occupational categories are less likely to file a charge citing accommodation compared with other occupational categories. This is very much in line with previous research suggesting that higher-level employees have more flexibility and make informal arrangements for accommodation in the workplace; that is, flexibility for breaks or an appointment is not something that needs to be requested through an accommodation process, as it might be for a lower-level job (Harlan and Robert 1998).

The most common type of accommodation requested in the charge data sample was reassignment or light duty work (e.g., move to another shift, different work location, or new position that does not aggravate disability [N = 21]), followed by leave as a reasonable accommodation (N = 17), requests for flexibility (e.g., in schedule, reduced hours, working from home, breaks during day [N = 12]), and adjusting the workspace or providing equipment (e.g., limiting noise, adjusting lights, adjusting ergonomics, vehicle with automatic transmission, headset for phone, new computer equipment [N =12]). The most common limitation cited was an accommodation of lifting or bending restrictions (N = 13), and 11 charges noted that disability was related to a workplace injury or illness. As presented in Table 1, the most common bases of charges were orthopedic impairments and medical impairments, each cited on close to 25% of sample charges.

Poor Communication Impacting the Accommodation Process

Out of 78 charges, 26 specifically discussed communication challenges during the reasonable accommodation process as the core issue. Individuals described topics such as whom they disclosed to, whom they requested the accommodation from, and where the process broke down. In general, the case notes highlight the importance of communication and the benefits of employer flexibility in accommodation. Among the most common complaints related to communication was the complete lack of an interactive process; that is, the employer would not engage in dialog about the accommodation after the accommodation was requested. In some cases, employees requested an accommodation and did not get any response; in other cases, the accommodation request was denied with no explanation.

The role of the manager can be important. In two cases, the manager discouraged the employee from requesting an accommodation, suggesting that the process will take months, or that the employer had not done anything in the past. In most cases, the individual's accommodation request was handled by an HR representative. Occasionally, unfavorable decisions were attributed to someone at a corporate office.

Another communication issue related to new managers or business owners who disregarded an employee's current accommodation. In some cases, a current accommodation was questioned by the new administration or supervisor and a request made for further medical documentation. Essentially, the accommodation request process needed to start over again and often resulted in a different and unfavorable outcome for the employee.

There were also several cases where the individual was accommodated then, after a limited time, the employer was not willing to continue the accommodation—for example, allowing an individual to work from home for a limited amount of time but then requiring that he or she return to the workplace or resign. If such an accommodation was now being viewed as an undue hardship for the employer, the hardship must be demonstrated, taking into account whether the accommodation caused a hardship when allowed previously.

Charging parties also discussed how they were treated differently as a result of an accommodation request. Examples include retaliation for an accommodation request, such as being forced onto unpaid leave and having benefits lapse, being taken off the regular schedule, threatened with unfavorable reviews, or informed that further promotion would not be available because of the limitations. In some cases, the request for an accommodation led to an accommodation that intentionally isolated the individual (e.g., placing an employee's desk in a corner away from others) or the accommodation led co-workers to treat the individual differently.

Interaction Between Leave and Accommodation

In several cases, when an employee was not accommodated, she or he felt forced out of the job. This outcome was most commonly associated with leave; 25 charges involving leave resulted in the charging party being discharged while on leave or having a return to work request denied or significantly stalled. Further discussion of the difficulties related to leave is presented below.

Often, individuals reported a conflict between the availability of leave and employer hesitation to allow an individual to return to work when there were still restrictions; this was more common in manual occupations. When returning to work after a leave, it was frequently observed in the charges that the individual was seeking reassignment or light duty or some other accommodation that would make a return to work feasible. Employers were reported to have often stipulated that the employee must be at 100% prior to returning to work and wanted to see medical documentation indicating no restrictions. It is important to note that the EEOC clearly states that an "employer will violate the ADA if it requires an employee with a disability to have no medical restrictions—that is, be 100% healed or recovered—if the employee can perform her job with or without reasonable accommodations" (US EEOC 2016). For example, an employee was not allowed to return to work with any restrictions because of "duties and responsibilities" of their job. The employee was told he needed a note to return to work with no restrictions by a certain date or he would lose his job; this employer did not engage in an interactive process around accommodation. In another case, to return to the job, an employee needed to be able to use specialized equipment that was available on the jobsite and being used by others. The employer would not allow the claimant to return to work with this accommodation, thus forcing the claimant to take leave beyond that allowed by the collective bargaining agreement of one year, so the claimant was discharged. If an employee can do the essential functions of the job—even if an accommodation is needed to do so—the employer may be violating the ADA by not allowing the employee to return.

In several cases, leave was taken without formal leave approval (e.g., FMLA). These situations arose when there was an unexpected hospitalization or a doctor's recommendation for immediate leave. In some cases, the employee did not know of the leave application process and was not informed by the employer of leave of absence policies. For example, an employee with a known disability was hospitalized, informing the employer daily by leaving a message on the company's sick line. The employer's policy indicated that leave should have been available, but the claimant did not know how to apply for leave and may not have been able to do so from the hospital. While still in the hospital, the employee called to check in and was told she was fired for being out too long. In such a case, it may be necessary for the employer to provide information about leave options per company policy, and when leave is not available, to inform the employee that leave as an accommodation is an option.

Under employer policies, some leave programs are not available for employees in select job classifications, such as new employees on a probationary period or part-time employees. One employee reported requesting a six-week medical leave, as prescribed by a doctor to adjust to new medication, but the individual was still in the probationary period. The human resources department therefore told this employee he was not covered by leave programs and could not get leave as a reasonable accommodation. When a leave is requested under these conditions and the employer leave policies do not cover disability-related leave, an employer must provide unpaid leave as an accommodation unless it can demonstrate that this leave would result in an undue hardship.

When leave programs cannot be extended further, employees may still request leave as an accommodation. An employee in a professional position had a leave of one year for new medications, but after that approved period, additional leave was needed. The employee wanted to return to work eventually and did not want to apply for long-term disability programs. However, the employer was concerned the employee would not return and therefore denied the additional leave. It is the responsibility of the employer to demonstrate undue hardship if denying leave as an accommodation.

The limitation of the charge data is that they tell only the story of the charging party, and in many cases, this is a very abbreviated story. However, the sample of charges presented here offers some context and examples for where employers are struggling to provide accommodation. How accommodation interfaces with existing leave programs is particularly challenging. Further, communication was often lacking in the accommodation process, and it seems that a consistent process for providing accommodations was not in place in many of the workplaces that appeared in our sample. As in other studies of accommodation, for the most part, the cost of accommodations was low, but resistance to providing supports or leave resulted in what was likely much higher costs both monetarily and to company reputation when accommodations were denied or implemented poorly.

OVERVIEW OF GOOD PRACTICE RELATED TO ACCOMMODATION

This chapter provides an overview of the laws and regulations related to providing disability-related workplace accommodation as well as a review of research about the perspective of employers and employees around the disclosure and accommodation process. The literature points to several practices that can be very effective in ensuring that people who require accommodations get what they need to be successful. In a study conducted by Erickson, von Schrader, Bruyère, and VanLooy (2014), eight accommodations practices were identified as promising based on a survey of the literature. Organizations surveyed had implemented an average of 3.8 practices out of the eight effective accommodation practices/policies listed in Figure 2. Large organizations (those with more than 500 employees) implemented significantly more of the practices than smaller organizations—4.1 compared with 3.4 on average. The study found no differences between industries. In this section, we will review each promising practice around providing reasonable accommodation.

FIGURE 2
Accessibility and Accommodation: Percentage of Organizations That Implemented Each Practice or Policy

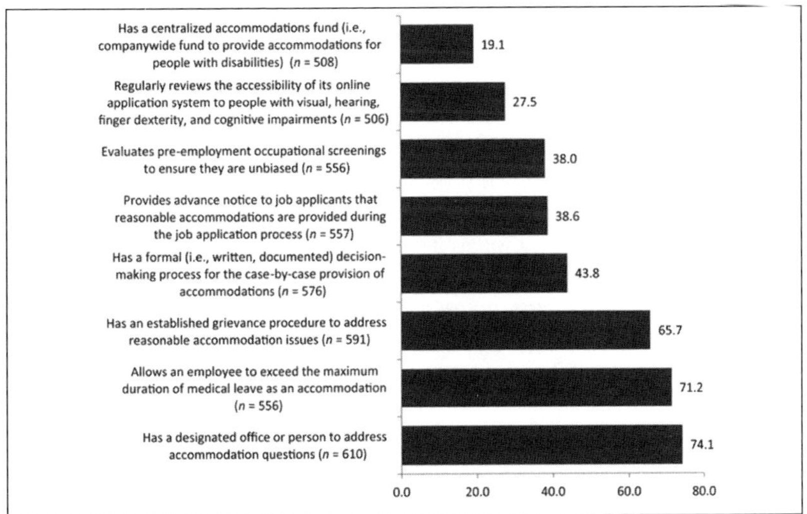

Note: Sample excludes "don't know" and missing responses.
Source: Erickson, von Schrader, Bruyère, and VanLooy (2014).

Formal Decision-Making Process for Accommodation

As discussed throughout this chapter, a clear policy and process to implement workplace accommodations is a critical component of consistent implementation of the reasonable accommodation process. In the absence of a policy and process, each manager, unit, or department will often make very different decisions when an employee requests an accommodation. This is a risky precedent because it greatly increases the likelihood of disparate treatment across the organization. Often, managers will "go with their gut" to approve or deny an accommodation request without regard to the requirement for an individualized analysis of each request. There are many excellent examples of effective reasonable accommodation policy and process available. The National Aeronautics and Space Administration, for example, is a leader in disability diversity whose reasonable accommodation policies and process are publicly available on their website at https://go.nasa.gov/2sU7pWB (NASA 2018).

Centralized Accommodation Process

Having a clear policy and process in place helps to ensure that all members of the workforce are treated fairly when they request an accommodation. However, several steps of the accommodation process require knowledge of the impact of disability at work, an understanding of how functional limitations of a disability will affect a certain task or essential function, and an awareness of potential solutions to mitigate the disability and allow for task completion. These are high-level skills that many managers may not possess. Therefore, it is advisable that organizations develop the skill and expertise to address these issues at a central level. Centralizing the accommodation process was the most commonly implemented practice in the Cornell University 2014 study (Erickson, von Schrader, Bruyère, and VanLooy 2014). Moving responsibility for the accommodation process to a centralized team streamlines the process and allows for a natural place for expertise on this topic to develop. Managers who need assistance or who have a team member request an accommodation know where to go for support, and the organization is better prepared to respond to requests. The central team can work with the manager to understand essential and marginal functions and the reasonableness of requests in the day-to-day operation of the unit. Most important, a central processing unit for accommodation reduces the opportunity for disparities to arise in processing requests for accommodation. This person or team can also assist with tracking accommodation requests, verifying accurate decision making around accommodations, and identifying potential cost savings for high-volume solutions (e.g., ergonomic interventions).

Centralized Accommodation Fund

While many accommodations required by employees are not overly costly (Loy 2017), concern over expense can still serve as a sticking point at the unit or departmental level. This is especially true when cost control is a part of the departmental evaluation of success. Centralizing an accommodation fund removes the concern of excessive cost from individuals units or departments and moves it to a central location within an organization that has budgeted to cover these expenses.

Accommodation Grievance Process

It is important to have an appeal process in place for the aggrieved employee who has a complaint about an accommodation request. This allows employees to assert their rights and receive an impartial analysis of whether the organization has met its obligations (Gutman 2015). To protect themselves and ensure sound decision making throughout the process, organizations should document every stage of the reasonable accommodation process. If an accommodation is not provided as requested, the EEOC recommends that the organization detail the reason it was denied (US EEOC 2005). Common issues include insufficient medical documents, removal of an essential function, a reduction in performance standards, likelihood that any accommodation would be ineffective in resolving the issue, or an undue hardship. Explain the reason for the denial to the employee who requested the accommodation. Where appropriate, offer an alternative accommodation. When the denial is shared with the employee, let him or her know who made the decision to deny the accommodation. Tell the employee that he or she has a right to appeal the decision. Provide a period for appeal and an office or individual who will review the request. Many organizations use an equal opportunity officer or HR manager to perform reviews. It's important to advise the employee what will happen after completion of the review as well. In some cases, an appeal may result in the employee getting an alternative effective accommodation. If the decision is upheld after appeal, the employee still has an option to file a discrimination charge with a state human rights protections office or with the EEOC. However, if the employer has done their due diligence, the likelihood is reduced that its actions will be found to be discriminatory.

Training Managers

To ensure that an organization is able to implement the reasonable accommodation policies and practices it creates, it is essential to train managers. Not only do managers play a key role in recognizing disability disclosure and requests for reasonable accommodation, but they also implement company policy and serve as the primary touch point for employees within an organization (Rudstam and Strobel Gower 2012). It is imperative to train managers on important issues such as how to challenge their own assumptions about the implications of disability at work, how to address performance issues when disability may be a contributing factor, and how to provide appropriate support using the benefits offered within the organization. Managers are very often the primary source of support for the employees they supervise, so it is critical that they are well equipped to understand the issues their employees may face and refer them to the appropriate organizational resources to get what they need to be successful.

While training managers is critical, it is not always easy, especially where disability is concerned. Commonly used traditional diversity training approaches in workplaces have been shown to have limited, if any, impact on desired diversity outcomes (Dobbin, Kim, and Kalev 2011; US EEOC 2017). According to Wang-Audia and Tauber (2014), instead of seeking training, about 70% of people turn to search engines to learn what they need to know to succeed at work. However, when employees search the Internet broadly for quick answers to their disability inclusion questions, there is the danger they will find inaccurate or inappropriate information. Organizations are more frequently turning to curated micro-content in order to provide accurate and timely information that can be easily absorbed (Walsh and Volini 2017). Organizations should regularly communicate critical stopping points, resources, and policies for managers when it comes to addressing disability issues in the workplace.

CONCLUSION

The reasonable accommodation provision of the ADA makes it possible for many people with disabilities to have equal employment opportunities as well as equal access to the privileges and benefits of employment. However, employees' concerns about the possible negative consequences of disability disclosure, coupled with employers' lack of understanding about their obligations under the law, can influence the accommodation process. This chapter provided an overview of the reasonable accommodation process and offered employers practical approaches to improve this process within their organizations by examining good employer practices as well as potential pitfalls from the perspective of both employee and employer. At the heart of the issue is supporting qualified employees to do their best work, which is in the best interest of employer and employee alike.

Reasonable accommodation requests begin with disability disclosure, which can be a complex choice for people with disabilities. This chapter began with two characters, Tracy and Roberto, with different disabilities, working in different types of workplaces. Both are hesitant to disclose a disability, and neither really understands her or his rights to accommodation under the ADA. For Tracy, the stigma associated with her bipolar disorder may influence her willingness to ask for help. For an older employee like Roberto, an accommodation to help him read spreadsheets may be the difference between early retirement and staying in the workforce as long as desired. From their perspective, disclosing a disability may change the way people in the organization feel about them or treat them. However, not accessing a needed accommodation can lead to performance issues and limit their contributions in the workplace. Workplaces can increase comfort with disclosure by demonstrating a commitment to disability inclusion, through actions such as including individuals with disabilities in promotional materials, encouraging applications from people with disabilities, and highlighting success stories of current employees with disabilities. Further, when an employer fosters an accommodating, flexible, and supportive work environment for all employees, employees with disabilities may not have to disclose in order for their workplace needs to be met.

When an employee does disclose and request an accommodation, managers should be prepared to recognize this as a reasonable accommodation request under the ADA. Developing a policy statement and a clear process for handling such requests can make the process more transparent for all parties. Most managers will not receive many accommodation requests; therefore, education about the ADA, recognizing a disclosure, disability awareness, and the organization's process for accommodation can support those involved in responding to and implementing accommodation requests.

In practice, some disclosure or accommodation requests are mishandled, opening the employer up to receiving a discrimination charge under the ADA, potentially a costly proposition. The charge data represent only ADA issues where the charging party filed with an outside organization, but they can inform employers about where conflict arises in the accommodation process. Two issues that were common in the charge data were poor communication and challenges around providing leave as an accommodation and supporting workers returning from leave. A clear and commonly understood accommodation process, including the critical step of an interactive dialog, can improve communication between employee and employer. Further, documenting accommodation requests and outcomes can help minimize the likelihood of confusion and/or discontinuation of an accommodation when turnover among managers and HR representatives takes place. While offering leave and returning an employee to work can be challenging on several fronts, flexibility and openness to considering accommodations support the effective transition back to the workplace. Additional complexities can arise in a unionized environment, specifically, when a reasonable accommodation is in conflict with a collective bargaining agreement (e.g., when offering light duty as an accommodation is in conflict with seniority rights). However, engaging all parties—the employer, union, and the individual—in dialog can help to identify whether there is an effective accommodation that does not affect the rights of other employees.

Communicating a clear, consistent, and transparent process for the case-by-case provision of accommodation, creating a centralized accommodation fund, training managers and employees about rights and responsibilities under the ADA, and offering a grievance process that is fair and unbiased can encourage people to disclose their disabilities and request needed support before work performance is significantly impacted. These strategies can also help to limit potential conflict throughout the accommodation process. When all employees are supported to do their best work, it benefits both employers and employees, and a transparent accommodation process is an important means of achieving these benefits.

ACKNOWLEDGMENTS

The contents of this chapter were developed under a grant from the National Institute on Disability, Independent Living, and Rehabilitation Research (NIDILRR) to Cornell University for the Northeast ADA Center (grant number 90DP0088-01-00). NIDILRR is a center within the Administration for Community Living (ACL), US Department of Health and Human Services (HHS). The Northeast ADA Center is authorized by NIDILRR to provide information, materials, and technical assistance to individuals and entities that are covered by the ADA. The contents of this chapter do not necessarily represent the policy of NIDILRR, ACL, or HHS, and should not be assumed as endorsement by the federal government.

The discrimination charge data statistics and summaries reported in this chapter are derived from data files obtained under an agreement from the US Equal Employment Opportunity Commission. Summaries of data are based on our aggregations and do not represent the EEOC's official aggregation of the data.

The authors would like to acknowledge Moriah Willow, social scientists and statistician, US Equal Employment Opportunity Commission, for assistance in obtaining and working with these data.

The authors would also like to thank Anne Hirsh, co-director; Lou Orslene, co-director; and Linda Batiste, principal consultant/legislative specialist, all of the Job Accommodation Network for their helpful suggestions on the chapter.

REFERENCES

Ameri, Mason, Lisa A. Schur, Meera Adya, Scott Bentley, Patrick F. McKay, and Douglas Kruse. 2015. "The Disability Employment Puzzle: A Field Experiment on Employer Hiring Behavior." NBER Working Paper Series, 21560. Cambridge, MA: National Bureau of Economic Research. doi:10.3386/w21560

American Bar Association. No date. "Collective Bargaining and NLRA Issues Raised by the Americans with Disabilities Act." http://bit.ly/2MBnBVK

Baldridge, D.C., and J.F. Veiga. 2001. "Toward Greater Understanding of the Willingness to Request an Accommodation: Can Requesters' Beliefs Disable the ADA?" *Academy of Management Review* 26: 85–99.

Baldridge, D.C., and J.F. Veiga. 2006. "The Impact of Anticipated Social Consequences on Recurring Disability Accommodation Requests." *Journal of Management* 32: 158–179.

Balser, D.B. 2000. "Perceptions of On-the-Job Discrimination and Employees with Disabilities." *Employee Responsibilities and Rights Journal* 12 (4): 179–197.

Barnard, Kathleen Phair. 2009 (Apr. 30). "Reasonable Accommodation in the Unionized Setting." American Bar Association Labor & Employment Law Section. Technology in the Practice & Workplace Committee Mid-Year Meeting: The Recent ADA Amendments and Use of New Technologies in Providing a Reasonable Accommodation. http://bit.ly/2Hb6N6O

Brohan, Elaine, Claire Henderson, Kay Wheat, Estelle Malcolm, Sarah Clement, Elizabeth A. Barley, Mike Slade, and Graham Thornicroft. 2012. "Systematic Review of Beliefs, Behaviours and Influencing Factors Associated with Disclosure of a Mental Health Problem in the Workplace." *BMC Psychiatry* 12 (1): 11. doi:10.1186/1471-244X-12-11

Bruyère, Susanne M., Sarah von Schrader, Wendy Coduti, and Melissa Bjelland. 2010. "United States Employment Disability Discrimination Charges: Implications for Disability Management Practice." *International Journal of Disability Management* 5 (2):48–58. doi:10.1375/jdmr.5.2.48

Campbell, F.A.K. 2008. "Exploring Internalized Ableism Using Critical Race Theory." *Disability & Society* 23 (2): 151–162.

Chang, H.Y., S. von Schrader, and W. Strobel Gower. 2018. "Examining Small Business Employers and ADA Implementation: Implications for Vocational Rehabilitation Professionals." Presented at the National Council on Rehabilitation Spring 2018 Conference.

Colella, A. 2001. "Coworker Distributive Fairness Judgments of the Workplace Accommodation of Employees with Disabilities." *Academy of Management Review* 26: 100–116.

Colella, Adrienne, Ramona L. Paetzold, and Maura A. Belliveau. 2004. "Factors Affecting Coworkers' Procedural Justice Inferences of the Workplace Accommodations of Employees with Disabilities." *Personnel Psychology* 57 (1): 1–23.

Cook, L.H., and K.J. Shinew. 2014. "Leisure, Work, and Disability Coping: 'I Mean, You Always Need That "In" Group.'" *Leisure Sciences* 36 (5): 420–438.

Cook, LaWanda. 2017 (Aug./Sep.). "The Workplace Disclosure Dilemma." *Ability Magazine*, pp. 42–43.

Dalgin, Rebecca Spirito, and James Bellini. 2008. "Invisible Disability Disclosure in an Employment Interview: Impact on Employers' Hiring Decisions and Views of Employability." *Rehabilitation Counseling Bulletin* 52 (1): 6–15. http://bit.ly/2sQ6shM

Dalgin, Rebecca Spirito, and Dennis Gilbride. 2003. "Perspectives of People with Psychiatric Disabilities on Employment Disclosure." *Psychiatric Rehabilitation Journal* 26 (3): 306–310.

Dobbin, F., S. Kim, and A. Kalev. 2011. "You Can't Always Get What You Need: Organizational Determinants of Diversity Programs." *American Sociological Review* 76 (3): 386–411. doi:10.1177/0003122411409704

Erickson, W., C. Lee, and S. von Schrader. 2017. "Disability Statistics from the American Community Survey (ACS)." Ithaca, NY: Cornell University Yang-Tan Institute on Employment and Disability. http://www.disabilitystatistics.org

Erickson, William A., Sarah von Schrader, Susanne M. Bruyère, and Sara A. VanLooy. 2014. "The Employment Environment: Employer Perspectives, Policies, and Practices Regarding the Employment of Persons with Disabilities." *Rehabilitation Counseling Bulletin* 57 (4): 195–208. doi:10.1177/0034355213509841

Feuerstein, Michael, Gina M. Luff, Cherise B. Harrington, and Cara H. Olsen. 2007. "Pattern of Workplace Disputes in Cancer Survivors: A Population Study of ADA Claims." *Journal of Cancer Survivorship: Research and Practice* 1 (3): 185–192. doi:10.1007/s11764-007-0027-9

Gutman, Arthur. 2015. "Disabilities: Best Practices for Vulnerabilities Associated with the ADA." In *Practitioner's Guide to Legal Issues in Organizations*, edited by C. Hanvey and K. Sady, pp. 163–182. Geneva, Switzerland: Springer. doi:10.1007/978-3-319-11143-8

Harlan, Sharon L., and Pamela M. Robert. 1998. "The Social Construction of Disability in Organizations: Why Employers Resist Reasonable Accommodation." *Work and Occupations* 25 (4): 397–435.

Hsieh, Hsiu-Fang, and Sarah E. Shannon. 2005. "Three Approaches to Qualitative Content Analysis." *Qualitative Health Research* 15 (9): 1277–1288. doi:10.1177/1049732305276687

Jammaers, Eline, Patrizia Zanoni, and Stefan Hardonk. 2016. "Constructing Positive Identities in Ableist Workplaces: Disabled Employees' Discursive Practices Engaging with the Discourse of Lower Productivity." *Human Relations* 69 (6): 1365–1386. doi:10.1177/0018726715612901

Johnston, L.M., S.M. Bruyère, and E. Reiter. 2011. "The ADA and Collective Bargaining Issues." Ithaca, NY: Cornell University ILR School. http://bit.ly/2MDjNmS

Kulkarni, Mukta. 2012. "Contextual Factors and Help-Seeking Behaviors of People with Disabilities." *Human Resource Development Review* 11 (1): 77–96. doi:10.1177/1534484311416488

Kulkarni, M., and M.L. Lengnick-Hall. 2013. "Obstacles to Success in the Workplace for People with Disabilities: A Review and Research Agenda." *Human Resource Development Review* 13 (2): 158–180. doi:10.1177/1534484313485229

Loy, Beth. 2017. "Workplace Accommodations: Low Cost, High Impact." Accommodation and Compliance Series. Morgantown, WV: Job Accommodation Network. http://bit.ly/2MEyjuq

Lutz, Barbara J., and Barbara J. Bowers. 2005. "Disability in Everyday Life." *Qualitative Health Research* 15 (8): 1037–1054.

Madaus, J., T. Foley, J. McGuire, and M. Ruban. 2002. "Employment Self-Disclosure of Postsecondary Graduates with Learning Disabilities: Rates and Rationales." *Journal of Learning Disabilities* 35 (4): 364–369.

Merriam-Webster. No date. *Merriam-Webster Unabridged Dictionary*. Online. "Disabled." http://bit.ly/2H8oV14

Murray, M., and S. von Schrader. 2014. "Educational Institutions as Model Employers of People with Disabilities." Presented to the Association for University Centers on Disability, Washington, DC.

National Aeronautics and Space Administration (NASA). 2018. "NASA Headquarters Reasonable Accommodation for Individuals with Disabilities." Washington, DC: National Aeronautics and Space Administration. https://go.nasa.gov/2sU7pWB

Nishii, L. 2013. "The Benefits of Climate for Inclusion for Gender Diverse Groups." *Academy of Management Journal* 56 (6): 1754–1774. doi:10.5465/amj.2009.0823

Nishii, Lisa, and Susanne M. Bruyère. 2014. "Research Brief: Inside the Workplace: Case Studies of Factors Influencing Engagement of People with Disabilities." Ithaca, NY: Cornell University ILR School. http://bit.ly/2MEuDZC

Oldfield, M., E. MacEachen, B. Kirsh, and M. MacNeill. 2016. "Impromptu Everyday Disclosure Dances: How Women with Fibromyalgia Respond to Disclosure Risks at Work." *Disability and Rehabilitation* 38 (15): 1442–1453. doi:10.3109/09638288.2015.1103794

Reed, Karla S., Michelle Meade, Melinda Jarnecke, Phillip Rumrill, and James S. Krause. 2017. "Disclosing Disability in the Employment Setting: Perspectives from Workers with Multiple Sclerosis." *Journal of Vocational Rehabilitation* 47 (2): 175–184. doi:10.3233/JVR-170893

Rudstam, Hannah, and Wendy Strobel Gower. 2012. "Beyond Instruction; Beyond a Website: Distance Learning, Disability Inclusiveness and Changing Workplace Practices." *Rehabilitation Research, Policy & Education* 26 (4): 345–354. http://bit.ly/2MBCYNS

Santuzzi, A.M., and P.R. Waltz. 2016. "Disability in the Workplace: A Unique and Variable Identity." *Journal of Management* 42 (5): 1111–1135. doi:10.1177/0149206315626269

Santuzzi, Alecia M., Pamela R. Waltz, Lisa M. Finkelstein, and Deborah E. Rupp. 2014. "Invisible Disabilities: Unique Challenges for Employees and Organizations." *Industrial and Organizational Psychology* 7 (2): 204–219.

Schur, Lisa, Kyongji Han, Andrea Kim, Mason Ameri, Peter Blanck, and Douglas Kruse. 2017. "Disability at Work: A Look Back and Forward." *Journal of Occupational Rehabilitation* 27 (4): 482–497. doi:10.1007/s10926-017-9739-5

Schur, Lisa, Douglas Kruse, Joseph Blasi, and Peter Blanck. 2009. "Is Disability Disabling in All Workplaces? Workplace Disparities and Corporate Culture." *Industrial Relations* 48 (3): 381–410.

Smith, David Harry, and Jean F. Andrews. 2015. "Deaf and Hard of Hearing Faculty in Higher Education: Enhancing Access, Equity, Policy, and Practice." *Disability & Society* 30 (10): 1521–1536. doi:10.1080/09687599.2015.1113160

Solovieva, Tatiana I., Denetta L. Dowler, and Richard T. Walls. 2011. "Employer Benefits from Making Workplace Accommodations." *Disability and Health Journal* 4 (1): 39–45. doi:10.1016/j.dhjo.2010.03.001

US Census Bureau. 2018. "American Community Survey, 2010–2014 American Community Survey 5-Year Estimates, Table S181." Calculations by S. von Schrader using American FactFinder. http://factfinder.census.gov

US Equal Employment Opportunity Commission (US EEOC). No date. "The ADA: Your Employment Rights as an Individual with a Disability." Washington, DC: US Equal Employment Opporunity Commission. http://bit.ly/2MCUlhl

US Equal Employment Opportunity Commission (US EEOC). 1993. "Memorandum of Understanding Between the General Counsel of the National Labor Relations Board and the Equal Employment Opportunity Commission (November 16, 1993)." Washington, DC: US Equal Employment Opporunity Commission. http://bit.ly/2MEvtWg

US Equal Employment Opportunity Commission (US EEOC). 2002. "Enforcement Guidance: Reasonable Accommodation and Undue Hardship Under the Americans with Disabilities Act." Washington, DC: US Equal Employment Opporunity Commission. http://bit.ly/2MEADBE

US Equal Employment Opportunity Commission (US EEOC). 2005. "Practical Advice for Drafting and Implementing Reasonable Accommodation Procedures Under Executive Order 13164." Washington, DC: US Equal Employment Opporunity Commission. http://bit.ly/2MDmTau

US Equal Employment Opportunity Commission (US EEOC). 2016. "Employer-Provided Leave and the Americans with Disabilities Act." Washington, DC: US Equal Employment Opporunity Commission. http://bit.ly/2MCiBQC

US Equal Employment Opportunity Commission (US EEOC). 2017. "Affirmative Action for Individuals with Disabilities in Federal Employment." Washington, DC: US Equal Employment Opporunity Commission. http://bit.ly/2GanUpr

US Equal Employment Opportunity Commission (US EEOC). 2018. "Charge Statistics (Charges Filed with EEOC), FY 1997 Through FY 2017." Washington, DC: US Equal Employment Opporunity Commission. http://bit.ly/2UusUJt

US Office of Federal Contract Compliance Programs (US OFCCP). No date. "Frequently Asked Questions: Section 503 Regulations." Washington, DC: US Office of Federal Contract Compliance Programs. http://bit.ly/2MEwRIs

US Office of Federal Contract Compliance Programs (US OFCCP). No date. "Regulations Implementing Section 503 of the Rehabilitation Act." Washington, DC: US Office of Federal Contract Compliance Programs. http://bit.ly/2ME4DxQ

von Schrader, Sarah, and Susanne M. Bruyère. 2018. "What Works? How Federal Contractors Are Implementing Section 503: Survey Report." Ithaca, NY: Cornell University Yang-Tan Institute on Employment and Disability. http://bit.ly/2ME4EBU

von Schrader, S., and W. Erickson. 2017. "Employment Discrimination Charges Filed Under the Americans with Disabilities Act (ADA)." Ithaca, NY: Cornell University Yang-Tan Institute on Employment and Disability. http://bit.ly/2MEZsxj

von Schrader, Sarah, Valerie Malzer, and Susanne M. Bruyère. 2014. "Perspectives on Disability Disclosure: The Importance of Employer Practices and Workplace Climate." *Employee Responsibilities and Rights Journal* 26 (4): 237–255. doi:10.1007/s10672-013-9227-9

von Schrader, Sarah, Xu Xu, and Susanne M. Bruyère. 2014. "Accommodation Requests: Who Is Asking for What?" *Rehabilitation Research, Policy, and Education* 28 (4): 329–344. doi:10.1891/2168-6653.28.4.329

Walsh, B., and E. Volini. 2017. "Rewriting the Rules for the Digital Age: 2017 Deloitte Global Human Capital Trends." Deloitte University Press. http://bit.ly/2MABsf1

Wang-Audia, W., and T. Tauber. 2014 (Nov. 26). "Meet the Modern Learner: Engaging the Overwhelmed, Distracted, and Impatient Employee." *Bersin Research Bulletin.*

Watson, N. 2002. "Well, I Know This Is Going to Sound Very Strange to You, but I Don't See Myself as a Disabled Person: Identity and Disability." *Disability & Society* 17 (5): 509–527.

West, Steven, Richard Roessler, Phillip Rumrill, Brian McMahon, Jessica Hurley, Linnea Carlson, and Fong Chan. 2008. "Employer Characteristics and Reasonable Accommodation Discrimination Against People with Disabilities under the Americans with Disabilities Act." *Rehabilitation Professional* 16: 209–220.

CHAPTER 5

Unwelcoming Workplaces: Bullying and Harassment of Employees with Disabilities

LAWANDA COOK
SARAH VON SCHRADER
VALERIE MALZER
JENNIFER MIMNO
Cornell University

INTRODUCTION

This chapter considers the impact of workplace climate and culture on the experiences of employees with disabilities. In it, we explore issues of bullying and harassment, such as those raised in the scenario below, and share relevant findings from an extensive review of the literature and two recent Cornell University studies. The first study examined US Equal Employment Opportunity Commission (EEOC) discrimination charges that cited harassment under the Americans with Disabilities Act (ADA). The second study inquired about personal and organizational factors that impact work–life balance and turnover intention among employees with disabilities, including whether they had faced harassment or discrimination in the past year.

Similar themes were noted across both studies, highlighting the experiences of workers with disabilities, who report having been harassed on the basis of disability and/or other personal characteristics such as gender, age, or race. We explain how and when anti-harassment law applies to disability-related bullying, discuss the rights of targeted people with disabilities, and consider the role of organizational leadership in appropriately addressing bullying and harassment and supporting employee well-being. We conclude with specific suggestions for creating healthier, more welcoming and inclusive workplaces.

To begin our discussion of workplace climate and culture in unwelcoming workplaces, we offer a scenario drawn from an actual case (*Murphy v. BeavEx, Inc.* 2008):

> "Cedric," who has progressive multiple sclerosis (MS), works as a dispatcher. He uses a cane for mobility and experiences weakness in his limbs, memory loss, cognitive impairment, and difficulty with bowel and bladder control. He is frequently ridiculed by his co-workers and often called derogatory names. Co-workers hide his cane so he has to ask for help to retrieve it. He has been the subject

of drawings displayed in the dispatch area—one of which depicted him as "Stupid Employee of the Month."

Are the behaviors of Cedric's colleagues merely examples of a workplace culture that includes "teasing," or is something more insidious going on? Are his co-workers' "jokes" examples of harassment? Are they part of a more serious pattern in the workplace? There are several factors to consider in determining whether his colleagues' behaviors are problematic and possibly illegal. Key considerations include Cedric's perception of their behavior toward him, how Cedric's colleagues view the behaviors, and whether his work performance and ability to maintain employment are adversely impacted. The fact that Cedric has MS, a health condition that affords him protections under the ADA, must also be taken into account in assessing this workplace situation.

RELEVANT LITERATURE

Bullying and other forms of harassment create negative work environments, resulting in significant, damaging consequences for employees and organizations. Workplace bullying and harassment occurs throughout the world and is an issue that has until recently received little attention in the United States (Duffy and Sperry 2007; Yamada 2010). Harassment based on protected group membership (e.g., race, color, religion, gender, disability, or age) is illegal in the United States and is defined as unwelcome behaviors that promote a hostile work environment that a "reasonable person" would find intimidating or abusive (Mattice and Shorago 2015).

Bullying can take many forms, but it is generally acknowledged as repeated unacceptable behavior involving a psychological power imbalance, in that when a target does not report the abuse, the perpetrator's behaviors are likely to become more frequent and more aggressive (Mattice 2018). Elame (2013) describes discriminatory bullying as a form of abuse and victimization linked to disability, gender, ethnic origin, sexual orientation, or religion that occurs repeatedly over the course of time by one or more individuals. Although the bullying Cedric experienced on a repeated basis was discriminatory, the court did not determine it to be illegal harassment. To understand why this is, it is important to understand how harassment is defined in the United States.

Harassment

The issue of workplace harassment is most commonly associated with unwanted sexual advances from one employee toward another, a very prevalent concern in the US workplace. In Stop Street Harassment's 2018 national study on sexual harassment and assault, 38% of women and 13% of men in the United States reported experiencing sexual harassment in the workplace (Kearl 2018). In that study, 77% of women reported having experienced some form of sexual harassment and/or assault in their lifetimes; the incidence of assault was higher among women with disabilities. Similarly, men in socially marginalized groups, including those with disabilities, also reported experiencing more harassment and assault. While the majority of incidents occurred in public spaces, the workplace was the third most common location of sexual assault and harassment of both men and women (Kearl 2018). Some targets file charges; Feldblum and Lipnic (2016) report that in 2015, 45% of workplace harassment charges brought to the EEOC by people employed by private employers or state or local governments alleged sexual harassment, and 44% of charges from federal employees alleged harassment on the basis of sex (Feldblum and Lipnic 2016).

Workplace harassment based on personal characteristics other than gender, gender identity, sexual orientation, or pregnancy, all of which are covered under protections against sexual harassment ("Coverage," US EEOC, no date), is also a significant workplace issue. In 2015, 34% of charges by individuals working for private employers or state or local governments claimed harassment on the basis of race, and 19% of harassment charges were on the basis of disability. Among federal employees, 36% of charges alleged harassment based on race, and 34% claimed harassment based on disability (Feldblum and Lipnic 2016).

Harassment is defined within US civil rights legislation as a form of employment discrimination that involves unwelcome conduct toward a person based on that person's membership in a protected category—race, color, sex, age, national origin, disability, or genetic information ("Harassment," US EEOC, no date; Mattice and Shorago 2015). Harassment becomes unlawful when at least one of these two conditions are met: (1) the person must endure the offensive conduct in order to maintain his or her job or (2) the conduct is severe or pervasive enough to create a work environment that a reasonable person would consider intimidating, hostile, or abusive ("Harassment," US EEOC, no date). In the case on which Cedric's story is based, the court ruled that neither of those two conditions were met, concluding that although insensitive, his co-workers' conduct was not severe and pervasive enough to have altered Cedric's working conditions (*Murphy v. BeavEx, Inc.* 2008).

Harassment is a common problem throughout the world, creating hostile work environments for employees in all types of occupations. While research suggests that blue-collar workers experience high levels of harassment, white-collar workers, such as public servants and people in the hospitality industry, may be especially susceptible to this type of maltreatment (Ariza-Montes, Arjona-Fuentes, Law, and Han 2017; Notelaers et al. 2011). Harassment can result in significant consequences for employees and organizations.

Bullying

Workplace bullying or "mobbing" is one form of harassment that has only recently been the subject of study in the United States (Sperry and Duffy 2009). This phenomenon is estimated to be experienced by between 5% and 24% of workers, depending on the country (Nielsen, Matthiesen, and Einarsen 2010). Although other countries have studied workplace bullying since the 1980s, the term was introduced to the United States in the popular press in 1998 by psychologists Gary and Ruth Namie (Yamada 2010). The Namies founded the Workplace Bullying Institute (WBI), the only US organization that integrates all aspects of workplace bullying: self-help advice for individuals, personal coaching, research, books, public education, union assistance, training for professionals, employer consulting, and legislative advocacy (Workplace Bullying Institute 2012). The WBI annually conducts a survey of bullying in the United States. Results of the WBI's 2014 Workplace Bullying Survey indicate that "27% of Americans have suffered abusive conduct at work; another 21% have witnessed it; 72% are aware that workplace bullying happens" (Namie 2014: 3).

In describing a model of a continuum of negative behaviors that constitute workplace bullying (Figure 1), the WBI emphasizes that bullying is an issue of "psychological violence" and states that "bullying is a form of workplace violence ... including everything from incivility and disrespect up to, but stopping short of, physical violence" (Workplace Bullying Institute 2013). Mattice and Shorago (2015) note that a psychological power imbalance between the perpetrator and target is a key feature of the bullying dynamic. Einarsen, Hoel,

FIGURE 1
Continuum of Negative Behavior

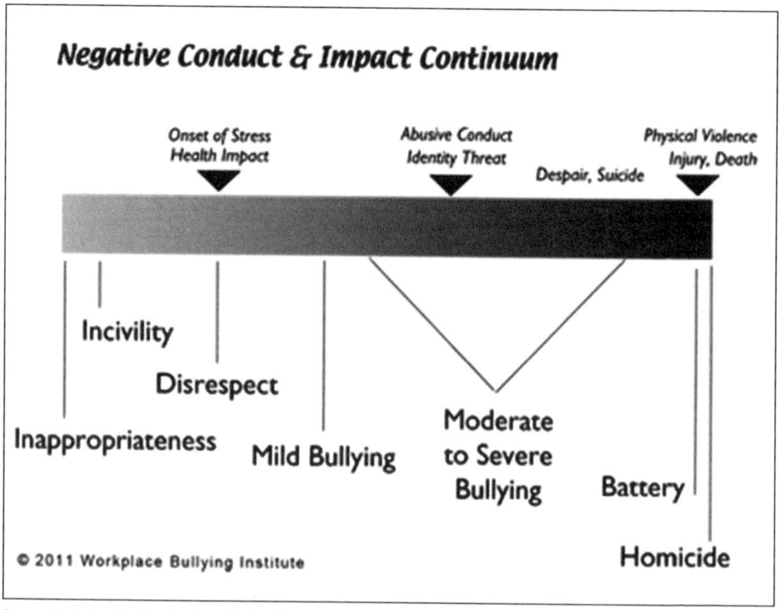

Source: Workplace Bullying Institute. Used with permission.

Zapf, and Cooper (2011) also highlight the psychological nature of bullying and advise that it includes persistent behaviors that are offensive, harassing, and socially excluding over a long period. Bullying includes work interference or sabotage, which prevents work from getting done (Namie 2014); this work-performance consequence of bullying is associated with its being viewed as illegal harassment (Taylor 2008).

Bullying and Employee Well-Being

Bullying behaviors fall within the US Occupational Safety and Health Administration's (OSHA) definition of "workplace or occupational violence." OSHA, a department of the US Department of Labor, defines workplace violence as "any act or threat of physical violence, harassment, intimidation, or other threatening disruptive behavior that occurs at the work site. It ranges from threats and verbal abuse to physical assaults and even homicide" (US OSHA, no date). While bullying and violence share similar traits and can overlap, "workplace violence is overt and physical, while bullying is insidious and manipulative" (Mattice 2018). The psychological violence demonstrated through workplace bullying can affect the target's well-being in a number of ways. Bullying can contribute to the onset or exacerbation of chronic health conditions such as type 2 diabetes (Xu et al. 2017), depression (McTernan, Dollard, and LaMontagne 2013), and post-traumatic stress disorder (Hansen et al. 2006). Bullying's negative impact on financial well-being is evidenced by research indicating that 26% of bullying targets do not find employment after leaving their jobs, and, of those who do, 52% earn less in their new positions (Namie 2011).

The long-term consequences of workplace bullying and harassment adversely impact employees' lives both on and off the job. A variety of factors, including workplace culture and availability of supportive workplace policies, influence perceptions of quality of work life and work–life balance (Greenhaus, Ziegert, and Allen 2012). Workplace culture and policies related to expected behaviors are critical considerations when addressing bullying and harassment (Morrall and Urquhart 2004; Namie and Lutgen-Sandvik 2010; Yamada 2010).

Disability-Related Bullying and Harassment

Research about bullying among school-aged youth with and without disabilities suggests that even in the same setting, children with disabilities, as well as those who are members of other marginalized groups, are more likely to be bullied than their nondisabled peers (Carter and Spencer 2006; Eisenberg, Gower, McMorris, and Bucchianeri 2015; National Center for Educational Statistics 2017). Less is known about the prevalence and antecedents of disability-related bullying in the workplace. For instance, although the WBI collects data about several background factors of bullying targets (e.g., age, race, ethnicity, and political affiliation) and considers the disabling impacts of bullying, the institute has not asked whether survey respondents have a pre-existing disability in nearly two decades of research about this critical workplace issue. However, the WBI's findings over multiple years suggest that members of other marginalized groups, including women and people of color, are more likely to be bullying targets; thus, it is reasonable to assume this may also be the case for workers with disabilities.

One indicator that workers with disabilities might be more often targeted by bullies is that the number of disability-related workplace harassment claims has increased in recent years (Feuerstein, Gehrke, McMahon, and McMahon 2017). Although there is no federal law against workplace bullying in the United States, bullying is a form of harassment. Thus, when a member of a protected group is targeted because of her or his membership in a protected category, the bullying may meet the definition of illegal harassment (Yamada 1999). Claims of disability-related harassment are addressed by Title I of the ADA and must meet all of the following criteria, which are based on the framework for sexual harassment claims (Taylor 2016):

- The individual has a disability as defined by the ADA.
- The individual was subjected to unwelcome harassment.
- The harassment was based on disability.
- The harassment was severe and pervasive enough to alter a term, condition, or privilege of employment.
- The employer knew or should have known of the harassment and failed to take prompt, remedial action.

The existing literature on disability-related workplace bullying and harassment suggests that employees with disabilities often feel that their employing organizations are not only unwelcoming but openly hostile toward them (Shigaki et al. 2012; Vickers 2017). Consequently, some individuals with disabilities engage in various forms of impression management (Goffman 1959)—conscious and unconscious behaviors undertaken to minimize stigma associated with disability or other stigmatized characteristics—when interacting with others in the workplace (Vickers 2017). These employees may feel the need to minimize the impact of their conditions and resist requesting reasonable accommodations, even in situations in which some type of adjustment in when, where, or how essential job functions get done would be beneficial (Shigaki et al. 2012).

As a group, people with disabilities are used to adapting and often find ways to manage, even when a setting is not particularly responsive to their personal needs. This ability to "make do," as Cedric did in the opening example, may explain the difficulty that bullied employees face when seeking recourse, especially when they have been able to maintain their employment. Ultimately, Cedric chose to leave his job because his co-workers' behaviors and supervisors' inaction created a workplace he experienced as unwelcoming and hostile.

The Cost to Organizations

Workplaces in which bullying and harassment are prevalent can create a negative work climate that can cause significant and expensive consequences for the organization. Problems such as poor morale and poor employee relations, loss of respect for managers and supervisors, poor performance, lost productivity, absence, resignations, and damage to company reputation can plague a workplace if bullying is allowed to go unchecked (Leymann 1990; Morrall and Urquhart 2004). Studies on the US workplace have shown that these effects, especially absenteeism and presenteeism (being present at work but completely disengaged), result in organizational loss, which becomes more costly when they result in the loss of qualified personnel and health-related claims (Manners and Cates 2016; Vega and Comer 2005; Wall, Smith, and Nodoushani 2017). For example, Hollis's (2015) investigation of workplace bullying within 175 four-year colleges and universities in the United States found that 62% of employees were affected by workplace bullying, resulting in an estimated organizational cost of $4,684,999 to $8,092,271 annually, depending on the size of the institution. This estimate takes into account all of the ways that bullying can financially impact an organization because of employee disengagement and related costs.

A hostile workplace affects not only targeted employees but anyone who is aware of the harassing behavior, including employees who witness maltreatment of others or who feel that they must support the harasser to avoid being targeted, too (Wall, Smith, and Nodoushani 2017). These potential impacts of workplace harassment mean that employees who are not personally targeted may also have legal rights if the consequences they experience create a hostile work environment, and the law protects witnesses who come forth from retaliation ("Facts About Retaliation" US EEOC, no date). When bullied employees do pursue legal action against employers for not protecting them against these behaviors, even if they are not successful, the legal costs to the company are considerable (Wall, Smith, and Nodoushani 2017). It is in an organization's best interest to learn to identify bullying and harassment and to know how to address these problematic behaviors that can be so costly and pervasive.

Employer Awareness

Employers may not always be aware of how pervasive the problem of bullying and harassment is in their workplaces. There are several reasons why this might be true. Crucially, employees are hesitant to report the abuse, in part because they fear retaliation and doubt that their employer will take meaningful action to protect them (SHRM 2018). Nearly 75% of those harassed at work never even talk to a supervisor about it (Feldblum and Lipnic 2016). Employees who do report their experiences often have their doubts confirmed; a recent survey on workplace bullying found that of the 27% of workers who reported feeling bullied to their human resources department, 57% said no action was taken to address their concerns (CareerBuilder 2012).

Another reason employers may be unaware of the magnitude of the problem may be because a targeted person makes claims of harassment based on his or her subjective view of the situation—meaning that what one employee finds offensive or harassing may not be viewed as such by others. Importantly, the legal standard for what constitutes illegal harassment is based on whether a "reasonable person" would view the behaviors as harassment. This may be difficult to determine, especially in cases of disability-related harassment when there are few, if any, colleagues who can relate to the target's lived experience of disability. Such complaints may be assumed to be due to the person's disability rather than indicative of the workplace climate and culture, and reporting the experience may result in the target being seen as even more "different." Branch and Murray (2015) found that nontargets often have difficulty empathizing with people who are bullied, not understanding or appreciating what they are experiencing. When managers and supervisors lack this empathy, they may not realize the extent of the problem. Finally, Namie and Lutgen-Sandvik (2010) propose that one of the biggest challenges to recognizing and addressing bullying is the tendency to think of it as conflict between individuals rather than considering the role of workplace culture. However, workplace culture may in fact encourage bullying—and undoubtedly helps to sustain it.

Even when the perpetrator's behaviors do not meet the legal definition of harassment, the experience can adversely affect both the work and personal life of the targeted individual. Below we describe two Cornell University studies that shed light on the workplace bullying and harassment faced by people with disabilities and consider what each study suggests about the personal and organizational factors that contribute to these experiences.

EEOC CHARGE DATA STUDY

As noted earlier in this chapter, there is relatively little research on the prevalence and experience of workplace harassment and bullying on the basis of disability. Employment discrimination charges filed with the EEOC are one data source that has been used for examining employment discrimination. Data on charges are collected in the EEOC's Integrated Mission System, documenting details of charges filed under Title I of the ADA and other employment-related anti-discrimination statutes enforced by the EEOC. While analysis of these data cannot directly shed light on the prevalence of harassment in the workplace, they do represent cases where an individual has chosen to file a charge with an outside agency. Prior research related to workplace harassment has revealed interesting patterns, such as that individuals with behavioral impairments are more likely to allege harassment compared with individuals with physical disabilities (Shaw,

Chan, and McMahon 2012). Further, among people with disabilities who file charges, those who are also people of color, are female, or are above age 35 are more likely to have alleged harassment compared with other workplace maltreatments (Shaw, Chan, and McMahon 2012). This research suggests that individuals who are members of more than one underrepresented group may be more likely to report feeling harassed. This finding is in line with a study of the Age Discrimination in Employment Act (ADEA) charges that found that age discrimination charges that cite other statutes, such as the ADA and Title VIII of the Civil Rights Act (CRA), are increasingly common and are more likely to cite harassment as an issue (von Schrader and Nazarov 2016).

The prevalence of charges that cite harassment among ADA charges is increasing annually (Figure 2). This pattern is not unique to ADA charges and is similar for Title VI of the CRA and ADEA charges (author calculation based on http://bit.ly/2UusUJt and http://bit.ly/2Yw1x3G). Over the ten-year period from 2005 to 2014, approximately 15% of charges cited harassment as an issue.

To understand more about the context and characteristics of ADA charges that cite harassment, we conducted a qualitative analysis of case notes from verified charges. Verified charges are those with a merit outcome for the charging party—that is, charges that were withdrawn or settled with benefits for the charging party or where the charge went to conciliation after an EEOC merit decision. Our analysis focused on case notes that describe the particulars of the perceived discriminatory act as reported by the charging party, collected using the EEOC's Form 5, Charge of Discrimination. Form 5 is used to collect facts from the charging party about the actions or policies that are being complained

FIGURE 2
Percentage of ADA Charges Citing Harassment as an Issue (2005–2014)

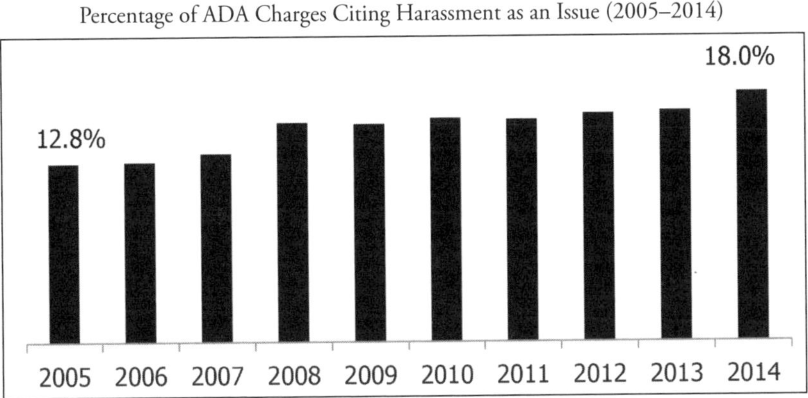

Source: Calculation by Sarah von Schrader, Cornell University Yang-Tan Institute on Employment and Disability, using data from EEOC's Integrated Mission System. Both EEOC and Fair Employment Practices Agency charges are included in aggregations. Summaries of data are based on our aggregations and do not represent the EEOC's official aggregation of the data.

about in order to establish whether the issue is covered by EEOC statutes (or other federal or state laws) and to collect information that will be used by EEOC to guide investigation and mediation efforts.

There were approximately 70,000 closed ADA charges in 2013 and 2014, and 21.4% of them had a merit outcome. Among ADA charges that cited harassment, the merit rate was slightly lower at 20%. It should be noted that these numbers do not match those reported by the EEOC because our data also include the 30% to 40% of all charges filed annually that are received by state and local Fair Employment Practice Agencies (FEPAs) rather than only those filed with the EEOC. Table 1 presents more information about the population of charges from which we drew our sample, presenting characteristics of all verified ADA charges, verified harassment charges, our sample of verified harassment charges with case notes, and our sample of verified harassment charges with Form 5 data (some case notes in the sample did not include Form 5 information).

In comparing verified harassment charges to verified charges more broadly under the ADA, we found that the proportion that cite another statute (ADEA or Title VII of the CRA) is greater. For example, the proportion of verified ADA harassment charges that also cite the ADEA is 22% compared with 16% of verified ADA charges overall. Likewise, 44% of verified ADA harassment charges also cite Title VII of the CRA, while only 27% of the verified ADA charges do so overall. This suggests that harassment charges are more likely to cite multiple bases beyond disability and is in line with research that suggests that individuals who are members of underrepresented groups are more likely to experience harassment (Nauen 2017). Another notable characteristic is that among verified harassment charges, behavioral issues and a subset of those charges—mental health issues—are cited more frequently. This suggests that individuals who disclose what are often nonvisible and more highly stigmatized disabilities are more likely to cite harassment as an issue on a charge.

Using a conventional content analysis approach (Hsieh and Shannon 2005), we analyzed a total sample of 73 charges from fiscal years 2013 and 2014 that met the criteria described above. While preliminary, the findings are interesting in that they provide information about the antecedent of the harassment, the perceived harassment, the impact on the charging party, and the organizational response to the reported harassment. These data, in contrast to the quantitative data on charges that have been analyzed in previous charge research, allow us new data points, specifically the occupation of the charging party and the relationship between the charging party and the perpetrator(s) of the harassment, but they also offer the context that is missing from the quantitative charge data.

Our analysis of the case notes included documenting the occupation of the charging party and the perpetrator of the harassment, as well as coding and developing themes representing characteristics of workplace harassment based

TABLE 1
Harassment-Related Case Note Analysis, Sample Characteristics (2013–2014)

	Sampled charges with Form 5 data (N = 73)	Sampled charges (N = 100)	All verified harassment charges (N = 2,364)	All verified ADA charges (N = 14,832)
Most common issues cited (a single charge can cite one or more)				
Discharge	37%	40%	43%	60%
Reasonable accommodation	45%	45%	35%	39%
Terms and conditions	21%	25%	31%	21%
Harassment	100%	100%	100%	16%
Type of disability* cited on charge (a single charge can cite one or more)				
Nonspecific	27%	34%	41%	43%
Orthopedic	14%	14%	13%	15%
Behavioral	25%	23%	24%	16%
Mental health disability (subset of behavioral)	19%	19%	20%	14%
Medical	29%	25%	18%	18%
Sensory	8%	8%	6%	5%
Neurological	8%	7%	6%	6%
Other statutes cited (a single charge can cite one or more)				
% citing ADEA	22%	22%	22%	16%
% citing Title VII of CRA	32%	35%	44%	27%
Charging party characteristics				
% male	43%	41%	39%	44%
Mean age	46.1 (N = 68)	47.1 (N = 90)	45.8 (N = 1,891)	45.8 (N = 10,959)
Respondent characteristic				
Large employer (500+ employees)	52% (N = 67)	48% (N = 85)	39% (N = 1,995)	37% (N = 12,305)
Office receiving charge				
FEPA receiving office	5%	12%	35%	39%

*Type of disability categories are defined in Feuerstein, Luff, Harrington, and Olsen (2007).
Note: Verified harassment charges are also included in the all verified ADA charge numbers presented.
Source: Calculation by Sarah von Schrader, Cornell University Yang-Tan Institute on Employment and Disability, using data from EEOC's Integrated Mission System from fiscal years 2013 and 2014. Both EEOC and FEPA charges are included in aggregations. Summaries of data are based on our aggregations and do not represent the EEOC's official aggregation of the data.

on disability. While the perspective is from the charging party, not the perpetrator or the employer, these descriptions offer important lessons for employees and employers alike. A few key findings from this analysis are related to the experiences of disability harassment, occupation of the charging party, the relationship to the perpetrator, and the (in)action of management in response. A summary of findings is presented below.

Experiences of Disability Harassment

Harassment on the basis of disability shares many of the same features of workplace harassment on the basis gender and race. However, in cases where the disability was not obvious, harassment often included disclosing information about the charging party's disability to those who would not need to know or subjecting the person to excessive questioning about whether they had a disability.

We identified five broad categories of experiences reflected in the case notes on verified charges of harassment:

- *Badgering comments related to disability.* The perpetrator often joked about the charging party's disability, making statements like "You should be euthanized" or distributing a flyer making fun of the individual's disability. These behaviors often took place in front of co-workers and/or customers and in some instances resulted in disclosure of confidential information about the disability to others.
- *Questioning the disability or need for workplace accommodation.* In some cases, the employer repeatedly asked about the validity of the person's disability or accommodation request, demanding excessive documentation of disability. The charging party in some cases was forced to provide additional, updated documentation related to disability, even in instances of permanent restriction, or to provide additional medical documentation when there was a change in supervisor.
- *Seeking to exacerbate disability.* The perpetrator sometimes acted with the intention of exacerbating a known disability—for example, by wearing perfume to aggravate a known allergy or assigning work that requires stair climbing when that is a known and previously accommodated limitation.
- *Excluding from work activities.* Charging parties described actions that were taken to exclude them from work activities—for example, by scheduling key team meetings during the person's regularly scheduled medical appointments or locking the targeted employee out of the building.
- *Discrediting and making it harder to demonstrate competence.* In several cases, there was an effort by others to discredit the targeted individual by creating conditions that made it more difficult for the person to complete job tasks. Examples include deleting the charging party's work-related accounts, damaging her or his work equipment, or assigning

> excessive work and/or unreasonable deadlines. In some cases after a disability was disclosed, the charging party's work performance was questioned unfairly. For example, case notes suggested that performance expectations for the individual increased significantly after disclosure and then they were placed on a performance improvement plan. Individuals described their experience as "walking on egg shells," that is, constantly being threatened with disciplinary action or with being fired.

In many of the descriptions of harassment, individuals discussed other forms of discrimination, including issues around failure to provide reasonable accommodation and terms and conditions of employment. Charging parties who cited harassment as an issue often described their treatment in comparison with others without disabilities; they reported being denied the same benefits or opportunities as those without a disability. Examples included being denied professional development training, the use of a flexible workplace/schedule, or permission to wear personal clothing instead of orgizational attire or a uniform.

Based on workforce numbers, the distribution of charges by occupation group was not significantly different from the distribution of employed people with disabilities. In the sample of harassment charges, charging parties' occupations were fairly evenly represented across four broad occupational categories: management, business, science, and arts occupations (22%), sales and office occupations (31%), service occupations (26%), and natural resources, construction, and maintenance occupations/production, transportation, and material-moving occupations (21%). Nationally, about 27% of the civilian-employed population with disabilities works in management, business, science, and arts occupations, 22% in service occupations, 25% in sales and office occupations, and 26% in natural resources, construction, and maintenance occupations/production, transportation, and material-moving occupations (US Census Bureau 2018). When comparing these proportions, we found no statistical evidence that individuals with disabilities in certain occupational categories are more or less likely to file charges on the basis of harassment.

Most perpetrators of harassment were supervisors or other "higher ups." The relationship between the charging party and the perpetrator(s) of the harassment was noted on 77% of the sample charges, and the vast majority indicated that the harassment was perpetrated by a supervisor or higher up (72%), an additional 14% were harassed by both a supervisor/higher up and co-workers, and the final 14% reported being harassed solely by co-workers.

Often harassment started immediately after a disability disclosure and/or an accommodation request. The most common situation seemed to be when an individual requested leave, often disclosing his or her disability to explain why the leave was needed. The leave was sometimes granted and sometimes denied, but the harassment typically began shortly after the request. The harassing behavior most often described included supervisors or others complaining excessively about the leave, badgering the charging party for more information about the disability, excessive monitoring of the charging party's whereabouts, or accusing the targeted employee of abusing leave policies. One might surmise, that in comparison with other types of accommodation requests, leave more directly affects or inconveniences the supervisor and/or co-workers who might have to cover for the individual, thus leading to a change in behavior toward the employee.

When harassment was reported, individuals were either ignored and/or retaliated against. In most cases, the charging party reported that when he or she advised human resources (HR) of the situation, which many targets did on multiple occasions, the response, if she or he received one, was generally not very helpful. Targeted employees reported that HR did not provide suggestions for handling the situation, but rather the harassment was ignored, and targets reported that they were told that it was an isolated incident or unfounded claim. Additionally, there were warnings from HR that reporting harassment could lead to retaliation, and actual retaliation was commonly reported in the harassment charges. The retaliation described included further harassment related to reporting, terminating the charging party, placing the individual on a performance improvement plan, or increasing efforts toward constructively discharging the employee.

WORK–LIFE BALANCE AND DISABILITY STUDY

The workplace issues identified in the examination of EEOC ADA harassment charge data described above are consistent with findings from our work–life balance and disability study. The study examined balance between participants' work and personal lives in an effort to understand (1) how employees with disabilities effectively manage work and other life demands and (2) what employers can do to support effective work–life balance among workers with disabilities. Because maltreatment in the workplace can adversely affect employees' in both their work and personal lives, this study included questions about workplace harassment and discrimination, as well as about personal strategies and employer practices that support the work–life management of employees with disabilities. In describing their workplace experiences, several participants shared stories of harassment and discrimination, in many cases referring to these situations as "bullying." The role of one's supervisor both in perpetuating bullying behavior and as a critical resource in effective work–life balance was also noted.

An online survey was disseminated between May and June 2014 through multiple organizations with collective access to tens of thousands of people with a wide range of disabilities, via their social media accounts, newsletters, and e-blasts. Eligible respondents met two requirements. They (1) self-identified as a person with a disability and/or chronic health condition, defined in the survey as "including, but not limited to, individuals with a physical or cognitive impairment, mental health condition, chronic health condition (such as heart disease or diabetes), or a vision or hearing impairment" and (2) were competitively employed or had worked competitively within the prior six months.

The survey contained four items related to workplace maltreatment. Respondents were asked whether they had experienced or witnessed workplace harassment or discrimination during the past 12 months, and, if so, to describe those experiences. The language for these questions was adapted from a bullying questionnaire developed by Einarsen, Raknes, and Matthiesen (1994). The survey can be accessed at http://bit.ly/2HnexEV.

Quantitative analysis included descriptive statistics, such as means, as well as exploration of relationships via correlation. Qualitative analysis of open-ended responses involved two researchers separately reviewing and coding the data, coming to consensus about the key themes and codes, and then reviewing these with a third researcher to ensure reasonableness of interpretation (Creswell 2007).

Five hundred sixty-one individuals met the screening criteria and responded to the survey. Ninety-four percent of respondents were in regular, permanent employment (full or part time). Respondents worked in a variety of job fields, most commonly community and social service (27%). On average, they worked 39 hours per week, although some worked as few as seven hours and others reported working 70 hours or more per week.

Seventy percent of respondents were female. The average age was 49 with a range from 20 to 79 years old. In general, they were highly educated (69% had a bachelor's degree or higher), White (68%), married/partnered (57%), and living with no minor children in the home (71%). The majority (59%) reported a pre-tax income of less than $75,000 per year, and 40% reported earning less than $50,000 annually.

The most frequently reported disability type was Other (Figure 3, next page). Some individuals who selected Other provided information about specific conditions (e.g., lupus, MS, diabetes), which would qualify for protections under the ADA but that did not obviously align with the standardized disability questions. The most common specific disability types reported were Ambulatory (47%) and Mental/ Emotional (40%). Seventy percent of respondents reported having two or more types of disability.

Key Findings Related to Harassment/Discrimination Questions

Twenty-three percent of survey respondents reported having personally experienced workplace harassment/discrimination in the previous 12 months, and 31% had witnessed others being harassed/discriminated against. Sixteen percent reported both having experienced and witnessed harassment/discrimination.

Personally experiencing harassment/discrimination was related to higher levels of work–life conflict (an indication of lower work–life balance), poorer manager–

FIGURE 3
Disability Types as Reported by Survey Respondents

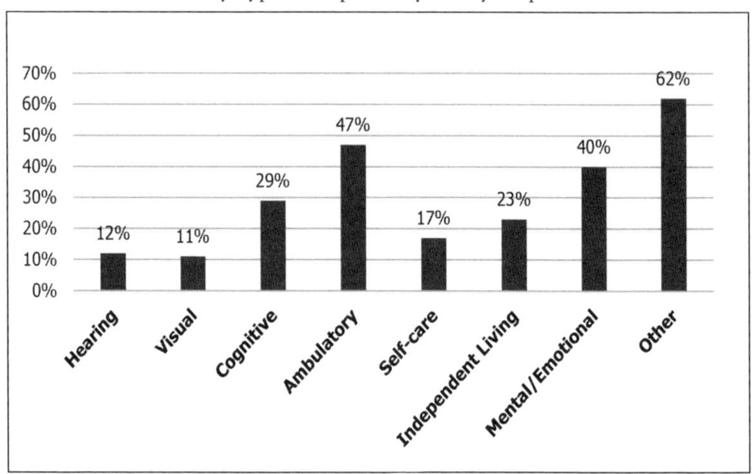

Source: Work–Life Balance and Disability Study (2014), Cornell University Yang-Tan Institute on Employment and Disability.

subordinate relationships, and a less inclusive workplace climate. Experiencing harassment/discrimination was also related to a higher reported turnover intention. A similar pattern was observed for individuals who had witnessed, but not personally experienced, harassment/discrimination.

Open-ended survey questions asked respondents to describe personal experiences of harassment/discrimination, as well as those they had witnessed. They described experiences involving both co-workers and supervisors, sometimes related to characteristics other than disability, including age, gender, sexual orientation, and religion. Their stories featured both subtle and more overt cases of harassment/discrimination. Ninety-seven respondents described a personal experience, and 113 wrote about those they had witnessed. Although not all would necessarily meet the legal definition of harassment, understanding behaviors that employees perceive to be harassing is important for employers who wish to maintain employee engagement and minimize the possibility of employees filing a charge. Several themes, consistent with the literature on workplace bullying and harassment, and similar to the themes identified in the EEOC charge data study, were noted within the work–life balance study respondents' descriptions, as follows.

Marginalization or Exclusion

Respondents described a range of ways in which they had been excluded and marginalized in the workplace, some of which could have a direct impact on job performance. Some respondents reported feeling that these were deliberate attempts to make the workplace unpleasant, at times as part of a perceived effort to encourage them to quit.

> "I have been moved to an undesirable location where I do not have the proper equipment for my job in an attempt to hide me! Other associates have been told not to talk to me."

> "I am underutilized and left out of projects and meetings and left to do menial work. I feel excluded."

> "I am only rarely invited to offsite meetings under the assumption that my wheelchair is why."

Lack of Professional Opportunities

Some respondents described feeling excluded from opportunities for advancement and professional development. In some cases, respondents reported feeling it was a direct result of disability-based discrimination. They described feeling devalued. Denial of such opportunities can adversely impact job performance as well as co-worker relationships, especially if colleagues view the person as not maintaining skills for current job expectations and feel that they need to "pick up the slack" because of the person's perceived lack of competence.

> "It isn't easy to define. But I have discovered that I am paid less than others who have less experience, knowledge, and skills than me.... I see others developing plans to get promoted, and I have tried to develop plans, but they are ignored."

> "I have been discriminated against because of my disability. I was not selected for promotion due to it, and I am losing my position due to it as well."

> "Lack of participation in professional development activities, strategic planning within the unit, and communication regarding strategic and operational directions taken by the unit. Lack of promotion, pay/salary increases."

Forced Disclosure/Confidentiality Breach

Respondents also spoke about the challenges of maintaining privacy about their disability/medical condition and related accommodations in the workplace. At times supervisors or HR staff inappropriately disclosed personal information about respondents to others, or requested an unnecessary amount of detail about a disability or accommodation request. In other cases, the visible nature of disability or provision of accommodation exposed respondents to invasive questions or harassment from co-workers. When there is a lack of trust and perceived support, workers may be reluctant to disclose a disability and may make considerable effort to minimize the influence that their disability has in the workplace. As a result, they may not seek accommodations that could enable them to perform essential job functions and avoid secondary health conditions, potentially reducing their job tenure and overall well-being.

> "More than once, details of an accommodation request were shared with people who did not need to know."

> "Forced to disclose why I have a state-issued handicap hang tag issued to me because I have an invisible disability and appear to look 'normal.' I was never so humiliated. Demanded I bring medical proof, and I've had this hang tag for over ten years and only worked at this job three weeks."

> "There is a person in my office who questions my schedule and what I do with my time. This person is not aware of any accommodations I may have and is harassing me about how I come and go. I am feeling like I am going to be forced to disclose my health impairment to get this person off of focusing on my coming and going."

Difficulty Getting Needed Accommodations

Among respondents who requested workplace accommodations, some encountered issues in obtaining and/or maintaining the accommodation. Some respondents described workplaces in which there was no policy for requesting an accommodation, or if there was a policy, it was disregarded. Others described encountering a general resistance to providing any accommodation at all. The effort of requesting an accommodation and then needing to extensively follow up represents a type of emotional labor (Hochschild 1983) that individuals with disabilities are expected to perform in addition to their job duties. Such expectations may affect the time and energy an employee can give to the job for which they were hired, thus, leaving the employee susceptible to being viewed as less capable than nondisabled colleagues.

> "[The] department did not want to pay for handicapped parking and still harasses me when I need a new book of temporary [parking] permits. In part, they didn't read the policy and think it is beneath them to deal with such trivia."

> "I had accommodations in place for two months. The new supervisor decided to 'revisit' the accommodations because she didn't agree with them. We're in year three of the first EEOC complaint, eight months into second EEOC complaint. There are no written policies or procedures for my position, so the administration feels they are free to make up rules that are contrary to the [F]MLA" [referring to the Family Medical Leave Act].

Hostile Interaction

Some respondents described hostile workplaces where superiors and, to a lesser extent, co-workers and/or subordinates, treated them with contempt or disregard, leading to issues with work performance and stress. Supervisors play a critical role in creating and maintaining workplace culture and climate. When their inappropriate behaviors go unchecked, others may actively participate in the harassment or support it by remaining silent.

> "One of the employees in a management position would yell at me in front of other employees and never listen to what my concerns were."
>
> "One of the staff I supervise has treated me with contempt and disregard on the basis of my disability, eroding the supervisor–staff relationship."
>
> "It is borderline harassment. My supervisor keeps things just this side of legal. She just makes the work situation difficult with lots of little things like a negative comment here or there, not approving things as quickly as she would for other co-workers, etc. It just creates a stressful and uncomfortable work environment for me, and I am in constant fear of losing my job."

As in the EEOC ADA harassment charge study, respondents in the work–life balance study reported being berated in front of others, excluded from work functions, denied accommodations, forced to disclose disability, and devalued as evidenced by lesser pay and fewer opportunities for professional development than their colleagues without disabilities. Some respondents in the work–life balance study described their experiences as having been "bullied," although this term was not used in the survey questions. Respondents who used the term "bully/bullying" were not specific in defining what they meant; however, their comments included such statements as "bullying is actually supported as a method to 'get the work done'" and "some faculty feel it is okay to bully staff." Again, this suggests that workplace bullying is more a matter of workplace culture than an issue among individual employees.

The high level of academic attainment among our survey respondents may help to explain the prevalence of reported harassment, as recent research suggests that bullies may be threatened by high performers (e.g., Khan, Moss, Quratulain, and Hameed 2016). As a group, more highly educated employees perform better at core job tasks and at citizenship behaviors such as helping and getting along with others, as well as adhering to workplace safety and showing other positive workplace behaviors (Johnson and Elder 2002; Ng and Feldman 2009). When employees with disabilities perform as well or better than their nondisabled colleagues and maintain positive standing within the workplace community "despite their disabilities," other workers may be concerned that this reflects poorly on their own job performance and interpersonal challenges they may have with colleagues.

The high prevalence of harassment reported by the work–life balance study respondents who had relatively high levels of educational attainment may further be explained by the fact that most were employed within the social service field and may therefore have been more familiar with their rights and more comfortable advocating for themselves. Meanwhile, the charge data from the EEOC study suggest that individuals in occupations typically requiring higher levels of education are less likely to file a charge citing harassment. Harassment in the workplace is clearly an issue for people with disabilities, and addressing the issue is challenging. Deciding whether to report a perpetrator's unwelcome behaviors to the employer and/or EEOC requires an employee to weigh the potential costs and benefits, and these may differ depending on the individual's occupation, disability, financial needs, and other factors.

CONCLUSION

There is increasing evidence of the pervasiveness of workplace bullying and harassment. The literature on this topic is still relatively new, and little is known about the workplace bullying experienced by people with disabilities. While the findings from these two studies have limitations, they align with and extend the previous research described in our introduction. They provide context for our understanding of the workplace harassment experienced by individuals like Cedric, and they help to illuminate some of the unique challenges and concerns workers with disabilities may have when it comes to reporting situations of bullying and harassment. Further, our studies add to evidence of the ways in which failure to address issues of workplace bullying and harassment can negatively impact organizations. Based on the findings of our studies and the other research we have cited, we offer the following suggestions for addressing bullying and harassment and creating more welcoming and inclusive workplaces.

Lead by Example

Expect company leadership to demonstrate good social intelligence and communication skills. When managers and supervisors model positive, respectful behaviors that take into account the needs and diverse backgrounds of employees, they set a vital example about the value of taking time to listen to and get to know workplace colleagues.

Educate Everyone

Educate staff at all levels about the potential impact and consequences of unwelcome behaviors. Bullying needs to be understood as a form of harassment with consequences that can be as detrimental as workplace sexual harassment. Helping all employees to see the ways that such behaviors adversely affect individuals and organizations provides an opportunity to move thinking away from bullying as an issue between individual employees and to foster a commitment to more positive workplace culture.

Expect Civility

Create civility codes and expect all to adhere to them. In the 2016 Civility in America poll, 95% of respondents said civility is a problem, with nearly three quarters (74%) saying civility has declined in the past few years. All employees should be expected to behave in ways that promote civility, fairness, and inclusion. Abusive behavior, in any form, should not be tolerated (Weber Shandwick 2018).

Respond Quickly

When maltreatment is reported and abusive situations do arise, they need to be handled swiftly. Quick action will demonstrate that the claims of targeted employees will be taken seriously, which could enhance the likelihood of disclosing feelings of bullying and harassment sooner, potentially decreasing the negative impact on the individual and the organization, which has a legal obligation to address situations of known harassment.

Terminate If Necessary

Be willing to terminate employees who do not meet these expectations. Holding top leadership and senior staff to the same standards of civility and subjecting them to the same consequences when the expectations are not met sends a clear message of the organization's commitment to a safe, healthy, and welcoming workplace.

Do Not Rely on Traditional Training

As Carpello (2017) cautions, "Mandated training is basically an illustration or two of bullying, and all that's doing is teaching people how to bully." Rather, organizations need to acknowledge bullying as a form of harassment and train leadership to deal with it in the workplace. Manners and Cates (2016) recommend that employees be offered effective leadership training, enabling them to feel comfortable and empowered to address any issues that arise, and also, importantly, to be able to recognize bullying behaviors that they themselves may practice. To enhance the workplace inclusion of people with disabilities, training should include exploration of implicit bias; ableism as evidenced in policies, practices, and physical design of workspaces; and increased understanding of the purpose and implementation of the ADA, as well as other anti-discrimination legislation.

Further, findings of the two Cornell studies we have highlighted in this chapter point to the need for training that considers the changing demographics of the US workforce. Given that members of marginalized groups are reportedly harassed more often, as the workforce becomes more diverse it is critical for employers to understand how the intersection of disability with other identities (e.g., gender identity, race, age, and sexual orientation) influences workplace experiences.

Bullying and harassment are significant concerns in the US workplace. Employees who are members of historically marginalized groups, such as individuals with disabilities, are more likely to be targets of these unwelcome behaviors. This phenomenon can negatively impact individuals' physical, emotional, and financial well-being. To maintain healthy, safe, and inclusive workplaces, employers should hold all employees to standards of civility and be prepared to take quick, decisive action when instances of maltreatment are observed or reported.

ACKNOWLEDGMENTS

Portions of the contents of this chapter were developed under two grants from the National Institute on Disability, Independent Living, and Rehabilitation Research (NIDILRR) to Cornell University. One grant funds the Northeast ADA Center (grant number 90DP0088-01-00), which is authorized by NIDILRR to provide information, materials, and technical assistance to individuals and entities that are covered by the ADA. The second grant (grant number 90IF0051-01-00) funded a research project entitled, "Getting and Keeping People with Disabilities in the Workforce: Negotiating Work, Life, and Disability." NIDILRR is a center within the Administration for Community Living (ACL), US Department of Health and Human Services (HHS). The contents of this chapter do not necessarily represent the policy of NIDILRR, ACL, or HHS and should not be assumed as endorsement by the federal government.

The discrimination charge data statistics and summaries reported in this chapter are derived from data files obtained under an agreement from the US Equal Employment Opportunity Commission. Summaries of data are based on our aggregations and do not represent the EEOC's official aggregation of the data.

The authors would like to acknowledge Moriah Willow, social scientist and statistician at the US Equal Opportunity Commission, for assistance in obtaining and working with these data.

The authors would like to acknowledge the thoughtful comments of Angela Winfield, associate vice president for inclusion and workforce diversity, Cornell University; and James Gross, professor of labor relations, law, and history, Cornell University, on an earlier draft of this chapter.

REFERENCES

Ariza-Montes, Antonio, Juan M. Arjona-Fuentes, Rob Law, and Heesup Han. 2017. "Incidence of Workplace Bullying Among Hospitality Employees." *International Journal of Contemporary Hospitality Management* 29 (4): 1116–1132. doi:10.1108/IJCHM-09-2015-0471

Branch, Sara, and Jane Murray. 2015. "Workplace Bullying. Is Lack of Understanding the Reason for Inaction?" *Organizational Dynamics* 44 (4): 287–295. doi:10.1016/j.orgdyn.2015.09.006

CareerBuilder. 2012 (Aug. 29). "CareerBuilder Study Finds More Workers Feeling Bullied in the Workplace." https://cb.com/2Hh52qK

Carpello, Alexis. 2017 (Nov. 13). "Bullying Continues to Be a Pervasive Threat in the Workplace." *Workforce*. http://bit.ly/2HmwvHx

Carter, Bonnie Bell, and Vicky G. Spencer. 2006. "The Fear Factor: Bullying and Students with Disabilities." *International Journal of Special Education* 21 (1): 11–23. http://bit.ly/2HjHD5W

Creswell, John W. 2007. *Qualitative Inquiry & Research Design: Choosing Among Five Approaches* (2nd ed.). Thousand Oaks, CA: Sage.

Duffy, Maureen, and Len Sperry. 2007. "Workplace Mobbing: Individual and Family Health Consequences." *The Family Journal* 15 (4): 398–404. doi:10.1177/1066480707305069

Einarsen, S., B.I. Raknes, and S.B. Matthiesen. 1994. "Bullying and Harassment at Work and Their Relationships to Work Environment Quality: An Exploratory Study." *European Work and Organizational Psychologist* 4 (4): 381–401.

Einarsen, Staale, Helge Hoel, Dieter Zapf, and C.L. Cooper. 2011. "The Concept of Bullying and Harassment at Work: The European Tradition." In *Bullying and Harassment in the Workplace: Developments in Theory, Research, and Practice*, edited by S. Einarsen, H. Hoel, D. Zapf, and C.L. Cooper, pp. 3–40. Boca Raton, FL: CRC.

Eisenberg, M.E., A.L. Gower, B.J. McMorris, and M.M. Bucchianeri. 2015. "Vulnerable Bullies: Perpetration of Peer Harassment Among Youths Across Sexual Orientation, Weight, and Disability Status." *American Journal of Public Health* 105 (9): 1784–1791.

Elame, Esoh. 2013. *Discriminatory Bullying: A New Intercultural Challenge*. New York, NY: Springer.

Feldblum, Chai, and Victoria A. Lipnic. 2016. "U.S. Equal Employment Opportunity Commission Select Task Force on the Study of Harassment in the Workplace: Report of Co-Chairs." Washington, DC: US Equal Opportunity Employment Commission. http://bit.ly/2RS09IU

Feuerstein, M., A.K. Gehrke, B.T. McMahon, and M.C. McMahon. 2017. "Challenges Persist Under Americans with Disabilities Amendments Act: How Can Oncology Providers Help?" *Journal of Oncology Practice* 13 (6): e543–e551. doi:10.1200/JOP.2016.016758

Feuerstein, Michael, Gina M. Luff, Cherise B. Harrington, and Cara H. Olsen. 2007. "Pattern of Workplace Disputes in Cancer Survivors: A Population Study of ADA Claims." *Journal of Cancer Survivorship* 1 (3): 185–192.

Goffman, Erving. 1959. *The Presentation of Self in Everyday Life*. Garden City, NY: Doubleday.

Greenhaus, J.H., J.C. Ziegert, and T.D. Allen. 2012. "When Family-Supportive Supervision Matters: Relations Between Multiple Sources of Support and Work–Family Balance." *Journal of Vocational Behavior* 80 (2): 266–275.

Hansen, Ase Marie, Annie Hogh, Roger Persson, Björn Karlson, Anne Helene Garde, and Palle Ørbæk. 2006. "Bullying at Work, Health Outcomes, and Physiological Stress Response." *Journal of Psychosomatic Research* 60 (1): 63–72. doi:10.1016/j.jpsychores.2005.06.078

Hochschild, A.R. 1983. *The Managed Heart: Commercialization of Human Feeling*. Berkeley, CA: University of California Press.

Hollis, Leah P. 2015. "Bully University? The Cost of Workplace Bullying and Employee Disengagement in American Higher Education. *SAGE Open*. doi:10.1177/2158244015589997

Hsieh, Hsiu-Fang, and Sarah E. Shannon. 2005. "Three Approaches to Qualitative Content Analysis." *Qualitative Health Research* 15 (9): 1277–1288. doi:10.1177/1049732305276687

Johnson, M.K., and G.H. Elder Jr. 2002. "Educational Pathways and Work Value Trajectories." *Sociological Perspectives* 45 (2): 113–138. doi:10.1525/sop.2002.45.2.113

Kearl, Holly. 2018. "The Facts Behind the #metoo Movement: A National Study on Sexual Harassment and Assault." Reston, VA: Stop Street Harassment. http://bit.ly/2RV4vPr

Khan, Abdul Karim, Sherry Moss, Samina Quratulain, and Imran Hameed. 2016. "When and How Subordinate Performance Leads to Abusive Supervision." *Journal of Management* 44 (7): 2801–2826. doi:10.1177/0149206316653930

Leymann, H. 1990. "Mobbing and Psychological Terror at Workplaces." *Violence and Victims* 5 (2): 119–126.

Manners, Ian, and Steven Cates. 2016. "Bullying in the Workplace: Does It Exist in United States Organizations?" *International Journal of Business and Public Administration* 13 (2): 99–114.

Mattice, Catherine M. 2018. "Bullying … Harassment … Violence: Key Workplace Differences Explained." Arlington, VA: International Employee Assistance Professionals Association. http://bit.ly/2RS0jQw

Mattice, Catherine M., and Alisa A. Shorago. 2015. "Bullying Versus Harassment: Understanding the Difference and the Legal Significance for Employers." HR WebAdvisor Webinar. DKG Media.

McTernan, Wesley P., Maureen F. Dollard, and Anthony D. LaMontagne. 2013. "Depression in the Workplace: An Economic Cost Analysis of Depression-Related Productivity Loss Attributable to Job Strain and Bullying." *Work and Stress* 27 (4): 321–338. doi:10.1080/02678373.2013.846948

Morrall, Stephen, and Charles Urquhart. 2004. "Bullying and Harassment in the Workplace." *Legal Information Management* 4 (3): 164–167. doi:10.1017/S1472669604001719

Murphy v. BeavEx, Inc. 2008. 544 F. Supp. 2d 139. Dist. Court, D. Connecticut.

Namie, Gary. 2011. "The WBI Website 2011 Instant Poll–B: Post-Bullying Financial Woes for Bullied Targets Post-Bullying." Clarkston, WA: Workplace Bullying Institute. http://bit.ly/2RYw5LF

Namie, Gary. 2014. "2014 WBI U.S. Workplace Bullying Survey." Clarkston, WA: Workplace Bullying Institute. http://bit.ly/2S1zGse

Namie, Gary, and Pamela E. Lutgen-Sandvik. 2010. "Active and Passive Accomplices: The Communal Character of Workplace Bullying." *International Journal of Communication* 4: 343–373. doi:10.1108/13527600710745723

National Center for Educational Statistics. 2017. "Indicator 11: Bullying at School and Cyberbullying Anywhere." *Indicators of School Crime and Safety*. http://bit.ly/2Hm8YEN

Nauen, Rachel. 2017 (Oct. 19). "3 in 10 Workers Report Feeling Bullied at Work." *CareerBuilder*. https://cb.com/2Hlc6AE

Ng, Thomas W.H., and Daniel C. Feldman. 2009. "How Broadly Does Education Contribute to Job Performance?" *Personnel Psychology* 62: 89–134. http://bit.ly/2RVuNkA

Nielsen, Morten Birkeland, Stig Berge Matthiesen, and Ståle Einarsen. 2010. "The Impact of Methodological Moderators on Prevalence Rates of Workplace Bullying. A Meta-Analysis." *Journal of Occupational and Organizational Psychology* 83 (4): 955–979. doi:10.1348/096317909X481256

Notelaers, Guy, Jeroen K. Vermunt, Elfi Baillien, Ståle Einarsen, and Hans De Witte. 2011. "Exploring Risk Groups Workplace Bullying with Categorical Data." *Industrial Health* 49 (1): 73–88. doi:10.2486/indhealth.MS1155

Shaw, L.R., F. Chan, and B.T. McMahon. 2012. "Intersectionality and Disability Harassment: The Interactive Effects of Disability, Race, Age, and Gender." *Rehabilitation Counseling Bulletin* 55 (2): 82–91. doi:10.1177/0034355211431167

Shigaki, C.L., K.M. Anderson, C.L. Howald, L. Henson, and B. Gregg. 2012. "Disability on Campus: A Perspective from Faculty and Staff." *Work* 42 (4): 559–571.

Society for Human Resource Management (SHRM). 2018. "Harassment-Free Workplace Series: A Focus on Sexual Harassment." Alexandria, VA: Society for Human Resource Management. http://bit.ly/2RPEAc3

Sperry, Len, and Maureen Duffy. 2009. "Workplace Mobbing: Family Dynamics and Therapeutic Considerations." *American Journal of Family Therapy* 37 (5): 433–442. doi:10.1080/01926180902945756

Taylor, Barry C. 2008. "Disability Harassment, Retaliation, and Discipline: Three Emerging ADA Issues." *Legal Briefings*. Chicago, IL: DBTAC Great Lakes ADA Center.

Taylor, Barry. 2016. "The Americans with Disabilities Act: What the Legal Research Reveals About Trends and Unanticipated Applications of the Law." Webcast. ADA National Network. http://bit.ly/2S3BL7n

US Census Bureau. 2018. "American Community Survey, 2010–2014 American Community Survey 5-Year Estimates, Table S1811." Calculations by S. von Schrader using American FactFinder. Washington, DC: US Census Bureau. http://factfinder.census.gov

US Equal Employment Opportunity Commission (US EEOC). No date. "Coverage." Washington, DC: US Equal Employment Opportunity Commission. http://bit.ly/2HpsO25

US Equal Employment Opportunity Commission (US EEOC). No date. "Facts About Retaliation." http://bit.ly/2YuQDeg

US Equal Employment Opportunity Commission (US EEOC). No date. "Harassment." Washington, DC: US Equal Employment Opportunity Commission. http://bit.ly/2RWD1Jc

US Occupational Safety and Health Administration (US OSHA). No date. "Workplace Violence." Washington, DC: US Occupational Safety and Health Administration. http://bit.ly/2RVIOP3

Vega, Gina, and Debra R. Comer. 2005. "Sticks and Stones May Break Your Bones, but Words Can Break Your Spirit: Bullying in the Workplace." *Journal of Business Ethics* 58 (1): 101–109. doi:10.1007/s10551-005-1422-7

Vickers, Margaret H. 2017. "Dark Secrets and Impression Management: Workplace Masks of People with Multiple Sclerosis (MS)." *Employee Responsibilities and Rights Journal* 29 (4): 175–195. doi:10.1007/s10672-017-9295-3

von Schrader, Sarah, and Zafar E. Nazarov. 2016. "Trends and Patterns in Age Discrimination in Employment Act (ADEA) Charges." *Research on Aging* 38 (5): 580–601. doi:10.1177/0164027515593989

Wall, Alison E., Robert A. Smith, and Omid Nodoushani. 2017. "Workplace Bullying: A Growing Epidemic." *Competition Forum* 15 (2): 251–258.

Weber Shandwick. 2018. "Civility in America VII: The State of Civility." http://bit.ly/2RTOVDQ

Workplace Bullying Institute. 2012. "History of the Workplace Bullying Institute." http://bit.ly/2RYZK7A

Workplace Bullying Institute. 2013. "Bullying Is Workplace Violence." http://bit.ly/2RUQLUY

Xu, Tianwei, L.L. Magnusson Hanson, T. Lange, L. Starkopf, H. Westerlund, I.E.H. Madsen, R. Rugulies, J. Pentii, S. Stenhold, J. Vahtera, A.M. Hansen, M. Kivimäki, and N.H. Rod. 2017. "Workplace Bullying and Violence as Risk Factors for Type 2 Diabetes: A Multicohort Study and Meta-Analysis." *Diabetologia* 61 (1): 1–9. doi:10.1007/s00125-017-4480-3

Yamada, David C. 1999. "The Phenomenon of Workplace Bullying and the Need for Status-Blind Hostile Work Environment Protection." *Georgetown Law Journal* 88 (3).

Yamada, David. 2010. "Workplace Bullying and American Employment Law: A Ten-Year Progress Report and Assessment." *Comparative Labor Law and Policy Journal* 32 (1): 251–284. http://bit.ly/2YyUeIp

Chapter 6

Welcoming (All) Veterans into Our Workplaces: The Employment of Veterans with Disabilities

Hannah Rudstam
Cornell University

James Whitcomb
Lorin Obler
US Government Accountability Office[1]

INTRODUCTION

Over the past two decades, employers have been eager to welcome veterans into their workforce, making special efforts to hire and retain veteran employees. Veterans bring significant value to a workplace: skills, discipline, loyalty, and teamwork. This is as true for veterans with disabilities as it is for those without. Unfortunately, though, for nearly half of recently returned Gulf War Era II veterans and for about one quarter of all veterans with a service-connected disability (US Bureau of Labor Statistics 2019; Erickson, Lee, and von Schrader 2017), the "Veterans Are Welcome" banners in the workplace have too often been lowered. For employers, this means a lost opportunity to tap into a significant source of skilled talent. For veterans with disabilities, this means a lost opportunity to work—a loss that takes both a financial and an emotional toll. Work is not just about a paycheck. For veterans with disabilities (and for others), work is an integral part of well-being during transition and beyond (Ainspan 2011; Bullock, Braud, Andrews, and Phillips 2009; Cohen, Suri, Amick, and Yan 2013; Kukla, Rattray, and Salyers 2015; Stern 2017).

Labor and employment relations (LER) practitioners are positioned to play a key role in mediating successful employment outcomes for veterans with disabilities. Being effective in this role involves understanding the range of employment issues facing veterans with disabilities. Often, these issues are not just related to veterans' impairments but are also rooted in how disability is viewed by others, particularly by employers. The ability of LER practitioners to balance the perspectives of both employers and workers makes them uniquely positioned to navigate the broad range of employment barriers facing veterans with disabilities.

The purpose of this chapter is to provide LER practitioners with the knowledge needed to be effective in improving employment outcomes for veterans with disabilities. To do this, we will address three areas: human, legal, and practical.

Human issues focus on the daily struggles faced by veterans with disabilities and the implications of these struggles for workplace policies. Legal issues revolve around the laws and programs for veterans with disabilities. Finally, practical considerations focus on creating workplace cultures and sustainable practices that truly welcome all veterans, including those with disabilities. To set the stage, we begin with a discussion of the prevalence and demographic findings on veterans with disabilities.

VETERANS, DISABILITY, AND EMPLOYMENT: AN OVERVIEW

In 2018, there were 19.2 million veterans over the age of 18 living in the United States, about 10% of whom were women (US Bureau of Labor Statistics 2019). This includes veterans who served during World War II, the Korean War, the Vietnam Engagement, Gulf War Era I (after August 1990 to August 2001), Gulf War Era II (after September 2001), and other service eras. In 2018, there were 4.1 million Gulf War Era II veterans over the age of 18 in the United States, about 17% of whom were women (US Bureau of Labor Statistics 2019).

The veteran population as a whole is aging, with 9.2 million veterans over age 65 in 2017 (US Census Bureau 2018). The education levels of veterans are similar to those of the overall population. In 2017, about 29% of veterans 25 years or older had completed at least a bachelor's degree compared with about 32% of nonveterans (US Census Bureau 2018).

Estimates of the prevalence of disability among veterans can vary considerably for several reasons. First, different data collection efforts use different definitions of disability, resulting in markedly different estimations of the number of veterans with a disability. For example, the definition of disability under the Americans with Disabilities Act Amendments Act (ADAAA) is different from the definition used by the US Department of Veterans Affairs (DVA) to calculate rates for veterans' disability compensation. Second, disability rates can vary depending on the age range included in the data. If individuals over age 65 are included, disability rates can be higher because of the higher prevalence of disability among older adults (von Schrader, Bruyère, Malzer, and Erickson 2013). Third, disability rates can vary depending on the point at which the data were collected in the veteran's transition to civilian life. Many veterans may not realize they have a disability immediately after ending their service, so data collected immediately upon discharge might not capture disabilities that are in the process of unfolding.

Fourth, most veteran disability data collection efforts have tended to underreport three of the most common types of disabilities among returning veterans: post-traumatic stress disorder (PTSD),[2] closed-head traumatic brain injury (TBI), and depression (Tanielan and Jaycox 2008). As will be discussed, underreporting is likely due to several reasons, such as dismissing subtle symptoms, fear of stigma, and the delayed onset of symptoms (Griffin and Stein 2015;

Tanielan and Jaycox 2008). Finally, veterans' disabilities can be either service connected (resulting from an injury or disease acquired or aggravated during military service) or unconnected to their military service. The number of veterans with *any* disability, of course, will be considerably higher than those with only service-connected disabilities.

Disability Rates Among Veterans

According to the US Census Bureau (2018), 29.5% of working-age veterans surveyed from across all service periods had a disability compared with 14.2% of nonveterans. Among veterans with a service-connected disability, 30.8% had a severe service-connected disability, and 63.7% had a nonsevere disability (Erickson, Lee, and von Schrader 2017).[3] About 5% of veterans with service-connected disabilities did not indicate their level of disability severity.

Forty-one percent of veterans who served during the Gulf War Era II (2001–present) reported a service-connected disability in 2018. Of these, nearly half were rated as having a disability that was close to or above a "severe" disability (at least 60% disabled) (US Bureau of Labor Statistics 2019).

Since 1990, the number of veterans reporting a service-connected disability has risen by about 60% (National Center for Veterans Analysis and Statistics 2014). This increase has been attributed to several factors related to the service experiences of Gulf War Era I and II veterans (Holder 2016; McNally and Frueh 2013; Tanielan and Jaycox 2008). Improved medical care onsite has resulted in more of these veterans surviving their injuries with a disability. The multiple deployments of Gulf War Era I and II veterans put them at greater risk for acquiring a disability. The increased exposure to improvised explosive devices (IEDs) and other explosives has led to more blast injuries among these veterans. Finally, there is a growing awareness among Gulf War Era veterans of the legitimacy of certain types of disabilities, such as PTSD or TBI, resulting in more diagnoses of these disabilities.

Employment of Veterans with Disabilities

Findings on the employment of veterans with disabilities can be confusing. Because age ranges and definitions (e.g., "employed" and "disability") can vary between studies, there is some disparity in the findings about the employment rates of veterans with disabilities. Further, it can be challenging to tease out how service-connected versus nonservice-connected disabilities impact employment outcomes. Whether a disability is service connected is not always straightforward. Disabilities existing prior to service can be exacerbated by a service-connected disability. Also, other disabilities can arise secondarily to a service-connected disability.

With these caveats in mind, we note that studies suggest veterans in general have better employment outcomes than nonveterans. However, the picture is complicated for veterans with disabilities. They face many of the same employment barriers as nonveterans with disabilities, yet veterans with service-connected disabilities tend to have better employment outcomes than either veterans with nonservice-connected disabilities or nonveterans with disabilities.

According to the US Bureau of Labor Statistics (2019), the unemployment rate in 2018 for all veterans of working age with no service-connected disability was 3.5% compared with 5.2% for veterans with a service-connected disability. For Gulf War Era II veterans (served since 2011), the unemployment rate for those without a service-connected disability was 3.3% compared with 5.3% of those with a service-connected disability. Across all periods of service, veterans with service-connected disabilities were more likely than those without those disabilities to work in the public sector. Thirty-two percent of veterans with a service-connected disability worked in the public sector compared with 18% of veterans with no disability.

Other statistics examine how having any disability versus a service-connected disability affects veterans' employment. Consider the following statistics (Erickson 2019):[4]

- 43% of veterans with both service-connected and nonservice-connected disabilities were employed.
- 42% of veterans with only nonservice-connected disability(ies) were employed.
- 76% of veterans with only service-connected disability(ies) were employed.
- 83% of veterans with no disability were employed.

Further studies on the employment outcomes of veterans have shown that veterans with disabilities generally have lower rates of competitive employment, are more likely to work in part-time jobs, and are paid lower wages than veterans without disabilities (American Council on Education 2009; Burnett-Zeigler et al. 2011). Smith (2015) found that disability was more powerful than veteran status in determining veterans' employment rates—that is, veterans and nonveterans with disabilities had similar rates of employment, and both had lower employment rates than either veterans or nonveterans without disabilities.

Veterans' Poverty Rate with Versus Without a Disability

Studies of the employment earnings of veterans with service-connected disabilities who returned to the civilian workforce between 2001 and 2006 showed an aggregate loss of earnings estimated at $556 million during 2010 (Heaton, Loughran, and Miller 2012). These findings were also reflected in Lauer and Houtenville's (2018) data on people from the United States ages 18 through 64:

- poverty rate of individuals without a disability: 6.5%
- poverty rate of civilian veterans without a disability: 6.5%
- poverty rate of individuals with a disability: 26.7%
- poverty rate of civilian veterans with a disability: 17.6%

What about veterans among the working poor?[5] According to the DVA, veterans overall are less likely than nonveterans to be among the working poor. Yet veterans with any disabilities are clearly more likely than veterans without disabilities to be among the working poor. Consider the following statistics from the DVA (2017c):

- 7.9% of veterans with a disability are among the working poor.
- 4.4% of veterans without a disability are among the working poor.
- 16.0% of nonveterans with a disability are among the working poor.
- 8.9% of nonveterans without a disability are among the working poor.

Several factors might explain why veterans generally fare better than the nonveteran population as far as their rates of being among those in poverty and the working poor. As will be discussed later, unlike civilians with nonservice-connected disabilities, veterans with service-connected disabilities can, with a few exceptions, get income from disability compensation whether or not they have employment earnings. Further, eligible veterans living in poverty can receive a veterans' low-income pension, and veterans who have any type of total or permanent disability qualify for that pension (USA.gov 2019). With this additional income, veterans with disabilities are more likely than nonveterans without disabilities to be above the poverty line. Also, veterans with service-connected disabilities are entitled to vocational rehabilitation counseling services, which could lead to improved employment earnings. Finally, veterans with disabilities have better access to services, such as healthcare and higher education, than do nonveterans with disabilities. These factors and others (e.g., aging demographics) could explain the lower number of veterans with disabilities among the working poor.

Though veterans generally have better economic and employment outcomes than nonveterans, veterans with disabilities do not fare as well as those without disabilities. Veterans with disabilities continue to face barriers to their economic and employment lives that are not faced by those without disabilities. What does research tell us about the nature of these barriers?

Where Has Research Attention Been Focused?

The bulk of attention devoted to understanding the employment rates of veterans with disabilities tends to be focused on issues related to veterans themselves, such as their willingness to work, the functional limitations of their disabilities, or the effectiveness of services designed to provide support to these veterans (Stern 2017). Though these are important issues, a key question has not been given sufficient attention: What role does disability discrimination play in the employment outcomes of veterans with disabilities? Veterans with disabilities fear job discrimination and report experiencing it (Cohen, Suri, Amick, and Yan 2013; Rudstam, Streeter-Wilson, and Gower 2012, Stern 2017; Stone and Stone 2015). Yet there are surprisingly few studies focused on how and why employment discrimination against veterans with disabilities occurs (Stern 2017).

The lack of research attention to employment discrimination issues for veterans with disabilities can be evidenced by a search for peer-based journal articles over the past ten years. For example, a recent ProQuest search of peer-reviewed articles using the search terms "veterans" and "disability(ies)" yielded 57 articles. A fully equivalent search adding the search term "employment" yielded 13 articles. Another fully equivalent search adding the search term "discrimination" yielded no articles.

There could be several reasons for the lack of attention to the role of disability-based job discrimination in veterans' employment outcomes. First, for reasons already discussed, veterans' disability rates can be difficult to describe accurately, and data analysis can be challenging on several levels. Second, there may be an implicit assumption that veterans with disabilities do not need to work because they get financial support from the DVA Disability Compensation Program (described below). The clear majority of veterans, however, do need to work even if they receive disability compensation. For example, in 2017, disability compensation for a veteran with no dependents and a 30% disabled rating was about $417 a month. The rate for a veteran with no dependents and a 50% disabled rating was about $855 month (US Department of Veterans Affairs 2017a). Hence, veterans with service-connected disabilities most often do need to work. Third, researching employers' perceptions and beliefs toward veterans with disabilities can be challenging. Many employers are unwilling to express negative perceptions of veterans with disabilities, *even if* these tacit perceptions might be driving their decisions around recruiting, hiring, and retaining these veterans. The failure to meaningfully include disability discrimination in the research conversation on the employment of veterans with disabilities has weakened the power of our efforts to impact employment outcomes for veterans with disabilities.

VETERANS WORKING WITH A DISABILITY: THE HUMAN EXPERIENCE

While many veterans have successfully transitioned to civilian life, others have experienced difficulties. The sentiments of Vincent Vargas on the experience of transitioning from military to civilian life has been echoed by other veterans: "War is ugly, but it's not the worst part of military service. I like to explain war as the 'easy' part. The 'hard' part is getting out" (Vargas 2017).

Tragically, too many veterans do not win this second battle. After adjusting for differences in age and gender, the suicide rate for veteran adults in 2016 was 22% higher for veterans than for nonveterans (US Department of Veterans Affairs 2017b).

Having a job can be an important part of the healing process for veterans with disabilities. Work is not just about making money; it is also about gaining a sense of accomplishment, connecting with others, and being driven by a purpose. Veterans with disabilities who are employed have better social relationships and community participation than similarly situated veterans who are not working (Bullock, Braud, Andrews, and Phillips 2009; Griffin and Stein 2015; Ottomanelli, Barnet, and Goetz 2013; Ownsworth and McKenna 2004).

The Nature of Veterans' Disabilities

The types of disabilities of Gulf War Era I and II veterans are somewhat unique. Nearly 80% of these veterans' service-connected disabilities were the result of blast or explosion injuries, mostly incurred during the detonation of IEDs or roadside bombs (Belmont et al. 2010; Owens et al. 2007). The injuries associated with these and other combat experiences are both obvious and nonobvious. The most frequent types of obvious injuries are orthopedic injuries. About 50% of Gulf War Era veterans' combat-related injuries were orthopedic injuries, including both soft-tissue and musculoskeletal wounds (Belmont et al. 2010; Owens et al. 2007; Peoples, Gerlinger, Craig, and Burlingame 2005). Other injuries of Gulf War Era veterans, however, are less obvious to others and often co-occur with other wounds. These are PTSD, TBI, or depression. The high prevalence of these more subtle injuries has led to their being referred to as the "signature disabilities" of Gulf War Era veterans.

The National Center for PTSD has determined that 11% to 20% of Gulf War Era veterans have PTSD (Gradus 2011). The impairments associated with PTSD vary considerably but can include withdrawal from others, recurring flashbacks of the trauma event, sleep disturbance, agitation, anxiety, emotional numbness, and difficulty concentrating. Many individuals report that these symptoms can be triggered by specific experiences, such as sudden loud noises or being in certain locations. These symptoms can be present immediately after the trauma event or can have delayed onset (National Center for PTSD 2016). PTSD is often successfully treated with a range of different medication and/or therapy options (Hepner et al. 2016).[6]

TBI, also considered one of the signature disabilities, is another leading cause of service-connected disability among veterans. Estimates of TBI frequency among Gulf War Era I and II vets vary, with estimates often ranging from 17% (Lindquist, Love, and Elbogen 2017) to 19% (Tanielan and Jaycox 2008). Often the result of blast injuries, TBI symptoms can be subtle and may not be diagnosed until well after the traumatic event (Lindquist, Love, and Elbogen 2017). TBI frequently co-occurs with other service-connected injuries, such as PTSD. Symptoms of TBI vary according to the nature and severity of the injury and may include headache, dizziness, tinnitus, sleep disturbances, memory problems, or cognitive/attention problems. TBI can change significantly over time, with healing occurring over a period of days or extending into years (Defense and Veterans Brain Injury Center 2018).

Estimates of the signature disabilities vary considerably because they may have delayed onset and are often not diagnosed until well after the trauma event.

Tanielan and Jaycox (2008) estimated that about 30% of veterans transitioning from Gulf War Era service screen positive for at least one of the three signature disabilities, making those among the most prevalent types of disabilities for returning veterans. Unfortunately, these disabilities also tend to be the most stigmatized and misunderstood by others—a factor that clearly impacts the employment lives and decisions of veterans with these disabilities.

Veterans' Employment Dilemmas

Veterans with disabilities (whether service connected or not) experience a number of dilemmas when getting or retaining work. First, their disabilities may be still unfolding while they are transitioning to civilian employment. Hence, these veterans, in addition to dealing with the transition to the civilian workforce, also face the challenge of navigating self-acceptance about having a disability and working through bureaucracies to get services and treatment (Griffin and Stein 2015). Second, the employment challenges of veterans with disabilities are often rooted not in the impairments themselves but in how others view them. Misperception and stigma about disabilities are all too common, particularly for the signature disabilities of PTSD, TBI, and depression. Employer beliefs and misperceptions include the belief that individuals with these disabilities cannot be treated, are to blame for their disability, do not recover, pose a danger to others, have weak personalities, or cannot be effectively accommodated (Rudstam, Gower, and Cook 2012). These misperceptions, though often unspoken, can drive how employers make decisions about veterans with disabilities.

In addition to fueling the decisions that drive employment discrimination, disability stigma affects how veterans with disabilities themselves make decisions about their work lives. Sixty-five percent of veterans with PTSD feared discrimination in hiring, and 57% feared discrimination during employment. Sixty-seven percent of these veterans did not intend to disclose their PTSD during hiring,[7] and 74% would not disclose the condition when employed. Seventy-two percent reported they were unlikely or very unlikely to ask for an accommodation when employed. Veterans with TBI who were surveyed had similar responses. Sixty-five percent said they feared discrimination in hiring, and 57% feared it during employment. Sixty-five percent would not disclose during hiring, and 62% would not disclose while employed. Finally, 83% were either unlikely or very unlikely to ask for an accommodation when employed (Rudstam, Streeter-Wilson, and Gower 2012).

Though veterans with the signature disabilities fear discrimination more than veterans with less stigmatized disabilities, veterans with other service-connected disabilities hold similar fears of discrimination in employment (Stern 2017). Nearly 60% of veterans surveyed who had disabilities other than PTSD or TBI said they had significant fears of disability discrimination in the workplace. Only 35% of these reported that they were likely or very likely to disclose their disability to their employer, and only 27% of veterans surveyed said they were likely or very likely to ask their employer for an accommodation (Rudstam, Streeter-Wilson, and Gower 2012).

How veterans with disabilities make decisions about disclosure and accommodations could, in turn, pose additional workplace problems for themselves. Hiding a disability from co-workers and managers could be stressful. Not coming forward to get an accommodation could impact job performance. Withdrawing from workplace social connections could result in lack of support, less access to knowledge channels in the workplace, and simply being unhappy at work.

Transitioning to the Civilian Workplace for Veterans with Disabilities

The transition from the military to civilian workplace culture can be a challenging adjustment for any veteran but is especially challenging for veterans with service-connected disabilities (Morin 2011). In addition to transitioning from a military to civilian workplace culture, veterans with disabilities may also be adjusting to a disability identity and internalizing the public stigma and misperceptions about their disabilities (Stern 2017). Also, these veterans may not yet fully understand their legal rights as applicants or employees with disabilities, particularly in the areas of disability disclosure and accommodation (Rudstam, Streeter-Wilson, and Gower 2012). Finally, while they are dealing with these challenges, they are also facing the challenges associated with accessing disability-related benefits, treatments, and services for veterans. These and other factors can significantly impact the employment lives of veterans with disabilities and how they make decisions about their work lives.

These findings suggest that veterans with service-connected disabilities can access social, financial, and service resources that are largely not available to people with disabilities in general. Though these resources can improve their employment and economic situations somewhat, much more needs to be done. Veterans with disabilities, whether service connected or not, face the same struggles and barriers to employment that others with disabilities face. Key among these struggles is disability discrimination. Does the law provide any protections to support veterans with disabilities?

LEGAL ISSUES AND SERVICES FOR VETERANS WITH DISABILITIES

A patchwork quilt of laws, programs, and services applies to the employment of veterans with disabilities. Navigating this complex landscape is a significant challenge for employers, service providers, and, most importantly, veterans themselves. No one single law applies specifically to the employment rights of veterans with disabilities. In addition to some state-specific laws, four federal laws apply to the employment of veterans with disabilities: the 2008 ADAAA (Publ. L. 110-325), the Uniformed Services Employment and Re-Employment Rights Act (USERRA), the Family and Medical Leave Act (FMLA), and the Vietnam Era Veterans Employment and Re-Employment Rights Act (VEVRAA).

The ADAAA and Veterans with Disabilities

The ADAAA applies to all individuals with disabilities, including veterans, who qualify for its protections. Veterans who meet the ADAAA definition of disability and are qualified to do the job are given the protections of the ADAAA, regardless of whether the disability is connected to military service. Also, whether an individual meets the definition of disability under the ADAAA is not connected to her or his Veterans Administration (VA) disability compensation rating. (The VA disability compensation program is further discussed below.) In most cases, however, veterans with service-connected disabilities are covered under the ADAAA's protections against disability discrimination.[8]

Research on veterans' understanding of their rights under the ADAAA has shown that veterans with disabilities surveyed were generally aware of the ADAAA but did not fully understand their ADAAA rights around disability disclosure and accommodations (Rudstam, Streeter-Wilson, and Gower 2012). Veterans were confused about several issues related to disability disclosure and the right to a job accommodation. For the many veterans with less obvious disabilities (such as PTSD and TBI), disability disclosure during hiring and employment is a choice. Many veterans did not understand that, even if they did not disclose a disability during hiring, they may still disclose it at any time during their employment. Further, many did not understand that, once employed, they have a right to an accommodation, whether or not they disclosed their disability when hired (Rudstam, Streeter-Wilson, and Gower 2012). Finally, veterans with newly acquired disabilities need to understand that the choice to not disclose a disability during hiring *is not a lie and is not dishonorable.* Rather, it is a choice that the veteran can make for each job application and employment situation. (An exception is that, once he or she is hired, some disability disclosure to the employer will be needed if the veteran chooses to request an accommodation. Both the veteran and employer should understand this disclosure cannot be shared with co-workers.)

Employers also may have areas of confusion around their compliance responsibilities to veterans with disabilities under the ADAAA. Many employers struggle with job design or environment accommodations, particularly for veterans with the signature disabilities of PTSD or TBI.[9] For example, only 30% could identify any accommodation for an employee with TBI (Rudstam, Gower, and Cook 2012). Like veterans, some employers were also confused about the disclosure choice, particularly whether veterans with PTSD must disclose this disability when applying for a job.

USERRA and the Employment of Veterans with Disabilities

USERRA was passed in 1994 to protect all returning veterans (including those with disabilities) from adverse employment impacts of military service. Employers are prohibited from failing to hire a qualified service member due to fear of her or his deployment, terminating an employee who is deployed, reducing the pay or position of a veteran returning to the job after a deployment, failing to provide training to attain job levels or receive promotions that would have been achieved if the employee had not been deployed, or forcing the employee to use vacation time during a deployment.

Enforced by the US Department of Labor, USERRA focuses on all veterans, not just those with disabilities. However, it does go beyond the ADAAA in terms of employer requirements involving veterans with disabilities. Unlike the ADAAA, USERRA applies to all employers, regardless of head count. Compliance requires employers to provide reasonable accommodations (such as changes in equipment, work schedules, or processes) to veterans with a service-connected disability returning to their jobs. If the veteran's service-connected disability is such that she or he can no longer perform the former job, even with an accommodation, USERRA also requires the employer to provide and pay for training or other supports so that the veteran can be placed in a job of equivalent status, seniority, and pay.

FMLA and Veterans with Disabilities

Also enforced by the Department of Labor, the FMLA was passed in 1993 and expanded in 2010 to include provisions for veterans and their families. FMLA requires employers to provide unpaid leave for qualifying family and medical reasons (such as pregnancy, personal illness, or illness of a direct family member) and to protect the jobs of workers who take this leave. An employee whose family includes an active service member is entitled to two types of leave. First, qualifying exigency leave provides up to 12 weeks of job-protected, unpaid leave to deal with the deployment of a family member (such as a spouse, son, daughter, parent, or next of kin). Second, military caregiver leave allows employees to take up to 26 weeks of unpaid, job-protected leave during a single 12-month period to care for a family member who is a veteran with a serious injury or illness. A veteran in this case is defined as a member of the armed forces, including members of the reserves and the National Guard, who was discharged under conditions other than dishonorable.

VEVRAA and Veterans with Disabilities

Passed during the Vietnam Era in 1974, VEVRAA originally focused on protecting returning Vietnam Era veterans from employment discrimination. In later years, however, VEVRAA evolved beyond Vietnam Era veterans and came to be applied to veterans generally. VEVRAA was amended in 2005 and, in 2014, new rules for VEVRAA took effect. Unlike USERRA, which applies to nearly all employers, VEVRAA applies to employers who have contracts/subcontracts of at least $100,000 with the federal government. However, like USERRA, VEVRAA is not limited to veterans with disabilities, though it does include disability issues in its employer requirements.

VEVRAA is enforced by the US Office of Federal Contract Compliance Programs (US OFCCP). A key requirement of VEVRAA is to hold covered employers more accountable for recruiting, hiring, and retaining veterans and, specifically, veterans with disabilities. Veterans covered by VEVRAA were originally defined as Vietnam Era veterans who served any time between February 1961 and May 1975. Later, the definition of veterans covered by VEVRAA expanded to include "protected veterans," which encompassed (among others) those with service-connected disabilities (US OFCCP 2015).

Employers covered under VEVRAA must take several measures to demonstrate their progress in recruiting, hiring, and retaining covered veterans. These measures include (but are not limited to) the following:

- using a hiring benchmark based either on a benchmark set by the OFCCP or a customized benchmark based on the employer's best available data on state/regional percentages
- inviting veteran applicants and employees to voluntarily self-identify as a covered veteran
- using self-identification data to track and report success in recruiting and retaining covered veterans
- partnering with and using recruiting sources that focus on protected veterans
- conducting planned evaluations of efforts taken to recruit and hire qualified protected veterans
- listing job openings in formats that can be accessed by state employment service delivery systems

Since the passage of new VEVRAA rules in 2014, employers have faced some compliance challenges, leading to recent changes in VEVRAA's reporting requirements. For example, the invitation for current employees to self-identify originally included a question asking veterans to identify their specific protected category. This has since been changed to include only a general question about whether the veteran falls under any protected category. Also, the OFCCP annually changes the benchmark numbers for veteran hiring and employment, requiring employers to stay updated on these changes. Finally, more employer supports have been put into place for compliance with VEVRAA, such as guidance on conducting internal evaluations of veteran recruitment efforts and expansion of the OFCCP Employer Referral Directory (a tool available on the Department of Labor website at http://bit.ly/2ufmYZB).

Survey research on employers' efforts to evaluate their own recruiting and hiring practices to comply with VEVRAA has shown that employers are confused about compliance issues, but that their compliance efforts resulted in positive workplace changes for veterans with disabilities (Colosimo, Gabbard, and Pryor 2015).

Veterans' Disability Compensation

Veterans with service-connected disabilities are entitled to tax-free disability compensation through the DVA Disability Compensation Program. As required by statute, this benefit is based on an average reduction in earning capacity across a group of individuals with a similar physical or mental impairment. Compensation rates are determined using a 0% to 100% scale, according to the level to which the service-connected disability limits average earning capacity. A veteran must be rated with at least a 10% level of disability to receive cash benefits. The cash benefits are increased based on the number of dependents, but the rating assigned is based on the average reduction in earning capacity for a given impairment, such as the loss of a limb. For example, veterans rated with a 10% level of disability would be determined to have a service-connected disability that will result in a 10% loss of their employment earnings; veterans rated at 100% would be determined to have a total loss of their employment earnings because of a service-connected disability. For the most part, veterans receiving VA compensation for a service-connected disability can work without their compensation benefits being affected.[10] Also, in many instances, a veteran must first receive a disability rating from the VA and then apply for VA services, such as health care and vocational rehabilitation, at his or her own discretion, as shown in Figure 1.

FIGURE 1
The VA Disability Benefits Process

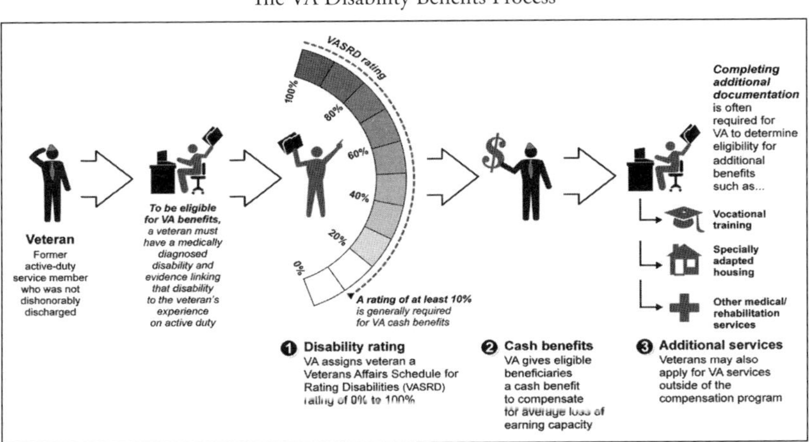

Source: US Government Accountability Office analysis of VA and Congressional Research Service documents.

The percentage of veterans collecting DVA disability compensation has increased over the past two decades (US Congressional Budget Office 2014). Several reasons have been posed for this increase: greater awareness of combat-related disabilities, the higher chance that these disabilities are diagnosed, increased awareness of disability compensation, the nature of combat in recent engagements, and improved battle-site medical care resulting in more veterans surviving their injuries. In 2016, the percentages of veterans ages 21 through 64 receiving a DVA disability rating were as follows:

- 4.7% of veterans with a service-connected disability had a 0% disability rating.[11]
- 27.4% had a 10% to 20% rating.
- 17.5% had a 30% to 40% rating.
- 14.1% had a 50% to 60% rating.
- 30.8% had a rating of 70% or higher (Erickson, Lee, and von Schrader 2017).

Programs and Services for Employment of Veterans with Disabilities

A wide array of programs and services is available to promote the employment of veterans. Some of these merely encompass veterans with disabilities; others are specifically designed for them. In addition to the federal programs described below, many states have developed their own programs and services for veterans with disabilities (National Council of State Legislators 2018).

The nonexhaustive list of federal programs shown in Table 1 highlights the main federal programs to benefit employment outcomes of veterans with disabilities and provides references for more information.

Vocational Rehabilitation and Employment Program

The Vocational Rehabilitation and Employment (VR&E) program focuses on employment assistance for veterans with service-connected disabilities (US Department of Veterans Affairs, no date). In addition to skills assessment, career counseling, classroom training and education, and job placement services to veterans, VR&E subsidizes veterans' salaries so that employers pay an apprentice-level wage while training veterans. As the veteran progresses, the employer pays a larger portion of the veteran's salary until the training program is completed, at which point the employer pays the full salary. In addition, VR&E can provide specialized tools, equipment, and workplace modifications to eligible veterans (i.e., assistive technology), allowing them to perform their duties. These services help veterans without additional cost to employers. Moreover, VR&E can provide employers with information about other federal programs offering incentives to companies that employ veterans.

TABLE 1

Overview of Federal Programs That Promote Employment for Veterans with Disabilities

Program	Services Provided					
	Career counseling and job placement	Vocational Training	On-the-Job Training and Apprenticeship	Assistance with Job Accommodations	Assistance with Recruiting and Creating Veteran-Friendly Environment	Tax Credit
Vocational Rehabilitation and Employment	✓	✓	✓	✓		
Post-9/11 GI Bill On-the-Job Training and Apprenticeship			✓			
America's Heroes at Work—Veterans Hiring Toolkit					✓	
Jobs for Veterans State Grants	✓				✓	
Work Opportunity Tax Credit						✓

Post-9/11 GI Bill On-the-Job Training and Apprenticeship Programs

This DVA GI Bill provides on-the-job training (OJT) and apprenticeship programs that offer alternatives to a college education for veterans who may not be interested in the higher education programs that are typically funded by the GI Bill. Veterans can use Post-9/11 GI Bill funds for up to two years of OJT and up to three years of an apprenticeship program. These funds provide a supplemental living stipend—beyond the wage paid by the employer—and support any related classroom training. The benefits are available to veterans with service-connected disabilities as well as the broader population of veterans.

Moreover, participating nonfederal employers receive a subsidy to compensate for training costs. Specifically, the GI Bill-approved OJT and apprenticeship programs for nonfederal employers or apprenticeship sponsors must generally be approved by a state apprenticeship agency (SAA), while the DVA approves OJT and apprenticeship programs sponsored by federal agencies (US Department of Veterans Affairs 2012). (SAAs are agencies designated by the state's governor that evaluate, approve, and monitor education and training programs for the GI Bill.)

In addition, Department of Labor staff at American Job Centers help match OJT participants to participating employers for employment and training opportunities. Upon establishing a contract for the provision of occupational training, participating employers receive a subsidy of up to 75% of the trainee's wages to compensate for training costs. To maintain their eligibility, employers must demonstrate a pattern of providing program participants with long-term employment and wages, benefits, and working conditions commensurate with unsubsidized employees of similar work experience.

America's Heroes at Work: Veterans Hiring Toolkit

This Department of Labor toolkit is designed to assist and educate employers who have decided to include transitioning service members, veterans, and veterans with disabilities in their recruitment and hiring initiatives. These resources also help inform employers about how to create a welcoming and inclusive environment for veterans, including veterans with disabilities (US Department of Labor 2018).

Jobs for Veterans: State Grants

This Department of Labor program supports staff at state workforce agencies who focus on helping veterans achieve employment. Disabled Veteran Outreach Program staff serve veterans with barriers to employment, including those with disabilities, and provide career counseling and job placement assistance. Also, Local Veterans Employment Representative staff engage with businesses to promote the hiring of veterans, with a focus on hiring veterans with disabilities.

Work Opportunity Tax Credit

Overseen by the Department of Labor, the veteran portion of the Work Opportunity Tax Credit (WOTC) is a federal tax credit available to employers who hire veterans and individuals from other eligible target groups with significant barriers to employment. Employers who hire targeted veterans—those who have a service-connected disability, are unemployed, or are receiving food stamp benefits—are eligible for tax credits of up to $9,600 per targeted veteran hired, with no limit on the number of individuals for whom an employer can claim the tax credit. In addition, the Returning Heroes Tax Credit and the Wounded Warrior Tax Credit within the WOTC program are still in effect after being passed in 2011 and have been authorized through December 31, 2019.

IN PRACTICE: INCLUDING VETERANS WITH DISABILITIES IN WORKPLACE CULTURES, POLICIES, AND PRACTICES

What does our discussion mean for LER practitioners as they support employers and veterans in creating a workplace that is truly welcoming for all veterans, including those with disabilities? As we have seen, the law does offer some protections for veterans with disabilities, and the programs and services available to veterans can provide the support that will boost their employment and economic outcomes.

But this will not be enough. Veterans with disabilities will also need workplaces where they are connected, accommodated, supported, and understood—workplaces that are free of disability-related misperception and stigma and are driven instead by evidence-based best practices of what works for veterans with disabilities. This is where the important work of LER practitioners comes in.

What follows are ten actions LER practitioners can consider taking when supporting employers in creating workplace cultures and practice that are truly welcoming to all veterans, including those with disabilities. Each action is followed by key action questions for LER practitioners to consider when working with employers.

1. Take a candid look: What happens to people with disabilities in the workplace will also happen to veterans with disabilities. Though most employers take pride in their efforts to create a veteran-friendly workplace, these efforts are weakened when they are not fully extended to the many veterans who have service-connected or other disabilities. Too often, when organizations reach out to veteran applicants and employees, disability is not a part of the conversation.

If the employer does not have the means to hear the voices of employees with disabilities, they also probably do not hear the voices of veterans with disabilities. In this chapter, we have discussed how the human experience of disability in the workplace is a powerful driver of how employees with disabilities make decisions that could significantly affect their job performance and retention, such as asking for an accommodation. Listening not just to veterans—but also to veterans with disabilities—is a critical part of having a veteran-friendly workplace.

This listening can take several forms: focus groups, communications with employee resource groups (discussed later), employee interviews, or invitations to provide anonymous feedback to organizational leaders. Whatever the form it takes, though, the key point is that leadership is capable of acting on these findings. Many of the resources highlighted in this chapter can provide a sense of best workplace practices for taking action.

Key questions for LER practitioners: Does the organization have in place a means to listen to the voices of employees and veterans with disabilities? Has the organization acted on what it hears?

2. Evaluate talent acquisition and hiring practices. As discussed, a significant number of veterans fear disability discrimination, especially in the hiring process. The assumptions about talent (who has it, where to find it) that drive an organization's talent acquisition process are too often tacit and unquestioned. These assumptions manifest less in an organization's public pronouncements about supporting veterans, and more in the tacit decisions around *where* the organization looks for talent and *who* is hired.

Key questions for LER practitioners: Does the organization implicitly screen out veterans with disabilities (and others)? What assumptions actually drive recruiters and hiring managers as they bring talent into the organization? Who is tacitly included or excluded when these assumptions are applied? Does the organization announce job openings in ways that can be accessed by organizations that typically work with veterans with disabilities (such as the Disabled Veterans Outreach Program or veterans rehabilitation services)?

3. Build partnerships with organizations focusing on veterans with disabilities. Though many organizations have built partnerships with veterans' organizations, fewer have examined and measured whether these partnerships meaningfully include veterans with disabilities. LER practitioners can encourage employers to take a closer look at their current partnerships with veterans' organizations to determine whether they screen out veterans with disabilities.

Many of the federal programs and services described above, such as the VR&E and the Local Veterans Employment Representative programs (with the Department of Labor) partner with employers to enhance the hiring of qualified veterans with disabilities.[12] In addition to considering national organizations, many state/regional organizations deal directly or indirectly with the employment of veterans with disabilities. Finally, ten regional ADA centers located across the country offer free and confidential guidance on applying the ADAAA to employment issues.[13]

Key questions for LER practitioners: Has the organization built and sustained partnerships with agencies that can assist with the hiring and employment of veterans with disabilities?

4. Put metrics into place and use them. Whether or not the employer is covered by VEVRAA, tracking and evaluating an organization's efforts to hire veterans should include veterans with disabilities. Some organizations might hesitate to collect information about disability, fearing this data collection could come into conflict with the ADAAA's disability disclosure requirements. However, the ADAAA does allow employers to make disability inquiries of applicants and employees under certain conditions: The data must be anonymized so it cannot be connected to an individual respondent; the data must be collected voluntarily with no penalty for respondents who choose not to participate; and the data can be used only to assess and improve human resources processes.[14] This tracking and evaluation effort can cover the application process, the accommodation process, and general employee engagement. Overall, the main question this effort should seek to answer is this: What actually happens to veterans with disabilities when they apply to or work in our organization? This larger question breaks down to the following questions that can be part of an organization's evaluation process:

- Are we listing our job openings in ways that can be accessed by agencies working with veterans with disabilities?
- Are we using recruiting resources that are likely to include veterans with disabilities?
- How many veteran applicants were referred from the recruiting sources used by the employer? Of these, how many were veterans with disabilities?
- Of the applicants who were extended job offers, how many were veterans? How many were veterans with a disability?
- How many veterans are among current employees? How many are veterans with disabilities?
- How many of these veterans requested reasonable accommodations? Of these, how many received an accommodation?
- How many veterans (and veterans with a disability) were promoted/transferred to roles of increasing responsibility?
- How many veterans have left the organization—voluntarily and involuntarily? What was their length of employment? How many of these were veterans with disabilities?
- (If employee engagement surveys are used.) How many veterans report that they get the supports they need to perform at their best in the workplace? Of these, how many are veterans with disabilities?

For the most part, these questions could be answered by using existing organizational data or surveys. To fully understand quantitative findings, however, survey data could be supplemented with data from focus groups and individual, open-ended interviews.

Key questions for LER practitioners: Does the organization have in place effective measures for tracking the progress of including veterans with disabilities across the spectrum of employment processes?

5. Address barriers to effective accommodations for veterans with disabilities. Though most employers are familiar with the job accommodation requirement, fewer are adept at accommodating veterans with disabilities. Five types of barriers stand in the way of these veterans getting the accommodations they need to perform at their best. First, they may be unwilling to come forward to request an accommodation. This unwillingness could be rooted in several issues. One of these is the difference between the military culture (where asking for "special" help could be equated with "not pulling your own weight") and the civilian workplace culture (where getting an accommodation is seen as a legally protected right).

The second barrier is the fear of disclosing a disability. For the many veterans with the signature disabilities (PTSD, TBI, or depression), this fear can be significant. Because these disabilities are more stigmatized and misunderstood, the fear of disclosing to a manager and co-worker can prevent veteran workers from coming forward.

The third barrier is simply that veterans might not be fully aware of their rights to an accommodation or might believe their medical condition does not "count" as a disability.

Fourth, procedural barriers can prevent veterans from coming forward. When the accommodation process is complex, involves multiple points of disclosure, is unclear to those involved, or is inconsistently applied, barriers to effective accommodations intensify.

To overcome these barriers, send a strong, clear message that accommodations are not "special favors" but are a key part of ensuring that everyone can fully contribute to organizational goals. This communication should also include clear, simple directions on how to request an accommodation and include a reminder that accommodation requests will not be shared with co-workers. Finally, employers need to become more adept at accommodating the full range of disabilities among veterans, including veterans with both visible and invisible disabilities.[15]

Key questions for LER practitioners: What actually happens to workers who request accommodations in this workplace? What barriers to getting effective accommodations exist in this workplace generally? These barriers are likely to be even greater for veterans with disabilities, who are more likely to have recently acquired disabilities.

6. Focus on managers/supervisors. Efforts to fully include veterans with disabilities in the workplace need to put the role of the manager or supervisor front and center. The workplace experience of veterans with disabilities will be determined more by their daily interactions with their boss and less by the formal pronouncements of organizational leaders on the importance of hiring veterans. As face-to-face leaders, managers and supervisors are key players in determining whether an organization is truly veteran friendly and disability friendly. In most workplaces, managers and supervisors make the bulk of decisions about who gets hired, trained, developed, and promoted and who gets left out. More importantly, they set the emotional tone of the work group. In many workplaces, managers and supervisors are given formal training on legal issues related to disability but are left on their own to set the day-to-day emotional tone around disability issues in the workplace. This emotional tone is what drives how veteran workers will answer the questions that most powerfully determine their decisions about working with a disability—questions such as the following:

- Is it safe to come forward with my disability?
- Will others find out?
- Will I be resented by co-workers if I use a reasonable accommodation?
- If I come forward with a disability, will others see me as part of the team?
- Am I able to perform at my best in this job?

Key questions for LER practitioners: Do managers/supervisors set a positive emotional tone for people (and veterans) with disabilities in the workplace? Are they competent in both the legal and human issues surrounding disability in the workplace? Does the employer have the means to answer these questions across the organization?

7. Create and/or leverage employee resource groups for veterans and workers with disabilities. Employee resource groups (ERGs) can be a powerful way for workers to connect with others who have similar life experiences. While the primary goal of ERGs is usually to provide connection and conversation, ERGs can also be used to open lines of communication with organizational leadership. Many employers have consulted ERGs to better understand the diversity culture within the workplace. ERGs can also be a valuable resource to inform broader business practices, such as reaching markets/stakeholders, interacting with customers, and creating effective talent acquisition practices. For many organizations, an ERG specifically for veterans with disabilities might not be workable because there simply are not enough employees to sustain it. Therefore, existing ERGs, focusing for example on either veterans or disability issues, might be an option if these existing ERGs understand the unique employment issues faced by veterans with disabilities. An alternative for smaller organizations, or those with only a few veterans, is to engage a buddy or mentor program providing ongoing connection and support for veterans with disabilities.

Key questions for LER practitioners: Are there ERGs in the workplace related to veterans' or disability issues? If so, are these ERGs effectively leveraged, not just as connection groups but also as a conduit to inform workplace policies/ practices?

8. Designate expertise in supporting veterans with disabilities. Employment issues for veterans with disabilities can be unique and complex. As we have seen, these issues span the human, legal, and process functions. Though a myriad of services and information exist in this area, leveraging these in ways that make sense for each organization can be challenging indeed. Though many organizations have designated expertise in dealing with veterans' issues generally, far fewer have this expertise when it comes to veterans with disabilities.

Key question for LER practitioners: Is there designated expertise in the organization around disability issues for veterans?

9. Emphasize knowledge, skills, and abilities—not charity. Hiring veterans, including those with disabilities, is not about charity. Like all veterans, veterans with disabilities bring skills, talent, and experience to the workplace. Though there are programs and incentives to employ veterans with disabilities, the primary reason to hire them is the measurable value they will bring to the business. LER practitioners should consider seeking the support of their Local Veterans Employment Representatives for further ideas about making the business case for hiring veterans with disabilities.[16] While there are tax and other incentives to hire veterans, particularly veterans with disabilities, ultimately it is veterans' knowledge, skills, and abilities that are more attractive in the long term for employers than these incentives.[17] Hence, though LER practitioners should be prepared to explain these incentives, they should focus on talents and strengths, not short-term financial incentives or charity.

Key questions for LER practitioners: How does the employer approach internal and external communications around veterans with disabilities? Is employing veterans with disabilities framed as a charity effort or as being good for the business?

10. Build connections and conversations that foster a climate of trust. Though many employers have created a climate of trust for veterans generally, far fewer have done so for veterans with disabilities. Doing this requires both top-down and bottom-up practices. Top-down practices involve sending the message that workers with disabilities are hired for their knowledge, skills, and abilities, and not solely out of a moral obligation. Emphasize specific ways in which veterans with disabilities can be expected to contribute to organizational goals. Also, top-down messages should involve dispelling misperceptions and increasing understanding about disabilities: People with PTSD are not more likely than others to be violent in the workplace, asking for an accommodation is not a weakness or a "special favor," and workers with disabilities have knowledge, talents, and skills that are valued in meeting business goals. Top-down messages should also be centered on *actions* such as building partnerships with agencies focused on veterans with disabilities, creating an effective process for providing effective accommodations, and laying the groundwork for meaningful ERGs that contribute to the business.

Bottom-up practices involve ensuring that there is an open line of communication from veterans with disabilities to organizational leadership so that the voice of these veterans can be understood and appropriately responded to by their managers and co-workers. It also involves ensuring that managers/supervisors are fully prepared to embrace the integration of veterans with disabilities on their teams.

Key questions for LER practitioners: Does the organization engage in both top-down and bottom-up communications around disability and veterans' issues? Do these communications encompass the unique disability issues faced by veterans?

CONCLUSION

LER practitioners can play a vital role in ensuring that the welcoming spirit for veterans is extended to all veterans, including those with disabilities. Being effective in this role will involve supporting employers in understanding the human, legal, and practical challenges faced by veterans with disabilities who are striving to get and sustain employment. Understanding the human issues faced by veterans with disabilities involves going beyond legal compliance and public pronouncements to look more deeply into how disability discrimination could be impacting veterans with disabilities and how this discrimination can play out (often tacitly) during everyday life in the workplace.

Supporting employers in dealing with legal issues involves making sense of the wide array of laws and services that touch on employing veterans with disabilities. Supporting employers in implementing practices that include veterans with disabilities involves curating both cultural and procedural efforts that span the organization's spectrum of workplace practices. However, the most important role LER practitioners can play is guiding employers in how to go beyond being a veteran-ready workplace by posing the question, "What actually happens to veterans with disabilities in our workplace?" For some, this may be an uncomfortable question that they cannot or do not want to answer. Yet addressing it effectively is central to achieving a truly veteran-inclusive workplace.

ACKNOWLEDGMENTS

The authors would like to thank James McCaffrey, BTL Investments, for his support of the Cornell efforts contributing to the completion of this paper. They would also like to thank Sherrill Curtis, Curtis Consulting Group; Bill Fowler, veterans' employment representative, New York State Department of

Labor; Julia Pollack, doctoral fellow, RAND Corporation; and Edgar Johnson, staffing consultant, Office of Workforce Recruitment and Retention, Cornell University, for providing reviews and feedback.

ENDNOTES

[1] Whitcomb and Obler are researchers at the US Government Accountability Office (GAO). Any errors are the authors' and should not be attributed to the GAO.

[2] The validity of the term "post-traumatic stress disorder (PTSD)" has been challenged because it assumes the condition is a "disorder." Hence, some authors use the term "post-traumatic injury" or simply "post-traumatic stress." We use "PTSD" here because it is the term most readers will recognize. To read more about this controversy, go to http://bit.ly/2FiF3ej.

[3] As will be discussed, the DVA uses a disability rating scale to determine the severity of service-connected disabilities. This scale is from 0% disabled to 100% disabled. The DVA defines a severe service-connected disability as one for which the work-earning potential of the veteran has been reduced by 70% or more as a result of the disability.

[4] Estimates are based on analysis of the 2011 ACS Public Use Microdata (PUMS) and limited to the noninstitutionalized working-age (21–64) civilian population.

[5] Defined as people between the ages of 18 and 64 who have worked or looked for work for at least 27 weeks but whose incomes still fall below the official poverty level.

[6] Although the media often link PTSD to veterans, it is in fact a relatively common condition in the general population and can arise from a range of traumatic experiences unrelated to military service, such as accidents, assaults, or abuse (National Institute of Mental Health 2017).

[7] This number would likely have been higher if it did not include the many veterans with newly acquired disabilities who did not understand their nondisclosure rights under the ADAAA.

[8] The main provisions of the ADAAA have been discussed elsewhere in this volume and will be discussed here only as they pertain to veterans with disabilities. Two documents from the Equal Employment Opportunity Commission provide a fuller overview of veterans' employment rights under the ADAAA: "Understanding Your Employment Rights Under the Americans with Disabilities Act: A Guide for Veterans" (http://bit.ly/2Fg6PYU) and "Veterans and the Americans with Disabilities Act: A Guide for Employers" (http://bit.ly/2uilqhm).

[9] Accommodation options for the signature disabilities and other service-connected disabilities can be found at the Job Accommodation Network document "Veterans and Service Members" (http://bit.ly/2uiTJVO).

[10] Some work limitations apply to veterans receiving Total Disability Based on Individual Unemployability (TDIU).

[11] A 0% disability rating is not the same as no disability. It means the veteran has a service-connected disability but, at the current time, the disability does not impact her or his occupational functioning.

[12] For more information, go to http://bit.ly/2uiUP40.

[13] ADA centers can be used by veterans themselves and by employers and LER practitioners. To find out more, go to http://bit.ly/2ug24cK.

[14] This anonymity can be problematic in workplaces that are either small or have a small number of veteran applicants or employees. For more information, contact the Equal Employment Opportunity Commission at (800) 669-4000, (800) 669-6820 (TTY for deaf/hard of hearing callers), or (844) 234-5122 (ASL video phone for deaf/hard of hearing callers), or email info@eeoc.gov.

[15] For guidance on accommodating veterans with disabilities, see the Job Accommodation Network brief, "Veterans and Service Members," at http://bit.ly/2uiTJVO. Also, Department of Veterans Affairs VR & E staff are trained on reasonable accommodations and can provide employers with support in putting effective accommodations into place at their workplaces.

[16] To find local representatives, go to http://bit.ly/2ugvzex.

[17] For more information on tax and other incentives for hiring veterans with disabilities, contact your regional ADA center at (800) 949-4232.

REFERENCES

Ainspan, N.D. 2011. "From Deployment to Employment for Veterans with Psychological Disabilities, Finding a Job Can Be as Effective at Treating Symptoms as Prescribing Medication." *U.S. Naval Institute Proceedings* 137 (2): 44–49.

American Council on Education. 2009. "Serving Those Who Serve: Higher Education and America's Veterans." http://bit.ly/2uhTpX8

Belmont Jr., P.J., G.P. Goodman, M. Zacchilli, M. Posner, C. Evans, and B.D. Owens. 2010. "Incidence and Epidemiology of Combat Injuries Sustained During 'The Surge' Portion of Operation Iraqi Freedom by a U.S. Army Brigade Combat Team." *The Journal of Trauma: Injury, Infection, and Critical Care* 68 (1): 204–210.

Bullock, E.E., J. Braud, L. Andrews, and J. Phillips. 2009. "Career Concerns of Unemployed U.S. War Veterans: Suggestions from a Cognitive Information Processing Approach." *Journal of Employment Counseling* 46: 171–181.

Burnett-Zeigler, I., M. Valenstein, M. Ilgen, A.J. Blow, L.A. Gorman, and K. Zivin. 2011. "Civilian Employment Among Recently Returning Afghanistan and Iraq National Guard Veterans." *Military Medicine* 176 (6): 639–646.

Cohen, S.I., P. Suri., M.M. Amick, and K. Yan. 2013. "Clinical and Demographic Factors Associated with Employment Status in US Military Veterans Returning from Iraq and Afghanistan." *Work* 44: 213–219.

Colosimo, J., R. Gabbard, and K. Pryor. 2015. "Survey of Federal Contractors on Effective Assessment of Outreach and Recruitment Efforts for Individuals with Disabilities and Protected Veterans." Washington, DC: DCA Consultants. http://bit.ly/2Ffegjc

Defense and Veterans Brain Injury Center. 2018. "TBI Basics." http://bit.ly/2WwHDIj

Erickson, W. 2019 (Apr. 22). Cornell University Yang-Tan Institute on Employment and Disability. Personal communication.

Erickson, W., C. Lee, and S. von Schrader. 2017. "Disability Statistics from the American Community Survey (ACS)." Ithaca, NY: Cornell University Yang-Tan Institute on Employment and Disability. http://www.disabilitystatistics.org

Gradus, J. 2011. "Epidemiology of PTSD." National Center for PTSD. http://bit.ly/2FmNHIG

Griffin, C., and A. Stein. 2015. "Self-Perception of Disability and Prospects for Employment Among U.S. Veterans." *Work* 50: 49–58. doi:10.3233/WOR-141929

Heaton, P., D.S. Loughran, and A. Miller. 2012. "Compensating Wounded Warriors: An Analysis of Injury, Labor Market Earnings, and Disability Compensation Among Veterans of the Iraq and Afghanistan Wars." Santa Monica, CA: Rand. http://bit.ly/2Fn3GXw

Hepner, K., C. Roth, E. Sloss, S. Paddock, P. Iyiewuare, M. Timmer, and H. Pincus. 2016. "Quality of Care for PTSD and Depression in the Military Health System. Santa Monica, CA: Rand. http://bit.ly/2FgrXhG

Holder, K. 2016. "The Disability of Veterans." US Census Bureau Report. Washington, DC: US Census Bureau. http://bit.ly/2MaMKd7

Kukla, M., N.A. Rattray, and M.P. Salyers. 2015. "Mixed Methods Study Examining Work Reintegration Experiences from Perspectives of Veterans with Mental Health Disorders." *Journal of Rehabilitation Research & Development* 52: 477–491.

Lauer, E.A., and A.J. Houtenville. 2018. "Annual Disability Statistics Compendium: 2017." Durham, NH: University of New Hampshire Institute on Disability.

Lindquist, L., H. Love, and E. Elbogen. 2017. "Traumatic Brain Injury in Iraq and Afghanistan Veterans: New Results from a National Random Study." *The Journal of Neuropsychiatry*. http://bit.ly/2Mf6gWa

McNally, R.J., and C. Frueh. 2013. "Why Are Iraq and Afghanistan War Veterans Seeking PTSD Disability Compensation at Unprecedented Rates?" *Journal of Anxiety Disorders* 27 (5): 520–526.

Morin, R. 2011. "The Difficult Transition from Military to Civilian Life." Washington, DC: Pew Research Center. https://pewrsr.ch/2FfoX5g

National Center for PTSD. 2016. "What Is PTSD?" Washington, DC: US Department of Veterans Affairs. http://bit.ly/2WywSVM

National Center for Veterans Analysis and Statistics. 2014. "Trends in Veterans with a Service-Connected Disability: 1985 to 2012." Washington, DC: US Department of Veterans Affairs. http://bit.ly/2FgB169

National Council of State Legislators (NCSL). 2018. "State Help for Returning Veterans." http://bit.ly/2FeQQKI

National Institute of Mental Health (NIMH). 2017. "Post-Traumatic Stress Disorder." http://bit.ly/2FloO0h

Ottomanelli, L., S.D. Barnett, and L.L. Goetz. 2013. "A Prospective Examination of the Impact of a Supported Employment Program and Employment on Health-Related Quality of Life, Handicap, and Disability Among Veterans with SCI." *Quality of Life Research* 22 (8): 2133–2141.

Owens, B.D., J.F. Kragh, J. Macaitis, S.J. Svoboda, and J.C. Wenke. 2007. "Characterization of Extremity Wounds in Operation Iraqi Freedom and Operation Enduring Freedom." *Journal of Orthopedic Trauma* 21 (4): 254–257.

Ownsworth, T., and K. McKenna. 2004. "Investigation of Factors Related to Employment Outcome Following Traumatic Brain Injury." *Disability and Rehabilitation* 26 (13): 765–784.

Peoples, G.E., T. Gerlinger, R. Craig, and B. Burlingame. 2005. "Combat Casualties in Afghanistan Cared for by Single Forward Surgical Team During the Initial Phases of Operation Enduring Freedom." *Military Medicine* 170 (6): 462–468.

Rudstam, H., W. Gower, and L. Cook. 2012. "Beyond Yellow Ribbons: Are Employers Prepared to Hire, Accommodate and Retain Returning Veterans with Disabilities?" *Journal of Vocational Rehabilitation* 36: 87–95.

Rudstam, H., J. Streeter-Wilson, and W. Gower. 2012. "Veterans with Disabilities in the Workplace." Presentation at the CDO Workforce NY Conference.

Smith, D.L. 2015. "The Relationship of Disability and Employment for Veterans from the 2010 Medical Expenditure Panel Survey (MEPS)." *Work* 51 (2): 349–363.

Stern, L. 2017. "Post 9/11 Veterans with Service-Connected Disabilities and Their Transition to the Civilian Workforce." *Advances in Developing Human Resources 19*(1): 66–77. doi:10.1177/1523422316682928

Stone, C., and D.L. Stone. 2015. "Factors Affecting Hiring Decisions About Veterans." *Human Resource Management Review* 25: 68–79.

Tanielan, T., and L.H. Jaycox (eds.). 2008. *Invisible Wounds of War: Psychological and Cognitive Injuries, Their Consequences, and Services to Assist Recovery.* Santa Monica, CA: Rand Center for Military Health Policy. http://bit.ly/2uiD5pa

USA.gov. 2019. "Veterans Disability Benefits." http://bit.ly/2Mf5qIY

US Bureau of Labor Statistics. 2019. "Employment Situation of Veterans—2018." News Release. Washington, DC: US Bureau of Labor Statistics. http://bit.ly/2MbxD3e

US Census Bureau. 2018. American FactFinder: "Veteran Status 2017." Washington, DC: US Census Bureau. http://bit.ly/2WoI6wc

US Congressional Budget Office. 2014. "Veterans Disability Compensation: Trends and Policy Options." Washington, DC: US Congressional Budget Office. http://bit.ly/2unjfch

US Department of Labor. 2018. "Employer Guide to Hire Veterans." Washington, DC: US Department of Labor. http://bit.ly/2Ws2AEh

US Department of Veterans Affairs. No date. "Vocational Rehabilitation and Employment (VR&E)." Washington, DC: US Department of Veterans Affairs. http://bit.ly/2ujFLmo

US Department of Veterans Affairs. 2012. "Post 9/11 GI Bill: How Do I Get My On-the-Job Training or Apprenticeship Program Approved?" Washington, DC: US Department of Veterans Affairs. http://bit.ly/2uiMMnz

US Department of Veterans Affairs. 2017a. "Veterans Compensation Benefits Rate Tables—Effective 12/1/17." http://bit.ly/2uiDHuY

US Department of Veterans Affairs. 2017b. "Veterans Suicide Statistics by State." Washington, DC: US Department of Veterans Affairs. http://bit.ly/2uhgoSb

US Department of Veterans Affairs. 2017c. "The Veteran Working-Poor: The Relationship Between Labor Force Activity and Poverty Status." Washington, DC: US Department of Veterans Affairs. http://bit.ly/2urlOuh

US Office of Federal Contract Compliance Programs (US OFCCP). 2015. "Fact Sheet: New Regulations on Vietnam Era Veterans' Readjustment Assistance Act (VEVRAA)." Washington, DC: US Office of Federal Contract Compliance Programs http://bit.ly/2uf9OvI

Vargas, V. 2017. "After the War: A Soldier's Struggle to Come Home." *History.com.* History Stories. http://bit.ly/2Mf2jR5

von Schrader, S., S. Bruyère, V. Malzer, and W. Erickson. 2013. "Absence and Disability Management Practices for an Aging Workforce." Ithaca, NY: Cornell University Yang-Tan Institute of Employment and Disability. http://bit.ly/2ui7h3R

CHAPTER 7

Youth with Disabilities: A Human Resource for the 21st-Century Workforce

THOMAS P. GOLDEN
KELLY CLARK
Cornell University

CATHERINE H. FOWLER
University of North Carolina–Charlotte

INTRODUCTION

Youth represent a significant portion of the population of individuals with disabilities in the United States and worldwide, with 12.4% of the 40,890,900 individuals reporting a disability being under the age of 21 (Erickson, Lee, and von Schrader 2018). Tapping into this population has been a fruitful strategy for many employers, who have successfully hired and trained these young people to achieve success while adding much-needed staff to their workforce (Erickson et al. 2014; Shandra and Hogan 2009). Employers may need to understand contextual factors impacting employment-related training and employment for this young population in order to tailor their approach to developing and integrating this talented workforce. Focused efforts can result in improved outcomes for their business and support national and international agendas on affirmative action (Lindsay et al. 2014).

This chapter provides a broad overview of factors related to positive employment outcomes for youth with disabilities, including the evolution of special education and mandates to support successful post-school success of youth with disabilities. Special education is an important contextual factor for employers to understand, as the law mandates critical services and supports that can aid and assist employers and schools working together to support the development of the future workforce.

This overview is followed by a description of predictors of post-school success for youth with disabilities and case examples from organizations and businesses that have successfully developed, recruited, trained, and hired youth with disabilities. These examples provide perspectives on the contributions of youth with disabilities to the profitability and overall work environment. In addition, these cases illustrate approaches that employers can take to initiate their own workforce development efforts or enhance existing programs, and also provide examples of resources that can assist businesses in accessing this untapped labor pool. Finally, this chapter will discuss efforts by the US government to promote a policy environment to support employment outcomes for youth with disabilities that reinforces and complements employer efforts toward fostering more inclusive workplaces. The purpose of this chapter is to bridge a gap that continues to exist between local secondary schools, post-secondary education institutions, and local and corporate businesses in working in partnership to effect positive post-school outcomes for youth with disabilities, while at the same time providing employers with a relevant and skilled workforce for tomorrow.

FORCES SHAPING THE 21ST-CENTURY WORKFORCE AND THE NEED FOR GREATER WORKPLACE INCLUSIVENESS

The workplace and workforce of tomorrow need to be prepared for and shaped today. Doing this will require an understanding of the structural forces and mechanisms impacting the workplace and workforce. Karoly and Panis (2004) identified three clear forces shaping the 21st-century workplace and workforce—shifting demographic patterns, advances in technology, and economic globalization. Shifting demographic patterns hold significant implications for labor force supply as the labor demand side attempts to keep pace with growing and ever changing needs of the domestic and global population. Among the primary forces that are shifting the demographic patterns of the workforce for tomorrow are sporadic workforce growth as certain markets waiver, the workforce ages, and the number of youth to replace existing workers decreases; increasing diversity of the workforce as un- or undertapped labor pools are accessed; and widening skills and opportunity gaps for future workers (Casner-Lotto and Barrington 2006; Karoly and Panis 2004; Snider, Hill, and Martin 2003).

At the intersection of these shifting demographics lies the un- and undertapped labor of youth with disabilities—representing a potentially formidable future workforce. Researchers rethinking diversity in the workplace are emphasizing multicultural models where both dominant and nondominant cultures coexist and thrive (Coleman Selden and Selden 2001). For example, disability does not discriminate and cuts across all facets of diversity from race and ethnicity to culture, gender, age, and religion. While many workplaces have accepted the challenge to embrace a multicultural and inclusive model, at the conclusion of the second decade of the 21st century there is evidence to suggest that businesses are not completely invested in this opportunity or have not fully realized their potential in this area. Contributing to this, the US secondary and post-secondary educational system continues to not meet its obligation to prepare the workforce of tomorrow, resulting in a growing skills gap in which youth may lack the necessary skills and work ethic needed for employment success (Symonds, Schwartz, and Ferguson 2011). While federal and state law since 1975 has clearly outlined services and supports to facilitate the skill development and improved post-school outcomes of youth with disabilities, these laws have yet to realize their full potential in successfully bridging school-to-work movement.

Evolution of Special Education and Transition Mandates to Support Post-School Success

Since the passage of the Education for All Handicapped Children Act (Publ. L. No. 94-142) in 1975, supporting states and localities in protecting the rights of youth with disabilities to receive free and appropriate public education has been a critical domestic policy agenda (Yell 1998). The early years after the passage of the act were focused on ensuring that local communities began educating the over 1.75 million students with disabilities who had until then received no educational services and that the appropriate services and supports were extended to over three million students who were not receiving them (Katsiyannis, Yell, and Bradley 2001; Turnbull and Turnbull 1998). In the early 1970s, domestic schools "educated only 20% of children with disabilities" (Katsiyannis, Yell, and Bradley 2001: 325).

In 1990, Public Law 101-476 called for significant changes to Public Law 94-142, placing additional emphasis on increasing graduation rates and successful post-school outcomes for youth with disabilities—requiring transition planning as part of the individualized education program, promoting inclusive living, learning, and earning outcomes as adults. These changes included retitling the Education for all Handicapped Children Act to the Individuals with Disabilities Education Act (IDEA). IDEA was amended in 1997 (Publ. L. No. 106-17) strengthening the role of the parent and emphasizing student progress toward student goals, and again in 2004, increasing emphasis on accountability and improved outcomes through reading, early intervention, and evidence-based instruction (Katsiyannis, Yell, and Bradley 2001).

The last two and a half decades of domestic special education policy have increased focus on improving transition education, services, and supports for youth with disabilities. This has been accomplished through federal, state, and local investment in the development and implementation of transition services, as well as identification of evidence-based practices leading to improved post-school outcomes (Kohler and Field 2003). Preparing youth with disabilities to join the competitive workforce has been a driving force in this effort—attempting to ensure that youth with disabilities are exiting school with the skills and capacities needed to be competitively employed in integrated settings with individuals without disabilities and in areas with the potential for career advancement—not simply job placement. While the National Longitudinal Transition Studies (NLTS) have documented general improvements over time in post-secondary education enrollment and employment rates, there are persistent education and employment outcome disparities associated with race/ethnicity and income level, as well as higher rates of employment termination, incarceration, and limited increases in earnings over time (Liu et al. 2018;

Newman et al. 2010; Wagner, Newman, Cameto, and Levine 2005). These continuing challenges have been driving forces in the development of contemporary domestic workforce policy.

Growing Prioritization of Youth Disability, Workforce Development, and Employment Policy

On July 22, 2014, the Workforce Innovation and Opportunity Act (WIOA) was signed into law—providing the first legislative reform in close to two decades. This landmark piece of legislation supersedes the Workforce Investment Act of 1998. The purpose of the WIOA is not only to strengthen the domestic public workforce system and support Americans in obtaining high-quality jobs and careers but also to assist employers in recruiting, hiring, retaining, and advancing skilled workers—including youth with disabilities and youth with significant barriers to employment. Toward that end, the US Departments of Labor, Education, and Health and Human Services have recognized the importance of working collaboratively to prepare all key stakeholders for implementation of the law and issuing guidance.

Title I of the WIOA clearly details a broad youth agenda that supports an integrated service delivery system—providing a framework for stakeholders to leverage additional resources to support in-school and out-of-school youth in preparing for employment. Services supporting this youth agenda include career exploration and guidance, support for continued educational attainment, skills training, job placement leading to a career, and/or enrollment in post-secondary education. Title IV of the WIOA, the Rehabilitation Act of 1973 as amended, further outlines specific provisions to ensure that students and youth with disabilities have opportunities to receive the training and other essential services and supports they need to achieve competitive integrated employment through the state/federal partnership for vocational rehabilitation. These provisions broadened student eligibility requirements, increased opportunities to practice and improve workplace skills through work-based learning, placed fiscal requirements on allotment of federal dollars that must support pre-employment transition services, established a continuum of services available to students and youth with disabilities, and placed restrictions on the payment of subminimum wages.

This prioritization of youth in contemporary disability policy is a direct response to a need to better equip marginalized populations in preparing for attaining and advancing in employment and to address current post-school challenges youth are facing. It recognizes that preparing youth with disabilities to join the competitive workforce is not exclusively the responsibility of the education system or local educational institutions but that it also requires partnerships across community stakeholders—including employers. Toward that end, research has shown that there are a number of key predictors of post-school success.

PREDICTORS OF POST-SCHOOL SUCCESS

What Is Post-School Success?

Post-school success after completing high school can include pursuing career goals by obtaining employment or enrolling in a post-secondary education program that may lead to the achievement of that goal. "Success" can also include living independently, navigating the community, or engaging in meaningful social relationships. Several reauthorizations of the IDEA (i.e., 1990, 1997, 2004) have emphasized the importance of providing support for students with disabilities while in high school in order to assist them in obtaining employment, pursuing post-secondary education or training, and living more independently after completing high school (Individuals with Disabilities Education Act of 2004). In addition, employment has been identified as a factor related to a higher quality of life for individuals with disabilities (Canha, Simões, Owens, and Matos 2013; Simões and Santos 2016).

Tracking Post-School Outcomes

To track how students fare after completing high school, states must collect and report post-school outcomes of youth with disabilities as measured through the State Performance Plan for Part B of the IDEA. The 14th of 17 indicators of state program compliance and outcomes specifically measures the percentage of youth who are no longer enrolled in secondary school, who had an individualized education program (IEP) in effect at the time they left school, and were within one year of leaving high school. These indicators are targeted to youth who are enrolled in higher education, enrolled in higher education or competitively employed, and enrolled in higher education or in some other post-secondary education or training program or competitively employed or in some other employment within one year of leaving high school (Office of Special Education Programs 2017). "Enrolled in higher education" means youth have been enrolled full time or part time in a community college or college or university for at least one complete term at any point during the year since they left high school. "Competitive employment" is defined as having worked for pay at or above minimum wage in an integrated setting with others without disabilities for a period of 20 hours per week for at least 90 days at any time during the year since leaving high school and includes military employment (Workforce Innovation Opportunity Act, 34 CFR § 361.5(c)(9)).

In addition to Indicator 14 data collection, the NLTS has collected data on post-school outcomes of individuals with disabilities three times since 1993 (Wagner et al. 2005). In 2011, the results from the National Longitudinal Transition Study 2 (NLTS2) included results from more than 11,000 youth with disabilities nationwide. Data were collected from 2001 to 2009 from students, parents, and schools and provided a national perspective of the experiences of youth with disabilities after high school. Data from the NLTS2 measured demographic characteristics, middle and high school experiences (e.g., schools, school programs, related services), experiences of youth with disabilities after high school, and other factors (e.g., community type, interagency collaboration, service agencies). Currently, the NLST (Lipscomb et al. 2017) is reporting data from 12,000 in-school youth—10,000 of those with IEPs across all disability categories. Research questions include a focus on how post-school outcomes of youth with disabilities compare to those without disabilities, as well as the variation of high school and post-secondary outcomes by student characteristics. The second phase of the study will follow the students through high school and beyond and use administrative data collected by the US Department of Education and other agencies.

Disparities for Youth with Disabilities

Despite efforts of policy makers and practitioners, a gap remains in post-school outcomes for youth with disabilities compared with their peers without disabilities. Data collected from the NLTS2 indicate post-school outcomes for individuals with disabilities continued to fall behind their peers without disabilities in education, employment, and independent living (Newman et al. 2011). According to the US Bureau of Labor Statistics (2017) employment rates for individuals with disabilities were 18% compared with 66% for those without a disability. Additionally, youth with disabilities reported working fewer hours and receiving lower wages compared with their peers without disabilities (Newman et al. 2011). In the area of post-secondary education, the NLTS 2012 found fewer youth with disabilities expected to enroll in some type of post-secondary education or training compared with their peers without a disability (76% vs. 94%), and they were almost half as likely as their peers to take college entrance and placement exams (42% vs. 70%; Lipscomb et al. 2017).

Youth with disabilities also fell behind their peers in planning and taking steps to obtain post-secondary education, as well as enrolling in and completing post-secondary education (Lipscomb et al. 2017). Lastly, youth with disabilities were also less likely to live on their own and have financial stability (Lipscomb et al. 2017; Newman et al. 2011). Findings from the NLTS 2012 demonstrated youth with disabilities were more likely than their peers without disabilities to be socioeconomically disadvantaged and to struggle with their health, communication skills, and ability to complete typical tasks independently (Lipscomb et al. 2017). Overall, engagement and use of school supports demonstrated improvements over the past decade (2003–2012) for youth with disabilities. Additionally, having a paid job not sponsored by school for youth with disabilities declined from 27% in 2003 to 19% in 2012; however, participation in school-sponsored work activities remained stable at 13% in 2003 and 14% in 2012 (Lipscomb et al. 2017).

Predictors of Post-School Success

The National Secondary Transition Technical Assistance Center and now the National Technical Assistance Center on Transition reviewed quality correlational research to identify school factors associated with positive post-school outcomes for students with disabilities. Test et al. (2009) and Mazzotti et al. (2016) together identified 20 predictors of post-school success for individuals with disabilities. The review conducted by Test et al. (2009) found the following predictors of post-school success:

- career awareness
- career and technical (or vocational) education
- community experiences
- high school diploma status
- inclusion in general education
- interagency collaboration
- occupational courses paid work experience
- parent involvement
- program of study
- self-care skills
- self-determination and self-advocacy
- social skills
- student supports
- work study

Recently, Mazzotti et al. (2016) identified four additional predictors: parent expectations, youth autonomy and decision making, travel skills, and goal setting. Table 1 (next page) contains a list of predictors and correlated outcome areas.

Consistently, early work experience was one of the most frequently identified predictors of post-school employment for students with disabilities (Carter, Austin, and Trainor 2012; Hasazi et al. 1985; Mazzotti et al. 2016; Test et al. 2009; Wehman et al. 2015). This was consistent across disability categories, socioeconomic status, and geography (Gold, Fabian, and Luecking 2013). Work experience has been defined by Rowe, Alverson, and Unruh (2015) as any activity with a student in an authentic workplace, including job shadowing, internships, paid employment, apprenticeships, and job sampling. Paid employment indicates compensation paid directly to the individual, at minimum wage or higher. According to Luecking (2009), work experience can take a variety of forms, and the most common types include the following:

- apprenticeships
- career exploration
- internships
- job shadowing
- paid employment
- service learning
- work sampling

Table 2 shows the definitions of the types of work-based learning experiences.

To provide work experiences during high school, collaboration among professionals and across stakeholders is necessary. Collaboration has been identified as a critical component of effective transition programs encouraging positive transition to work and adult-life outcomes (Wehman 2013). In fact, when collaboration focuses on students with disabilities' outcomes combined with stakeholders providing services together, rather than a referral from one party to the next, the likelihood of high school completion and post-school employment rates increase (Fabian and Luecking 2015). Employers play a key role in providing viable and authentic work experiences for students with disabilities. Several

TABLE 1
In-School Predictors of Post-School Success and Outcome Areas

	Outcomes		
Predictors	Education	Employment	Independent Living
Career awareness	✓	✓	
Career and technical education	✓	✓	
Community experiences		✓	
Exit exam/high school diploma		✓	
Goal setting	✓	✓	
Inclusion in general education	✓	✓	✓
Interagency collaboration	✓	✓	
Occupational courses	✓	✓	
Paid employment/work experience	✓	✓	✓
Parent expectations	✓	✓	✓
Parental involvement		✓	
Program of study		✓	
Self-advocacy/self-determination	✓	✓	
Self-care/independent living	✓	✓	✓
Social skills	✓	✓	
Student support	✓	✓	✓
Transition program	✓	✓	
Travel skills		✓	
Work study		✓	
Youth autonomy/decision making	✓	✓	

TABLE 2
Work-Based Learning Experiences

Type	Definition
Career exploration	"Career exploration involves visits by youth to workplaces to learn about jobs and the skills required to perform them. Visits and meetings with employers and people in identified occupations outside of the workplace are also types of career exploration activities from which youth can learn about jobs and careers" (Luecking 2009: 13).
Job shadowing	"Job shadowing is extended time, often a full workday or several workdays, spent by a youth in a workplace accompanying an employee in the performance of his or her daily duties" (Luecking 2009: 13).
Job sampling/work sampling	"Work sampling is work by a youth that does not materially benefit the employer but allows the youth to spend meaningful time in a work environment to learn aspects of potential job task and 'soft skills' required in the workplace" (Luecking 2009: 13).
Service learning	"Service learning is hands-on volunteer service to the community that integrates with course objectives. It is a structured process that provides time for reflection on the service experience and demonstration of the skills and knowledge required" (Luecking 2009: 13).
Internships	"Internships are formal agreements whereby a youth is assigned specific tasks in a workplace over a predetermined period of time. Internships may be paid or unpaid, depending on the nature of the agreement with the company and the nature of the tasks" (Luecking 2009: 13).
Apprenticeships	"Apprenticeships are formal, sanctioned work experiences of extended duration in which an apprentice learns specific occupational skills related to a standardized trade, such as carpentry, plumbing, or drafting. Many apprenticeships also include paid work components" (Luecking 2009: 13).
Paid employment	"Paid employment may include existing standard jobs in a company or customized work assignments that are negotiated with an employer, but these jobs always feature a wage paid directly to the youth. Such work may be scheduled during or after the school day. It may be integral to a course of study or simply a separate adjunctive experience" (Luecking 2009: 13).
Mentoring	"[A mentor] is a person who through support, counsel, friendship, reinforcement, and constructive example helps another person, usually a young person, to reach his or her work and life goals. Mentoring relationships provide valuable support to young people, especially those with disabilities, by offering not only academic and career guidance but also effective role models for leadership, interpersonal and problem-solving skills" (Office of Disability Employment Policy 2012).

employers have developed programs to provide work experiences for students with disabilities to address workforce labor needs. The following section provides examples of employers working to provide work experiences for youth and young adults with disabilities, including paid work experiences.

CASE EXAMPLES

Marriott Bridges

Marriott Foundation for People with Disabilities developed the Bridges from School to Work program, which has served over 15,000 youth since 1989. It operates in ten major areas across the United States, including Atlanta, Baltimore, Boston, Chicago, Dallas, Los Angeles, Oakland, Philadelphia, San Francisco, and Washington, D.C. The Bridges program was originally designed to create paid internships with local companies for youth with disabilities during their last year of high school (Tilson, Luecking, and Donovan 1994). Since that time it has evolved to provide services to in- and out-of-school youth, with a focus on vocational development in addition to initial job placement, and it provides extended follow-up to help to ensure initial job placement success. The critical roles for employers with this program are serving as a site for job development and hiring trained employees.

Two fundamental principles guide the services provided by Bridges. First, it is an employer-driven model, giving priority to the needs of the employer in all employment-related activities, to create job placements that are sustainable over time. Second, there is a focus on abilities rather than disabilities, to place students in jobs that match their strengths. Bridges believes that every youth with a disability has the potential to be a contributing employee and assists students to fully realize their potential by ensuring that the job match is a good one between the student's skills and interests and the needs of the company, both the workplace and the student are willing to make the job placement work, and appropriate supports are available to ensure success over time, particularly early in the employment relationship.

Bridges core elements include initial career counseling and job search, placement in a paid position with training and support from program staff to assist in job success, and placement after the program with follow-up support and the ability to track participants and measure vocational growth and success. Local employers assist in providing competitive placements and are key partners in this process. To identify youth with disabilities who may benefit from the program, Bridges collaborates closely with school systems, vocational rehabilitation, and workforce agencies in local communities. Together these partners work to assist youth with disabilities in gaining and maintaining competitive employment. Without the cooperating Marriot properties, however, the program could not succeed. Being willing to allow students to learn on the job with the supports of program staff is a critical role that businesses can plan in workforce development.

Hiring youth who have participated in comprehensive job training programs similar to Bridges is, of course, another critical role. Employers with a wide array of employee sectors can serve as excellent partners for workforce development efforts like Bridges. Additionally, they benefit from an eventual hire of an employee with a deeper understanding of the position and a better match between the employee and the tasks to be completed.

Landmark College Works

Landmark College Works is an on-campus employment preparation program operated by Landmark College in Putney, Vermont. Landmark College is exclusively for students who learn differently—including, but not limited to, students with learning disabilities, autism, and attention-deficit/hyperactivity disorder. Landmark College champions a strength-based model and is a fully accredited, not-for-profit institution—offering both bachelor's and associate's degrees. Career Connections is the department at Landmark responsible for providing employment readiness skill-building opportunities and internships. It provides job search and placement support, as well as follow-up support to alumni. Further, the program assists employers in managing diversity posed by disability in the workplace. Career Connections at Landmark helps students connect to work-based learning opportunities within corporations such as Hasbro, SAP, JPMorgan Chase & Co., BroadFutures, BioTek, and Vermont Genetics Network. The program was expanded through the Six-College Collaborative Internship Program through partnership with the Brattleboro Development Credit Corporation—offering paid internships with area businesses. Landmark also has on-campus internship opportunities across different fields and disciplines.

To increase employment opportunities for youth with disabilities, Landmark focuses on a holistic approach to preparing their students for their lives after college. It offers a short-term, intensive, Employment Readiness Experience—integrating an on-campus job experience with classroom work focusing on communication, professional skills, and career exploration. The approaches to supporting students toward a career path are tailored to fit each student's level of job skills and experiences.

As evidenced by the Landmark College Works model, employers do not need to establish work-based learning programs in isolation. There are many postsecondary education colleges and universities that operate similar programs, working in partnership with private and public sector employers to create work-based learning opportunities through internships and formal mentoring programs. An essential benefit of these types of collaborative partnerships are the supports a program like Landmark College Works can provide to business and industry to prepare them to meet the needs of learning diverse students and how to foster enhanced inclusive workplace practices. Further information regarding

Landmark College Works including success stories and their impact can be found online at http://bit.ly/2VlpA3T.

Employers can benefit from the developing labor pool served by programs like Landmark's by being open to offering internships for high school and college students with disabilities. The educational component of the internship is arranged through an educational institution. The employer remains the expert on the career field and provides work-based learning opportunities—simultaneously meeting a task or skill need in the company and an educational and career development need for a young person. Additionally, the employer has a role in advising the program regarding industry-wide or specific business needs that might be addressed by interns and students in a program such as Landmark's.

Neurodiverse Hiring Initiative

The Neurodiverse Hiring Initiative (NHI) in Rochester, New York, is a relatively new partnership established at the Rochester Institute of Technology (RIT) between their Spectrum Support Program and Office of Career Services and Cooperative Education. RIT is home to leading creators, entrepreneurs, innovators, and researchers. Founded in 1829, RIT enrolls 19,000 students in more than 200 career-oriented and professional programs, making it among the largest private universities in the United States. The university is internationally recognized for academic leadership in business, computing, engineering, imaging science, liberal arts, sustainability, and fine and applied arts. It is also a globally recognized leader in preparing deaf and hard-of-hearing students for employment success, offering unparalleled support services to the over 1,100 deaf and hard-of-hearing students living, learning, and earning on the RIT campus. RIT's cooperative education program is one of the oldest and largest in the nation, and the university has global partnerships, including satellite campuses in China, Croatia, Dubai, and Kosovo.

The focus of NHI is to connect qualified RIT students on the autism spectrum with employers seeking to diversify their workplace and workforce. NHI recognizes the large untapped labor pool that is represented by neurodiverse job seekers and works through the services and supports they provide to match labor supply and demand. NHI offers an array of resources for employers that build a more inclusive workplaces. Their "Employer Guide to Supervising Individuals with Autism Spectrum Disorder" seeks to aid employers in working more effectively with this population. In addition, they offer distance learning programs and training to educate employers, host pre-employment programs for participating RIT students, network employers and participating RIT students through career fairs, and aid in job matching.

As a result of the efforts of NHI, many neurodiverse job seekers have secured employment. NHI's efforts have included working with public and private sector employers, including Fortune 500 companies as well as federal contractors and small start-ups through RIT's technology business incubator, Venture Creations. Employer testimonials about hiring job seekers through NHI report unique attributes for each employee—reinforcing the heterogeneity of the neurodiverse population.

NHI varies from the Landmark College Works model in that it is an inclusive post-secondary education setting where students both with and without disabilities attend. It is similar in that it recognizes that some subpopulations of students require unique sets of services and supports to equally advantage them in their job search process. It is also similar in that it supports employers in fostering and enhancing workplace and workforce diversity. The role of the employers in the NHI model is informing the program of their interest in diversifying their workplace and advising on needed skills and talents. Resources described at the end of this chapter provide suggestions that any company can access to make these efforts in their own communities.

Empire Beauty School

The Empire Beauty School (EBS) in Providence, Rhode Island, is one of many EBS locations nationally. The school provides an accredited cosmetology and esthetician education, as well as salon services to clients in Providence. EBS has become a key player in the employment of an individual with an intellectual disability. Like many small businesses, the school's role as an employer occurred through a seemingly informal yet intentional process.

A young woman who had completed her public school education and received work-skills training on campus was later receiving employment and case management services through the Fogarty Center in Providence. Fogarty Center is a nonprofit provider of residential, employment, and self-directed day supports for children and adults with intellectual, developmental, and other disabilities. Through a series of strengths-focused meetings with the job seeker, her family members, and her case manager with Fogarty Center, EBS was identified as a place where this woman would want to continue learning beyond high school, owing to her interest in the beauty and fashion industry.

The Fogarty Center assisted in navigating the application process. EBS was open to the job seeker in completing a three-month paid work experience—allowing her to assist instructors and students in the hands-on coursework, as well as be exposed to the client interaction aspects of the salon. During this initial period, vocational rehabilitation funds paid for a job coach from the Fogarty Center to support the job seeker, as well as minimum wage hourly pay and assistance. As a school, Empire has historically accepted students with disabilities historically and provided necessary accommodations in accordance with the Americans with Disabilities Act. The accommodations and supports needed for this student to be successful were greater but opened the door to another possibility of permanent employment, according to the director of

EBS in Providence. When the school determined that hiring the job seeker was a good move for their business, there were concerns expressed from their legal department about potential liability owing to the individual's medical support needs. Again, staff from the Fogarty Center were able to provide information that alleviated any concerns, and the school moved forward with offering her a job.

The results for EBS have been positive. "[We] feel strongly that—especially with small businesses [hiring an individual with evident disabilities] changes the culture positively. Our clients arrange their appointments to see her.... Her interactions with our students help them put things in perspective," according to the school's leadership. After a year, the employee has taken on a wider variety of tasks at work and expanded the number of hours she works.

Value of Case Studies

Businesses linked with university programs or large enough to support a human resources department may have embraced a philosophy and developed policies to focus on the recruitment, retention, and advancement of youth employees with disabilities; however, this effort may seem more daunting to employers with a smaller workforce. Small businesses make up 99% of businesses in the United States and employ over 47% of the US workforce, according to US Small Business Administration data (2018). However, the most common way that a youth gains employment while in high school is through a personal relationship. Service providers may assist individuals and their families in identifying natural connections to employers and businesses in their community. As described in the case study with EBS, the employer can be open to this experience and benefit from this undertapped labor source of students and youth with disabilities.

These case studies represent simply a few of the ways that a variety of types of employers have engaged in the mutually beneficial efforts to develop a future workforce. Whether large, national companies with a wide array of positions or small, local businesses with a few employees, businesses serve as critical partners for educators, service providers, families, and young people seeking work experiences and training in a career. This role makes businesses invaluable to the success of the young person. In turn, businesses benefit from a trained, committed, creative workforce.

IMPLICATIONS AND RECOMMENDATIONS

These case examples, as well as much supporting research, have implications for employers and suggest that creating an inclusive workplace to support a 21st-century workforce can take various forms. As illustrated here, employers can work to create an inclusive workplace by partnering with schools, agencies, and other organizations to provide work-based learning opportunities for youth and young adults with disabilities. There are also resources available from several organizations who can assist in providing training, technical assistance, and other practical resources to help a company become inclusive of individuals with disabilities.

Types of Work-Based Learning Opportunities

Work experience has consistently been identified as the most important predictor of post-school employment success for individuals with disabilities (Carter, Austin, and Trainor 2012; Mazzotti et al. 2016; Test et al. 2009). Work experiences are useful in all phases of career development and can take various forms. The most common types were listed and defined in Table 2. These experiences can be effective in preparing youth with disabilities for employment, particularly when they occur in authentic workplaces where they can learn key skills and behaviors needed for work, as well as identify the types of accommodations and supports they may need. To create these experiences, effective partnerships are crucial.

Developing critical partnerships requires creation of a mutually supportive relationship, with a focus on a specific goal that is beneficial to all parties. The common goal may be to improve employment outcomes for the community's youth with disabilities, but each partner in the process can benefit in different ways. For example, businesses may gain opportunities to meet current workforce needs, prepare their future workforce, improve company engagement in the community, and find talent that may increase workplace diversity and inclusion. Related research confirms that companies that have internships (targeting individuals with disabilities) are six times more likely to have successfully hired a person with a disability in the past year (Erickson et al. 2014). Government agencies may increase their ability to meet mandates for service outcomes. Schools could better meet special education law requirements by being able to offer students more authentic work experiences.

Table 3 (next pages) describes how these partnerships may affect businesses by describing the role of the business, potential partners involved, and anticipated benefits for each type of work-based learning experience. Each of these experiences can provide students with disabilities the opportunities needed to explore careers, develop their skills, and discover their strengths in the workplace. Getting involved in these types of partnerships may assist businesses in (1) meeting an industry-wide need such as preparing future workers to develop skills needed for a specific industry (e.g., technology, retail, medical); (2) meeting a specific company need (e.g., filling open positions, increasing production, or meeting a service need); and (3) meeting a community need by assisting students with disabilities in developing skills needed to be independent and productive citizens, which may increase the business's presence and community engagement (Luecking 2009).

When a business, school, company, or community organization wants to initiate a partnership, they will follow several steps such as identifying partners and bringing them together, organizing and establishing meeting structures, and serving as the primary communicator to all groups. According to the National

TABLE 3
Partnerships, Roles, and Benefits of Work-Based Learning (WBL) Experiences for Businesses and Students

WBL Type	Role of Business
Career exploration	• Allow schools/groups to visit a workplace • Provide a tour and overview of the different jobs available
Job shadowing	• Allow students/individuals to shadow an employee for a day to learn aspects of a specific job
Job sampling/ work sampling	• Allow students to try certain aspects of the jobs available at a company and spend time in the work environment to learn soft skills
Service learning	• Work with a teacher to provide hands-on volunteer service to the community that aligns with the teacher's course objectives
Internships	• Engage in a formal agreement where a student or individual is assigned specific tasks for a certain period of time. This can be paid or unpaid depending on the agreement.
Apprenticeships	• Formal, sanctioned work experiences of extended duration in which an apprentice learns specific occupational skills related to a standardized trade
Paid employment	• Existing standard jobs in a company or customized work assignments that are negotiated with an employer, but these jobs always feature a wage paid directly to the youth
Mentoring	• A mentor is a person who provides support, counsel, friendship, reinforcement, and constructive feedback to help another person, usually a young person, to reach his or her work and life goals.

Likely Partner(s)	Benefit to Business and Student
• Schools and school staff • Vocational programs • Vocational rehabilitation counselors • Community rehabilitation providers	• Exposure for students to different occupations • Company may gain new interest in position at their company
• Schools and school staff • Vocational programs • Vocational rehabilitation counselors • Community rehabilitation providers	• Student will learn the aspects of a job she or he is interested in • Mentoring opportunity for an employee • Main gain is more interest in specific jobs at your company
• Schools and school staff • Vocational programs • Vocational rehabilitation counselors • Community rehabilitation providers	• Students can explore jobs at a company and spend time in the work environment • This may provide opportunities for leadership among staff and the ability for them to learn skills to train others
• Secondary schools and school staff • Vocational programs • Colleges/universities	• Students gain course credit for the opportunity and can learn about a company while also learning job skills • Provides the company with opportunities to recruit future employees from partners
• Secondary schools • Colleges/universities • Vocational programs • Career and technical education centers	• Student gains valuable work experience • Company gains a paid or unpaid position depending on the agreement to do specific jobs • Could assist in developing new jobs for a company and gaining new talent
• Career and technical education centers • Vocational technical schools • Community colleges • High schools	• Students gain experiences that lead to a credential in a specific area • Employer could gain future employees, better trained staff, and exposure of jobs available within the company
• Vocational rehabilitation • Adult agency providers • Schools and school staff	• Employers gain valuable employees they can train beyond entry-level skills • Students gain paid work experience during high school
• Adult agency providers • Schools and school staff • Community colleges	• Employers can provide community outreach by mentoring youth in achieving their work and life goals • Employees who serve as mentors may be able to assist students in exploring their career goals and share their employment experiences with them • Students gain a connection in the community that may assist them in exploring their career interests and provide a person who is a role model for them in the community

Technical Assistance Center on Transition (Luecking et al. 2015), important responsibilities and activities of the leader (no matter what sector the leader is from) include the following:

- establishing meeting agendas to maintain a consistent focus from meeting to meeting
- facilitating discussions and keeping the group's focus on the agenda
- ensuring all members are comfortable in participating in discussion and activities
- making sure agreed-upon actions are carried out
- making sure consistent notes are taken at meetings and distributed to all members
- ensuring there are clear roles for all partners
- providing representation of the partnership to external groups

If a business wants to establish a partnership to work with a school or community organization, they should identify who their potential partners would be, define what they hope to accomplish, set up some meeting times to discuss logistics, and create a plan to build a sustainable partnership over time.

Resources to Support Development

There are several resources that can be used to support the development of a program that will provide work-based learning experiences for youth with disabilities. One such resource is Disability:IN (formerly the US Business Leadership Network, www.disabilityin.org), which has a variety of resources for employers. This member organization provides guidance and resources for human resources departments to promote the inclusion and success of individuals with disabilities in the workplace. Available resources include assessments of workplace accessibility and specific guidance on recruiting, hiring, and retaining employees. Disability:IN has affiliates across the United States to help businesses increase their knowledge of community outreach, recruiting, interviewing, accommodations, and barriers to employment. Through these affiliates, businesses can participate in a business-to-business dialog in order to learn how to use their organization for success. Disability:IN also offers events, committees, and articles on how employers are working with individuals with disabilities and creating inclusive environments.

The Job Accommodations Network (www.askjan.org) is another such group, and it provides information for employers and employees regarding workplace accommodations. The network can connect employers, job seekers, and employees with useful resources to facilitate access to reasonable accommodations at work.

Another group providing resources is the Association of People Supporting Employment First (APSE; www.apse.org). APSE provides resources including training opportunities through webinars and e-learning courses where professionals, employers, and organizations can learn to overcome challenges and create inclusive work environments. APSE can provide organizational transformation workshops at a business's site. APSE also provides resources for employers on how to recruit, hire, retain, and advance individuals with disabilities, as well as information on the benefits of hiring individuals with disabilities, tax incentives, new rules and regulations, and guidance documents for legislation for individuals with disabilities.

Finally, the Employer Assistance Resource Network on Disability Inclusion (EARN; www.askearn.org) provides support for employers in their efforts to recruit, hire, retain, and advance qualified individuals with disabilities. EARN provides education and resources through an online hub that includes employer-focused tools, resources, and publications on disability inclusion. They also provide online training on topics such as disability etiquette, interviewing job candidates with disabilities, and reasonable accommodations. They frequently offer HR Certification Institute credits through their webinars. They provide up-to-date information on the latest disability employment news, research-based tools, and exemplary examples of employers who are getting it right when it comes to disability inclusion.

CONCLUSION

As articulated earlier in this chapter, the workplace and workforce of tomorrow need to be shaped, guided, and prepared for today. Employers applying strategies that allow them to respond with agility to shifting demographic patterns, advances in technology, and economic globalization will be better positioned to remain competitive. This chapter emphasized understanding the important role of the un- and undertapped labor pool of youth with disabilities in developing such strategies. As presented, both work-based and partnerships models of rethinking diversity in the workplace provide a structuring approach to cultivate and support multicultural models where both dominant and nondominant cultures coexist and thrive. The prioritization of youth, not only in contemporary disability policy but also inclusive workplace practice, is a direct response to better equip marginalized populations such as youth with disabilities to address post-school challenges in preparing for, attaching to, and advancing in employment. This focus recognizes that preparing the untapped labor pool of youth with disabilities to join the competitive workforce is not exclusively the responsibility of the education system or local educational institutions; rather, it requires multiple partnerships across community stakeholders, including employers.

ACKNOWLEDGMENTS

The authors and editor would like to thank Jacqueline Hyatt and Ruth Allison, senior research associates with TransCen, for their review and comment on this chapter.

REFERENCES

Canha, L., C. Simões, L.A. Owens, and M. Matos. 2013. "The Importance of Perceived Quality of Life and Personal Resources in Transition from School to Life." T*he European Journal of Social and Behavioral Sciences* 69: 1881–1890.

Carter, E.W., D. Austin, and A.A. Trainor. 2012. "Predictors of Postschool Employment Outcomes for Young Adults with Severe Disabilities." *Journal of Disability Policy Studies* 23: 50–63.

Casner-Lotto, J., and L. Barrington. 2006. "Are They Really Ready to Work? Employers Perspectives on the Basic Knowledge and Applied Skills of New Entrants to the 21st Century U.S. Workforce." Report. Washington, DC: Partnership for 21st Century Skills. http://bit.ly/31nXTKs

Coleman Selden, S., and F. Selden. 2001. "Rethinking Diversity in Public Organizations for the 21st Century." *Administration & Society* 33 (3): 303–329.

Education for All Handicapped Children Act of 1975. Publ. L. No. 94-142, 94th Congress. (1975) (Enacted).

Erickson, W., C. Lee, and S. von Schrader. 2018. "2016 Disability Status Report: United States." Ithaca, NY: Cornell University Yang-Tan Institute on Employment and Disability.

Erickson, W., S. von Schrader, S.M. Bruyère, S. VanLooy, and D. Matteson. 2014. "Disability-Inclusive Employer Practices and Hiring of Individuals with Disabilities." *Rehabilitation Research, Policy and Education* 28 (4): 309–328.

Fabian, E., and R. Luecking. 2015. "Does Interagency Collaboration Improve Rehabilitation Outcomes for Transitioning Youth?" Research Brief 1, 15. Rockville, MD: Center on Transition to Employment for Youth with Disabilities and TransCen, Inc.

Gold, P.B., E.S. Fabian, and R.G. Luecking. 2013. "Job Acquisition by Urban Youth with Disabilities Transitioning from School to Work." *Rehabilitation Counseling Bulletin* 57: 31–45.

Hasazi, S.B., L.R. Gordon, and C.A. Roe. 1985. "Factors Associated with the Employment Status of Handicapped Youth Exiting High School from 1979 to 1983." *Exceptional Children* 51: 455–469.

Individuals with Disabilities Education Act (IDEA), 20 U.S.C. § 1400 (2004).

Karoly, L.A., and C.W.A. Panis. 2004. "The 21st Century at Work: Forces Shaping the Future Workforce and Workplace in the United States." Santa Monica, CA: Rand.

Katsiyannis, A., M.L. Yell, and R. Bradley. 2001. "Reflections on the 25th Anniversary of the Individuals with Disabilities Education Act." *Remedial and Special Education* 22 (6): 324–334.

Kohler, P., and S. Field. 2003. "Transition-Focused Education: Foundation for the Future." *Journal of Special Education* 37(3): 174–183.

Lindsay, S., T. Adams, R. Sanford, C. McDougall, S. Kingsnorth, and D. Menna-Dack. 2014. "Employers' and Employment Counselors' Perceptions of Desirable Skills for Entry-Level Positions for Adolescents: How Does It Differ for Youth with Disabilities?" *Disability & Society* 29 (6): 953–967.

Lipscomb, S., J. Haimson, A.Y. Liu, J. Burghardt, D.R. Johnson, and M. Thurlow. 2017. "Preparing for Life After High School: The Characteristics and Experiences of Youth in Special Education. Findings from the National Longitudinal Transition Study 2012. Volume 2: Comparisons Across Disability Groups: Full Report (NCEE 2017-4018)." Washington, DC: US Department of Education, Institute of Education Sciences, National Center for Education Evaluation and Regional Assistance.

Liu, A.Y., J. Lacoe, S. Lipscomb, J. Haimson, D.R. Johnson, and M.L. Thurlow. 2018. "Preparing for Life After High School: The Characteristics and Experiences of Youth in Special Education.

Findings from the National Longitudinal Transition Study 2012. Volume 3: Comparisons over Time (Full Report) (NCEE 2018-4007)." Washington, DC: US Department of Education, Institute of Education Sciences, National Center for Education Evaluation and Regional Assistance.

Luecking, R. 2009. *The Way to Work: How to Facilitate Work Experiences for Youth in Transition.* Baltimore, MD: Paul H. Brookes.

Luecking, R., A. Deschamps, R. Allison, J. Hyatt, and C. Stuart. 2015. "A Guide to Developing Collaborative School–Community–Business Partnerships." Washington, DC: National Technical Assistance Center on Transition.

Mazzotti, V.L., D.A. Rowe, J. Sinclair, M. Poppen, W.E. Woods, and M.L. Shearer. 2016. "Predictors of Post-School Success: A Systematic Review of NLTS2 Secondary Analyses." *Career Development and Transition for Exceptional Individuals* 39: 195–215.

Newman, L., M. Wagner, R. Cameto, A. Knokey, and D. Shaver. 2010. "Comparisons Across Time of the Outcomes of Youth with Disabilities Up to Four Years After High School: A Report of Findings from the National Longitudinal Transition Study (NLTS) and the National Longitudinal Transition Study-2 (NLTS-2)." Washington DC: US Department of Education, Institute of Educational Services, National Center for Special Education Research.

Newman, L., M. Wagner, A.M. Knokey, C. Marder, K. Nagle, D. Shaver, and M. Schwarting. 2011. "The Post-High School Outcomes of Young Adults with Disabilities Up to 8 Years After High School: A Report from the National Longitudinal Transition Study–2 (NLTS2; NCSER 2011-3005)." Menlo Park, CA: SRI International.

Office of Disability Employment Policy. 2012. "Cultivating Leadership: Mentoring Youth with Disabilities." Washington, DC: US Department of Labor. http://bit.ly/2ttHghA

Office of Special Education Programs (OSEP). 2017. Part B SPP/APR Indicator/Measurement Table. Washington, DC: US Department of Education. http://bit.ly/2Im9gfH

Rowe, D.A., C.Y. Alverson, and D.K. Unruh. 2015. "A Delphi Study to Operationalize Evidence-Based Predictors in Secondary Transition." *Career Development and Transition for Exceptional Individuals* 38: 113–126.

Shandra, C.L., and D.P. Hogan. 2009. "School-to-Work Program Participation and the Post-High School Employment of Young Adults with Disabilities." *Journal of Vocational Rehabilitation* 29 (2): 117–130.

Simões, C., and S. Santos. 2016. "Comparing the Quality of Life of Adults With and Without Intellectual Disability." *Journal of Intellectual Disability Research* 60: 378–388.

Snider, J., R.P. Hill, and D. Martin. 2003. "Corporate Social Responsibility in the 21st Century: A View from the World's Most Successful Firms." *Journal of Business Etiquette* 48 (2): 175–187.

Symonds, W.C., R. Schwartz, and R.F. Ferguson. 2011. "Pathways to Prosperity: Meeting the Challenge of Preparing Young Americans for the 21st Century." Cambridge, MA: Pathways to Prosperity Project, Harvard University Graduate School of Education. http://bit.ly/2GbsYcq

Test, D.W., V. Mazzotti, A.L. Mustian, R. Fowler, L. Kortering, and P. Kohler. 2009. "Evidence-Based Secondary Transition Predictors for Improving Postschool Outcomes for Students with Disabilities." *Career Development for Exceptional Individuals* 32: 160–181. doi:10.1177/0885728809346960

Tilson Jr., G.P., R.G. Luecking, and M.R. Donovan. 1994. "Involving Employers in Transition: The Bridges Model." *Career Development for Exceptional Individuals* 17: 77–89.

Turnbull, R.H., and A.P. Turnbull. 1998. *Free Appropriate Public Education: The Law and Children with Disabilities.* Denver, CO: Love Publishing.

US Bureau of Labor Statistics. 2017. "Persons with a Disability: Labor Force Characteristics–2015." Publication No. 16-1248. Washington, DC: US Bureau of Labor Statistics.

US Small Business Administration. 2018. "2018 Small Business Administration Profile." Washington, DC: US Small Business Administration. http://bit.ly/2Iklw06

Wagner, M., L. Newman, R. Cameto, and P. Levine. 2005. "Changes over Time in the Early Postschool Outcomes of Youth with Disabilities: A Report of Findings from the National Longitudinal Transition Study (NLTS) and the National Longitudinal Transition Study-2 (NLTS-2)." Menlo Park, CA: SRI International.

Wehman, P. 2013. *Life Beyond the Classroom: Transition Strategies for Young People with Disabilities* (5th ed.). Baltimore, MD: Paul H. Brookes.

Wehman, P., A.P. Sima, J. Ketchum, M.D. West, F. Chan, and R. Luecking. 2015. "Predictors of Successful Transition from School to Employment for Youth with Disabilities." *Journal of Occupational Rehabilitation* 25: 323–334.

Yell, M. 1998. *The Law and Special Education.* Old Tappan, NJ: Merrill/Prentice Hall.

CHAPTER 8

Mental Illness and Employment: Understanding a Major Disability Population in the US Workforce

HANNAH RUDSTAM
HSIAO-YING (VICKI) CHANG
HASSAN ENAYATI
Cornell University

INTRODUCTION: A MAP OF THE TERRITORY

Over the past two decades, labor and employment relations (LER) practitioners have made significant strides in understanding disability in the workplace and in supporting people with disabilities in getting and keeping jobs. Mental illness, however, poses a unique set of dilemmas for LER practitioners. People with mental illness comprise one of the largest categories of disability in workplaces both in the United States and across the globe (Steel et al. 2014; Vigo, Thornicroft, and Alun 2016; World Health Organization 2011). They are also one of the largest disability groups given rights and protections under the United Nations Convention on the Rights of Persons with Disabilities (United Nations 2006; World Health Organization 2013) and the Americans with Disabilities Amendments Act (ADAAA) (US EEOC 2009a). Yet they are arguably the least understood, the most stigmatized, and the most likely to be blamed for their condition—attitudes that fuel a deeply entrenched discrimination in the workplace (Baldwin 2016; Corrigan, Markowitz, and Watson 2004; Follmer and Jones 2018; Witaj et al. 2014). Further, mental illness is often not visible to others, making disability disclosure a choice. These and other issues make for a unique set of dilemmas surrounding mental illness disabilities in the workplace.

Navigating these dilemmas is not just about disability or legal compliance. It is also a business issue. About 18% of an organization's applicant pool and workforce will consist of people with mental illness, and this number is growing (NIMH 2016). Employers cannot afford to ignore one fifth of their current and potential workforce. Hence, these issues are increasingly seen as a key element of organizational effectiveness (Follmer and Jones 2018).

Into the future, employers will turn to LER practitioners to guide them in building workplaces where the large group of workers with mental illness can continue to be productive when working with a disability. The purpose of this chapter is both to provide LER practitioners with information about mental illness in the workplace and to build perspective. LER practitioners are well positioned to bring about intelligent action that can both benefit business and reduce ineffective discriminatory practices against this large segment of the talent pool and current workforce.

Though there is an extensive body of literature on mental illness and employment (see, for example, Banerjee, Chatterji, and Lahiri 2017; Follmer and Jones 2018; Harrington 2014; McDowell and Fossey 2015; NAMI 2014; OECD 2012), much of the work in this area has bypassed the key issue of employment discrimination. An important challenge for LER practitioners lies not just in "fixing" the individual but also in changing the social dynamic of the workplace to enable people with mental illness to sustain productivity when working with a disability. Four thematic perspectives run through this literature. First, the medical perspective, of course, focuses on the causes, prevention, and treatment of mental illness. Second, the occupational health perspective focuses on promoting mental health in the workplace (Aldridge and Harris 2017), addressing return-to-work issues for workers with mental illness (Pomaki 2017), mitigating the factors that contribute to mental illness in the workplace (such as stress or overwork) (Aldridge and Harris 2017), or reducing the risk of workplace violence (Clayson 2012; Krupa, Kirsh, Cockburn, and Gewurtz 2009). Third, the industrial–organizational psychology and human resources (HR) perspectives focus on legal compliance and building organizational climates to optimize productivity (Gurchiek 2015; Loehrke 2017). Fourth, the vocational rehabilitation perspective focuses on job placement for people with mental illness (and other disabilities), focusing mainly on people with serious mental illness (de Malmanche and Robertson 2015; Dean, Pepper, Schmidt, and Stern 2016; Hasson, Andersson, and Bejerholm 2011).

Though the need for these four thematic perspectives is self-evident, the issue of workplace discrimination against people with mental illness tends to exist only in their margins. Hence, the automatic (and often unquestioned) assumptions driving employment discrimination against people with mental illness are too seldom voiced in this literature. Mental illness is not just a medical condition. It exists within a broader social dynamic fueled by how people with mental illness are viewed by others—fueled by the social meaning of mental illness. A shift of attention to the social meaning of mental illness brings the issue of employment discrimination front and center. People with mental illness are limited not just by their impairment but also by the negative attitudes and misperceptions of others (Kinn, Holgersen, Aas, and Davidson 2014). Particularly in the realm of employment, the social meaning of mental illness can powerfully shape the employment experiences, decisions, and outcomes of people with mental illness.

Since Irving Goffman's early work on the nature of stigma, discrimination against people with mental illness has long been documented (see, for example, Baldwin 2016; Brohan et al. 2012; Brohan and Thornicroft 2010). Several misperceptions drive this employment discrimination: People with mental illness are seen to be more morally culpable for their impairment than people with other disabilities; they are seen to be dangerous, incompetent, and unpredictable; and they are seen as having intractable and permanent impairments. These misperceptions drive a structural discrimination that is a contributing factor to the negative employment outcomes for people with mental illness (Corrigan, Markowitz, and Watson 2004; Sharac, McCrone, Clement, and Thornicroft 2010; Stuart 2006). Much of the attention to mental illness in the workplace focuses on how to fix individuals by, for example, reducing stress in the work environment, providing better access to treatment, or improving supported employment services. Though these measures are certainly needed, a significant part of the picture is missing. How can we fix not just the individual but also the negative misperceptions of mental illness that give rise to employment discrimination?

In this chapter, we consider people with mental illness as one homogeneous group. In truth, of course, they are not. People with different mental illness diagnoses vary significantly in terms of treatment options, workplace support needs, the nature of discrimination they face, and employment outcomes. Yet there are important work–life experiences commonly shared by people with all types of mental illness. Their disability is often not immediately obvious to others, so disclosure can be a choice. They face widespread stigma and misperceptions because of their disability. Though they most often want to be employed, they encounter employment discrimination because of these misperceptions. They struggle to get effective treatment. The same employment laws and policies often apply to them, regardless of their mental illness diagnosis. They would benefit from changes in workplace cultures and policies that pave the way for effective individualized supports, such as accommodations. In most cases, LER practitioners will be dealing with these employment issues commonly faced by people with mental illness, instead of dealing with diagnosis-specific issues. For these reasons, our scope here is admittedly broad, encompassing the wide range of people with different types of mental illness.

DEFINITIONS AND DEBATES

Generally, mental illness in the United States is defined as any one of the nearly 300 disorders identified by the American Psychiatric Association's *Diagnostic and Statistical Manual of Mental Disorders* (2013). Yet there are ongoing debates around defining and categorizing mental illness. The term *mental illness* itself has been questioned because it invokes a narrow medical conceptualization that renders invisible how mental illness exists within a broader social dynamic that is rife with misperceptions and stigma. Throughout Europe and in other parts of the world, the term *mental disorder* has been preferred. Likewise, the idea that mental illness is the linear opposite of mental health has been called into question because it assumes that *mental illness* and *mental health* are mutually exclusive. Mental illness can be a chronic condition, but it is also a condition that is usually successfully treated (Harvey and Gumport 2015; Hunsley, Elliott, and Therrien

2013). Hence, one can live with a chronic disability but still be in a state of health (Follmer and Jones 2018; Keyes 2005). Also, mental illness is often co-morbid, occurring alongside other physical or mental diagnoses. Thirty-four million people have a co-occurring medical issue in addition to their mental illness diagnosis (Druss and Walker 2011). Finally, there has been controversy surrounding the issue of whether autism spectrum disorders (ASDs) should be considered a mental illness (O'Reilly, Karim, and Lester 2015; Rettew 2015). At issue is whether ASDs (especially Asperger Syndrome) are not mental illnesses but a different neurological state—simply a different way of thinking (Austin and Pisano 2017).

Prevalence of Mental Illness in the United States

According to the National Survey on Drug Use and Health (CBHSQ 2015), 43.4 million adults, or 17.9% of all US adults age 18 or older, experience some form of mental illness, indicating the high prevalence of mental illness in the US population. Among adults in the United States with *any* mental illness (AMI), 9.8 million (or 22% of those with AMI) report *serious* mental illness (SMI). Generally, SMI refers to mental illness diagnoses with more severe and longer-term daily living impairments, such as schizophrenia or major depression. The percentage of adults in the United States with AMI and SMI has remained steady from 2008 to 2015 (CBHSQ 2015).

An analysis of 2005–2008 mental illness surveillance data from the Centers for Disease Control and Prevention reveals differences in prevalence rates for particular mental illness diagnoses (Reeves et al. 2011). Specifically, 6.8% of US adults ages 18 and over reported currently having depression, and approximately 16% of adults had received a diagnosis of depression sometime in their lives (Reeves et al. 2011). The lifetime prevalence rates for anxiety, bipolar disorder, and schizophrenia are lower. Approximately 12% of adults reported having anxiety, 1.7% of adults reported bipolar disorder, and 0.6% of adults reported schizophrenia (Reeves et al. 2011).

Access to Treatment and Recovery

The majority of people treated for mental illness do recover. For example, about 70% to 85% of people with bipolar disorder or depression, 70% of people with anxiety disorders, and 50% of people with schizophrenia (a serious mental illness) do significantly improve with treatment (Insel 2015). Yet access to mental health treatment is uneven and depends mostly on state laws and policies. States that passed laws in favor of implementing the Affordable Care Act Medicaid Expansion and the Mental Health Parity Act had significantly higher levels of treatment access for people with mental illness (Mental Health America 2017). In 2017, 17% of adults with mental illness had no health insurance and, hence, no access to treatment. Among adults with mental illness who had health insurance, about 57% did not receive any mental health treatment (Mental Health America 2017).

MENTAL ILLNESS IN THE WORKPLACE

Mental Illness, Employment Outcomes, and Job Discrimination

Despite their ability and willingness to work (Drake et al. 2016; McQuilken et al. 2003; Secker and Membrey 2003), people with mental illness continue to report higher unemployment rates and worse employment outcomes than people without mental illness. Luciano and Meara (2014) examined the employment status of 77,326 working-age adults with and without mental illness using data from the 2009–2010 National Survey on Drug Use and Health. They found that, as mental illness becomes more severe, the unemployment rate increases and the full-time employment rate decreases. People without mental illness have a higher full-time employment rate (61.7%) than people with mild (50.9%), moderate (46.6%), or serious (38.1%) mental illness. Additionally, people without mental illness have a lower unemployment rate (7%) than people with mild (9.4%), moderate (10.2%), or serious mental illness (10.5%).

That mental illness is linked to lower income has been shown in a number of studies. For example, Luciano and Meara (2014) found that people with mental illness earn less than people without mental illness. Specifically, of those who are employed, 21.4% of people with SMI earn less than $10,000, compared with only 12.3% of people without mental illness (Luciano and Meara 2014).

Both national survey data and administrative datasets are useful in understanding the intersection of mental illness and workplace discrimination (Enayati and von Schrader 2016; Erickson, Karpur, and Hallock 2016). von Schrader (2011) reviewed US Equal Employment Opportunity Commission (EEOC) data and Americans with Disabilities Act (ADA) charges filed from 2005 through 2010 by people who had experienced workplace discrimination because of their disabilities. The analysis showed that 6% of the ADA charges concerned depression and 3.5% of the charges concerned anxiety disorders. The number of ADA charges that cited mental disorders increased between 2005 and 2010, with anxiety disorders having the largest increase. von Schrader (2011) showed that 58.4% of these charges were related to discharge, and 28.2% of the charges involved issues regarding reasonable accommodations. In short, charges brought by people with mental illness are a significant and increasing source of EEOC employment discrimination charges.

Several studies have examined how employers' beliefs about people with mental illness fuel employer decisions that negatively affect employment outcomes. For example, Brohan and Thornicroft's (2010) survey of 502 employers showed that the top five concerns employers had about hiring people with mental illness included (in order of prevalence) fears of co-worker safety, inability to handle stress, strange or unpredictable behaviors, impaired job performance, and absenteeism. Krupa, Kirsh, Cockburn, and Gewurtz (2009) found similar employer assumptions about workers with mental illness, such as being unable to do the job, being a danger to others, exacerbating the employee's symptoms and being relied on for charity.

Over the past three decades, several studies have shown how these negative beliefs affect employers' decisions about applicants and employees with mental illness (Sharac, McCrone, Clement, and Thornicroft 2010; Stuart 2006). In one study, half of US employers said they would hesitate to hire someone with a history of mental illness and 70% would not hire someone who was currently taking psychiatric medication or had a history of substance abuse (Scheid 1999; Stuart 2006). Similarly, Manning and White (1995) found that half of employers surveyed would almost never hire an applicant if they knew the person had a psychiatric disability and nearly 25% would dismiss an employee if it was found out she or he had a psychiatric disability. Studies of applicants and employees with mental illness further illustrate how these beliefs and practices impact the work lives of people with mental illness. Applicants and employees with mental illness have described experiences such as being dismissed from the hiring process, avoided by co-workers, micromanaged by supervisors, and excluded from meetings after having disclosed a mental illness (Mental Health Foundation 2002; Thornicroft et al. 2009). These (and other) studies point to the role of stigma in the employment outcomes of people with mental illness. Yet more research is needed to discern the roles of individual effects (such as lack of skills or poor job performance) and discrimination in employment outcomes for people with mental illness.

How does this stigma unfold in the workplace? Ben-Zeev, Young, and Corrigan (2010) have identified three ways stigma affects life outcomes: public stigma, self-stigma, and label avoidance. This framework enables a more nuanced look at how mental illness discrimination occurs in the workplace.

Public stigma involves commonly held stereotypes that determine how employment decisions (such as hiring, promotion, or termination) are made about people with mental illness. The effect of public stigma on employment opportunities for people with mental illness has been clearly shown (Baldwin and Johnson 2004; Link 1987; Scheid 2005; Stuart 2006).

Self-stigma occurs when people with mental illness internalize public stigma and negatively judge their own competence or potential on the job (Corrigan, Larson, and Rusch 2009; Link et al. 2001). Though more subtle than public stigma, self-stigma can powerfully impact employment outcomes in several ways: failing to seek development or training opportunities, fearing participation in group meetings, isolating oneself from mentoring or workplace social connections, and exacerbating stress. These workplace behaviors can, in turn, worsen mental illness symptoms.

Label avoidance occurs when a fear of stigma inhibits seeking support or treatment (Kessler et al. 2009). Label avoidance can prevent people from coming forward to get needed supports or accommodations, resulting in lowered job performance, increased absences, or failure to voluntarily disclose mental illness in response to the employer's reporting activities—behaviors which, again, can result in exacerbation of symptoms, The negative impact of self-stigma and label avoidance has been shown in a recent survey. In one study, 95% of employees who took time off because of stress-related depression reported hiding the real cause of their absence from their employer, and 49% reported being uncomfortable with talking to their employer about mental health (Deloitte UK Centre for Health Solutions 2017).

These (and other) studies highlight the multilayered and entrenched nature of employment discrimination against people with mental illness. Automatic assumptions about mental illness not only keep qualified applicants out of the workplace, but they also prevent employees from seeking treatments and workplace supports that could sustain their job performance.

Yet the picture is not all bleak. Employers who have had experience employing people with mental illness are more likely than those who have not to hire more people with mental illness (Hand and Tryssenaar 2006; Ozawa and Yaeda 2007).

What does this mean to LER practitioners? Advocating for reduced workplace stress, better services, and improved access to treatment for workers with mental illness will always be part of what LER practitioners need to do to improve employment outcomes for people with mental illness. But this alone won't be enough. LER practitioners also need to direct their efforts toward changing workplace culture and climate in ways that will enable the presence and performance of workers with mental illness. The concluding section of this chapter discusses these actions in greater detail.

Mental Illness and Job Performance

Though there is a significant body of research on mental illness in the workplace, fewer studies examine work performance or competence. Generally, these studies suggest that workers with mental illness have greater rates of absenteeism (Dewa, Lesage, Goering, and Caveen 2004; Goetzel et al. 2004) and reduced productivity (Ashman and Gibson 2010; De Lorenzo 2013; Kessler et al. 2009).

Yet there are a few caveats to consider when translating these findings into workplace practices. First, unlike studies that examine the job performance of people with other disabilities (see, for example, DePaul University 2007; Institute for Corporate Productivity 2014; Wood and Marshall 2010), studies on the job performance of people with mental illness have often assessed performance levels *without* accommodations or other mitigating measures in place (Arends et al. 2014; Sallis and Birkin 2014). Second, measures of the job performance of people with mental illness have largely relied on self-reporting (see, for example, Gilmour and Patten 2007; Sallis and Birkin 2014). Individuals with the most prevalent types of mental illness (depression and anxiety disorders) are likely to self-stigmatize (Drapalski et al. 2013) and could be prone to under-reporting their productivity. Third, the majority of people with a mental illness diagnosis do not have serious mental illness. People with serious mental illness make up about 22% of those with any mental illness (CBHSQ 2015), yet much of the research on mental illness and workplace issues (such as job retention and violence) is carried out on people with serious mental illness (see, for example, Arends et al. 2014; Desmarais et al. 2014; Gladman and Waghorn 2016).

About Mental Illness and Workplace Violence

A commonly held belief driving workplace policies and practice regarding people with mental illness is that they are dangerous to others (Krupa, Kirsh, Cockburn, and Gewurtz 2009; Tsang et al. 2007). When a violent incident occurs in the workplace, it is often automatically assumed that mental illness was the cause of the violence. The fact that this belief is largely not supported by evidence is surprising to many employers.

The fear of workplace violence is largely influenced by social media, movies, and public speech, where mental illness and violence are often portrayed as synonymous. A recent study conducted by McGinty, Kennedy-Hendricks, Choksy, and Barry (2016) examined news stories from 1995 to 2014 and found that more than half of the news articles on violence linked the violent events in question to mental illness. They also found increased coverage of mass shootings with consistent (but unfounded) attribution to mental illness issues. The impact of social media coverage emphasizing mental illness and violence significantly enhances the deeply ingrained stigma that shapes public perceptions of people with mental illness.

What is the evidence? People with mental illness, who comprise about 18% of the US population, account for less than 1% of all gun-related homicides and about 6% of mass-shooting events (Knoll and Annas 2016). Further, Fazel and Grann (2006) found that nearly 95% of any violent crimes (such as homicide, common assault, threatening behavior, or robbery) were committed by people who did not have mental illness. Looking only at people with SMI, Steadman et al. (2015) showed that less than 2% committed gun-related violence within one year after discharge from the hospital. In fact, most people with mental illness are victims rather than perpetrators of violence (Desmarais et al. 2014). People with SMI are 11 times more likely to be victims of a crime than people without mental illness (Teplin, McClelland, Abram, and Weiner 2005).

Framing violence in the workplace as a mental health issue is an oversimplification that both marginalizes people with mental illness and will not make the workplace safer. The action implications for LER practitioners involves supporting employers in creating policies that are evidence based and that truly improve safety in the workplace.

DISABILITY EMPLOYMENT LAW AND MENTAL ILLNESS

Mental Illness and the ADA

The intent of Congress to protect people with mental illness from job discrimination is apparent in the very definition of disability contained in the original ADA of 1990 and the ADAAA of 2008 as "a *physical or mental* (italics ours) impairment" (US EEOC 2012). Yet employers remain confused about how to apply the ADAAA to mental illness issues (De Lorenzo 2013; Fairclough, Robinson, Nichols, and Cousley 2013), and people with mental illness continue to struggle to assert their rights under the ADAAA (McAlpine and Warner 2002; Melkumyan 2013; von Schrader and Erickson 2017).

When the ADAAA was passed in 2008, the definition of disability was expanded and clarified (US EEOC 2008). It was hoped that the ADAAA would provide more protections to people with mental illness in several ways (Center and Imparato 2003; Schopick 2012). First, disability was now to be determined without mitigating measures (such as medications or therapy) in place. For people with mental illness, this meant that the many people who were being treated for mental illness were more likely to be included in ADAAA's protections against employment discrimination. Second, though the ADAAA did not change the phrase "substantially limited in one or more major life activity," the expansion of a clarifying list of major life activities now included some activities that would seem to align with common symptoms of mental illness, such as interacting with others and concentrating. Third, the ADAAA strengthened the "regarded as" prong of the definition of disability. With mental illness being one of the most stigmatized and misunderstood disabilities, it was hoped that this strengthening would give people with mental illness additional protections against employment discrimination (Engelmeier and Marshall 2014; Schopick 2012).

Regulations for the ADAAA were not issued until 2011, so case law on employment discrimination and mental illness is still evolving. Overall, however, a few trends have been identified. For employment discrimination cases involving any kind of disability under the ADAAA, the number of cases dismissed through summary judgment has clearly decreased after the passing of the ADAAA. Yet this decrease has been far greater for cases involving physical disabilities than for those involving mental disabilities. One study conducted between 2010 and 2013 found the rate of summary judgment dismissal for post–Amendments Act cases involving physical disabilities was 20.7%, compared with 40% for those involving mental disabilities (Befort 2013; Kaminer 2016).

Though a complete review of post-ADAAA case law on mental illness is outside the scope of this chapter, we can touch on three issues around how courts have reacted post-ADAAA to cases involving mental illness and employment. First, since passage of the ADAAA, the attention of the courts has shifted away from whether the individual has a disability and toward whether the individual is qualified to do the job. Passing the "qualified individual" hurdle has been more problematic for people with mental illness than for those with physical disabilities (Befort 2013; Kaminer 2016; Schopick 2012). Being qualified to do the job is not just about education and experience credentials; it has more revolved around whether the employer can defend its definition of essential job functions that define "qualified." Attendance as an essential job function has often been at the heart of this argument. Because attendance is a particularly problematic job function for workers with mental illness, they have struggled to show that they are "qualified individuals" who can get the protections of the ADAAA (Kaminer 2016; Schopick 2012). Second, courts have been less likely to rule that the discrimination events brought by workers with mental illness "count" as adverse impact as often as they do for people with physical disabilities (Kaminer 2016). Third, though the "regarded as" prong of the ADAAA protections should have particularly benefited individuals with mental illness (as they protect against discrimination based on stigma and misperception), this prong has only rarely been used (Befort 2013; Kaminer 2016).

Several documents recently issued by EEOC can clarify these rather complex issues. In 2016, EEOC issued a new document, "Depression, PTSD, & Other Mental Health Conditions in the Workplace: Your Legal Rights," which provides an overview of the rights of applicants and workers with mental illness (US EEOC 2016). Further, a full explanation of how the ADAAA applies to employment interactions involving mental illness is available in the EEOC document, "EEOC Enforcement Guidance on the Americans with Disabilities Act and Psychiatric Disabilities" (US EEOC 2009a).

Mental Illness and the Disability Disclosure Dilemma

The ADAAA limits when an employer can inquire about applicants' or employees' disabilities (US EEOC 2009b). Mental illness is often not immediately obvious to others. Hence, except when the person is asking for a reasonable accommodation, disclosure is, in many employment situations, a legally protected choice. However, it is a choice that people with mental illness (and many employers) may not always realize they have, particularly those who are newly diagnosed (Brohan et al. 2012). An important role for LER practitioners is to spread awareness among both employers and people with mental illness that disclosure during hiring and employment is, in many employment situations, a choice.

Even when people with mental illness understand their disclosure choices, they often see this as a high-stakes gamble with both costs and possible benefits (Brohan et al. 2012; Jones 2011). The choice to disclose a mental illness can be proactive (such as asking for an accommodation or a desire to not have to hide the mental illness) or reactive (such as explaining a workplace behavior) (Jones 2011). For obvious reasons, most applicants with mental illness choose not to disclose to potential employers (Brohan et al. 2012; Jones 2011; Marwaha and

Johnson 2005). When working, they may (except when asking for an accommodation) choose to disclose a mental illness, the level of detail they use when disclosing, and the words used to describe their mental illness. Ellison, Russinova, MacDonald-Wilson, and Lyass (2003) found that voluntary disclosure rates for workers with mental illness (including both serious and nonserious mental illness) varied by employment sector. Forty-six percent of workers in the human services sector voluntarily disclosed, compared with 30% in the business, educational, or technical services sectors. Another study, focusing only on workers with serious mental illness, examined the consequences of disclosing to someone at work (Pandya et al. 2011). In this study, 42% reported no change in how they were treated at work after disclosing, 38% reported being treated worse, and 20% reported being treated better. From the applicants' and workers' perspectives, disclosing a mental illness is a risk most are unwilling to take unless they have a reasonable expectation of benefiting from this disclosure. These benefits could include getting an accommodation, building connections with others, explaining a behavior, or simply not having to hide their mental illness.

From the employers' perspective, the disclosure dilemma is often played out when the employer believes an employee has mental illness that she or he has not disclosed. According to the ADAAA, any disability inquiry the employer makes in this situation must be job related and consistent with business necessity (US EEOC 2009b). Two key questions determine this criterion. First, does the employer have a *reasonable belief* that the worker has a disability that impacts performance of essential job functions? Second, is there a *reasonable belief* that the employee poses a direct threat to others? A reasonable belief is one based on objective evidence—not vague speculation or unlikely scenarios (US EEOC 2009b). If the answer is yes to either of those two questions, the employer may make a disability inquiry and/or require a medical exam.

The action implications for LER practitioners involve understanding the human, legal, and practical issues related to disclosing a mental illness and balancing the needs of employers and applicants/employees with mental illness. As a first step, build awareness of disclosure as a legally protected choice among both employees and employers. Second, balance employers' motivation to know with applicants' and workers' motivation to conceal. Third, if employers want more people with mental illness to come forward, pose questions about why they do not. What actually happens to people who come forward with a mental illness in their workplace? Ultimately, it is what actually happens that will influence the disclosure decision more powerfully than will pronouncements or workplace policies.

Accommodations for People with Mental Illness

People with mental illness are one of the largest groups with a legal right to a reasonable accommodation in the American workplace. Yet employers struggle to provide them with effective accommodations (McDowell and Fossey 2015) and are more hesitant to provide accommodations for people with mental illness than with physical disabilities (McAlpine and Warner 2002; Shankar et al. 2014). Research suggests several reasons for this reluctance. Employers tend to believe workers with mental illness are less deserving of accommodations than people with other disabilities (McDowell and Fossey 2015; Shankar et al. 2014). Accommodations for workers with mental illness are less straightforward and tangible than for other types of disabilities (Mancuso 1990; McDowell and Fossey 2015). For example, the need to build a ramp or modify furniture is more tangible than the need to change the supervisory style for a worker with an anxiety disorder. In fact, because of the less tangible nature of accommodations for workers with mental illness, many employers actually do accommodate them but do not recognize these efforts as an accommodation (Mizzoni and Kirsh 2006).

Further, employers have less knowledge of accommodation options for workers with mental illness than for those with physical impairments (Unger and Kregel 2003). There is less consensus in the literature on how to identify and implement effective accommodations for people with mental illness (McDowell and Fossey 2015; Secker, Membrey, Grove, and Seebohm 2003). Finally, workers with mental illness themselves might be less willing to request an accommodation. They may not recognize that mental illness "counts" as a disability, or they might believe the risk of disclosing is not worth the possibility of getting an accommodation (Brohan et al. 2012).

When workers are not accommodated, they are not as productive (Loy 2015). Given the large number of people in the workplace with mental illness, finding ways to overcome these barriers to accommodation is a key issue for LER practitioners. What are the action implications for LER practitioners? First, practitioners need to broaden their understanding of the types of accommodation options for people with mental illness. The US Department of Labor's Job Accommodation Network (JAN) describes more than 100 types of accommodations to be considered for workers with mental illness (Job Accommodation Network 2015), such as increased reminders for completing work tasks, work from home, time off for attending treatment, short breaks for fatigue related to medication adjustments, changing marginal job tasks, or using white-noise earphones for reducing ambient noise.

Second, practitioners must recognize that the interactive process to find effective accommodations for people with mental illness requires an individualized approach. Given the wide range of functional limitations associated with mental illness, there is no one-size-fits-all for finding accommodations. Even individuals with the same diagnosis could need very different types of accommodations, depending on the person, the job, and how the person's condition impacts the job. Also, accommodation needs can change as treatment and the mental illness conditions change.

Third, the ADAAA requires employers to engage in an interactive process to identify a reasonable accommodation. Because of the widely varying needs of workers with mental illness, this interactive process for them may require more listening, more attention to the individual's unique functional impairments related to the job, and more expertise in the range of accommodations that can be considered. This level of expertise is often outside the job description and competence of managers and supervisors. Having a centralized accommodation function, which takes the main responsibility for the interactive process away from managers and supervisors, can ensure a more effective accommodation process for workers with mental illness (and others).

Fourth, LER practitioners need to reach out to employees/applicants themselves. People with mental illness themselves may have internalized the sense that, unlike physical impairments, mental illness is not a "real" disability (Drapalski et al. 2013). Hence, they might not believe they have a right to or deserve an accommodation.

Applying the ADAAA to Mental Illness: Some Employer Dilemmas

In what follows, we highlight three specific dilemmas involving mental illness in the workplace where employers are often challenged in applying the ADAAA.

Employee First Discloses a Mental Illness After a Negative Performance Evaluation or Disciplinary Action

Workers might disclose a mental illness to a supervisor in response to a negative performance evaluation or disciplinary action. When this happens, the supervisor should treat this as a request for a reasonable accommodation, and the organization's process for reasonable accommodation should be set into motion. However, the employee can be held accountable for his or her performance leading up to the disclosure. The employer does not have to withdraw performance evaluations or disciplinary actions taken prior to the disclosure of a mental illness (US EEOC 2009a). However, future performance evaluations should be conducted only after a reasonable accommodation is in place.

Employer Wants to Terminate a Worker Because of a Mental Illness

An employee with a mental illness (or any other disability covered under the ADAAA) can be terminated if she or he is unqualified to do the job or if there is sound evidence that she or he poses a direct threat to others.

The definition of "qualified individual" goes beyond levels of education and experience. More broadly, the ADAAA defines "qualified" as being able to perform the essential functions of the job with or without a reasonable accommodation (US EEOC 2009a). Employers might encounter two pitfalls when determining whether a worker with mental illness can be considered unqualified and, hence, terminated. First, the employer might fail to have identified and justified essential job functions. Essential functions are those that justify the existence of the job (such as driving for a food delivery worker), require a set of skills specific to the job role, and cannot easily be performed by co-workers. For example, giving patients intravenous medications would be an essential job function for a hospital nurse, but delivering meals to patients would not because it does not involve a specific skill set and could be done by others in the workplace. The second pitfall involves determining too quickly that the worker is unqualified. Employers sometimes do not understand that "unqualified" is, in most cases, determined after, not before, a reasonable accommodation has been put into place.

The other common grounds for terminating employees with mental illness is "direct threat," defined as "a significant risk of substantial harm to the health or safety of the individual or others that cannot be eliminated or reduced by reasonable accommodation" (US EEOC 2009a). Under the ADAAA, employers do have a right to terminate employees who pose a direct threat to co-workers or the public. However, this direct threat must be based on a reasonable belief and evidence, not on vague speculation or unlikely scenarios. As discussed above, research does not support the idea that a mental illness diagnosis *in itself* constitutes a threat to others. To terminate an employee with mental illness on the basis of direct threat, the employer must show specific employee behaviors that pose a clear and imminent danger to others (such as verbally threatening co-workers or menacing the public) (US EEOC 2009a).

Employer Has a Policy of Zero Tolerance for Alcohol or Illegal Drug Use on the Job

About 8.4% of American adults (20.2 million people) were classified with addictive disorder in 2014 (SAMHSA 2015), making it one of the most prevalent types of mental illness in the American workplace. Addictive disorder may also co-occur with other types of mental illness. Many employers view addictive disorders not as a disability or a mental illness but as a choice (National Safety Council 2015). Hence, they tend to be less accepting of people with this condition and have more difficulty in applying the ADAAA to employment situations involving addictive disorders. The laws in this area can be confusing and even contradictory, with state disability laws sometimes differing from federal law (SAMHSA 2015). The ADAAA does not require employers to tolerate alcohol or illegal drug use on the job (US EEOC 2009a). Workers who are impaired by alcohol or illegal drugs while on the job can be disciplined or terminated when they violate zero-tolerance policies that have been fairly and uniformly applied. Employers may conduct screens for illegal drug use among applicants and employees, but certain guidelines must be followed. The drug screen cannot be a medical inquiry, meaning that it must use the five-panel test, which focuses on screening for illegal drugs not legally prescribed drugs. In some cases, however, even the five-panel test will detect certain legally prescribed drugs, such as some drugs used to control anxiety disorders. If this happens, employers cannot discriminate against individuals who have these false positives by, for example, withdrawing a job offer or terminating employment (US EEOC 2009a). Finally, applicants and workers with addictive disorders are given some protections under the ADAAA. Applicants and workers cannot be discriminated against because of a history of an addictive disorder for which they are now in recovery. Also, employees who are recovering from an addictive disorder may have a right to an accommodation, such as time off for attending treatment (US EEOC 2009a).

The action implications for LER practitioners involve supporting employers in avoiding certain pitfalls regarding mental illness and employment. These pitfalls revolve around certain questions to pose to employers. Does everyone across the organization (and specifically managers/supervisors) understand that mental illness is often defined as a disability under the law? Have they defined essential versus marginal job functions? Are drug screens being used appropriately? Does everyone who recruits or hires fully understand the ADAAA's limitations on disability inquiries? Are managers/supervisors able to recognize and move forward accommodation requests from workers with mental illness? Is the direct threat criterion being invoked appropriately?[1]

CONCLUSION: LER PRACTITIONERS AND ORGANIZATIONAL CHANGE

Changing Organizational Climate

LER practitioners stand at the nexus of organizational leaders, managers, and employees with disabilities. Hence, they are uniquely positioned to be a powerful force in addressing the issues discussed in this chapter. Underlying all these issues is the need to create an organizational climate that enables workers with mental illness to fully contribute to organizational goals. Given the substantial number of applicants and employees with mental illness, this becomes not just a medical issue or a problem of legal compliance. It is also a business issue. Whether employers know it or not, about one fifth of their applicant pools and workforce will have mental illness. Being unable to fully engage this large segment of available talent has significant consequences for organizational effectiveness in meeting business goals.

Many of our previous points have revolved around the subtle, tacit nature of the misperceptions that often drive employment discrimination toward individuals with mental illness. Changing this discrimination will involve going beyond formal policies and practices to reach more deeply into the informal realm of everyday assumptions that drive workplace interactions. In other words, it will involve changing the organizational climate. A substantial literature focuses on organizational climate and its role in employee engagement and performance (see, for example, Albrecht, Breidahl, and Marty 2018; Findley Musgrove, Ellinger, and Ellinger 2014; Menguc, Auh, Yeniaras, and Katsikeas 2017). Other studies have looked at the effect of organizational climate on outcomes related to employee attitudes, safety, ethics, and general employee health (Parker et al. 2003; Schluter, Winch, Holzhauser, and Henderson 2008). The few studies examining how organizational climate impacts mental illness among employees are based on a medical model of mental illness (see, for example, Bronkhorst, Tummers, Steijn, and Vijverberg 2015) and have tended to focus narrowly on worker stress or burnout (see, for example, Gershon et al. 2007). The purpose of this research has mainly been on *preventing or reducing* mental illness among workers (MacDavitt, Chou, and Stone 2007; Michie and Williams 2003; Stansfeld and Candy 2006). Though useful, these studies have largely bypassed how the social identity of mental illness plays out in the workplace and how stigma and misperception drive workplace interactions in ways that lead to discrimination across HR functions. How can LER practitioners support employers in creating an organizational climate that not only reduces mental illness but also ensures that workers can, as much as possible, retain their jobs and continue to be productive when a mental illness arises?

Ehrhart, Schneider, and Macey (2014: 69) defined organizational climate as "the shared meaning organizational members attach to the events, policies, practices, and procedures they experience and the behaviors they see being rewarded, supported, and expected." Organizational climate is negotiated in the everyday fabric of lived experience and personal interactions in the workplace. It is the backdrop informing the subtle but powerful social meaning of mental illness in each workplace. Against this backdrop, people make in-the-moment decisions that collectively determine whether a workplace is inclusive or discriminatory. These in-the-moment decisions pivot around key questions: How should I treat a co-worker with mental illness? Should I hire a veteran even if I think she has PTSD? Should I hire an applicant who has been active in mental illness advocacy groups? If I have a mental illness, do I have a right to an accommodation? Who else will find out about my mental illness? Will my job performance be judged fairly? Will my co-workers see my accommodation as unfair? How these questions are answered shapes a myriad of larger questions about productivity, inclusiveness, work environment, retention, talent acquisition, and legal compliance. Though organizational climate is subtle, it is powerful in shaping an inclusive workplace. And changing it can be challenging.

Impacting organizational climate involves going beyond formal policies and procedures to reach more deeply into the fluid, tacit fabric of everyday life in the workplace. Because most research has been directed at how to prevent mental illness in the workplace, little evidence exists to inform how to facilitate organizational climates that prevent discrimination and build trust for people with mental illness. However, general research on interventions to change organizational climate have suggested three areas of focus: leadership, group practices and interactions, and communication flow (Bronkhorst, Tummers, Steijn, and Vijverberg 2015; Gershon et al. 2007). We adapt these three areas to the unique challenges in building organizational climates conducive to maximizing the productivity of workers with mental illness.

Leadership and Organization-Wide Processes

Because of the deep stigma and misperceptions associated with mental illness, organizational leaders have often hesitated to take a stand on discrimination against people with mental illness. A first step in building a positive organizational climate around mental illness in the workplace is to encourage leaders to publicly recognize the business costs of this discrimination, such as lost opportunities to acquire talent, lost productivity, higher turnover, and a hostile work environment.

Second, leaders should be urged to start new conversations in the workplace by publicly challenging the misperceptions surrounding mental illness and setting the tone for building trust with the roughly one fifth of the workforce who is impacted by mental illness. Though this step will take courage (given the deeply rooted assumptions about mental illness), taking it will be a powerful way to change how workers think about mental illness in their work groups.

Third, some of the steps described below (such as changing the accommodation process or creating an employee resource group) may involve changes in resource allocations. Decisions about resource allocations should always be made in the context of a full consideration of the business costs of not supporting workers with mental illness, such as increased employee turnover, reduced productivity, and lost opportunities for effective talent management.

Fourth, despite the passing of the Mental Health Parity Act in 2016, many health insurance plans do not provide access to effective treatment for physical and mental conditions (NAMI 2016). The clear majority of people with mental illness do get better with treatment (Insel 2015). Barriers to effective treatment for workers with mental illness lead to increased work absence and reduced productivity. Leaders should examine their employee health insurance plan to ensure that there is service parity for mental and physical health.

Fifth, organizational leadership must determine the organization-wide process for requesting and implementing accommodations. Many organizations have found that a centralized accommodation function is more effective than a one-off approach to requesting and implementing accommodations. This is especially the case for accommodations for employees with mental illness (McDowell and Fossey 2015). For many employees, the stigma surrounding mental illness is a significant barrier to requesting an accommodation from a manager or supervisor (Jones 2011). Further, finding effective accommodations for people with mental illness is beyond the expertise of most managers and supervisors (Brohan et al. 2012; McDowell and Fossey 2015). Creating a centralized accommodation function can ensure that the expertise needed to create effective accommodations for workers with mental illness is available. Finally, having employee assistance program practitioners who understand the legal and human issues in accommodating workers with mental illness can assist in the accommodation process.

Organizational leaders can reach out to create new partnerships with agencies addressing mental illness issues in the workplace. Some of these organizations are state based while others are national (such as the Center for Workplace Mental Health of the American Psychiatric Association or the Stigma-Free Company initiative of the National Alliance on Mental Illness). Forming these partnerships not only provides valuable services and insights, but it also sends employees within the organization a message about how people with mental illness will be treated.

Group Practices and Interactions

Changing organizational climate involves reaching beyond leadership to understand everyday life in work groups and informal interactions. A first step is to recognize the importance of managers and supervisors as arbiters of organizational climate for all workers (Buckingham and Coffman 1999; Momeni 2009; Osterman 2009) but particularly for workers with mental illness (Follmer and Jones 2018; Patrician, Shang, and Lake 2010). These face-to-face leaders play a powerful role in determining whether the climate of a work group is perceived as hostile or safe for employees with mental illness. Also, managers/supervisors are often on the front line of how workers with mental illness make decisions about requesting accommodations, and they often play a key role in implementing accommodations. Preparing managers and supervisors to deal effectively with mental illness issues in their work groups will involve a range of development experiences: training, awareness building, and communicating expectations for work group leadership.

Second, employee resource groups (ERGs) can be very helpful for employees with mental illness themselves and can also promote positive changes in how others in the workplace view mental illness issues (DiversityInc 2013). The most successful ERGs are those that can benefit both the group members and the organization. In addition to providing support for the individuals in the group, ERGs can also provide a voice to inform policies and practices in the larger organization (Welbourne and McLaughlin 2013). ERGs focusing on mental illness could do this by, for example, building awareness across the organization for the business need to provide a positive workplace environment for the sizable portion of the workforce who has a mental illness themselves or has a family member with a mental illness.

Third, most organizations have some way of "taking the pulse" of the organizational climate, usually through employee surveys. Given the significant percentage of employees working with a mental illness, these climate survey efforts could be made more powerful by including some questions on mental illness in the workplace. Normally, climate and work satisfaction surveys only touch on mental illness issues by assessing stress and burnout levels among workers. They usually do not assess whether workers with mental illness feel their environment is conducive to their productivity, view their work environment as supportive, are willing to request accommodations, or trust enough to come forward to be counted as a person with a disability for organizational reporting efforts.

Communications

While the medical meaning of mental illness is relatively fixed and cuts across settings, the social meaning of mental illness is often fluid, tacit, and grounded in the context of each workplace. Hence, communications plans about mental illness will need to be organization specific, with each workplace considering its unique situation when crafting a communications plan. If possible, involve the employee resource group in forming these communications. Organizational communications about mental illness need to have both an informational and an emotional–interactional component.

Informational Component

Information dissemination about mental illness in the workplace is relatively straightforward. First, simply get the word out that "disability" means both physical and mental disabilities. Many managers and workers may not realize that mental illness is a type of disability covered under the law. Likewise, they may not realize that people with mental illness can request accommodations and can and should come forward to be counted as a person with a disability for the organization's federal reporting requirements. As discussed, accommodations for workers with mental illness may not be as obvious as accommodations for physical disabilities. Providing examples of accommodations for workers with mental illness can be helpful. Second, ensure that the accommodation process is transparent to all employees and managers. When formulating an accommodation process, many companies focus only on the process itself without giving due attention to how the process will be communicated. Third, because of the stigma about mental illness, a key question posed by employees is if I come forward to report my disability or ask for an accommodation, who will find out about my diagnosis? Make this messaging more effective by including a simple statement addressing confidentiality.

Emotional–Interactional Component

Changing the automatic misperceptions that drive discrimination against people with mental illness involves going beyond information dissemination. Communications to change the emotions and perceptions that give rise to everyday workplace interactions can include several elements. First, as discussed, managers and supervisors set the emotional tone for how mental illness issues will be treated in the work group. Hence, reaching them is a cornerstone of any communication effort to build awareness of mental illness. Second, storytelling can be a powerful way to challenge assumptions and change perceptions (Boyce 1996; Dixon 2014). Real-life narratives about individuals working with mental illness, even when presented anonymously, can humanize mental illness and bring it out from the shadows. These narratives can also help employees draw the connections between an accepting organizational climate and business success. Third, surprise people. To challenge the assumption that people with mental illness cannot or should not work, highlight the personal stories of well-known people in the business world and other areas of life with mental illness who have made valued contributions to their careers or to society. Many recognizable people have publicly shared their stories about working with mental illness (Each Mind Matters 2013). The surprise element of these stories may cause some to rethink their automatic assumptions about the capabilities of people with mental illness. Fourth, provide forums for safe two-way conversations about mental illness. One organization sponsored a series of both virtual and face-to-face lunch-and-learn events that included discussions with mental illness experts and a panel consisting of ERG members, employees, and leaders who were willing to share their experiences. The final session consisted of HR and organizational leaders responding to anonymously collected employee feedback about what the organization was doing well and what needed improvement. After the session, the effort was sustained through guided virtual conversations between HR leaders and employees and by continuing the session discussion each year.

WHAT'S TO BE DONE?

Though a significant body of work on mental illness in the workplace has produced useful findings for LER practitioners, something is missing. In the workplace, how mental illness is viewed by others—the social meaning or stigma of mental illness—is often more limiting than the mental illness itself. Further, when this stigma is internalized by people with mental illness themselves, they make decisions about their own work lives that profoundly impact their employment outcomes: *What kind of job should I seek? Am I able to work? Will I get fired? What will my colleagues think? Should I ask for an accommodation?*

The points discussed above are not just a to-do checklist. Rather, they are shifts in attention—shifts that will take the organization beyond policies driven by misperception or distrust and toward more effective employment practices that leverage the full range of talent available to the organization. We have discussed several of these attention shifts in this chapter. What can LER practitioners do?

- Go beyond focusing solely on fixing the individual to focusing on creating organizational climates where workers feel safe in coming forward to get support.

- Go beyond focusing on preventing stress or burnout to focusing on preventing discrimination.
- Go beyond assessing job performance of workers with mental illness without accommodations to assessing performance with an accommodation in place.
- Go beyond top organizational leaders to build awareness of mental illness issues among mid-level managers/supervisors who are on the front line of mental illness issues in the workplace.
- Go beyond seeing mental illness policies as a marginal HR issue to seeing it as a key talent management imperative that impacts business success.
- Go beyond using health insurance plans with substandard treatment for mental illness to demanding insurance plans that put mental illness treatment on par with other medical issues.
- Go beyond allowing misperceptions to guide workplace policy to focusing on creating policies rooted in valid evidence.

The role of LER practitioners in this journey is pivotal. Creating effective workplaces for what is arguably the largest and the most invisible disability population in our workplaces today is one of the most important LER challenges of the future. And much work needs to be done.

ACKNOWLEDGMENTS

The authors thank Marjorie Baldwin, professor of economics, Carey School of Business, Arizona State University; and Adam Litwin, associate professor of industrial and labor relations, Cornell University ILR School, for their reviews of this manuscript.

ENDNOTE

[1] See several resources for more information on these issues. First, the ten ADA centers located across the United States can provide free and confidential support to LER practitioners or employers with questions in these areas. Go to www.adata.org/find-your-region or call (800) 949-4232 (toll free) to reach the ADA center in your region. Second, to contact the EEOC, look in your telephone directory under US Government. For information and instructions on reaching your local office, call (800) 669-4000 (toll free). Third, to contact the Job Accommodation Network, see www.askjan.org/contact-us.cfm.

REFERENCES

Albrecht, S., E. Breidahl, and A. Marty. 2018. "Organizational Resources, Organizational Engagement Climate, and Employee Engagement." *Career Development International* 23 (1): 6785.

Aldridge, Jodie, and Anne Harriss. 2017. "Depression in the Workplace: The Role of OH." *Occupational Health & Wellbeing* 69 (7): 27–29.

American Psychiatric Association. 2013. *Diagnostic and Statistical Manual of Mental Disorders* (5th ed.). Arlington, VA: American Psychiatric Publishing.

Arends, Iris, Niklas Baer, Veerle Miranda, Christopher Prinz, and Shruti Singh. 2014. *Mental Health and Work: Achieving Well-Integrated Policies and Service Delivery.* Paris, France: Organisation for Economic Co-operation and Development.

Ashman, I., and C. Gibson. 2010. "Existential Identity, Ontological Insecurity and Mental Well-Being in the Workplace. (Report)." *Contemporary Readings in Law and Social Justice* 2 (2): 126–148.

Austin, R., and G. Pisano. 2017 (May–Jun.). "Neurodiversity as a Competitive Advantage." *Harvard Business Review.*

Baldwin, M. 2016. *Beyond Schizophrenia: Living and Working with a Serious Mental Illness.* Lanham, MD: Rowman & Littlefield.

Baldwin, M.L., and W.G. Johnson. 2004. "Labor Market Discrimination Against Men with Disabilities." *Journal of Human Resources* 29 (1): 1–19.

Banerjee, S., P. Chatterji, and K. Lahiri. 2017. "Effects of Psychiatric Disorders on Labor Market Outcomes: A Latent Variable Approach Using Multiple Clinical Indicators." *Health Economics* 26 (2): 184–205.

Befort, Stephen F. 2013. "An Empirical Examination of Case Outcomes Under the Americans with Disabilities Amendments Act." 70 *Washington & Lee Review* 2027.

Ben-Zeev, Dror, Michael A. Young, and Patrick W. Corrigan. 2010. "DSM-V and the Stigma of Mental Illness." *Journal of Mental Health* 19 (4): 318–327. doi:10.3109/09638237.2010.492484

Boyce, M. 1996 "Organizational Story and Storytelling: A Critical Review." *Journal of Organizational Change Management* 9 (5): 5–26.

Brohan, E., C. Henderson, K. Wheat, E. Malcolm, S. Clement, E. Barley, M. Slade, and G. Thornicroft. 2012. "Systematic Review of Beliefs, Behaviours and Influencing Factors Associated with Disclosure of a Mental Health Problem in the Workplace." *BMC Psychiatry* 12: 11. doi:10.1186/1471-244X-12-11

Brohan, E.C., and G. Thornicroft. 2010. "Stigma and Discrimination of Mental Health Problems: Workplace Implications." *Occupational Medicine* 60 (6): 414–415.

Bronkhorst, B., L. Tummers, B. Steijn, and D. Vijverberg. 2015. "Organizational Climate and Employee Mental Health Outcomes: A Systematic Review of Studies in Health Care Organizations." *Health Care Management Review* 40 (3): 254–271.

Buckingham, M., and C. Coffman. 1999. *First Break All the Rules: What the World's Greatest Managers Do Differently*. New York, NY: Simon & Schuster.

Center, Claudia, and Andrew J. Imparato. 2003. "Redefining 'Disability' Discrimination: A Proposal to Restore Civil Rights Protections for All Workers." 14 *Stanford Law and Policy Re*view 321.

Center for Behavioral Health Statistics and Quality (CBHSQ). 2015. "Behavioral Health Trends in the United States: Results from the 2014 National Survey on Drug Use and Health." HHS Publication No. SMA 15-4927, NSDUH Series H-50. http://bit.ly/2tAXWUu

Clayson, Tracy. 2012. "Mental Health: Employers' Roles in Creating Healthy Workplaces." *Materials Management and Distribution* 57 (3): 29.

Corrigan, P.W., J.E. Larson, and N. Rusch. 2009. "Self-Stigma and the 'Why Try Effect' Impact on Life Goals and Evidence Based Practices." *World Psychiatry* 8 (2): 75–81.

Corrigan, P.W., F. Markowitz, and C. Watson. 2004. "Structural Levels of Mental Illness Stigma and Discrimination." *Schizophrenia Bulletin* 30 (3): 481–491.

Dean, David, John Pepper, Robert Schmidt, and Steven Stern. 2016. "The Effects of Vocational Rehabilitation Services for People with Mental Illness." *Journal of Human Resources* 52 (3): 826–858.

Deloitte UK Centre for Health Solutions. 2017 (Mar.). "At a Tipping Point? Workplace Mental Health and Wellbeing." London, UK: Deloitte UK Centre for Health Solutions http://bit.ly/2KnMxli

De Lorenzo, Mirella Sarah. 2013. "Employee Mental Illness: Managing the Hidden Epidemic." *Employee Responsibilities and Rights Journal* 25 (4): 219–238.

de Malmanche, J., and L. Robertson. 2015. "The Experience of KAI MAHI, an Employment Initiative for People with an Experience of Mental Illness, as Told by Zarna, Zeus, Lulu, Mary, Paul, and Hemi." *Community Mental Health Journal* 51 (8): 880–887.

DePaul University. 2007. "Exploring the Bottom Line: A Study of the Costs and Benefits of Workers with Disabilities." Chicago, IL: DePaul University. http://bit.ly/2V8U2hp

Desmarais, Sarah L., Richard A. Van Dorn, Kiersten L. Johnson, Kevin J. Grimm, Kevin S. Douglas, and Marvin S. Swartz. 2014. "Community Violence Perpetration and Victimization Among Adults with Mental Illnesses." *American Journal of Public Health* 104 (12): 2342–2349.

Dewa, C.S., A. Lesage, P. Goering, and M. Caveen. 2004. "Nature and Amplitude of Mental Illness in the Workplace." *Healthcare Papers* 5 (2): 12–25.

DiversityInc. 2013 (Jan. 31). "How to Create a Mental-Health-Friendly Workplace." http://bit.ly/2tDmwns

Dixon, J. 2014 (Oct. 27). "Building a Storytelling Culture." *Stanford Social Innovation Review*.

Drake, R.E., G.R. Bond, H.H. Goldman, M.F. Hogan, and M. Karakus. 2016. "Individual Placement and Support Services Boost Employment for People with Serious Mental Illnesses, but Funding Is Lacking." *Health Affairs* 35 (6): 1098–1105.

Drapalski, A., A. Lucksted, P. Perrin, J. Aakre, C. Brown, B. DeForge, and J. Boyd. 2013. "A Model of Internalized Stigma and Its Effects on People with Mental Illness." *Psychiatric Services* 64 (3): 264–269.

Druss, B., and E. Walker. 2011. "Mental Disorders and Medical Comorbity." Research Synthesis Report Number 21. Princeton, NJ: Robert Wood Johnson Foundation. http://bit.ly/2H4EIyq

Each Mind Matters. 2013. "Are Celebrities Changing How We Talk About Mental Illness?" http://bit.ly/2Rkukpn

Ehrhart, M., B. Schneider, and W. Macey. 2014. *Organizational Climate and Culture: An Introduction to Theory, Research, and Practice*. New York, NY: Routledge.

Ellison, M., Z. Russinova, K. MacDonald-Wilson, and A. Lyass. 2003. "Patterns and Correlates of Workplace Disclosure Among Professionals and Managers with Psychiatric Conditions." University of Massachusetts Medical School Systems and Psychosocial Advances Research Center Publications and Presentations. http://bit.ly/2tEXlRG

Enayati, H., and S. von Schrader. 2016. "Using Administrative Data." In *Disability and Employer Practices: Research Across the Disciplines*, edited by S. Bruyère, pp. 79–96. Ithaca, NY: Cornell University Press.

Engelmeier, Sheila, and Thomas E. Marshall. 2014 (May 1). "The Challenge of Mental Health and Impairment in the Workplace: Compassion, Accommodation, and Discipline." *Pacific Coast Conference Proceedings*. Pacific Coast Labor & Employment Law Conference. http://bit.ly/2RlukFt

Erickson, W.A., A. Karpur, and K.F. Hallock. 2016. "Exploring National Survey Data." In *Disability and Employer Practices: Research Across the Disciplines*, edited by Susanne M. Bruyère. Ithaca, NY: Cornell University Press.

Fairclough, S., R. Robinson, D. Nichols, and S. Cousley. 2013. "In Sickness and in Health: Implications for Employers When Bipolar Disorders Are Protected Disabilities." *Employee Responsibilities and Rights Journal* 25 (4): 277–292.

Fazel, S., and M. Grann. 2006. "The Population Impact of Severe Mental Illness on Violent Crime." *American Journal of Psychiatry* 163 (8): 1397–1403.

Findley Musgrove, C., A. Ellinger, and E. Ellinger. 2014. "Examining the Influence of Strategic Profit Emphases on Employee Engagement and Service Climate." *Journal of Workplace Learning* 26 (3/4): 152–171.

Follmer, Kayla B., and Kisha S. Jones. 2018. "Mental Illness in the Workplace: An Interdisciplinary Review and Organizational Research Agenda." *Journal of Management* 44 (1): 325–351.

Gershon, R., P. Stone, J. Faucett, K. MacDavitt, and S. Chou. 2007. "Organizational Climate and Nurse Health Outcomes in the United States: A Systematic Review." *Industrial Health* 45 (5): 622–636.

Gilmour, H., and S.B. Patten. 2007. "Depression at Work." *Perspectives on Labour and Income* 19 (4): 57–62, 64–69.

Gladman, B., and G. Waghorn. 2016. "Personal Experiences of People with Serious Mental Illness When Seeking, Obtaining and Maintaining Competitive Employment in Queensland, Australia." *Work* 53 (4): 835.

Goetzel, R.Z., S.R. Long, R.J. Ozminkowski, S. Wang, and W. Lynch. 2004. "Health, Absence, Disability, and Presenteeism Cost Estimates of Certain Physical and Mental Health Conditions Affecting U.S. Employers." *Journal of Occupational & Environmental Medicine* 46 (4): 398–412.

Gurchiek, K. 2015 (Jan. 20). "Coping with Employees' Mental Illnesses Can Be Challenging." *Society for Human Resource Management Journal.*

Hand, C., and J. Tryssenaar. 2006. "Small Business Employers' Views on Hiring Individuals with Mental Illness." *Psychiatric Rehabilitation Journal* 29 (3): 166–173.

Harrington A. 2014. "Mental Health at Work." In *Contemporary Occupational Health Nursing: A Guide for Practitioners*, edited by G. Thombory, pp. 121–141, Oxfordshire, UK: Routledge.

Harvey, A., and N. Gumport. 2015. "Evidence-Based Psychological Treatments for Mental Disorders: Modifiable Barriers to Access and Possible Solutions." *Behavior Research and Therapy* 68: 1–12.

Hasson, Henna, Mats Andersson, and Ulrika Bejerholm. 2011. "Barriers in Implementation of Evidence-Based Practice." *Journal of Health Organization and Management* 25 (3): 332–345.

Hunsley, J., K. Elliott, and Z. Therrien. 2013. "The Efficacy and Effectiveness of Psychological Treatments." *Canadian Psychology/Psychologie Canadienne* 55 (3): 161–176.

Insel, Thomas. 2015 (May 15). "Mental Health Awareness Month: By the Numbers." Bethesda, MD: National Institute of Mental Health. http://bit.ly/2Ko70qc

Institute for Corporate Productivity. 2014. Employing People with Developmental and Intellectual Disabilities. Seattle, WA: Institute for Corporate Productivity. http://bit.ly/2Rm0qRA

Job Accommodation Network. 2015. "Accommodation and Compliance: About Mental Health Impairments." Job Accommodation Network Accommodation and Compliance Series. http://bit.ly/2Kqthng

Jones, Amanda. 2011. "Disclosure of Mental Illness in the Workplace: A Literature Review." *American Journal of Psychiatric Rehabilitation* 14 (3): 212–229.

Kaminer, D. 2016. "Mentally Ill Employees in the Workplace: Does the ADA Amendments Act Provide Adequate Protection?" *Health Matrix: Journal of Law and Medicine* 26 (1): 206–253.

Kessler, R.C., S. Aguilar-Gaxiola, J. Alonso, S. Chatterji, S. Lee, J. Ormel, T.B. Üstün, and P.S. Wang 2009. "The Global Burden of Mental Disorders: An Update from the WHO World Mental Health (WMH) Surveys." *Epidemiologia e Psichiatria Sociale* 18 (1): 23–33.

Keyes, C.L. 2005. "Mental Illness and/or Mental Health? Investigating Axioms of the Complete State Model of Health." *Journal of Consulting and Clinical Psychology* 73 (3): 539–548.

Kinn, Liv Grethe, Helge Holgersen, Randi W. Aas, and Larry Davidson. 2014. "'Balancing on Skates on the Icy Surface of Work': A Metasynthesis of Work Participation for Persons with Psychiatric Disabilities." *Journal of Occupational Rehabilitation* 24 (1): 125–138.

Knoll, J., and G. Annas. 2016. "Mass Shootings and Mental Illness." In *Gun Violence and Mental Illness*, edited by Lisa H. Gold and Robert I. Simon. Washington, DC: American Psychiatric Association. http://bit.ly/2tIe0Uy

Krupa, Terry, Bonnie Kirsh, Lynn Cockburn, and Rebecca Gewurtz. 2009. "Understanding the Stigma of Mental Illness in Employment." *Work* 33 (4): 413–425.

Link, B.G. 1987. "Understanding Labeling Effects in the Area of Mental Disorders: An Assessment of the Effects of Expectations of Rejection." *American Sociological Review* 52: 96–112.

Link, B.G., E.L. Struening, S. Neese-Todd, S. Asmussen, and J. Phelan. 2001. "Stigma as a Barrier to Recovery: The Consequences of Stigma for the Self-Esteem of People with Mental Illness." *Psychiatric Services* 52: 1621–1626.

Loehrke, K. 2017. "Employees' Mental Health Really Is Your Business." *The Business Journals*. http://bit.ly/2tGwSDp

Loy, B. 2015. "Workplace Accommodations: Low Cost, High Impact." Job Accommodation Network Accommodation and Compliance Series. Job Accommodation Network. http://bit.ly/2tEHv9s

Luciano, A., and E. Meara. 2014. "Employment Status of People with Mental Illness: National Survey Data from 2009 and 2010." *Psychiatric Services* 65 (10): 1201–1209.

MacDavitt, K., S. Chou, and P. Stone. 2007. "Organizational Climate and Health Care Outcomes." *The Joint Commission Journal on Quality and Patient Safety* 33 (11, Suppl.): 45–56.

Mancuso L. 1990. "Reasonable Accommodation for Workers with Psychiatric Disabilities." *Psychosocial Rehabilitation Journal* 14 (2): 3–19.

Manning, C., and P. White. 1995. "Attitudes of Employers to the Mentally Ill." *Psychiatric Bulletin* 19: 541–543.

Marwaha, S., and S. Johnson. 2005. "Views and Experiences of Employment Among People with Psychosis: A Qualitative Descriptive Study." *International Journal of Social Psychiatry* 51 (4): 302–316.

McAlpine, D.D., and L. Warner. 2002. "Barriers to Employment Among Persons with Mental Illness: A Review of the Literature." Report. New Brunswick, NJ: Center for Research on the Organization and Financing of Care for the Severely Mentally Ill, Institute for Health Care Policy and Aging Research, Rutgers University.

McDowell, C., and E. Fossey. 2015. "Workplace Accommodations for People with Mental Illness: A Scoping Review." *Journal of Occupational Rehabilitation 25* (1): 197–206.

McGinty, E.E., A. Kennedy-Hendricks, S. Choksy, and C.L. Barry. 2016. "Trends in News Media Coverage of Mental Illness in the United States: 1995–2014." *Health Affairs* 35 (6): 1121–1129.

McQuilken, M., J.H. Zahniser, J. Novak, R.D. Starks, A. Olmos, and G.R. Bond. 2003. "The Work Project Survey: Consumer Perspectives on Work." *Journal of Vocational Rehabilitation* 18 (1): 59–68.

Melkumyan, Vladimir. 2013. "The Effects of the Americans with Disabilities Act Amendments Act of 2008 on People with Mental Illness." Ph.D. dissertation, California State University, Long Beach.

Menguc, B., S. Auh, V. Yeniaras, and C.S. Katsikeas. 2017. "The Role of Climate: Implications for Service Employee Engagement and Customer Service Performance." *Journal of the Academy of Marketing Science* 45 (3): 428–451.

Mental Health America. 2017. "The State of Mental Health in America 2018." Alexandria, VA: Mental Health America. http://bit.ly/2H7qTPB

Mental Health Foundation. 2002. "Out of Work: A Survey of the Experiences of People with Mental Health Problems Within the Workplace." London, UK: Mental Health Foundation.

Michie, S., and S. Williams. 2003. "Reducing Work Related Ill-Health and Sickness Absence: A Systematic Literature Review." *Occupational and Environmental Medicine* 60 (1): 3–9.

Mizzoni C., and B. Kirsh. 2006. "Employer Perspectives on Supervising Individuals with Mental Health Problems. *Canadian Journal of Community Mental Health* 25 (2): 193–206.

Momeni, N. 2009. "The Relation Between Managers' Emotional Intelligence and the Organizational Climate They Create." *Public Personnel Management* 38 (2): 35–48.

National Alliance on Mental Illness (NAMI). 2014. "Road to Recovery: Employment and Mental Illness." Arlington, VA: National Alliance on Mental Illness. https://www.nami.org/work

National Alliance on Mental Illness (NAMI). 2016. "The Doctor Is Out: Continuing Disparities in Access to Mental and Physical Health Care." Arlington, VA: National Alliance on Mental Illness. http://bit.ly/2H7rjp9

National Institute of Mental Health (NIMH). 2016. "Mental Illness Definitions and Prevalence." Bethesda, MD: National Institute of Mental Health. http://bit.ly/2H89k1Z

National Safety Council. 2015. "Proactive Role Employers Can Take: Opioids in the Workplace." http://bit.ly/2tHAMMa

O'Reilly, M., K. Karim, and J.N. Lester. 2015. "Should Autism Be Classified as a Mental Illness/Disability? Evidence from Empirical Work." In The Palgrave Handbook of Child Mental Health, edited by M. O'Reilly and J.N. Lester. London, UK: Palgrave Macmillan.

Organisation for Economic Co-operation and Development (OECD). 2012. "Sick on the Job? Myths and Realities About Mental Health and Work." Paris, France: Organisation for Economic Co-operation and Development. http://bit.ly/2tD0xx6

Osterman, P. 2009. *The Truth About Mid-Level Managers: Who They Are, How They Work, and Why They Matter*. Cambridge, MA: Harvard Business Review Press.

Ozawa, A., and J. Yaeda. 2007. "Employer Attitudes Toward Employing Persons with Psychiatric Disability in Japan." *Journal of Vocational Rehabilitation* 26 (2): 105–113.

Pandya, A., C. Bresee, K. Duckworth, K. Gay, and M. Fitzpatrick. 2011. "Perceived Impact of the Disclosure of a Schizophrenia Diagnosis." *Community Mental Health Journal* 47 (6): 613–621.

Patrician, P., J. Shang, and E. Lake. 2010. "Organisational Determinants of Work Outcomes and Quality Care Ratings." *Research in Nursing & Health* 33 (2): 99–110.

Parker, C.P., B. Baltes, S. Young, J. Huff, R. Altmann, H. Lacost, and J.E. Roberts. 2003. "Relationships Between Psychological Climate Perceptions and Work Outcomes: A Meta-Analytic Review." *Journal of Organizational Behavior* 24 (4): 389–416.

Pomaki, Georgia. 2017. "Return-to-Work Strategies for Employees with Mental Health Conditions." *Benefits Quarterly* 33 (1): 50–55.

Reeves, W.C., T.W. Strine, L.A. Pratt, W. Thompson, I. Ahluwalia, S.S. Dhingra, and B. Morrow. 2011. "Mental Illness Surveillance Among Adults in the United States." *MMWR Supplement* 60 (3): 1–29.

Rettew, D. 2015 (Oct. 8). "Is Autism a Mental Illness?" *Psychology Today*. http://bit.ly/2tGaslq

Sallis, Anna, and Richard Birkin. 2014. "Experiences of Work and Sickness Absence in Employees with Depression: An Interpretative Phenomenological Analysis." *Journal of Occupational Rehabilitation* 24 (3): 469–483.

Scheid, T.L. 1999. "Employment of Individuals with Mental Disabilities: Business Response to the ADA's Challenge." *Behavioral Science Law* 17 (1): 73–91.

Scheid, T.L. 2005. "Stigma as a Barrier to Employment: Mental Disability and the Americans with Disabilities Act." *International Journal of Law and Psychiatry* 28 (6): 670–690.

Schluter, J., S. Winch, K. Holzhauser, and A. Henderson. 2008. "Nurses' Moral Sensitivity and Hospital Ethical Climate: A Literature Review." *Nurse Ethics* 15 (3): 304–321.

Schopick, Abigail. 2012. "The Americans with Disabilities Act: Should the Amendments to the Act Help Individuals with Mental Illness?" *Legislation and Policy Brief* 4 (1): 1–33.

Secker, J., and H. Membrey. 2003. "Promoting Mental Health Through Employment and Developing Healthy Workplaces: The Potential of Natural Supports at Work." *Health Education Research* 18 (2): 207–215.

Secker J., H. H. Membrey, B. Grove, and P. Seebohm. 2003. "The How and Why of Workplace Adjustments." *Psychiatric Rehabilitation Journal* 27 (1): 3–9.

Shankar, J., L. Liu, D. Nicholas, S. Warren, D. Lai, S. Tan, R. Zulla, J. Couture, and A. Sears. 2014. "Employers' Perspectives on Hiring and Accommodating Workers with Mental Illness." *SAGE Open* 4 (3).

Sharac, J., P. McCrone, S. Clement, and G. Thornicroft. 2010. "The Economic Impact of Mental Health Stigma and Discrimination: A Systematic Review." *Epidemiologia e Psichiatria Sociale* 19 (3): 223–232.

Stansfeld, S., and B. Candy. 2006. "Psychosocial Work Environment and Mental Health: A Meta-Analytic Review" *Scandinavian Journal of Work and Environmental Health* 32 (6): 443–462.

Steadman, H.J., J. Monahan, D.A. Pinals, R. Vesselinov, and P.C. Robbins. 2015. "Gun Violence and Victimization of Strangers by Persons with a Mental Illness: Data from the MacArthur Violence Risk Assessment Study." *Psychiatric Services* 66 (11): 1238–1241.

Steel, Z., C. Marnane, C. Iranpour, T. Chey, J. Jackson, V. Patel, and D. Silove. 2014. "The Global Prevalence of Common Mental Disorders: A Systematic Review and Meta-Analysis 1980–2013." *International Journal of Epidemiology* 43 (2): 476–493.

Stuart, H. 2006. "Mental Illness and Employment Discrimination." *Current Opinion in Psychiatry* 19 (5): 522–526.

Substance and Mental Health Services Administration (SAMHSA). 2015. "Mental and Substance Abuse Disorders." Rockville, MD: Substance and Mental Health Services Administration. http://bit.ly/2tGBklB

Teplin, L.A., G.M. McClelland, K.M. Abram, and D.A. Weiner. 2005. "Crime Victimization in Adults with Severe Mental Illness: Comparison with the National Crime Victimization Survey." *Archives of General Psychiatry* 62 (8): 911–921.

Thornicroft, G., E. Brohan, D. Rose, N. Sartorius, and M. Leese. 2009. "Global Pattern of Experienced and Anticipated Discrimination Against People with Schizophrenia: A Cross-Sectional Survey." *Lancet* 373 (9661): 408–415.

Tsang, H.W., B. Angell, P.W. Corrigan, Y.T. Lee, K. Shi, C.S. Lam, S. Jin, and K.M.T. Fung 2007. "A Cross-Cultural Study of Employers' Concerns About Hiring People with Psychotic Disorder: Implications for Recovery." *Social Psychiatry and Psychiatric Epidemiology* 42 (9): 723–733.

Unger, D., and J. Kregel. 2003. "Employers' Knowledge and Utilization of Accommodations." *Work* 21 (1): 5–14.

United Nations. 2006. "Convention on the Rights of Persons with Disabilities." http://bit.ly/2Kpj0I2.

US Equal Employment Opportunity Commission (US EEOC). 2008. "The Americans with Disabilities Act Amendments Act of 2008." Washington, DC: US Equal Employment Opportunity Commission. http://bit.ly/2H4KFvi

US Equal Employment Opportunity Commission (US EEOC). 2009a. "EEOC Enforcement Guidance on the Americans with Disabilities Act and Psychiatric Disabilities." Washington, DC: US Equal Employment Opportunity Commission. http://bit.ly/2H7w81J

US Equal Employment Opportunity Commission (US EEOC). 2009b. "Enforcement Guidance on Disability-Related Inquiries and Medical Examinations of Employees Under the Americans with Disabilities Act (ADA)." Washington, DC: US Equal Employment Opportunity Commission. http://bit.ly/2tEqts3

US Equal Employment Opportunity Commission (US EEOC). 2012. "Fact Sheet on the EEOC's Final Regulations Implementing the ADAAA." Washington, DC: US Equal Employment Opportunity Commission. http://bit.ly/2tHDe5k

US Equal Employment Opportunity Commission (US EEOC). 2016. "Depression, PTSD, & Other Mental Health Conditions in the Workplace: Your Legal Rights." Washington, DC: US Equal Employment Opportunity Commission. http://bit.ly/2tHDhy2

Vigo, D., G. Thornicroft, and R. Alun. 2016. "Estimating the True Global Burden of Mental Illness." *Lancet Psychiatry* 3 (2): 171–178.

von Schrader, S. 2011. Calculations from EEOC Charge Files. RRTC on Employer Practices Related to Employment Outcomes Among Individuals with Disabilities. Ithaca, NY: Cornell University.

von Schrader, S., and W. Erickson. 2017. "Employment Discrimination Charges Filed Under the Americans with Disabilities Act (ADA)." Ithaca, NY: Cornell University Yang-Tan Institute on Employment and Disability. http://www.disabilitystatistics.org/eeoc

Welbourne, T.M., and L.L. McLaughlin. 2013. "Making the Business Case for Employee Resource Groups." *Employment Relations Today* 40 (2): 35–44. http://bit.ly/2ZI4dLr

Witaj, P., A. Chrostek, P. Grygiel, J. Wciórka, and M. Anczewska. 2014. "Exploring Factors Associated with the Psychosocial Impact of Stigma Among People with Schizophrenia or Affective Disorders." *Community Mental Health Journal* 23: 1–9.

Wood, D., and E. Marshall. 2010. "Nurses with Disabilities Working in Hospital Settings: Attitudes, Concerns, and Experiences of Nurse Leaders." *Journal of Professional Nursing* 26 (3): 182.

World Health Organization. 2011. "Mental Disorders Affect One in Four." Press Release. Geneva, Switzerland: World Health Organization. http://bit.ly/2tIWkI4

World Health Organization. 2013. "Disability and Rehabilitation: Convention on the Rights of Persons with Disabilities." Geneva, Switzerland: World Health Organization. http://bit.ly/2tI2g4as

CHAPTER 9

Employment in High-Tech Industries: What Does It Mean for People with Disabilities?

William Erickson
Sara VanLooy
Wendy Strobel Gower
Cornell University

INTRODUCTION

Over the past several decades, automation and offshoring have caused the loss of many US jobs, while new technologies and social changes have eliminated many others. Jobs that once were the mainstay of the middle class have disappeared, while industries that did not exist in the last century are now major employers. As traditional manufacturing jobs have become less common, political and economic leaders have repeatedly pointed to these new "high tech" industries as the answer to the question "Where are the jobs?"

President Obama, speaking in 2013, put forth the idea of "turning regions left behind by global competition into global centers of cutting-edge jobs." This would include training workers in those regions to "earn the skills that high-tech jobs demand" within their home communities (Bump 2013). In 2015, the White House rolled out the TechHire Initiative, a program to "train workers for jobs in the digital age." In announcing this initiative, President Obama emphasized that "High-tech jobs … are a ticket into the middle class" (Leonard 2015).

A scan of recent online news coverage highlights governors, senators, political hopefuls, chambers of commerce, and business representatives all touting the needs and promise of "high tech." Utah's governor boasts of his state's "high-tech savvy," while candidates in races in California, Wisconsin, Maryland—and more—vie to be the most welcoming to "high-tech manufacturing."

The issue of quality jobs that provide a path out of poverty and access to the middle class is of particular concern to people with disabilities, who have historically lagged behind their nondisabled peers in access to higher-paying work. While 11% of Americans of ages 21 to 64 report having some form of disability, their employment rate was only 36%—compared with a rate of 79% for Americans without disabilities. This 43-point difference in employment rates (combined with similar disparities in access to full-time employment) contributes to a poverty rate that is over twice that of people without disabilities (26.6% vs. 10.9%) (Erickson, Lee, and von Schrader 2018)

Given these inequalities and the increased opportunities available in the high-tech industries, this chapter will examine the status of people with disabilities in high-tech employment. While the US Equal Employment Opportunity Commission (US EEOC) collects data on diversity in the high-tech workforce, its 2016 report notes that employers are required to provide data on race, color, and national origin of their workforce, but data on disability or age is not collected. The EEOC is "aware that both groups are under-represented in the tech workforce, suggesting the need to understand the causes and potential solutions" (US EEOC 2016).

That report clearly identifies the need for some measurement of disability participation in high-tech industries; however, there is currently no readily available data regarding the assumption of under-representation. This paper addresses this lack of information by developing estimates based on analysis of the US Census Bureau's American Community Survey (ACS) Public Use Microdata Sample (PUMS), examining the employment of people with disabilities in high-tech industries, as well as the STEM and STEM-related bachelor's degrees pipeline into employment. Following our description of these analyses, we discuss the implications of our findings for people with disabilities and the high-tech sector more generally.

We begin by describing what high-tech industries are and their importance to the US economy. We then develop a definition of "high tech" that can be operationalized using the ACS data, based on the proportion of workers in STEM occupations, providing a breakdown for two high-tech industry sectors: (1) traditional core high-tech industries and (2) healthcare high-tech industries. The proportions of people with disabilities employed by these two high-tech industries relative to other industries are examined, revealing discrepancies. From the literature and through further analysis, we then explore potential reasons why these differences might exist. Given the important role that STEM education plays as a pipeline leading to STEM occupations, we discuss the literature regarding STEM education and identify the proportion of younger working-age people (ages 21 to 35) by disability status who have recently graduated with STEM degrees, STEM healthcare–related degrees, or other bachelor's degrees. Several employment measures are examined by the different bachelor's degree fields of study and disability status, including labor force participation, unemployment rates, and employment within high-tech industries. Finally, we discuss the findings and implications of our results as they relate to high-tech industries and employment outcomes for people with disabilities.

High-Tech and STEM: Related Concepts with No Standard Definition

Despite the amount of discussion about high-tech industries, the term "high-tech" is not well defined in the literature (Wolf and Terrell 2016). When policy makers and business leaders talk about high-tech industries and jobs, they usually mean industries with a high concentration of science, technology, engineering, and mathematics (STEM) workers, and jobs that require education and training in STEM topics. This popular-culture definition generally encompasses high-skill jobs in science fields, which typically require knowledge of, and the ability to use, computers and advanced machines with some expertise, all of which require significant post-secondary education (Texas Workforce Investment Council 2015).

The status of the US workforce in high-tech industries, those that focus on STEM jobs, is an ongoing concern in discussions of global competitiveness and innovation. Issues relating to STEM workers and their preparation regularly crop up in education policy and immigration discussions (National Science Board 2015). Concern about the availability of workers to fill important STEM roles across multiple segments of the US economy has cycled repeatedly into public policy since World War II (Charette 2013). STEM careers offer incredible opportunities for skilled workers—excellent job growth, higher median wages, and abundant openings for people new to the workforce (Mugglestone and Allison 2015).

STEM Jobs, High-Tech Industries, and the US Workforce

High-tech firms play an important role in income, employment, and productivity growth overall and are often among the set of cutting-edge businesses that can drive economic growth. For example, information technology jobs make up 14% of all open jobs across the country, and 10 of the 25 "best jobs in America" identified by job-search website Glassdoor.com are in IT. High-tech industries are a vital part of the US economy, with the subset of high-tech manufacturing and services employing almost 17 million workers in 2014 and accounting for nearly 12% of total employment. Those industries contributed $7.1 trillion (23%) of total US output (Wolf and Terrell 2016). Projections indicate this sector will add another 691,000 jobs between 2014 and 2024. STEM occupations and STEM healthcare–related occupations are the two job clusters expected to grow the fastest through 2020 (Carnevale, Smith, and Strohl 2013)

Despite growing opportunities in high-tech/STEM fields, concern remains over the need for STEM workers to stay competitive and continue to innovate in the global marketplace (Charette 2013). The importance of scientific and technical knowledge to the American way of life is embodied in the Constitution's grant to Congress of the power to issue patents (Rothwell 2013), and was affirmed in the Morrill Act of 1862, which led to the creation of land-grant colleges to fund real-world studies in agriculture and engineering (Anft 2013). In 1945, Vannevar Bush helped initiate the National Science Foundation with his report to President Roosevelt stating the need for "a stream of new scientific knowledge to turn the wheels of private and public enterprise" (Rothwell 2013).

The need for STEM knowledge across the workforce is rising (National Science Board 2015) and is increasingly required even in jobs not traditionally thought of as STEM jobs. More job prerequisites include STEM skills. Rothwell (2013) differentiates between super-STEM jobs, which score highly across STEM fields, and high-STEM jobs, which require expertise in one or two aspects of STEM. In 2011, 9% of jobs were super-STEM, while the more inclusive high-STEM definition encompassed 20% of all US jobs (26 million). Given this movement toward a greater demand for STEM skills, how does one acquire them to increase employment opportunities?

Paths to High-Tech/STEM Employment

The path to STEM careers begins in school, where students are first introduced to STEM subject matter, choose STEM classes, and are placed into various levels of STEM coursework. The global shift from traditional manufacturing economies to economies based on STEM knowledge and skills has created a significant need for students to have an understanding of STEM (Fisher 2017). STEM education at the secondary level is of two types: applied and academic.

Applied STEM courses are part of career and technical education curricula, designed to teach the application of STEM concepts to real-world situations. These courses aim to impart skills and knowledge that can be put directly to work in STEM jobs. Approximately half of all STEM jobs in the US workforce are available to workers without a four-year degree, and these jobs pay, on average, 10% higher wages than non-STEM jobs with similar educational requirements (Texas Workforce Investment Council 2015).

Academic STEM, the education on which we have data available and this paper examines, follows the traditional academic curriculum, teaching concepts in the classroom, and documenting knowledge via exams and papers. People who enter high-tech/STEM fields in this way generally have bachelor's degrees in a STEM or STEM-related field.

Achieving an academic STEM/bachelor's degree, however, is a major stumbling block for students with disabilities, as they are less likely to enroll in post-secondary education: 43% do not pursue post-secondary education compared with 37% of students without disabilities. In 2012, about 11% of undergraduates reported a disability. On average, undergraduates with disabilities are older than their nondisabled peers and are slightly less likely to attend a four-year college (versus a two-year or other institution) (National Science Foundation 2017). For those individuals who do achieve a four-year degree, one would expect a wide variety of employment opportunities to be open, especially to those with a STEM or STEM-related degree.

Diversity in High-Tech/STEM Employment

The high-tech/STEM fields are not traditionally known for their diversity. Many technology companies are slowly working toward hiring more women and minorities into their ranks and into leadership positions. In general, women, African Americans, Hispanics, and Native Americans are under-represented in science and engineering fields. The amount of under-representation varies by specific field, and its roots lie in under-representation in pre-college coursework and college major choice (National Science Foundation 2017). Later in this chapter, we present statistics regarding the population of people with disabilities who achieve a bachelor's degree or higher, and we examine their fields of study (STEM, STEM-related, and non-STEM). Degrees in key fields are the pipeline to high-tech employment opportunities, and we will examine the employment situation of people with STEM and STEM-related degrees. First, however, we need to more clearly define STEM occupations and high-tech industries.

Defining STEM Occupations

While the state of STEM education and high-tech employment in the United States is frequently discussed, these conversations are complicated by the lack of a consistent definition of STEM and differing conceptualizations of the composition and character of the STEM workforce and career pathways (Landivar 2013a, 2013b; National Science Board 2015).

In response to the lack of consensus over who qualifies as a STEM worker, the US Office of Management and Budget (OMB) requested that the Standard Occupational Classification Policy Committee create guidelines for the classification of STEM workers. The final recommendations identified three main occupational domains within the category: (1) science, engineering, mathematics, and information technology occupations; (2) science and engineering-related occupations, and (3) nonscience and engineering occupations. STEM occupations are primarily in the computer and mathematical fields; engineering; and the life, physical, and social sciences. STEM healthcare–related occupations include both practitioners and technicians. These recommendations were reviewed and approved by OMB in April 2012 (Landivar 2013a, 2013b).

To identify high-tech industries, we apply a variation of the approach of the US Bureau of Labor Statistics that was developed by Heckler (2005) and was further enhanced by the Texas Workforce Information Council (2015). This approach is based on official STEM positions within industries:

Example STEM Core Occupations

- life and physical sciences (e.g., chemists, biologists, astronomers, life scientists, and zoologists)
- engineering (e.g., mechanical engineers, electrical engineers, and biomedical engineers)
- mathematics (e.g., mathematicians, statisticians, and actuaries)
- information technology occupations (e.g., computer systems analysts, programmers, and database administrators)

- social science occupations (e.g., sociologists, psychologists, economists, and political scientists)
- architecture occupations (e.g., architects, cartographers, and surveyors)

Example STEM Healthcare Occupations

- physicians
- nurses
- dentists
- pharmacists
- physical therapists

HIGH-TECH/STEM EMPLOYMENT TRENDS

Using the US Census Bureau's 2014 ACS PUMS, we classify all employed individuals as working in either core STEM, healthcare STEM, or non-STEM occupations. We then map the proportion of STEM workers within each industry. Following the approach of the Bureau of Labor Statistics, we exclude agricultural, management of companies and enterprises, and public administration industries from the analysis. Industries with the highest concentration of STEM workers are those identified as high-tech core or high-tech healthcare industries. The high-tech core industries are those that fall into the 90th percentile and include 24 industries in all. These industries have STEM occupation concentrations ranging from 16% to 64% (see Table 1 for the top ten list).

We use a similar procedure to identify the STEM high-tech healthcare industries focusing on the STEM healthcare occupations. However, because the distribution of healthcare STEM occupations has a clear drop-off at the 95th percentile, that cutoff point was used instead of the 90th. Table 2 summarizes the healthcare high-tech industries and the concentration of STEM healthcare occupations within each.

Based on this classification scheme, nearly half (47%) of all employees working in STEM occupations are employed within the 24 core high-tech industries. Almost nine out of ten (86%) individuals working in STEM healthcare occupations work in one of the 12 healthcare high-tech industries identified. Overall, more than one in five (21%) of all employed individuals are working in one of these two high-tech industry categories, with 13.6 million employed in the core high-tech industries and 17.2 million employed in the healthcare high-tech industries (Figure 1, page 240).

Disability and High-Tech/STEM Employment: A Look at the Data

Having defined high-tech industries, the next step is to understand how people with disabilities fare with respect to employment within those categories. In doing

TABLE 1
Top Ten (of 24) Core High-Tech Industries

Rank	Census Industry Name	Concentration of STEM Occupations
1	Computer systems design and related services	64%
2	Architectural, engineering, and related services	56%
3	Scientific research and development services	51%
4	Software publishers	49%
5	Colleges and universities, including junior colleges	42%
6	Aerospace product and parts manufacturing	39%
7	Computer and peripheral equipment manufacturing	38%
8	Electronic component and product manufacturing, not elsewhere classified	34%
9	Business, technical, and trade schools and training	32%
10	Internet publishing and broadcasting and web search portals	31%

Source: 2014 ACS PUMS; analysis by H. Enayati.

TABLE 2
Healthcare High-Tech Industries

Rank	Census Industry Name	Concentration of STEM Healthcare Occupations
1	Hospitals	56%
2	Offices of optometrists	51%
3	Veterinary services	50%
4	Offices of chiropractors	46%
5	Offices of physicians	44%
6	Outpatient care centers	43%
7	Offices of other healthcare practitioners	42%
8	Pharmacies and drug stores	42%
9	Offices of dentists	38%
10	Other healthcare services	38%
11	Nursing care facilities	30%
12	Home healthcare services	21%

Source: 2014 ACS PUMS; analysis by H. Enayati.

FIGURE 1
Total Employment (in millions) by High-Tech Industry Category

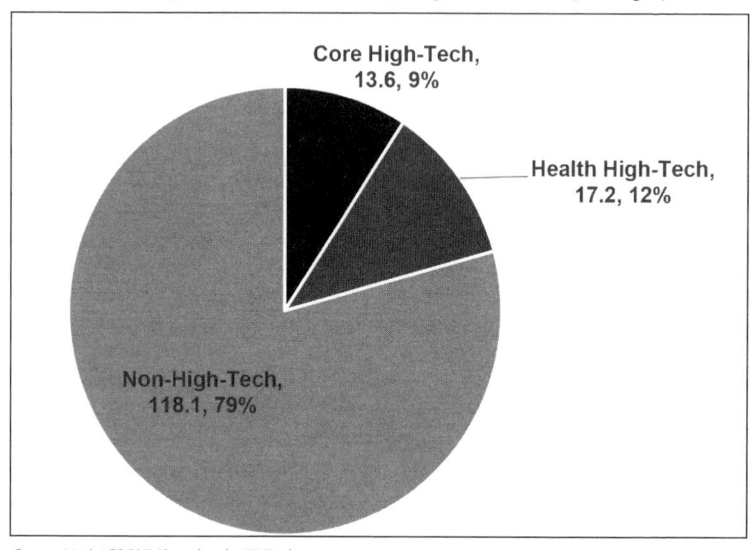

Source: 2014 ACS PUMS; analysis by W. Erickson.

so, we again use the 2014 ACS PUMS. To define disability, we use the ACS six-question disability sequence. These questions identify people with the following disability types: vision, hearing, ambulatory, cognitive, self-care (difficulty dressing or bathing), and independent living (difficulty doing errands alone such as visiting a doctor's office or shopping). Any individual who reports one or more of these six disability types is identified as a person with a disability.

Working with this definition, what is the status of disability employment in the two high-tech industry sectors? Approximately 5.1% of employees have a disability in the healthcare high-tech sector; in the core high-tech sector, only 4.1% have a disability. These proportions are both lower than the 5.7% of individuals with disabilities working in non-high-tech industries.

What might explain this lower disability employment rate in high-tech industries relative to other industries? The remainder of this chapter will explore this question, considering possible explanations and examining the data to gain insight into the potential issues and barriers to people with disabilities.

STEM Education and High-Tech Employment

As noted previously, a large proportion of individuals employed in core high-tech industries have a bachelor's degree or higher (59%), as do those working in healthcare high-tech industries (40%). This is significantly higher than the 29% of workers with this level of education in non-high-tech industries. From this, it is apparent that individuals lacking a post-secondary education, especially in STEM and STEM-related fields, are less likely to have employment in high-tech industries.

Previous research has found that people with disabilities overall have lower levels of educational attainment and are less likely to achieve a bachelor's degree than those without disabilities (Erickson, Lee, and von Schrader 2018). Educational attainment is closely linked to employment; 54% of people ages 21 through 64 with a disability who have a bachelor's degree or higher are employed compared with 31% of those with only a high school diploma. Note that, while employment prospects do improve with educational attainment, it is not a panacea. Even people with a bachelor's degree (or higher) experience employment disparities—54% of those with disabilities are employed compared with 84% of those without disabilities—a full 30 percentage point gap (Erickson, Lee, and von Schrader 2018).

Students with disabilities often encounter barriers to STEM education at an early age that their peers without disabilities do not face. Mathematics, for example, is one of the foundations of STEM knowledge, and access to the mathematics curriculum is the entryway into more advanced STEM coursework. Researchers have found that fifth-grade teachers' perceptions of a student's math ability is predictive of coursework recommendations for eighth-grade algebra—a major milestone on the path to STEM (Gottfried, Bozick, Rose, and Moore 2016). Many students with disabilities have lower scores in math on national tests, often lack role models in STEM professions, and have parents and teachers who may have lower expectations of their ability to participate in the STEM curriculum (Hawley, Cardoso, and McMahon 2013). Students with learning disabilities are frequently denied access to STEM classes or are placed in instructionally weak special programs separate from the main STEM curriculum (Gottfried, Bozick, Rose, and Moore 2016).

Even when gatekeepers allow entry to STEM coursework, environmental barriers may exist. High school science labs frequently are not designed for physical access, and STEM teachers at the secondary level are not always familiar with how to facilitate accommodations for students who have physical, visual, or auditory disabilities (Hawley, Cardoso, and McMahon 2013). Students with visual and hearing impairments are especially challenged by science curricula that rely heavily on videos, hands-on demonstrations, and physical observations. These factors mean that students with disabilities may lack exposure and hands-on experience to prepare them for the STEM workforce (Gottfried, Bozick, Rose, and Moore 2016).

Access to STEM internships and opportunities in high school is also limited by inaccessible internship application websites, the unwillingness of internship employers to accommodate, and inaccurate information given to families about the effect of paid internships on disability benefits (Hawley, Cardoso, and

McMahon 2013). Despite these barriers, students with disabilities continue to pursue the promise of the high-quality jobs that STEM studies offer.

The High-Tech Pipeline: Graduating with a STEM or Related Bachelor's Degree

As noted earlier, post-secondary education has become increasingly vital for people to gain quality employment, and this is especially the case with STEM-related occupations. Although fewer people with disabilities attain a bachelor's degree, researchers have found that they enter STEM fields of post-secondary study at the same rate, or even higher rates, as people without disabilities (Lee 2011). The next logical question is are they continuing their studies in STEM and actually graduating with a STEM or STEM-related degree at the same rate as college students without disabilities? If their degree profile differs from what they initially pursue, that could create a discrepancy in the proportion of those with a bachelor's degree in STEM or STEM healthcare–related fields. This could result in fewer qualified people with disabilities for high-tech industries.

To examine this question, we restrict our analysis to focus on only young, working-age people (ages 21 through 35) who have received a bachelor's degree or higher. That allowed us to examine the degree profiles of a relatively recent cohort of college graduates with disabilities. The ACS survey asks individuals with post-secondary degrees about their major field of study, which allows us to examine and compare the bachelor's degree majors between people with and without disabilities, focusing specifically on STEM and STEM healthcare–related fields.

Figure 2 reveals that young working-age individuals with and without disabilities have virtually identical profiles with regard to general fields of study. For people ages 21 to 35 with a bachelor's degree or higher, little difference exists between those with and without a disability in the proportion who graduated with a STEM or STEM healthcare–related bachelor's degree. Thirty-nine percent of those with and without a disability graduated with a bachelor's degree in a STEM field. Similar proportions of young people with and without disabilities (6.3% and 7.4%, respectively) graduated in a STEM healthcare–related field. The remaining 53.6% to 54.8% had degrees outside of STEM or STEM healthcare–related fields. These results agree with National Science Foundation statistics (2017) that show that students with and without a disability enroll in science and engineering fields in similar proportions at both the undergraduate and graduate levels.

STEM-Educated Candidates Entering the Labor Market

So we have shown that young college graduates with and without disabilities are just as likely to have a STEM bachelor's degree and nearly as likely to graduate in STEM healthcare–related fields. This tells us that the differences in employ-

FIGURE 2
Bachelor's Degree Field by Disability Status
(ages 21–35, not attending school, with a bachelor's degree)

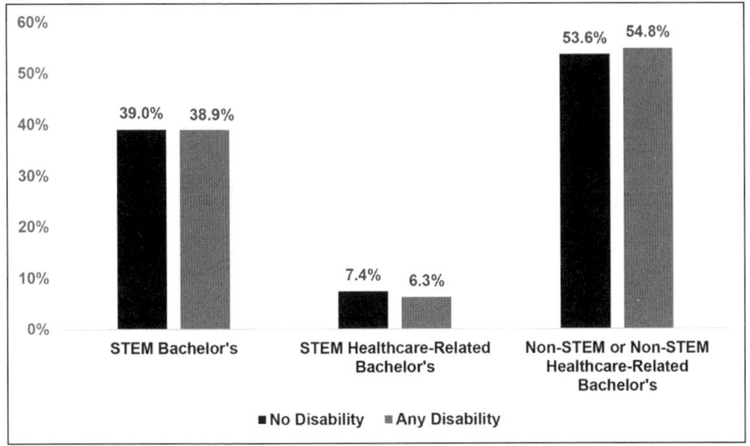

Source: 2014 ACS PUMS; analysis by W. Erickson.

ment in the high-tech industries cannot be explained by differences in their chosen fields of study or completion of STEM undergraduate programs.

Given all that, our next question is how do young, working-age individuals with a bachelor's degree or higher who have breached the various educational barriers, fare overall in terms of labor force status—especially those with degrees in STEM and STEM healthcare–related fields?

We again limit our focus to the young working-age population to address this question because a significant proportion of individuals age into a disability. About half of the scientists and engineers with disabilities report that they acquired their disability after the age of 40. About one third of scientists and engineers with disabilities became disabled before the age of 20, such that they entered the labor market for the first time with a disability. Because we are particularly interested in individuals with disabilities entering into the workforce, we limit our analysis to younger working-age people (ages 21 through 35) who received their bachelor's degree relatively recently and are not attending school (excludes those who are pursuing a graduate or professional degree). These younger individuals with disabilities are more likely to have had their disability when they began to search for employment, and this approach would exclude the majority of those who acquired a disability post-hire. Restricting our analysis in this way allows us to examine the experience of people with disabilities in the educational pipeline into STEM-related occupations and into high-tech industries.

We begin by looking at the labor force status of individuals with at least a four-year college degree and not attending school. By definition, individuals in the labor force are those who are either employed or have been actively looking for work in the past four weeks. As can be seen in Figure 3, around one in five (18% to 21%) young, working-age people with a bachelor's degree with a disability are out of the labor force compared with only 7% to 8% of those without a disability. Individuals with disabilities are nearly 2.5 times as likely to be out of the labor force regardless of their field of study. Why are these well-educated individuals with disabilities more likely to be out of the labor force—especially those with bachelor's degrees in STEM and STEM-related fields with such a high demand?

Focusing specifically on individuals who are in the labor force, we proceed to examine how they fare in the labor market. The unemployment rate is calculated by dividing the number of unemployed individuals who are actively looking for work by the number of all labor force participants (whether employed or actively seeking employment). Figure 4 shows the stark differences for those with a bachelor's degree or higher by field of study. Individuals with a STEM bachelor's degree with a disability are 3.8 times more likely to be unemployed than individuals without disabilities (13.1% divided by 3.5%). Those in STEM healthcare–related fields are 2.5 times more likely to be unemployed, and those with non-STEM or non-STEM-related degrees are 2.7 times more likely to be unemployed. This is a huge discrepancy—why are well-qualified young people with disabilities educated in fields with high demand for skilled employees so much more likely to be looking for work than those without disabilities, especially those studying STEM?

FIGURE 3
Bachelor's Degree Field of Study by Disability and Labor Force Status
(ages 21–35, not attending school)

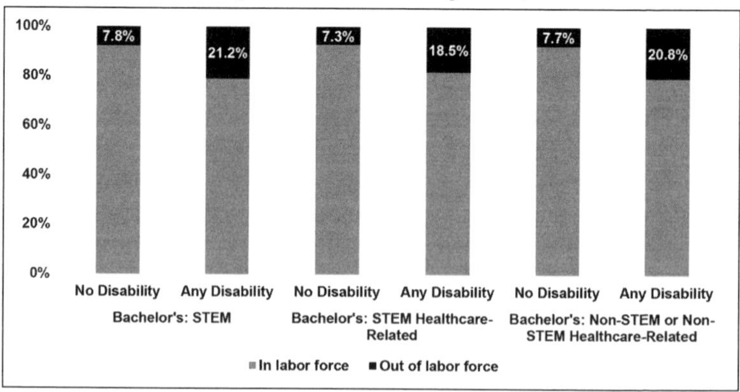

Source: 2014 ACS PUMS; analysis by W. Erickson.

FIGURE 4
Unemployment Rate by Bachelor's Degree Field and Disability Status
(ages 21–35 not attending school)

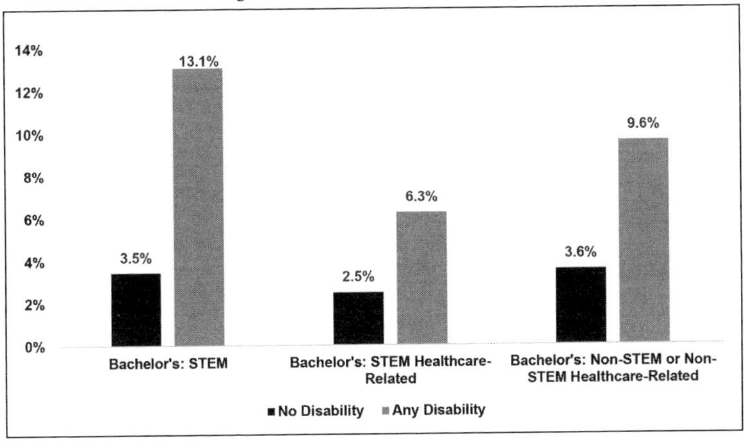

Source: 2014 ACS PUMS; analysis by W. Erickson.

STEM-Educated Candidates in the High-Tech Sector Workforce

Coming full circle, we now re-examine the employment of young individuals in high-tech industries identified earlier in this chapter, this time focusing on the population of younger workers with a bachelor's degree or higher in either a STEM or STEM-related field. These individuals are well qualified to be employed in those industries. Figure 5 (next page) compares the proportion of younger workers by disability status within the high-tech sector. It clearly shows that young, working-age people with disabilities with a STEM or STEM-related degree are actually less likely to be employed in their respective high-tech industries than persons without disabilities and are more likely to be employed *outside* of STEM core sectors.

Almost one quarter of young STEM-educated individuals without a disability who are employed are working in core high-tech sectors; this is 1.3 times higher than for those with a disability (18%). For those with a STEM healthcare–related degree, the disparity in employment rates in the high-tech health sector is even more striking. Over half (52.8%) of young employed workers with a STEM healthcare–related degree without a disability are employed in healthcare high-tech, being 1.4 times more likely than individuals with a disability (38%) to have such employment. This means that young, *employed* people with disabilities are more likely than those without a disability to be employed *outside* of the high-tech industry.

Simply put, young people with disabilities who make it past the obstacles in the STEM education pipeline are less likely to find or retain jobs in these two high tech–industry sectors.

FIGURE 5
Employment in High-Tech Industries by Bachelor's Degree and Disability Status (workers ages 21–35, not attending school)

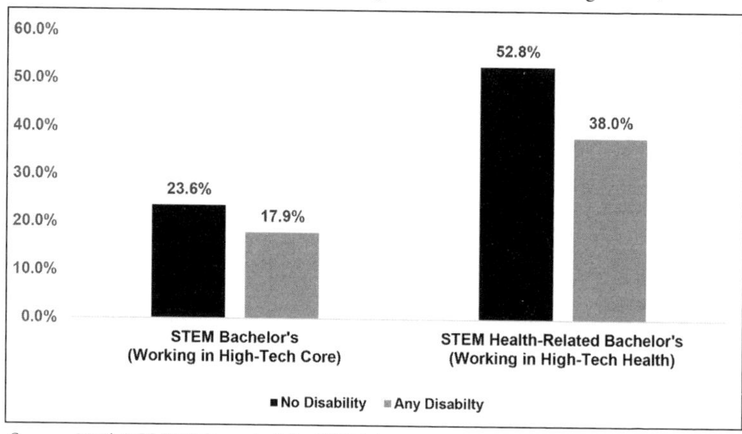

Source: 2014 ACS PUMS; analysis by W. Erickson.

SUMMARY

We began by defining disability and the concepts of high-tech industries using STEM occupations and the 2014 ACS data to identify high-tech core and high-tech healthcare industries. Using the ACS data, we determined that people with disabilities are under-represented in high-tech industries relative to other sectors. Given how vital higher education is to the majority of STEM occupations, we limited our analysis to examine younger people with a bachelor's or higher, specifically focusing on those with STEM or STEM healthcare–related undergraduate degrees. These are excellent backgrounds for moving into STEM or STEM healthcare occupations, the majority of which are in high-tech industries.

We determined that the general field of degree choices of young people with disabilities is similar to those without disabilities—so selection of bachelor's degree fields was not a likely cause for lower levels of high-tech industry employment. Further analysis determined that young, working-age people with disabilities were significantly less likely to be in the labor force than those without a disability, regardless of the degree field of study. Even those with a STEM or STEM healthcare–related degree were as likely to be out of the labor force as those with degrees in other fields. The unemployment rate of young, working-age people with disabilities is far higher relative to those without disabilities in the same fields of study—especially for those with a STEM degree, a surprising finding given the high industry demand.

Finally, we came full circle to look at employment in high-tech sectors, this time focusing on young workers with STEM and STEM healthcare–related degrees. We discovered that these well-qualified people with disabilities were less likely to be employed in high-tech industries than those without disabilities, especially in the healthcare industry. The following section discusses possible reasons for these discrepancies, points where interventions could have an impact, and potential ways to address them.

IMPLICATIONS

According to the Kessler Foundation National Employment and Disability Survey (2018), employers are actively seeking to recruit, hire, train, and retain people with disabilities in their organizations. We also know that people with disabilities want to work. Sixty-eight percent of people with disabilities are currently working, looking for work, or have worked since the onset of their disability (Kessler Foundation 2015). Yet many people with disabilities are still struggling to find employment. Although access to employment for people with disabilities is improving with an upward trend that began in the last quarter of 2016 and persisted for 21 consecutive months (Brendan-Curry 2018), employment for people with disabilities still lags well behind that of people without disabilities. To match employer demand for skilled workers with a population that is striving to work, it is critical that people with disabilities have equal access to high-growth job areas, such as those available in the tech industry.

In the following section we present what research has found regarding employment barriers to persons with disabilities that are likely contributing factors to the lower employment rates our analysis has found. Additionally, recognizing that a bachelor's degree in a STEM field doesn't happen in a vacuum, we also discuss literature regarding educational barriers that individuals with disabilities may encounter that dissuade them from studying STEM to begin with, limiting their options prior to applying or considering entering into STEM higher education and possibly affecting their job search after graduation. Along with the discussion of the barriers, we present possible ways of addressing educational and employment issues to improve opportunities for people with disabilities in STEM and the high-tech industries.

Barriers to Employment

The Kessler Foundation National Employment and Disability Survey (2015) identified barriers that people with disabilities face in seeking employment. These barriers begin in the job-search stage and include, among other things, lack of education and training (41.1%) and assumptions about the ability to perform the tasks of the job (36%). Once in the workplace, reported barriers included pay differentials (16.5%), poor attitudes on the part of supervisors (15.7%), and attitudes on the part of their co-workers (15.5%). Let us examine how these barriers can impede the employment opportunities of people with disabilities in the high-tech industry.

Impact of Assumptions

A certain prestige surrounds employment in the high-tech industry. Many of the jobs are desirable because they involve a high level of skill and ability and are lucrative. As noted in the Kessler study (2015), erroneous assumptions about the competence of people with disabilities in school and employment settings make it appear as though many of them will not succeed in the high-tech world. Assumptions begin early—budding technologists or scientists may be dissuaded from pursuing higher-level classes as early as high school. Teachers might tell them that the course of study will be "too hard" or that the functional limitation associated with their disability makes participation in high-tech study impossible (Brown 2016). Brown (2016) reports that "success requires desire, grit, and ingenuity." These are characteristics that many people with disabilities develop early in order to make their way in a world that is not designed to meet their needs.

Purposeful inclusion of students with disabilities in STEM preparatory programs can help to bridge the gap. A preparatory school in the US Midwest brought students from a variety of backgrounds together for STEM preparatory work. Teachers reported that students with disabilities were no more demanding of teacher time or attention than students without disabilities. The school was integrated in that teachers for each subject area developed individualized instruction for all students, regardless of disability, in order to ensure greater engagement and success in the curriculum (Bargerhuff 2013). The program focused on qualities that are important for those entering high-tech fields: persistence, inquiry, communication, creativity, and collaboration, and its outcomes show that all students can thrive when given an appropriate learning environment (Bargerhuff 2013).

This is no less true when people with disabilities seek to enter the workforce. The same assumptions that work to track students with disabilities away from STEM coursework are also at play in the job application and hiring process. One of the most damaging misconceptions employers sometimes hold is that people with disabilities, even when they have sufficient education and training, will not be able to do the precision work called for in the high-tech industry. This barrier often begins at the hiring stage because hiring managers and recruiters often see only the physical barriers to performing the work when evaluating candidates with disabilities. Hiring managers and recruiters often serve as gatekeepers to positions in STEM fields and prevent meaningful access to people with disabilities. The idea that assumptions about ability interfere with access is borne out in the research as well. A recent experiment conducted by Rutgers and Syracuse universities submitted résumés for employment for accounting positions in several organizations. Each résumé represented an applicant who was well qualified. In some application materials, a disability was disclosed; in others it was not. The applicants who identified as having a disability were 26% less likely than those without a disability to hear from the employer (Ameri et al. 2015).

Approaching one's work in a nonstandard way can add to the concerns an employer may have. If, for example, an employee who has low vision must use a magnification device to examine a lab sample, employers may be concerned that the results will not be as accurate as when the example is analyzed in the way that has been traditionally used in the past. It is critical to make the space for reasonable accommodation in high-tech settings because many people with disabilities approach their work in a different but equally effective way. Employers rightly focus on quality in the work that they do but must not assume it is only possible to achieve this quality with specific consistent processes. It is important for employers to take the time to consider the effectiveness of accommodations made by and for people with disabilities. Accommodations can include changes to the physical environment as well as alterations to make workplace systems, policies, and practices more flexible. Some of these changes may require a shift in the way employers think about the way work gets accomplished. Many of these changes could benefit all employees regardless of disability status. While employees with disabilities are more likely to request workplace accommodations, most accommodation requests actually come from employees without disabilities (Schur et al. 2014; von Schrader, Xu, and Bruyère 2014). Provision of workplace accommodations to those who request them contributes to the creation of a flexible and supportive workplace, which in turn improves employee attitudes across the board (Schur et al. 2014).

Employers sometimes make additional assumptions about the work of people with disabilities. Some employers believe that people with disabilities will require more supervision time from managers, pose a greater risk of accidents in the workplace, and require more off-work time than other employees do. Employers often worry about the ability of a person with a disability to meet production standards. A landmark study conducted by DePaul University and Disability Works (Hernandez and McDonald 2007) contradicts many assumptions about bottom-line impacts, yet these assumptions persist. Managers and supervisors play a critical role in any organization's ability to hire, retain, and promote people of all abilities in the workforce (Rudstam and Strobel Gower 2012). Therefore, it is critical to train managers on how best to include people with disabilities in the workplace. Managers and supervisors require training on critical concepts such as disability etiquette, the business case for inclusion, disclosure, reasonable accommodation policy and practice within their organization, and performance management. They need training and education to support their employees, with disabilities and without, on how they can work together to create an inclusive team and environment that respects the abilities of everyone who works within the organization. Owing to the significant turnover of managers and supervisors, online education and continued messaging are critical in facilitating ongoing training and support for managers (Rudstam et al. 2014).

Employers also express concern that once a person with a disability is hired, they cannot be fired, even if their performance is poor. They often point to the protections of the Americans with Disabilities Act (ADA) as proof of this last statement. However, according to the EEOC (2002a), the ADA does not require employers to lower production standards for people with disabilities. Neither does the ADA protect employees who fail to perform the essential functions of their job or meet evenly applied performance standards from being terminated (US EEOC 2002b). Providing training to managers on the basics of the ADA and how to effectively manage performance for people with disabilities is also helpful in dispelling myths about the legal ramification of hiring and firing people with disabilities.

Access to Middle-Skill High-Tech Jobs Also an Issue

Our findings illustrate how many people with disabilities have received an appropriate post-secondary education in STEM fields and yet still struggle to gain employment. The tech industry features jobs in both high- and middle-skill areas. High-skill STEM jobs require a bachelor's degree or greater in order to be qualified, while middle-skill STEM jobs are often accessed through career and technical education or on-the-job training programs. As noted previously, middle-skill jobs are also in high demand; in 2015, these types of jobs accounted for 53% of employment opportunities in the United States. These jobs will remain a viable option for work through 2024, and middle-skill jobs that require digital skills and STEM training outnumber those that do not (Burning Glass Technologies 2015).

Middle-skill careers have historically been the path to the middle class for most Americans, and they currently represent over 45% of all employment. In the past, a high school diploma was sufficient to obtain these jobs, but increasingly they require post-secondary education, though not necessarily four-year degrees. It is estimated that 65% of all future jobs will require some post-secondary education or training, and nearly half of those jobs will be middle-skill occupations (Texas Workforce Investment Council 2015). Despite the high demand for middle-skill jobs, only 43% of the country's workers are adequately trained for this level of employment (National Skills Coalition 2015). The lack of human capital trained for middle-skill jobs has slowed down economic improvement. Workers who are unable to secure sufficient training will face challenges in entering these high-demand jobs (Modestino 2016). The situation is particularly disadvantageous for people with disabilities, with a difference in labor force participation of 31 percentage points (Erickson, Lee, and von Schrader 2018). As described above, a number of factors contribute to this, including low expectations for K–12 students with disabilities, preparatory systems that do not offer equal opportunities to participate in key training sessions, and assumptions about what job seekers with disabilities can do at work.

In fact, systems that support employment continue to funnel people with disabilities through segregated employment that often does not provide access to existing training programs. The recent implementation of the Workforce Innovation and Opportunity Act (US Department of Labor, no date), which requires access for people with disabilities in Title I training programs, may lead to improvements in access to these middle-skill jobs.

Although institutional gating and tracking mean that many people with disabilities are insufficiently prepared to enter these critical fields, it is particularly concerning that our research shows that even well-prepared individuals with disabilities who have appropriate higher education in high-demand fields of study are still disadvantaged in the workplace.

Bridge programs that seek to facilitate the transition of a diverse student population into higher education programs are on the rise (Ashley, Cooper, Cala, and Brownell 2017). These programs often target under-represented minorities, female students, academically unprepared students, or highly academically prepared students. Bridge programs also have great potential to support students with disabilities who could use early engagement to identify necessary accommodations, develop plans to navigate difficult environments and social situations, and connect with faculty and student support programs to enhance their success at the post-secondary level.

Work Experience

When people with disabilities enter the workforce, they often enter into positions that are not a good fit (Lyons et al. 2016). This is a concern for both the employee and employer (Smith, Webber, Graffam, and Wilson 2004). Meanwhile, employers commonly cite the lack of qualified applicants as a barrier to hiring people with disabilities (Domzal, Houtenville, and Sharma 2008; Erickson, von Schrader, Bruyère, and VanLooy 2013; Kessler/National Organization on Disability 2010). Evidence suggests that only a minority of employers, between 11% and 34%, actively recruit workers with disabilities, with smaller employers being less likely to recruit (Dixon, Kruse, and Van Horn 2003; Domzal, Houtenville, and Sharma 2008; Lengnick-Hall, Gaunt, and Collison 2003). In light of these findings, there has been a push in the field to use internships and community partnerships as a tool to enhance the hiring of people with disabilities (Domzal, Houtenville, and Sharma 2008; Nicholas, Kauder, Krepcio, and Baker 2011).

Employers' most frequently cited barriers to employing people with disabilities are lack of skill, experience, and training (Erickson et al. 2014). As noted above, individuals with disabilities are less likely to have a bachelor's degree or higher; however, our findings indicate that a significant discrepancy still exists even after limiting this analysis to those with a bachelor's degree. This suggests that organizations are more likely to employ recent college graduates without disabilities than to employ those with a disability with an equivalent education. The fact that people with disabilities have lower employment and wage levels than people with disabilities is an ongoing issue. A 2015 study by Rutgers and Syracuse universities demonstrated that even experienced applicants were screened out if disability was disclosed. The study found that applicants with disabilities were about 26% less likely to receive an expression of interest from an employer (Ameri et al. 2015).

Internships may help to address these barriers by building job seekers' skills and demonstrating those skills to employers. Employers with an internship program for individuals with disabilities were almost six times more likely to have hired a person with a disability than those who did not (Erickson et al. 2014). Likewise, school-to-work programs have been shown to increase the likelihood of later adult employment among individuals with disabilities (Enayati, Karpur, and Golden 2016; Shandra and Hogan 2008). Internships offer valuable training and support and sometimes credentials that can boost job opportunities and earnings (Burgstahler and Bellman 2009; Grossman et al. 2015). Further research is needed to better support employers' effective implementation of this promising practice for bringing more people with disabilities into the talent pipeline. Programs such as Entry Point!, a program created and operated by the American Association for the Advancement of Science, specifically target talented graduate and undergraduate students with disabilities into a ten-week summer internship program with employer partners. The program recruits, screens, and refers qualified candidates to company and university research partners to gain valuable, real-world experience. Eighty-five percent of Entry Point! alumni are now successfully working in high-tech careers (American Association for the Advancement of Science 2018).

Retention

Across all students, with and without disabilities, many with STEM degrees are not working in STEM fields after graduation—as many as 40% of all STEM graduates choose not to pursue careers in STEM occupations, and of the remainder, nearly half will leave their field within ten years of entry (Hawley, Cardoso, and McMahon 2013). This rate of attrition applies to students and employees with disabilities as well—and combined with their already-lower rate of post-secondary attendance—this has a serious impact on the ultimate representation of people with disabilities in STEM occupations. Gaining a better understanding of what is behind this attrition, especially for persons with disabilities, could help identify what could be done to address this "leakage" of qualified individuals from STEM occupations.

Clues may be found in the reasons that women and ethnic/racial minorities report for leaving STEM occupations: A review of evidence of diversity and inclusion in high-tech workplaces by the US EEOC (2016) cites a 2015 survey of female scientists that found most experienced frequent workplace questioning of their expertise and competence—two thirds reported having to prove themselves repeatedly. Many felt isolated in the workplace and said that workplace socialization led to greater demands to prove competence rather than increased inclusion. The same EEOC review also cites a 2016 survey, in which similar reasons were given for leaving STEM studies in college.

Mentoring Programs

Mentoring programs provide young professionals with disabilities access to more experienced workers in their field. Even virtual mentoring, with support delivered online or over the phone, produced more confidence and self-efficacy in STEM skills and increased persistence in STEM activity participation (Gregg et al. 2017). Mentor programs can help people with disabilities to enter their field of choice and help prevent the attrition of talented, well-educated employees with disabilities. Mentor relationships are essentially interpersonal relationships; as a result, it is difficult to define the role of a mentor. The US Department of Labor's Office of Disability Employment Policy encourages mentorship programs that include well-qualified mentors who are screened and matched to appropriate candidates. Appropriate levels of visibility and accountability are encouraged (ODEP, no date). Mentoring provides firsthand exposure to the workplace and access to someone who can answer questions about critical soft skills and approaches to problem solving, thereby increasing the likelihood of employee retention.

Mentoring is very beneficial not only for employees but for youth interested in high-tech careers as well. Mentoring results in improved academic performance, increased attendance rates at school, better attitudes about school, higher college enrollment rates and aspirations, and stronger relationships with parents, teachers, and peers. A number of studies have found that mentoring has a positive impact on STEM-related knowledge and interest for students with disabilities (Sowers et al. 2017). Overcoming assumptions about what others believe a person with a disability is capable of accomplishing in the high-tech employment landscape can be challenging for those seeking employment. Mentoring not only improves the confidence of youth interested in STEM employment but also changes parents' perception of their child's abilities (Sowers et al. 2017). Mentoring, especially of older teenagers, may increase engagement in STEM activities, interest in STEM careers, and confidence in taking on STEM tasks (Sowers et al. 2017). As qualified workers become more difficult to find, it will be increasingly difficult for companies to disregard talented job seekers with disabilities. The creation of inclusive preparatory programs will become critical to the high-tech industry. Inclusive education and preparatory programs are already beginning to appear, but they should be expanded. Programs that highlight ways to increase universal design, as well as effective accommodations in high-tech environments (see Bellman, Burgstahler, and Chudler 2018, for example), will become increasingly important to ensure the success of this increasingly diverse workplace.

CONCLUSION

The path to high-tech careers is not easy for people with disabilities who face barriers along the way. Students without disabilities find career and technical education programs effective at sustaining interest and performance as they transition from STEM education to STEM jobs. Unfortunately, evidence suggests these programs are not as effective for students with disabilities (Gottfried, Bozick, Rose, and Moore 2016). Individuals acquire STEM knowledge and skills across multiple venues, including out-of-school programs such as extracurricular clubs, trips, and events sponsored by schools, libraries, community centers, colleges, philanthropic foundations, and corporations. Participation in extracurricular programs can increase grades, encourage engagement in school, and create interest in STEM studies and careers. However, many of these extracurricular activities also present barriers to students with disabilities, who are often discouraged from attending and are insufficiently accommodated when they do attend (Fisher 2017).

No matter the path students with disabilities pursue, Gottfried and colleagues (2016) conclude that current approaches to STEM education and career preparation for students with disabilities can only be described as "unsuccessful." Improvements in access to internships, mentorships, apprenticeships, and STEM education will all help facilitate involvement in high-tech careers for people with disabilities. We must continue to challenge assumptions around both what students with disabilities can accomplish and the capabilities of people with disabilities to perform in the workplace. Until educators and employers believe that success in the high-tech world is possible, no amount of preparation will make a difference.

The analysis presented in this paper shows that, even when young people with disabilities are equivalently prepared for employment (e.g., with a college degree in STEM or STEM-related fields), they are not being equally employed at the same rate as those without disabilities. One potential limitation is that individuals without disabilities are more likely to pursue advanced degrees—might those with advanced degrees widen the gaps? To examine the possibility that this is a potential contributing factor, we reanalyzed the data while excluding persons with advanced degrees and determined that the same patterns were found, suggesting that unequal pursuit of advanced degrees is not the cause of the discrepancies.

The fact that people with disabilities who have STEM and STEM-related degrees are less likely to be employed in high-tech industries is deeply concerning. One might expect that individuals who have overcome the educational barriers would be highly valued by employers, but it appears that additional barriers exist even for these well-prepared potential employees. Further research is needed to better understand what underlies these findings. Do educators' previously identified beliefs about students with disabilities to accomplish STEM studies carry over to the workplace? Are high-tech industries less likely to hire individuals with disabilities and/or provide accommodations? Are there issues with the types of jobs available in the high-tech industries that make them less attractive to individuals with disabilities? Might there be unique aspects of employment in high-tech industries that lead to greater retention discrepancies between those with and without disabilities?

Future research could examine the quality of job match of those with and without disabilities with STEM and STEM-related degrees both in and outside of high-tech industries. Are individuals with disabilities with college degrees employed in positions less well suited to their educational field relative to those without disabilities? This chapter used the ACS overall disability category based on six disability types; additional research that examines differences by ACS disability type with regard to STEM education and employment in high-tech may be illuminating. The descriptive analysis presented in this paper is only a beginning, but it has identified an issue. It will require additional research aimed at understanding the underlying mechanisms to effectively address this issue to remove barriers and improve employment opportunities for people with disabilities in STEM and high-tech industries.

ACKNOWLEDGMENTS

The authors appreciate reviews and feedback provided by Andrew Eddy, director, Untapped Group; Michael Fieldhouse, director, emerging businesses and federal government, DXC Technology; and David Jones, workforce analyst, US Department of Labor Employment and Training Administration.

REFERENCES

Ameri, Mason, Lisa A. Schur, Meera Adya, Scott Bentley, Patrick F. McKay, and Douglas Kruse. 2015. "The Disability Employment Puzzle: A Field Experiment on Employer Hiring Behavior." NBER Working Paper Series 21560. Cambridge, MA. doi:10.3386/w21560

American Association for the Advancement of Science (AAAS). 2018. "About Entry Point!" Washington, DC: American Association for the Advancement of Science. http://bit.ly/2SHhkht

Anft, Michael. 2013 (Nov. 11). "The STEM Crisis: Reality or Myth?" *Chronicle of Higher Education*. http://bit.ly/2ts9jOg

Ashley, Michael, Katelyn M. Cooper, Jacqueline M. Cala, and Sara E. Brownell. 2017. "Building Better Bridges into STEM: A Synthesis of 25 Years of Literature on STEM Summer Bridge Programs." *CBE Life Sciences Education* 16 (4). doi:10.1187/cbe.17-05-0085

Bargerhuff, Mary E. 2013. "Meeting the Needs of Students with Disabilities in a STEM School." *American Secondary Education* 41 (3): 3–20.

Bellman, Scott, Sheryl Burgstahler, and Eric H Chudler. 2018. "Broadening Participation by Including More Individuals with Disabilities in STEM : Promising Practices from an Engineering Research Center." *American Behavioral Scientist*. doi:10.1177/0002764218768864

Brendan Curry, Anna. 2018 (Jan. 5). "nTIDE December 17 Jobs Report: Year-End Job Numbers Cap Record Year for Americans with Disabilities." *Research on Disability*. http://bit.ly/2V0f4lS

Brown, Eryn. 2016. "The Fight for Accessibility." *Nature* 532 (7597): 137–139. doi:10.1038/NJ7597-137A

Bump, Philip. 2013 (Jul. 24). "Read: Obama's Speech on the Middle Class." *The Atlantic*. http://bit.ly/2V3esIv

Burgstahler, Sheryl, and Scott Bellman. 2009. "Differences in Perceived Benefits of Internships for Subgroups of Students with Disabilities." *Journal of Vocational Rehabilitation* 31 (3): 155–165. doi:10.3233/JVR-2009-0485

Burning Glass Technologies. 2015 (Mar.). "Crunched by the Numbers: The Digital Skills Gap in the Workforce." Boston, MA: Burning Glass Technologies. http://bit.ly/2V3LTdS

Carnevale, Anthony P., Nicole Smith, and Jeff Strohl. 2013. "Recovery: Job Growth and Education Requirements Through 2020 (Full Report)." Washington, DC: Georgetown Public Policy Institute Center on Education and the Workforce. http://bit.ly/2UZ48kG

Charette, Robert. 2013. "The STEM Crisis Is a Myth." *North American* 2 (c): 1–5.

Dixon, K.A., D. Kruse, and C.E. Van Horn. 2003. "Restricted Access: A Survey of Employers About People with Disabilities and Lowering Barriers to Work." New Brunswick, NJ: Rutgers University Heldrich Center for Workforce Development.

Domzal, C., A. Houtenville, and R. Sharma. 2008. "Survey of Employer Perspectives on the Employment of People with Disabilities: Technical Report. (Prepared Under Contract to the Office of Disability and Employment Policy, US Department of Labor)." McLean, VA: CESSI.

Enayati, Hassan, Arun Karpur, and Thomas Golden. 2016. "The Role of Participating in Career Development Activities on the Impact of Adolescent Poverty on Employment and Education Outcomes for Youth with Disabilities." Ithaca, NY: Cornell University Yang-Tan Institute on Employment and Disability.

Erickson, William A., Camille Lee, and Sarah von Schrader. 2018. "2016 Disability Status Report—United States." Ithaca, NY: Cornell University Yang-Tan Institute on Employment and Disability. doi:10.1111/j.1475-6765.2007.00760.x

Erickson, William A., Sarah von Schrader, Susanne M. Bruyère, and Sara A. VanLooy. 2013. "The Employment Environment: Employer Perspectives, Policies, and Practices Regarding the Employment of Persons with Disabilities." *Rehabilitation Counseling Bulletin* 57 (4): 195–208. doi:10.1177/0034355213509841

Erickson, William A., Sarah von Schrader, Susanne M. Bruyère, Sara A. VanLooy, and David S. Matteson. 2014. "Disability-Inclusive Employer Practices and Hiring of Individuals with Disabilities." *Rehabilitation Research, Policy, and Education* 28 (4): 309–328. doi:10.1891/2168-6653.28.4.309

Fisher, Karin. 2017. "The Importance of Extracurricular STEM Activities for Students with Disabilities." In *Proceedings of the Interdisciplinary STEM Teaching and Learning Conference* doi:10.20429/stem.2017.010103

Gottfried, Michael A., Robert Bozick, Ernest Rose, and Ravaris Moore. 2016. "Does Career and Technical Education Strengthen the STEM Pipeline? Comparing Students With and Without Disabilities." *Journal of Disability Policy Studies* 26 (4): 232–244. doi:10.1177/1044207314544369

Gregg, Noel, April Galyardt, Gerri Wolfe, Nathan Moon, and Robert Todd. 2017. "Virtual Mentoring and Persistence in STEM for Students with Disabilities." *Career Development and Transition for Exceptional Individuals* 40 (4): 205–124. doi:10.1177/2165143416651717

Grossman, Jean, Linda Kato, Tony Mallon, Sheila Maguire, and Maureen Conway. 2015. "The Value of Credentials for Disadvantaged Workers: Findings from the Sector Employment Impact Study." Washington, DC: Workforce Strategies Initiative at the Aspen Institute. http://bit.ly/2tta7Ti

Hawley, Carolyn E., Elizabeth Cardoso, and Brian T. McMahon. 2013. "Adolescence to Adulthood in STEM Education and Career Development: The Experience of Students at the Intersection of Underrepresented Minority Status and Disability." *Journal of Vocational Rehabilitation* 39 (3): 193–204. doi:10.3233/JVR-130655

Hernandez, Brigida, and Katherine McDonald. 2007. "Exploring the Bottom Line: A Study of the Costs and Benefits of Workers with Disabilities." Chicago, IL: DePaul University. http://bit.ly/2V8U2hp

Heckler, Daniel E. 2005 (Jul.). "High-Technology Employment: A NAICS-Based Update." *Monthly Labor Review*, pp. 57–72. http://bit.ly/2KBMKS1

Kessler Foundation. 2015. "2015 National Employment & Disability Survey: Report of Main Findings." West Orange, NJ: Kessler Foundation.

Kessler Foundation. 2018. "2017 Kessler Foundation National Employment and Disability Survey: Supervisor Perspectives." West Orange, NJ: Kessler Foundation. http://bit.ly/2KCcaii

Kessler/National Organization on Disability. 2010. "The ADA, 20 Years Later." New York, NY: National Organization on Disability. http://bit.ly/2N7eccb

Landivar, Liana Christin. 2013a (Sep.). "The Relationship Between Science and Engineering Education and Employment in STEM Occupations." *American Community Survey Reports*, 2–19. http://bit.ly/2Nrkxjd

Landivar, Liana Christin 2013b (Sep. 9). "Who Is a STEM Worker?" *Census Blogs*. http://bit.ly/2V5PtEe

Lee, Ahlam. 2011. "A Comparison of Postsecondary Science, Technology, Engineering, and Mathematics (STEM) Enrollment for Students With and Without Disabilities." *Career Development for Exceptional Individuals* 34 (2): 72–82. doi:10.1177/0885728810386591

Lengnick-Hall, M., P. Gaunt, and J. Collison. 2003. "Employer Incentives for Hiring Individuals with Disabilities." Alexandria, VA: Society for Human Resource Management.

Leonard, Bill. 2015 (Mar. 11). "Obama Announces TechHire Initiative." *SHRM News*. Alexandria, VA: Society for Human Resource Management. http://bit.ly/2trO0MR

Lyons, B.J., L.R. Martinez, E.N. Ruggs, M.R. Hebl, A.M. Ryan, K.R. O'Brien, and A. Roebuck. 2018. "To Say or Not to Say: Different Strategies of Acknowledging a Visible Disability." *Journal of Management* 44 (5): 1980–2007. doi:10.1177/0149206316638160

Modestino, Alicia Sasser. 2016. "The Importance of Middle-Skill Jobs." *Issues in Science and Technology* 33 (1). http://bit.ly/2tpTO9E

Mugglestone, Konrad, and Tom Allison. 2015 (Oct. 27). "The Best Jobs for Millennials." Indianapolis, IN: Lumina Foundation. http://bit.ly/2tsyUqE

National Science Board. 2015. "Revisiting the STEM Workforce—A Companion to Science and Engineering Indicators 2014." Arlington, VA: National Science Board.

National Science Foundation. 2017. "2017 Women, Minorities, and Persons with Disabilities in Science and Engineering." Washington, DC: National Science Foundation. http://bit.ly/2tsHFRq

National Skills Coalition. 2015. United States' Forgotten Middle." Fact Sheet. Washington, DC: National Skills Coalition. http://bit.ly/2Nbj3t6

Nicholas, Robert, Ronnie Kauder, Kathy Krepcio, and Daniel Baker. 2011. "Ready and Able: Addressing Labor Market Needs and Building Productive Careers for People with Disabilities Through Collaborative Approaches." New Brunswick, NJ: NTAR Leadership Center, Rutgers University. http://bit.ly/2KBKqdK

Rothwell, Jonathan. 2013. "The Hidden STEM Economy." Washington, DC: Brookings Institution. https://brook.gs/2tsz41e

Rudstam, Hannah, Thomas P. Golden, Wendy Strobel Gower, Ellice Switzer, Susanne M. Bruyère, and Sara A. VanLooy. 2014. "Leveraging New Rules to Advance New Opportunities: Implications of the Rehabilitation Act Section 503 New Rules for Employment Service Providers." *Journal of Vocational Rehabilitation* 41 (3): 193–208. doi:10.3233/JVR-140713

Rudstam, Hannah, and Wendy Strobel Gower. 2012. "Beyond Instruction; Beyond a Website: Distance Learning, Disability Inclusiveness, and Changing Workplace Practices." *Rehabilitation Education* 26 (4): 245–255. doi:10.1891/216866512805252524

Schur, Lisa, Lisa Nishii, Meera Adya, Douglas Kruse, Susanne M. Bruyère, and Peter Blanck. 2014. "Accommodating Employees With and Without Disabilities." *Human Resource Management* 53 (4): 593–621. http://bit.ly/2tqBehF

Shandra, Carrie L., and Dennis Hogan. 2008. "School-to-Work Program Participation and the Post-High School Employment of Young Adults with Disabilities." *Journal of Vocational Rehabilitation* 29 (2): 117–130. http://bit.ly/2towlFY

Smith, Kaye, Lynne Webber, Joe Graffam, and Carlene Wilson. 2004. "Employer Satisfaction, Job-Match and Future Hiring Intentions for Employees with a Disability." *Journal of Vocational Rehabilitation* 21 (3): 165–173.

Sowers, Jo-Ann, Laurie Powers, Jessica Schmidt, Thomas E. Keller, Alison Turner, Amy Salazar, and Paul R. Swank. 2017. "A Randomized Trial of a Science, Technology, Engineering, and Mathematics Mentoring Program." *Career Development and Transition for Exceptional Individuals* 40 (4): 196–204. doi:10.1177/2165143416633426

Texas Workforce Investment Council. 2015. "Defining Middle-Skill STEM Occupations in Texas." Austin, TX: Texas Workforce Investment Council. http://bit.ly/2tsHXYw

US Department of Labor. No date. "Laws and Regulations: The Workforce Innovation & Opportunity Act (WIOA)." Washington, DC: US Department of Labor. http://bit.ly/2trJo9u

US Equal Employment Opportunity Commission (US EEOC). 2002a. "ADA: Reasonable Accommodations." EEOC FOIA Letters. Washington, DC: US Equal Employment Opportunity Commission. http://bit.ly/2V4JCiI

US Equal Employment Opportunity Commission (US EEOC). 2002b. "Enforcement Guidance: Reasonable Accommodation and Undue Hardship under the Americans with Disabilities Act." Washington, DC: US Equal Employment Opportunity Commission. http://bit.ly/2MEADBE

US Equal Employment Opportunity Commission (US EEOC). 2016. "Diversity in High Tech." Washington, DC: US Equal Employment Opportunity Commission. http://bit.ly/2tshbiM

US Office of Disability Employment Policy (US ODEP). No date. "Cultivating Leadership: Mentoring Youth with Disabilities." Washington, DC: US Office of Disability Employment. http://bit.ly/2ttHghA

von Schrader, Sarah, Xu Xu, and Susanne M. Bruyère. 2014. "Accommodation Requests: Who Is Asking for What?" *Rehabilitation Research, Policy, and Education* 28 (4): 329–344. doi:10.1891/2168-6653.28.4.329

Wolf, Michael, and Dalton Terrell. 2016. "The High-Tech Industry: What Is It and Why It Matters to Our Economic Future." *Beyond the Numbers: Employment and Unemployment* 5 (8): 1–7. http://bit.ly/2ttc3v2

Chapter 10

Autism at Work: Targeted Hiring Initiatives and What We Can Learn for Other Groups

Susanne M. Bruyère
Cornell University

INTRODUCTION

One of the most significant barriers to positive employment outcomes for individuals with disabilities has been stigma and stereotypes about their capabilities. A striking recent innovation in disability inclusive policies and practices in industry has been the creation of affirmative hiring initiatives tailored to individuals with autism (Parmar 2017; Szczerba 2016). Employers in the technology and technology-intensive sectors have implemented targeted hiring initiatives for autistic people, who offer a different perspective (Hedley et al. 2016; Hurley-Hanson and Giannantonio 2017). These companies are trying to understand how to leverage the unique characteristics of autistic individuals in select jobs in the technology industry. This perspective sees their differences not as a problem to be solved but rather as a business advantage—one that takes the benefits of the diverse workteam concept to a whole new level of inclusion. Framing neurodiversity as a strategic advantage offers a paradigm shift that may not only benefit individuals with autism specifically but could also improve employment outcomes for individuals with disabilities more broadly.

Why might employers be particularly interested in autism? According to the Centers for Disease Control and Prevention, autism is a "developmental disability that can cause significant social, communication and behavioral challenges" (CDC 2019). It is also known as "autism spectrum disorder" (ASD). People with this diagnosis have characteristic learning, thinking, and problem-solving abilities that can range from gifted to severely challenged (CDC 2019). Select characteristics of autism appear to contribute to an ability to focus intently and perceive patterns, which is why some employers are now actively seeking out these individuals for their jobs. This consideration of a difference that would previously have caused a group to be marginalized from labor-force participation is what makes this business trend interesting and ultimately very useful. Individuals who gain employment through such programs report significant positive personal impact as a result. These positive outcomes are not only economic; people also report increased self-confidence and pride in the ability to use their skills to contribute to their company and communities.

This issue is not just an American concern. It is global. Autism occurs in every country, every ethnic group, and every socioeconomic class (Shore and Rastelli 2006). It therefore affords an opportunity for a far-reaching conversation and broadened perspective about the human capital pipeline and ways to facilitate workforce inclusion across a much greater proportion of the American and global populations.

The overarching focus of this chapter will be the need to improve employment outcomes for individuals with autism and ways that employers, employment service providers, and labor and employment relations professionals can capitalize on the emerging interest and contribute to the ultimate success of this trend. This chapter provides information about what autism is, statistics on the current prevalence of autism and employment status of individuals with autism, workplace and human resources (HR) policies and practices currently being implemented, challenges in successful implementation, and steps being taken to further facilitate success.

PEOPLE WITH AUTISM IN THE UNITED STATES

To convey the significance of these initiatives, this chapter first provides information about autism to lay a foundation for understanding the characteristics that underlie this label. It then follows with select statistics about the prevalence of this condition in the United States and the employment disparities that make pursuit of improved employment outcomes for this group most urgent, and therefore these affirmative hiring initiatives of high interest.

Definitions and Characteristics of Autism and Neurodiversity

According to the American Psychiatric Association (2019),

> autism spectrum disorder (ASD) is a complex developmental condition that involves persistent challenges in social interaction, speech and nonverbal communication, and restricted/repetitive behaviors. The effects of ASD and the severity of symptoms are different in each person. ASD is usually diagnosed in children, sometimes as young as three years old, and it is a lifelong condition. However, many people who are diagnosed with ASD live independent, productive, and fulfilling lives.

Autism differs greatly from person to person. Individuals with ASD demonstrate a wide range of abilities and characteristics, and it is important to understand that people with the same diagnosis may present themselves quite differently. The ways in which autism manifests in an individual can also change over time. The following characteristics are listed by the American Psychiatric Association as possibly occurring among individuals with ASD:

- encountering difficulties in communication and social interactions, including back-and-forth conversation, sharing interests or emotions, processing social cues such as eye contact and facial expressions, and developing, maintaining, or understanding relationships
- speaking in a unique way (such as using unusual patterns or pitches in speaking or "scripting" from favorite shows)
- engaging in repetitive or restricted behavior patterns, interests, or activities, such as having significant need for a predictable routine or structure, or enjoying intense interests in certain topics or activities
- experiencing the sensory aspects of the world in an unusual or extreme way, such as indifference to pain/temperature, the need to smell or touch objects, fascination with lights and movement, or being overwhelmed with loud noises

While many people with autism have normal intelligence or above, others have mild or significant intellectual delays. In addition, people with ASD are at greater risk for some medical conditions such as sleep problems, seizures, and mental illnesses (American Psychiatric Association 2019).

The characterization of autism is an evolving phenomenon. For example, the diagnosis of Asperger Syndrome, which was part of the fourth edition of the *Diagnostic and Statistical Manual of Mental Disorders* (DSM-IV) from 1994 through 2017, was removed in the latest edition. Yet many individuals who previously had this diagnosis still identify as having Asperger Syndrome despite its no longer being included in the DSM-V (Scheiner 2019b).

Historically, the medical community has used the phrase "autism spectrum disorder," but others prefer the terminology "autism spectrum condition." This preference for the word "condition" rather than "disorder" is an effort to recognize or convey that autism is a set of characteristics unique in each person and to remove the negative connotation that the word "disorder" might hold. It is also important to be aware that, while the wider disability community generally has a strong preference for discussing disability in terms of "person first language," in which a person with an ASD diagnosis would be described as "a person with autism," this is not always the case. "Identity first" language is growing in importance among individuals and advocates. "In the autism community, many self-advocates and their allies prefer terminology such as 'Autistic,' 'Autistic person,' or 'Autistic individual,' because we understand autism as an inherent part of an individual's identity—the same way one refers to 'Muslims,' 'African Americans,' or others" (Autism Self Advocacy Network 2019).

Finally, the term "autism" is also increasingly being broadened to include a larger group of people who can fit under the umbrella of the term "neurodiverse" (Sumner and Brown 2015). The term "neurodiversity" is credited to Judy Singer, who in her book *Neurodiversity: The Birth of an Idea*, talks about how autism has risen from a medicalized diagnosis to become a social movement (2016). "Neurodiversity is a concept where neurological differences are to be recognized and respected as any other human variation. These differences can include those labeled with Dyspraxia, Dyslexia, Attention Deficit Hyperactivity Disorder, Dyscalculia, Autistic Spectrum, Tourette's Syndrome and others" (National Symposium on Neurodiversity at Syracuse University 2011; Sumner and Brown 2015). For the purposes of this chapter, we will move between the terms described above and use them interchangeably as appropriate.

Status of People with Autism in the United States

Prevalence Rates

The discussion on definitions of autism and the broader term "neurodiversity" sets the stage for an appreciation of the difficulty researchers face when trying to provide accurate estimates of the size and composition of this population. The CDC estimates that 1 in 59 children has autism. The same estimates suggest that autism spectrum disorder is three to four times more common in boys than in girls (CDC 2018). This gender difference continues to be controversial; the difference may be attributable to the fact many girls with ASD exhibit less obvious signs compared to boys, but further investigation is under way (Lai et al. 2015; Rivet and Matson 2011). The CDC acknowledges the difficulties in tracking the prevalence of autism across time because of the "heterogeneity in symptom presentation, lack of biological diagnostic markers, and changing diagnostic criteria." In 2000 through 2002, these estimates were 1 in 150 children, and 1 in 68 during 2010 through 2012. What is worthy of note is the significant change in prevalence rates over time from what the CDC has recorded consistently to date (CDC 2018).

It is also important to note here, however, that autism today has a broader set of diagnostic criteria than it did historically, and some of the older population maybe not have been diagnosed because little was known previously about autism (Silberman 2015). There are likely many individuals who have autistic characteristics without the diagnostic label because their level of functioning or lack of awareness of ways ASD can manifest meant they never sought or were referred for a professional assessment that would provide a formal label (Wyatt 2017). In addition, there are inherent limitations in data on individuals with disabilities in general because many individuals do not disclose information about their disability in responding to surveys, owing to the stigma and biases of others around labels relating to perceived disability (Wyatt 2017).

The CDC prevalence estimates suggest that the autistic population is growing both in the United States and globally, and this also is a group whose educational access and employment future are significantly under-realized. This is why attention to these disparities is imperative. Below, we document these educational and employment disparities.

Higher Education Rates

Most youth with autism are intellectually capable of earning a post-secondary degree; about half have average to above-average intellectual ability (CDC 2018). Despite this, these youth are less likely to enroll in post-secondary education (two-year or four-year) than their peers with most other types of disabilities, such as speech/language impairments and specific learning disabilities (Wei et al. 2013). Moreover, while approximately 60% of students without disabilities enrolled in four-year colleges ultimately earn a bachelor's degree (National Center for Education Statistics 2019), a far smaller proportion (about 41%) of students with disabilities (including ASD) do so.

Employment Participation Rates

Approximately 58% of young adults with autism have had at least one paid job between high school and their early 20s (Roux et al. 2015). In addition, they seem to be disproportionately under-employed compared with their age-mates without such a diagnosis and with those with other kinds of diagnoses, including individuals with other neurodiversity characteristics; results from the National Longitudinal Transition Study-2 show that, in their early 20s, young adults with autism had far lower rates of employment than their peers. Approximately 95% of those with learning disabilities reported having ever worked after high school, compared to 58% of those with autism (Roux et al. 2015).

These dramatic disparities in employment participation illustrate the urgency of addressing these issues, and the significance of the increasing number of businesses that are looking to hire individuals with autistic characteristics. We will spend the remainder of this chapter discussing factors driving business interests, the evolution of this interest, and the challenges and opportunities that are emerging from these efforts.

BUSINESSES' INTEREST IN AUTISTIC CHARACTERISTICS

Why Is Business Interested?

The success of any company is dependent on having the right talent to fill its needs. With the unemployment rate at a 17-year low of 4.1%, many companies are finding it challenging to recruit the talent they need, particularly in select job areas (Kost 2018). In addition to a shortage of labor to fill open jobs, employers are also facing a skills gap for those already in the workforce (Maurer 2017). By 2030, it is estimated that the demand for skilled workers will outstrip supply, resulting in a global talent shortage of more than 85.2 million people (Korn Ferry 2018). These shortages are not an issue only for large businesses—a report from the National Federation of Independent Business details that 45% of small businesses were unable to find qualified applicants to fill job openings in the first quarter of 2017 (Dunkelberg and Wade 2017).

Interest in accessing the largely untapped talent pool of people with autism, and perhaps neurodiverse individuals more broadly, is largely being driven by the need of businesses to identify ways to fill the talent shortages they are already experiencing and those they anticipate in the future (Barnett 2018; Chu 2015). Some companies have also recognized that certain characteristics of a person with autism (autistic individual), such as an ability to focus intently, allow her or him to see patterns in data or contribute unique perspectives that others might not identify, which might be a competitive advantage. These traits are skills that can be applied to specific and necessary tasks such as cybersecurity or code debugging, where perhaps these individuals can outperform their "neurotypical" worker peers (Austin, Fieldhouse and Quinn 2017; Pisano and Austin 2016a).

Companies are experiencing other benefits as a result of these initiatives. Media interest in these efforts is increasing the companies' public relations cachet (CBS News 2018; EY 2018). Participating companies also report an increase in internal goodwill (EY 2018; Pisano and Austin 2016b). With the high prevalence rate of autism in the United States, companies are finding that many current employees either have a family member with autism or know of others in their community who do (EY 2018). In addition, employees already in the workforce who have not disclosed their own autism, seeing their employer's hiring initiatives, are now reportedly more comfortable coming forward to self-identify as a person with autism.

Evolution of Interest in Autism Hiring

Although most interest in affirmative hiring of autistic individuals has occurred in the past five years, there are longer-standing efforts in this area. Among these is an initiative by the Israeli Defense Department. The Roim Rachok (Looking Ahead) program is an innovative program designed to train adults on the autism spectrum in professions required by the Israeli Defense Forces (IDF). Israeli youth who have historically been exempt from military service now have a place to contribute their skills and abilities in Unit 9900, a selective intelligence squad, where their heightened perceptual skills are viewed as an asset (Rubin 2016). More recently, through a partnership with Ono Academic College, these recruits are also being trained for civilian jobs. The first training course was to decipher aerial and satellite photography. It is based on the idea that people on the autistic spectrum are very visually oriented, and many of them have the ability to focus on details that the work requires. The program has since been expanded to train participants in other professions needed in the IDF and civilian job market, such as software quality assurance, information sorting, and electro-optics work (Ono Academic College 2019).

The Federal Home Loan Mortgage Company (Freddie Mac) was also an early innovator in the area of autism hiring. Freddie Mac partnered with the Autism Self Advocacy Network in 2012 to create the Autism Internship Program, which was designed to match the business needs of a company with what is perceived to be the unique capabilities of individuals with autism. The program focused on young adults with college degrees in the field of computer science, mathematics, and finance (Coy 2015; Freddie Mac 2012).

This trend has caught on in other large multinational software services and cybersecurity companies, as well as more recently in the finance and accounting sectors. SAP began its Autism at Work program in 2013 with an aspirational objective of having 1% of its workforce represented by employees with autism (Bort 2013; Pisano and Austin 2016b). The company now has more than 150 employees with autism, and the program is operating in 12 countries. The types of positions have expanded tenfold over the program's evolution, and employees with autism have now been placed into 20 job types, including human resources, software development, customer service, and data protection functions. The program has not only brought new talent into the company across many job lines but also created significant media coverage for the business. For example, in February 2018, *CBS Sunday Morning* highlighted efforts by companies such as SAP and Microsoft to build workplaces that are more inclusive of autistic individuals. Company leaders, managers, and individuals with autism who have been given opportunities to use their skills and creativity were given a stage on which to discuss the significant benefits of these new talent-sourcing initiatives to both individuals and businesses. These companies are not only benefiting from the new talent but also from public recognition of their demonstration of the concept of neurodiversity in recognizing and respecting neurological differences as a normal human variation and proving it can be an asset in the workplace.

DXC Technology, formerly Hewlett Packard Enterprise, established its Dandelion Program in 2015, an added service offering for the company's clients, drawing on the talents of people with autism and initially building off of an approach used by Specialisterne (Austin and Sonne 2014). The company deploys "pods," organized around eight or nine employees with autism, to function as high-performance mini-ecosystems; these have been shown to be 30% more effective than average service teams in some areas (Pisano and Austin 2016a). The model, created in Australia, was initially applied to cybersecurity work being done by Hewlett Packard under contract to the Australian Defense Department for cybersecurity-related positions (Fieldhouse 2017). The program has now been broadened to include other types of industries, most notably finance, and is also being extended to other countries.

Microsoft's Autism Hiring Program began in 2015, and the company states that it was designed to identify and remove the barriers that would prevent those with autistic spectrum disorders from finding meaningful employment in the company. Microsoft reports that the program has enabled the company to access a previously untapped talent pool and that it is also a part of the company's evolving approach to increase diversity in its workforce. The company recruits broadly for talent across its open positions and has been successful to date in hiring in such technical roles as software engineer, service engineer, build engineer, lab engineer, data analyst, and data scientist (Microsoft 2019).

As interest in these programs has spread, Autism at Work hiring initiatives have expanded to the finance and accounting industries. JPMorgan Chase launched Autism at Work in July 2015 as a four-person pilot. Since then, it has grown to include over 125 people in seven countries. People are hired into a variety of roles (reportedly now 40-plus roles in ten lines of business) in technology functions such as software engineering, app development, quality assurance, technology operations, and business analysis, with one employee reported to be a personal banker. James Mahoney, the global head of JPMorgan Chase's Autism at Work program, reports that the company's aspiration is to get 300 people in the program by 2020 in 14 locations worldwide (JPMorgan Chase 2019). The company also reports that the employees in this program are outperforming their peers in comparable positions (Mahoney 2017). Those employees in the Autism at Work program were reported to be "48 percent more accurate and as much as 92 percent more productive" (JPMorgan Chase 2019).

EY (Ernst and Young, LLP) hired four individuals with autism to work in a new Philadelphia Neurodiversity Center of Excellence (CoE), proximate to universities with good STEM (science, technology, engineering, and mathematics) and autism-specific programs. In 2017, EY launched its second CoE in Dallas, where the team focuses on cybersecurity, robotic process automation, and complex analytics. The company also has been keeping comparative performance metrics on its CoE employees and reports that they perform a wide range of highly advanced tasks with remarkable quality and efficiency, with low error rates. With a combination of time savings and quality improvements, the program has resulted in an estimated $100,000 in cost savings (EY 2018).

More recently, companies involved in these initiatives have recognized their common needs for information and synergies that can be gained through collaboration, and they have established a consortium, which has proved invaluable as they evolve their programs in parallel. To respond to this need, SAP instituted the Autism at Work Summit in 2016. Today it takes place in four countries (Australia, India, New Zealand, and the United States) and will soon be expanded to Argentina and Brazil. In addition, to reach into higher education institutions more effectively, SAP also has expanded into a "specialty" summit, the Autism at Work University Series (Velasco 2019). Another example of expanding visibility is the Autism @ Work Employer Roundtable facilitated by DisabilityIN, a membership organization of employers who are working toward improving workplace disability inclusion. The purpose of the roundtable is to involve more employers in the Autism at Work initiatives, thereby improving employment outcomes for autistic people nationally and ultimately globally (DisabilityIN 2019).

With companies such as these reporting continuing expansion of their Autism at Work programs and documenting significant performance results, many other organizations are beginning to explore how to establish these programs. The remainder of this chapter describes some of the policies, practices, protocols, and continued iterative adjustments that experienced companies are successfully using, and it suggests approaches that other companies are trying and integrating into their own place settings and talent pipelines.

HUMAN RESOURCES/WORKPLACE POLICIES AND PRACTICES SUPPORTING SUCCESS

In this section, we provide an overview of some of the key considerations in establishing an Autism at Work program, drawn from the related literature on good practices and from reports from companies who are implementing such programs. The areas selected for focus are messaging from top leadership, supervisor training, and considerations in recruitment, selection, interviewing, hiring, and retention.

Messaging from Top Leadership

Any changes in an organization—whether sweeping changes such as alterations in lines of business; amendments to the core mission, vision, or values; mergers and acquisitions; or even seemingly more mundane changes like parking access or hours of gym availability—require thoughtful messaging from management (Nishii, Khattab, Shemla, and Paluch 2018). This is critical for letting the organization know that the change is occurring and to engender grassroots support for such changes. Research conducted by Cornell University on workplace disability inclusion has confirmed the importance of building a receptive workplace climate for affirmative hiring initiatives and building internal support (Erickson et al. 2014; Linkow et al. 2013).

These considerations have also proven crucial to the initiation and successful implementation of Autism at Work programs. Both internal and external company communication are essential to the longer-term success of such initiatives. Sending the message that affirmative hiring of autistic individuals is a part of the company's strategic direction affirms that employees need to take this initiative seriously and treat it as a business imperative rather than a "corporate social responsibility" or community engagement opportunity. Setting concrete goals, such as the "1% of the workforce by 2020" initially set by SAP when starting its program, confirms that the business goal is real and is an organizational priority. Related research has found that these goals are effective for broader disability-focused hiring initiatives; company representatives that reported having strong senior management commitment to diversity were five times more likely to have hired a person with a disability in the past year (Erickson et al. 2014). The same study found that supporting these goals via explicit communication about expectations and manager performance goals, establishing concrete organizational hiring goals for people with disabilities, and specifically mentioning disability in diversity and inclusion plans, each increased the likelihood of successfully hiring a person with a disability by three to four times (Erickson et al. 2014). Setting and publicly broadcasting goals that show the organization is committed to the initiative as a business strategy is critical.

Supervisor Training

Managers are critical to every employee's workplace experience, including those with disabilities (Sherbin and Kennedy 2017), and this is perhaps even more important in Autism at Work initiatives. When selecting locations to launch initial Autism at Work initiatives, companies report making the selection based on talent needs and volume of open positions—and also in areas where supervisors are receptive to taking on the new talent. To smooth the process and ensure success, participating companies have been exploring a wide variety of ways to better equip supervisors for success both prior to and during their involvement with the program.

Across these new initiatives, supervisors may play a wide number of roles in program initiation and maintenance, including assisting with screening, providing initial coaching about the position, providing ongoing support and performance management guidance, developing individual techniques to maintain or improve an individual's productivity, and helping to integrate individuals into the workplace. While these activities are a natural part of any supervisor's role, they are particularly critical in initiatives such as Autism at Work programs. The new employees may have little or no prior work experience and may need additional grooming and managerial support to successfully integrate into the workplace.

To assist supervisors who are stepping into this type of role, companies are creating internal training programs and are also accessing an emerging set of programs developed by external vendors. Companies sometimes have supervisors join the new employee recruits in their own one- to six-week screening and orientation programs, or they conduct several hours of targeted internal training to orient supervisors to the company's expectations for the program and the attendant role that the company expects the supervising manager to play (DXC Technology 2016a). Simultaneously, consultation services and related training programs and materials are materializing to support companies in this process and complement their internal efforts (select examples of such services and resources can be found at Goldstein 2019a, Integrate Autism Employment Advisors 2019, Scheiner 2017, and Uptimize 2019).

Considerations in Recruitment, Selection, Interviewing, Hiring, and Retention

As with any affirmative hiring program for a targeted population, a number of issues must be considered for successful planning, rollout, implementation, and maintenance of such initiatives. Among these are considerations in the recruitment, selection, interviewing, and hiring parts of the talent pipeline development process.

Recruitment Considerations

Companies that have relationships with community partners that provide employment services for individuals with autism are significantly more likely to successfully recruit these individuals. In the previously cited Cornell University study, companies that reported having relationships with community service providers and actively recruiting individuals with disabilities were three times more likely to have hired a person with a disability in the past year (Erickson et al. 2014). The companies described earlier in this chapter have each worked to identify community organizations that can be a talent pipeline of qualified neurodiverse individuals.

Indeed, as previously mentioned, locations for pilot programs have been selected based on the perceived availability of such talent and the co-location of local STEM training programs and service providers who can not only help find talent but also provide ongoing support services to new employees. Companies have looked to such pioneer providers as Specialisterne, often credited with the initial inspiration for such programs (Specialisterne 2019), national nonprofit networks such as The Arc (2019), or long-standing service providers such as state divisions of vocational rehabilitation (Employer Assistance and Resource Network on Disability Inclusion 2019) and local-area service providers (Integrate Autism Employment Advisors 2019). Companies are also beginning to broaden their search to talent focused in other than STEM areas, where there is also a wealth of autistic talent.

Selection and Interviewing Considerations

Autism at Work hiring initiatives have been characterized as selective hiring programs for autistic individuals with specific characteristics that are desirable for certain jobs in the tech sector, such as software testing, programming, and related tasks. Some of the common characteristics of autistic people described previously can make traditional job interviews challenging, such as problems with social interaction and communication or difficulty making eye contact or responding to social cues. Frequently used selection tools, such as cognitive skill tests, personality tests, and even interviews and work samples, could disadvantage individuals with neurological differences (Sumner and Brown 2015). Knowing this, many companies who were early adopters used a prescriptive protocol developed by Specialisterne, which involves using Lego Mindstorms education robotics technology to select and train candidates with the desired characteristics and propensities (Austin and Sonne 2014; Szczerba 2016; Wareham and Sonne 2008). The purpose of this approach was to test for the required job skills without the need for the verbal communication and social interaction that are often required for successful interactions with recruiters (Hendrickx 2009).

Over time, as it became clear that candidates often had a more diverse array of qualifications for a broader array of positions than previously believed, each company began evolving its strategies accordingly (Annabi 2019; DXC Technology 2016b). Many organizations have adopted a model of candidate selection that has more interdependency with various community service providers to assist with initial identification and screening of appropriate applicants for the program. In addition, companies have implemented training of recruiters and hiring managers about the strategic autism hiring initiatives. Each company has designed and implemented processes that reflect the company's talent needs, positions available, and organizational structure, as well as the community's needs (Annabi 2019). Across all efforts, the intended result is for more autistic candidates to transition into the company's applicant pool and through the initial screening process than would have otherwise done so in the past.

Hiring and Retention Considerations

Companies have developed a wide array of internal and external supports designed to help newly hired employees maintain successful attachment to the workforce. This may start with a comprehensive orientation program that introduces new hires to workplace culture and behavioral expectations and gives them information about resources and people available to assist with addressing potential issues. The nuanced observations required to understand workplace culture can be challenging for autistic individuals (Goldstein 2019b). Orientation may occur as a natural part of every new employee's experience, but some companies with affirmative autism hiring programs have tailored them exclusively to the targeted considerations for the Autism at Work program hires. In addition, some companies have created mentoring and "buddy" roles for co-worker volunteers, who provide support in navigating the company environment and facilitate social inclusion. Some companies feel these efforts are critical to the near and longer-term success of the individual in the social environment of the organization. Because social interactions and social contexts can be particularly challenging for some individuals with autism, helping them understand and fit into the workplace culture has been a critical factor to longer-term success (Pence and Svyantek 2017).

While preparing new employees for the cultural norms and behavioral and social expectations of the workplace, many companies are also preparing the workplace for its new recruits. As previously described, communication from the top about the strategic business imperative of the initiative is critical, as is the training of supervisors and readying of internal resources. Employee assistance programs, which can be very useful for providing employee support, will likely need to include topic-specific training for their counseling professionals to give them the skills they need to deal with the unique behavioral and mental health considerations for autistic individuals. Moreover, companies have found that partnering with seasoned, external community agencies and support services to provide supervisor training as well as job coaching services for autistic employees heightens the likelihood that supervisors and the company as a whole will be able to respond to the needs of individual employees when accommodations or interventions are needed.

CHALLENGES, LEARNINGS, AND OPPORTUNITIES FOR THE WAY FORWARD

The chapter thus far has provided an overview of the status of individuals with autism in the United States, in terms of prevalence rates, education and employment participation rates, some basic information about autism, motivations for the increasing interest of select employers in creating Autism at Work programs, and a high-level overview of the approaches being used by companies in recruiting, hiring, and retaining these individuals. The intent in providing this information has been to raise awareness of the disparities in employment for this population, how select industry sectors are creating opportunities to address these disparities, and some of the approaches employers are using to address existing impediments to workforce entry.

The section that follows describes some of the challenges experienced to date in these initiatives and explains employer approaches to address these challenges, showing how companies and the networks working with them function together. Future implications for improving employment outcomes for autistic individuals and those with other "differences" whose characteristics have been previously perceived as liabilities rather than benefits are also discussed.

Pipeline Issues and Ways to Address Them

Initial information about the availability of Autism at Work programs was met with enthusiasm by autistic individuals and their family members. This was facilitated in part by the affirmative outreach by companies and their affiliated employment service provider organizations, as well as by community members' response to a known need. Since its initiation, companies have expanded the numbers of people to whom they are opening their positions, the types of positions, and the locations for implementation of Autism at Work programs both domestically and globally, and have therefore also worked to expand ways to source talent. Finding larger numbers of qualified individuals has been a challenge for some companies, and a recognition that disclosure of disability and willingness to come forward may also be as big an impediment as finding the right pipeline for desired talent that will fulfill the particular company's and industry's needs (Bissonette 2015).

Many of these companies have moved toward intensive collaborations with local area and national higher education institutions, either because of their proximity to the company location or because the universities have the types of training programs that graduate appropriately skilled talent. In addition, companies are designing proactive efforts to encourage students to come forward and consider their programs through special initiatives. One example is the design and implementation of a Neurodiversity Hub model by DXC Technology, which is being implemented at Swinburne University in Melbourne, Australia, and also being tested in several US university settings (DXC Technology 2017). The Neurodiversity Hub design focuses on improving employability and creating opportunities for neurodiverse students by assisting them in obtaining work experience and internships with DXC and DXC's partner organizations. The hub also assists the company in building a pipeline of students for neurodiverse-friendly employers and leveraging DXC's expertise in this area "to drive research and derive further insights" (DXC Technology 2017). DXC Technology is making the Neurodiversity Hub model widely available globally through an online platform, which will include an array of resources for students, employers, university faculty and staff, and family members (DXC Technology 2019).

Another example of a similar company–university effort is the Spectrum Scholars program designed by JPMorgan Chase with the University of Delaware (UD) (Davis 2018). This initiative is backed by a ten-year grant from JPMorgan Chase and administered by UD's Center for Disabilities Studies. Spectrum Scholars provides a comprehensive support system and career exploration opportunities to UD students with autism majoring in computer and information sciences or in electrical and computer engineering. The initiative also includes training for UD faculty and staff and community businesses on working effectively with people with autism. The company is expanding its Autism at Work model to the United Kingdom and has a program with the University of Bath's Centre for Applied Autism Research. The collaboration supports an Employment Spring School for Autism at JPMorgan Chase's Bournemouth campus. The first cohort was launched in Bath in 2018, with 30 current students and recent graduates. The day experience for students at JPMorgan Chase's Bournemouth campus includes a tour of the innovation space, a panel session from employees with ASD, and an activity to provide insight and guidance for graduate interviews (University of Bath 2018).

Autism at Work initiatives also have implications for national and regional workforce and economic development efforts. Federal- and state-supported laborforce development initiatives are often directed toward under-represented minorities, but individuals with disabilities are frequently excluded. Individuals who are neurodiverse are a recognized disability population with a past experience of employment disparities that makes them a similarly worthy target group for a public policy intervention with a focus on enhancing employment opportunities. This blend of interests is demonstrated in other recent efforts of JPMorgan Chase, which is contributing funding to higher education initiatives that improve economic development in inner cities and teach technology skills to local-area high school students (Le Moyne College 2019).

Expanding Workplace Supports

Experience in these programs to date has underscored the importance of having appropriate preparation for the new autistic employees, as well as for their supervisors and the workplace as a whole. Companies have iteratively refined their selection, orientation, and training processes for the new employee candidates and have modified their supervisor training programs in response to these needs. Moreover, as issues such as socialization barriers or mental health concerns have surfaced, companies have proactively responded with solutions such as identification of appropriate community supports and refinement of pre-existing company resources (Hedley, Uljarevic, and Hedley 2017). Examples are the establishment of "buddies" to assist the new hires as they acclimate to the social aspects of the work environment and to facilitate inclusion in lunchtime socialization with colleagues or after work activities. Some companies have actually established socialization clubs consistent with the interests of the new autistic employees, such as gaming nights or similar outings.

Community agencies with job coaches have sometimes been called on to support the change process during challenging times, such as when job tasks or supervisors change, during difficult performance management dialogs, or when career progression and stretch assignments are being explored. Examples of company responses to mental health issues, when they may have surfaced, include identification of mental health practitioners in the community who can be available, enhancements to employee assistance program services to address the needs of the target population, and exploration of the use of wearable devices with applications designed to facilitate greater self-awareness among these employees of their own daily moods that might trigger heightened stress-related responses to work environment situations.

Continuously Evolving Approaches and Philosophies

Company-led efforts to share information across businesses and industries to further the impact of these initiatives have been remarkable. They have contributed to a continuous evolution of these programs through a discovery, transformation, and sharing cycle both within company structures and across companies. Although they have afforded opportunities for iterative program refinements and improvements, there exist significant variations between company approaches as well. This may present an added challenge to individuals who become aware of these programs and move between programs as they try to take advantage of the opportunity to finally make it into employment. An individual who is not successful with one program may try another, only to find the intake process, skill vetting, orientation, and training are entirely different and therefore confusing and ultimately discouraging.

Companies introducing Autism at Work programs have often required the collection and analysis of outcome metrics to assess the return on investment for such initiatives. A number of companies have shared early analyses, the results of which are very encouraging. They show that the autistic individuals hired are not only able to perform tasks at rates comparable to their peers, but in some cases these workers far exceed standards for accuracy, speed, or other related metrics. In the longer term, however, companies will need to consider the value and perhaps ethicality of making comparisons that they would not make for other minority populations. We can hope that once these programs have proven themselves, and individuals with autistic characteristics are more readily included in the workforce, companies will be able to initiate programs without making comparisons, and it will be sufficient to say that autistic employees performed to company standards, were very much engaged, and could bring their whole selves to the task at hand.

Implications for Labor and Employment Relations Professionals and the Workplace

The focus of this chapter has been how companies are responding to the critical need for talent in certain sectors, especially in the tech sector, with innovations in hiring neurodiverse talent. The examples of company practices have implications for labor and employment, as well as other workplace professionals who may have to navigate the issues that might arise with such affirmative hiring programs. Examples of specific issues include perceived preferential hiring or treatment, leading to resentment by co-workers; awkward and sometimes even inappropriate interactions with co-workers that lead to conflict; and health and safety issues that might occur as a result of a mental health–related or behavior outburst incident. One of the biggest barriers can be that autistic traits frequently violate workplace norms and very much fit the description of antisocial behavior, so they may be misinterpreted, particularly in environments where broader education has not as yet occurred (Goldstein 2019b). Willingness to disclose is also an issue. An individual who is already in the workforce and may have disclosed to a limited number of others (their hiring manager and some key close colleagues) early on in the employment process may need to disclose again as they are assigned to new teams, take on new projects, or get promoted. Such individuals may not be willing to make this broader disclosure themselves or have others discuss it on their behalf (Scheiner 2019a).

Proactive communication by the company and education of the workforce as a whole are critical to mitigate potential issues before they arise. Training of the specific supervisor and work unit where the autistic employee will work is imperative, but information should also be shared with workplace professionals who are positioned to address these issues when they occur, such as labor and employment professionals; these actions will be critical if the programs are to serve their intended purpose. Applying metrics to assess performance of individuals who came in through the programs and of the initiative as a whole is a responsible way to assess program effectiveness. Yet such metrics must be applied with care.

Autism at Work programs present a significant opportunity not only for individuals with autism around the world who are often significantly underemployed, but also for the workforce more generally. The perspective of seeing the characteristics of people with autism—once perceived by employers as an undesirable difference as an asset to be valued, pursued, and supported to success—is one that could benefit many other historically under-represented people in the labor force. Replicating these innovations can assist all of us to be seen for our skills and attributes rather than for our differences and deficits, and thereby better support each of us to be able to fully contribute our talents and energy to our workplaces and our communities.

ACKNOWLEDGMENTS

The author would like to acknowledge the following individuals who provided helpful reviews and comments on drafts of this manuscript: Ariel Avgar, associate professor of labor relations, Cornell University ILR School; Tim Goldstein, neurodiverse communication specialist; Kari Kelly, founder and CEO, Atypical Workplace; Marcia Scheiner, president, Integrate autism employment advisors; and José Velasco, vice president of products and innovation, SAP.

REFERENCES

American Psychiatric Association. 2019. "What Is Autism Spectrum Disorder?" Philadelphia, PA: American Psychiatric Association. http://bit.ly/2Mf38JV

Annabi, H. 2019. "Autism @ Work Playbook." Seattle, WA: Information School, University of Washington. http://bit.ly/2Mf3MXR

Austin, R.D., M. Fieldhouse, and P. Quinn. 2017 (Dec. 7). "Why the Australian Defence Organization Is Recruiting Cyber Analysts on the Autism Spectrum." *Harvard Business Review.* http://bit.ly/2Msxmcz

Austin, R.D., and T. Sonne. 2014 (May 19). "The Dandelion Principle: Redesigning Work for the Innovation Economy." *MIT Sloan Management Review.* http://bit.ly/2Mog8gq

Autism Self Advocacy Network. 2019. "Identity-First Language." Washington, DC: Autism Self Advocacy Network. http://bit.ly/2Me22he

Barnett, N. 2018 (Apr. 2). "Individuals with Autism Can Bring Untapped Talent to Every Business." *Microsoft Accessibility Blog.* http://bit.ly/2WlSp4f

Bissonette, B. 2015 (Oct. 1). Understanding Disclosure and Workplace Accommodations." *The OARACLE: News & Events.* Arlington, VA: Organization for Autism Research.

Bort, J. 2013 (May 31). "SAP Just Vowed to Hire a Whole Bunch of People with Autism." *Business Insider.* http://bit.ly/2Wv84OG

CBS News. 2018 (Feb. 11). "The Growing Acceptance of Autism in the Workplace." *Sunday Morning.* https://cbsn.ws/2WrJ8r7

Centers for Disease Control and Prevention (CDC). 2018 (Apr. 28). "Prevalence of Autism Spectrum Disorder Among Children Aged 8 Years—Autism and Developmental Disability Monitoring Network, 11 Sites, United States, 2014." *Surveillance Summaries* 67 (6): 1–23. http://bit.ly/2Mh4ALI

Centers for Disease Control and Prevention (CDC). 2019. "What Is Autism Spectrum Disorder?" Atlanta, GA: Centers for Disease Control and Prevention. http://bit.ly/2M9VZdE

Chu, J. 2015 (Jun.). "50,000 People with Autism Need Jobs This Year. Here's Why You Should Hire Them." *Inc.* http://bit.ly/2WlSC7x

Coy, C. 2015 (May 25). "Why Freddie Mac Is Recruiting Employees with Autism." *Rework*. http://bit.ly/2MsyInF

Davis, Z. 2018 (Sep. 18). "Spectrum Scholars: UD and JPMorgan Chase Collaborate to Offer Undergrads with Autism Opportunities for Success." Newark, DE: Center for Disability Studies, University of Delaware. http://bit.ly/2Wtm4s8

DisabilityIN. 2019. "Autism @ Work Employer Roundtable: Frequently Asked Questions." http://bit.ly/2Wx4ROo

Dunkelberg, W., and H. Wade. 2017. "NFIB Small Business Economic Trends, March 2017." Washington, DC: National Federation of Independent Business. http://bit.ly/2MdAngq

DXC Technology. 2016a. "Dandelion Program Management Training Handout: Autism Spectrum Consultant Strategy." Melbourne, Australia: DXC Technology. http://bit.ly/2WrM7Ql

DXC Technology. 2016b. "Dandelion Roadmap." Melbourne, Australia: DXC Technology. http://bit.ly/2MoiLPk

DXC Technology. 2017 (Nov. 14). DXC Establishes First Neurodiversity Hub with Swinburne University. News release. November 14, 2017. Melbourne, Australia: DXC Technology. http://bit.ly/2MdB0qi

DXC Technology. 2019. "Neurodiversity Hub." Melbourne, Australia: DXC Technology. https://www.neurodiversityhub.org

Employer Assistance and Resource Network on Disability Inclusion (EARN). 2019. "State Vocational Rehabilitation Agencies." Albertson, NY: Employer Assistance and Resource Network on Disability Inclusion. http://bit.ly/2MeJGwQ

Erickson, W.A., S. von Schrader, S.M. Bruyère, S.A. VanLooy, and D. Matteson. 2014. "Disability-Inclusive Employer Practices and Hiring of Individuals with Disabilities." *Rehabilitation Research, Policy, and Education* 28 (4): 309–327. doi:10.1891/2168-6653.28.4.309

EY. 2018. "Neurodiversity: Driving Innovation from Unexpected Places." https://go.ey.com/2M9Ivyr

Goldstein, T. 2019a. "Engaging Technical Workers." http://timgoldstein.com

Goldstein, T. 2019b (Apr. 18). Neurodiverse communication specialist. Personal communication.

Federal Home Loan Mortgage Company (Freddie Mac). 2012. "Autism as an Asset in the Workplace." McLean, VA: Federal Home Loan Mortgage Company http://bit.ly/2Mbs0Cd

Fieldhouse, M. 2017 (Nov. 1). "Implementing a Neurodiversity Program." Melbourne, Australia: DXC Technology. http://bit.ly/2Mf5NmT

Hedley, D., M. Uljarevic, L. Cameron, S. Halder, A. Richdale, and C. Dissanayake. 2016. "Employment Programmes and Interventions Targeting Adults with Autism Spectrum Disorder: A Systematic Review of the Literature." *Autism* 21 (8): 929–941. doi:10.1177/1362361316661855

Hedley, D., M. Uljarevic, and D.F.E. Hedley. 2017. "Employment and Living with Autism: Personal, Social and Economic Impact," In *Inclusion, Disability and Culture: An Ethnographic Perspective Traversing Abilities and Challenges*, edited by S. Halder and L.C. Assaf, pp. 295–311. Cham, Switzerland: Springer. http://bit.ly/2Wx6nA4

Hendrickx, S. 2009. *Asperger Syndrome & Employment: What People with Asperger Syndrome Really, Really Want*. London, UK: Jessica Kingsley.

Hurley-Hanson, A.E., and C.M. Giannantonio, eds. 2017. Special Issue: Autism in the Workplace. *Journal of Business and Management* 22 (1).

Integrate Autism Employment Advisors. 2019. Website. https://www.integrateadvisors.org

JPMorgan Chase. 2019. "Neurodiverse Hiring Brings Social and Business Benefits." http://bit.ly/2xfQyzE

Korn Ferry. 2018. "Future of Work: The Global Talent Crunch." Los Angeles, CA: Korn Ferry. http://bit.ly/2MfSYbX

Kost, B. 2018 (Oct. 8). "Shrinking the Talent Gap: Supporting Your Biggest Asset." *HR Daily Advisor*. http://bit.ly/2Mfx2xt

Lai, M., M. Lombardo, B. Auyeung, B. Chakrabarti, and S. Baron-Cohen. 2015. "Sex/Gender Differences and Autism: Setting the Scene for Future Research." *Journal of the American Academy of Child & Adolescent Psychiatry* 54 (1): 11–24.

Le Moyne College. 2019 (Apr. 18). "Le Moyne to Benefit from $3 Million JPMorgan Grant as Part of AdvancingCities Program." News Release. Syracuse, NY: Le Moyne College. http://bit.ly/2MdGpOo

Linkow, P., L. Barrington, S. Bruyère, I. Figueroa, and M. Wright. 2013 (Feb.). "Leveling the Playing Field: Attracting, Engaging, and Advancing People with Disabilities." Research Report R-1510-12-RR. New York, NY: The Conference Board. http://bit.ly/2Wspyv6

Mahoney, J. 2017 (Oct. 2). "Putting Untapped Talent to Work." *The OARACLE: News & Events*. http://bit.ly/2MelevD

Maurer, R. 2017 (Sep. 7). "Training People for Jobs to Fill the Skills Gap: Employers Have Responsibility to Upskill Their Workforce." Alexandria, VA: Society for Human Resource Management. http://bit.ly/2MhbfFI

Microsoft 2019. "Our Inclusive Hiring Programs." http://bit.ly/2M9Pvvd

National Center for Education Statistics. 2019. *The Condition of Education 2019*. NCES 2019-144. Washington DC: National Center for Education Statistics. http://bit.ly/2Rzotg0

National Symposium on Neurodiversity at Syracuse University. 2011. http://bit.ly/2WtesWC

Nishii, L.H., J. Khattab, M. Shemla, and R.M. Paluch. 2018. "A Multi-Level Process Model for Understanding Diversity Practices Effectiveness." *Academy of Management Annals* 12 (1): 37–82.

Ono Academic College. 2019. "Roim Rachok Program." Kiryat Ono, Israel: Ono Academic College. http://bit.ly/2MorBfY

Parmar, N. 2017 (Nov.). "Why Microsoft, Chase and Others Are Hiring More People with Autism." *Entrepreneur*.

Pence, S., and D. Svyantek. 2017. "Person–Organization Fit in the Workplace." *Journal of Business and Management* 22 (1): 117–134.

Pisano, G., and R. Austin. 2016a (Sep.). "Hewlett Packard Enterprise: The Dandelion Program." Harvard Business School Case 617-016. Boston, MA: Harvard University.

Pisano, G., and R. Austin 2016b (Jan.). "SAP SE: Autism at Work." Harvard Business School Case 616-042. Boston, MA: Harvard University.

Rivet, T.T., and J.L. Matson. 2011. "Review of Gender Differences in Core Symptomatology in Autism Spectrum Disorders." *Research in Autism Spectrum Disorders* 5: 957–976.

Roux, A., P. Shattuck, J. Rast, J. Rava, and K. Anderson. 2015. "National Autism Indicators Report: Transition into Young Adulthood." Philadelphia, PA: Life Course Outcomes Research Program, A.J. Drexel Autism Institute, Drexel University.

Rubin, S. 2016 (Jan. 6). "The Israeli Army Unit That Recruits Teens with Autism." *The Atlantic*. http://bit.ly/2WAKDDK

Scheiner, M. 2017. *An Employer's Guide to Managing Professionals on the Autism Spectrum*. London, UK: Jessica Kingsley.

Scheiner, M. 2019a (Apr. 18). President, Integrate Autism Employment Advisors. Personal communication.

Scheiner, M. 2019b (Apr. 20). President, Integrate Autism Employment Advisors. Personal communication.

Sherbin, L., and J.T. Kennedy. 2017 (Dec. 27). "The Case for Improving Work for People with Disabilities Goes Way Beyond Compliance." *Harvard Business Review*. http://bit.ly/2WoJUW5

Shore, S., and L. Rastelli. 2006. *Understanding Autism for Dummies*. Hoboken, NJ: Wiley.

Silberman, S. 2015. *Neurotribes: The Legacy of Autism and the Future of Neurodiversity*. New York, NY: Penguin Random House.

Singer, J. 2016/2017. *Neurodiversity: The Birth of an Idea*. Published as a Kindle e-book in 2016; published in print in 2017.

Specialisterne. 2019. "Welcome to Specialisterne." http://specialisterne.com

Sumner, K., and T. Brown. 2015. "Neurodiversity and Human Resource Management: Employer Challenges for Applicants and Employees with Learning Disabilities." *The Psychologist-Manager Journal* 18 (2): 77–85.

Szczerba, R. 2016 (Jan. 19). "This Visionary May Completely Disrupt the Tech Industry as We Know It." *Forbes*. http://bit.ly/2WwuvTv

The Arc. 2019. "A Leader in Disability Rights." Washington, DC: The Arc. https://www.thearc.org/who-we-are

University of Bath. 2018. "University and JPMorgan Chase Collaborate to Improve Employment Chances for People with Autism." Bath, UK: Centre for Applied Autism Research, University of Bath. http://bit.ly/2MeV7oi

Uptimize. 2019. "Developing Autistic Talent." Training Program. http://www.uptimize.com

Velasco, J. 2019 (Apr. 24). Vice president, products and innovation, SAP. Personal communication.

Wareham, J., and T. Sonne. 2008. "Harnessing the Power of Autism Spectrum Disorder. Innovations Case Study: Specialisterne." *Innovations: Technology, Governance, Globalization* 3 (1): 11–27. http://bit.ly/2WsBUU0

Wei, X., J.W. Yu, P. Shattuck, M. McCracken, and J. Blackorby. 2013. "Science, Technology, Engineering, and Math (STEM) Participation Among College Students with an Austism Spectrum Disorder." *Journal of Autism Developmental Disorders* 43 (7): 1539–1546. doi:10.1007/s10803-012-1700-z

Wyatt, J. 2017 (Fall). "Autism Spectrum Disorder in the Workplace." *Regional Labor Review*. Hempstead, NY: Hofstra University Center for the Study of Labor and Democracy.

Chapter 11

Global Perspectives on Employment for People with Disabilities

Matthew C. Saleh
Cornell University

GLOBAL PERSPECTIVES ON THE RIGHT TO WORK FOR PEOPLE WITH DISABILITIES

This chapter explores issues of employment for people with disabilities from a global perspective, providing an overview of thematic barriers, international regulatory frameworks, and contextual factors at regional and national levels. For labor and employment relations specialists, new developments in disability employment policy represent opportunities to re-imagine labor problems and the employment relationship itself. This is especially true in countries with rapidly changing economies and relatively recent commitments to disability employment as both a human rights requisite and a potentially vital source of policy solutions for trenchant and emerging problems pertaining to unemployment, poverty, population aging, urbanization, industrialization, technologization, and more.

Increasingly, policy efforts in this domain aim not only to improve jobseeker prospects but also to positively compel or encourage employer behavior. For labor and employment relations specialists, the rapid changes that are occurring represent opportunities to guide employers toward improving and "future proofing" their talent pools—while avoiding government sanctions or liabilities—by reorienting their policies and practices toward prospective employees with disabilities. Policy directives, we will see, become more substantial as governments increasingly recognize the importance of disability employment policy in human rights, labor, and poverty alleviation efforts. Employers in multiple domestic contexts—along with an ever-growing number of multinationals—can only benefit from guidance in how to comply with, and even maximize the benefits of, these expansive new policy changes.

In any national context, public policy governs the legal responsibilities of employers toward current and prospective employees with disabilities. Meanwhile, local economic conditions—such as dominant economic sectors; the number, size, and type of employers in a region; legal compliance and affirmative efforts by employers; and the capacities of regional employment services—moderate the practical impact of regulatory efforts (Sainsbury and Coleman-Fountain 2014). National frameworks vary in terms of the breadth of anti-discrimination requirements as well as the degree of rehabilitation and social services available to enhance labor market outcomes. Similarly, different nations are in different phases of implementing international human rights norms, most notably the United Nations Convention on the Rights of Persons with Disabilities (CRPD), an international treaty adopted in 2006 and entered into force in 2008. Nardodkar et al. (2016), for instance, found that of all UN Member States, 27% did not explicitly define the term "disability" in their laws, 30% had no explicit or implied legal provisions for providing reasonable accommodation to people with disabilities, and 51% had no explicit legal protections from dismissal, termination, or suspension of employment on health grounds.

Prevalence and Unemployment Rates Globally

Disability affects an estimated one billion people globally. That's about 15% of the total world population, making people with disabilities one of the world's largest minority groups (United Nations 2018; World Health Organization and World Bank 2011), and this is before accounting for the effects of disability on families and support networks, which cause the impact to be felt by a far greater number of individuals. Certain demographic patterns characterize the scope of the global challenge. Approximately 88% of people with disabilities live in the world's poorest countries, while 90% live in rural areas (Marks 1999, cited by Goodley 2017). Here, it is worth noting that low-income nations are generally experiencing more rapid urbanization than higher-income nations, a fact that will alter these demographics in coming decades and that carries its own set of policy challenges pertaining to urban/rural divides in education, employment, healthcare, transportation, and other domains (Eckert and Kohler 2014).

Evidence of Employment Inequality

According to the most recent estimates, the employment rate for people with disabilities globally is 44%, compared with 75% of the population without disabilities (World Health Organization and World Bank 2011). The inactivity rate for working-age people with disabilities is almost 2.5 times higher (World Health Organization and World Bank 2011). While these estimates are a few years old, recent national and regional figures indicate that the disparity remains intact. Rates of unemployment also vary significantly by type and severity of disability; studies from multiple contexts demonstrate lower employment rates for more severe disabilities, specifically for people with mental health and intellectual disabilities (Turcotte 2012; World Health Organization and World Bank 2011), and often these groups receive weaker legal protections than other disability categories (Hoffman, Sritharan, and Tejpar 2016).

Even industrialized nations with highly developed rehabilitation and social services offerings have trends of employment inequality. For example, in 2015, approximately 35% of working-age people with disabilities in the United States attained employment in the open labor market, compared with 78% of people without disabilities (Erickson, Lee, and von Schrader 2016). Similarly, in Organisation for Economic Co-operation and Development (OECD) countries, the average employment rate for people with disabilities was just over 40%, compared with approximately 75% for people without disabilities (OECD 2009). Unemployment rates from Asian and Pacific countries show similarly stark disparities in Australia (26.7% employment for people with disabilities; 61.7% for the total population), New Zealand (45%; 64.1%), Republic of Korea (37%; 59.5%), Thailand (40%; 71.4%), Cambodia (42.6%; 67%), Turkey (20%; 45.9%), and others (UN Economic and Social Commission for Asia and the Pacific 2015).

Further studies demonstrate employment gaps in a range of low- and middle-income contexts around the globe (Hoogeveen 2005 [Uganda]; Lamichhane and Okubo 2014 [Nepal]; Mitra 2018 [Tanzania, Uganda, Ethiopia, Malawi]); Mitra and Sambamoorthi 2008 [India]; Mizunoya and Mitra 2013 [Bangladesh, Brazil, Burkina Faso, Dominican Republic, Mauritius, Mexico, Pakistan, Paraguay, Philippines]; Mizunoya, Yamasaki, and Mitra 2016 [Vietnam]; Trani and Loeb 2010 [Afghanistan, Zambia]). In other words, the disability employment gap is very much a global problem.

Country Response in Training and Nondiscrimination Legislation

The main approach of industrialized welfare states has been investment in employment readiness and training programs, anti-discrimination legislation, and hiring quota schemes (Grover and Piggott 2007; Humpage 2007). The history of providing public protection to working-age individuals with disabilities is long in most industrialized nations. Early on, most of these programs aimed to reduce the financial burden resulting from disability through cash assistance and other benefits but over time moved toward pro-work programs aimed at improving labor market outcomes. The components of disability programs have changed over time, owing to a number of factors including "rapid growth in program costs; greater awareness that people with impairments are able and willing to work; and increased recognition that protecting the economic security of people with disabilities might best be done by keeping them in the labor market" (Burkhauser, Daly, and Ziebarth 2016: 367).

In high-income countries, research began to show that pure cash assistance programs may serve as potential "poverty traps" that "contribute to exclusion from the labor market and result in a comparably low life income" by making maintenance of benefits levels contingent on low work and minimal outside income (Eide and Ingstad 2011: 5). In noting this shift, it is important to address the need for caution in advocating restrictions to public assistance in favor of pro-work programs, and such policy efforts must prioritize *transition* to competitive wage work—not merely limitations on public aid in favor of precarious or low-wage employment.

Critics of the Council of the European Union's 2015 Guidelines for the Employment Policies of the Member States noted, for instance, that "work first" measures—such as the council's dictum that "social protection systems should promote social inclusion by encouraging people to actively participate in the labour market and society"—often place pressure on individuals to leave or phase out of benefits programs, sometimes resulting in the deterioration of financial position and security for individuals who struggle to find adequate employment (Waddington, Pedersen, and Ventegodt Liisberg 2016). Concerns of this sort have led to bridging arrangements in a number of national examples, where policies allow individuals with disabilities to combine wages with disability benefits until they reach a threshold limit of wages. Moreover, in countries where poverty is endemic, the introduction of disability grants or pensions can lead to markedly improved standards of living (Loeb et al. 2008).

The shift toward pro-work policies meant the enforcement of policy measures such as nondiscrimination laws and regulations as well as individual-level (vocational rehabilitation and training), employer-level (tax incentives and wage or other subsidies, quotas/levy systems), and mixed affirmative policy approaches (job matching and supported employment services). Later on, this chapter provides a sampling of the growing number of ways that governments are trying to open the labor market up to people with disabilities through affirmative policy approaches. Many countries either have yet to—or are in the extremely early stages of—implementing any comprehensive measures aimed at improving employment outcomes for people with disabilities. Analysis of four southern African nations, for instance, found high levels of difficulty accessing rehabilitation services (between 26% and 55% obtaining needed services) and vocational training (between 5% and 23%) (World Health Organization and World Bank 2011). Beyond vocational rehabilitation and training efforts, 59% of UN Member States have some type of affirmative action policy toward hiring people with disabilities, including tax exemptions, incentives, public and/or private sector quotas, and sanctions for failure to meet hiring guidelines, usually in the form of mandatory contributions to disability welfare funds (Nardodkar et al. 2016).

Impact on World Economies

While typically framed as primarily a human or civil rights issue, one often-overlooked aspect of unemployment trends for people with disabilities is the impact on national economies. While all people deserve the right to equal access to work and a livable wage, the aggregate negative social and economic consequences of discriminatory hiring policies tend to get short shrift. Exclusion of people with disabilities from the workplace leads to lost labor, trillions in annual loss in GDP (Metts 2000; Ozawa and Yeo 2006), and structural and social costs such as high benefit levels and health and social inequalities (Sainsbury and Coleman-Fountain 2014).

Governments are beginning to come around to the notion that change must also occur at the level of organizational culture as well, and employers in manifold contexts must similarly strive to overcome self-imposed environmental and cultural limitations upon their talent pools (Kulkarni and Gopakumar 2014). Thus, garnering higher employer buy-in is an increasingly important component of disability policy efforts. The "business case" for improving labor market outcomes for people with disabilities operates under notions of direct and indirect productivity. First, that when provided with an enabling environment, people with disabilities represent a qualified but undertapped pool of potential workers (direct productivity) (International Labour Organization 2010). Second, that such practices entail collateral benefits, such as lower costs of discrimination and liability, greater organizational problem solving and innovation, and stronger appeal to a diverse customer base (indirect productivity) (Yap and Konrad 2009; Saleh and Bruyère 2018).

CONTEXTUAL FACTORS RELEVANT TO DISABILITY EMPLOYMENT POLICY

Many of the policy considerations discussed above are on schedule to grow more pressing. Projections indicate that both the number and proportion of people with disabilities will continue to rise owing to factors such as population aging, chronic health conditions, and workplace incidents (Harper 2013; Houtrow et al. 2014; Vos et al. 2015). At the same time, our collective notions of what disability means are evolving to include a broader spectrum of impairments and to account for the role of disabling environmental and social conditions. As with urbanization trends, many demographic changes will be more acute in low- and middle-income nations, where populations are aging at more rapid rates than industrialized nations and where the history of treating aging or disability as major public policy concerns is shorter (Shrestha 2000).

In observing present and future policy issues in light of changing demographics, other important trends bubble to the surface. These include links between the global expansion of precarious employment and harmful work conditions (Quinlan, Mayhew, and Bohle 2001), pollution as a potential cause of disability (Stieb et al. 2002), and the effects of free-market deregulation measures promoting "flexible" labor by relaxing wage controls, union protections, social services offerings, and workplace standards (Hogstedt, Wegman, and Kjellstrom 2006). Growing trends in work involving atypical employment contracts, job insecurity, low wages detached from seniority and promotion frameworks, and limited benefits and entitlements disproportionately harm workers in marginalized social positions, such as people with disabilities (Vosko 2006).

Impact of Urbanization

Because many people with disabilities reside in rural areas, the mass commercialization and mechanization of agriculture is another important consideration, with a resulting impact on traditional social roles, disability identity, and the availability of work (Cotter 2007). In many contexts, agriculture is a vital source of employment for people with disabilities (Eurostat 2014). Related trends of rapid or unplanned urbanization in low- and middle-income nations also give rise to "insufficient housing, poor sanitary conditions and crowding, all of which can accelerate the spread of diseases," and all of which intersect with disability and health issues (Eckert and Kohler 2014: 8). As processes of urbanization occur, individuals in remote and rural areas face growing barriers related to transportation, distance, isolation, the availability of work, and consolidation of services in high-concentration population areas (Gething 1997). One analysis of rural versus more developed urban regions in four African nations (Kenya, Sierra Leone, Uganda, and Zambia) found that development indicators are often associated with widening, rather than narrowing, employment and socioeconomic gaps for people with disabilities, in part because social protections lag behind rapid development and urbanization trends (Leonard Cheshire Disability 2018).

Finally, we must not ignore the complex interrelation between disability and poverty, as research from low-, middle-, and high-income nations alike connects the conditions of poverty to exposure to disability conditions (Eide and Ingstad 2011; Fujiura and Yamaki 2000). Lower income levels also affect people with disabilities differently: additional costs for personal support, medical care, and/or assistive devices can lead to a higher likelihood of experiencing financial hardship (e.g., catastrophic health expenditure) (Loyalka, Liu, Chen, and Zheng 2014). Some countries use personal assistance schemes to help bridge these gaps, but the schemes vary in terms of the disability categories covered and other eligibility criteria, levels of funding provided, types of activities, assistance, and tasks funded, and more; in many other countries, people with disabilities are not able to obtain funded personal assistance from their government (Jolly 2010).

Poverty and rurality overlap on a global scale: Over 70% of the people living in extreme poverty reside in rural settings reliant on farming, livestock, aquaculture, and other agricultural means of income and subsistence (World Bank 2014). China, with its rapid economic growth in the past three decades and disability population estimated at between 82 and 85 million people, illustrates some of the common urban/rural policy challenges. About 70% of China's population of working-age people with disabilities live in rural areas; this population has lower income and socioeconomic status and is more likely to live in poverty related to family living costs, inaccessibility of healthcare and other services, and other factors (ILO Global Business and Disability Network 2013). Studies also show that rural populations in China have higher incidence of depressive disorders and substance addictions (Phillips et al. 2009), wide urban/rural health disparities favoring urban populations (Peng et al. 2010), and an association between rural residence and steep functional decline in older adults (Liu et al. 2009).

Globalization of Work

Many low- and middle-income countries are currently undergoing processes of industrialization and economic development, which are gradually altering their qualitative and quantitative economic characteristics, shifting emphasis to mass production, technological proliferation, and division of labor. Changing patterns of employment and wages in advanced and emerging markets pose their own challenges relating to net employment effects, "future-proofing" workforce skills, and near-term planning for the disruptive effects of the fourth industrial revolution on particular job families (e.g., declines in manufacturing and production jobs) (World Economic Forum 2016). Meanwhile, globalization continues to link economic livelihoods across national borders through trade, international finance, and the actions of transnational corporations, leading to the "integration of national economies into a world economy where the dominant themes are economies of scale and competition between nations and enterprises for the most cost-efficient production of goods and services" (Hogstedt, Wegman, and Kjellstrom 2006). Together, trends like these change not only the labor market conditions and employment prospects on the ground but also the ways that we conceive of labor.

In many cases, trends toward globalization—and the movement of factors of production across borders—have favored powerful industrialized nation-states and their economic, political, and cultural interests (Barnes and Mercer 2010). Multinational corporations play a powerful role in many of these trends. Multinationals from industrialized nations have expanded rapidly, driven by relocation of facilities or assets to other countries in search of greater efficiency, often characterized by lower wages and relaxed regulatory environments in the areas of finance, workplace safety, worker rights, and the environment (Monshipouri, Welch, and Kennedy 2003). Developing countries themselves are increasingly home to multinationals and overseas acquisitions, in part because of the increasing degree to which such nations account for the world GDP (Salehizadeh 2007).

From the perspective of social responsibility among multinationals and the governments that regulate them, it becomes increasingly important to look at inequality between individuals beyond the confines of the nation-state but in a manner that is cognizant of local and regional political, legal, and cultural customs. In one example, the Council of the European Union adopted a formal directive on disclosure of nonfinancial and diversity information, aiming to increase transparency and accountability for approximately 6,000 companies in the EU, requiring them to report on issues including sustainable development, social and employee-related rights, and human rights (Global Reporting Initiative 2014).

Productivity and Sector Employment Considerations

The concept of "productivity" in labor is often contingent on which economic sectors predominate in a given region: lower-income nations tend to feature agrarian economies where the primary sectors (agriculture, forestry, and mining) account for the majority of jobs, while in middle- and high-income countries, the secondary (manufacturing) and tertiary (services) sectors predominate. Which sectors predominate is an important policy consideration because certain sectors are more amenable to better employment outcomes for people with disabilities.

In the United States, for instance, an analysis of the distribution of disability employment by sector found that, in 2014, the largest proportion of workers with disabilities (21.2%) worked in education and health services, while the smallest share (0.9%) worked in the mining, quarrying, and oil and gas extraction industry (US Bureau of Labor Statistics 2015). While agricultural and related jobs made up only 2.7% of employment for people with disabilities, this was higher than for people without disabilities (1.5%), with a particularly marked difference for men with disabilities (4%) and men without disabilities (2.1%) (US Bureau of Labor Statistics 2015). Similar trends exist in Europe, where higher-than-average proportions of the total employed population of people with disabilities work in agriculture and related fields, particularly in Greece (27% compared with 11% of employed population without disability), Poland (28%; 12%), Croatia (39%; 11%), Romania (54%; 24%), and Turkey (44%; ~20%) (Eurostat 2014).

Informal Employment Markets

Many low- and middle-income countries feature largely informal labor markets; for example, in India, 87% of employed people with disabilities work in the informal sector (Mitra and Sambamoorthi 2008). Estimates for the size of the informal sector are highest in South Asia (82%; ranging from 62% in Sri Lanka to 87% in India), Sub-Saharan Africa (66%; from 33% in South Africa to 82% in Mali), and East and Southeastern Asia (65%; from 42% in Thailand to 73% in Indonesia) (Vanek et al. 2014). Comparatively, the informal sectors are smaller in Latin America (51%; from 40% in Uruguay to 75% in Bolivia); the Middle East and North Africa (45%; from 31% in Turkey to 57% in West Bank and Gaza), and Eastern Europe and Central Asia (10%; from 6% in Serbia to 16% in Moldova). The presence of large informal sectors highlights the importance of promoting opportunities for self-employment, entrepreneurship, and the development of cooperatives as important policy efforts (Article 27(f) of the CRPD addresses this need). Even in the formal sector, people with disabilities are less likely to work full-time: An analysis of EU countries found that employed people with disabilities (defined as "limitation in work caused by a longstanding health problem and/or a basic activity difficulty") are more likely to work part-time than employed individuals without disabilities (33% compared with 18%) (Eurostat 2014).

The size and scope of the informal sector in high-income countries has proven more difficult to estimate, but is generally smaller than in lower-income nations (Gunn 2004). Estimates of the shadow economy in OECD countries are typically below 20% of GDP, with intermittent disruptions owing to economic factors, and even lower rates (<10%) in high-income non-European OECD countries such as Australia, Canada, Japan, New Zealand, and the United States (Schneider 2015). Similarly, rates of "temporary employment" as a percentage of total wage workers vary by country and region. An analysis of select Asian countries found, for instance, that temporary work accounted for "an important proportion of wage employment" in the Philippines (24.3%), Indonesia (25.2%), Cambodia (53.2%), Vietnam (67.4%), and Pakistan (71.9%), far exceeding figures from the OECD and Japan (12% and 14%, respectively) (Nguyen, Nguyen-Huu, and Le 2016: 5). Research from Egypt shows that employment informality is the norm rather than the exception for young, working-age people in the country, an under-addressed policy complication that further marginalizes disenfranchised populations (Barsoum 2016).

DISABILITY PERCEPTION AND IDENTITY

Disability Identity and Context

Scholars of disability studies and political economy have long noted that both culture and economics play a powerful role in shaping disability identity for individuals with disabilities themselves, for societies, and for employers. While the presence of disability (as we now conceive it) has been a constant throughout human history, "culturally shared responses to [disability] vary greatly across time and social context" (Scheer and Groce 1988: 23) and are often compounded by complex local gender, ethnic, geographic, and other sociodemographic identities (Annable et al. 2003). Too frequently, policy discourses overlook the fact that disability is one identity among many. Moreover, legal and administrative definitions of disability do not always map closely to functional and subjective definitions, with other demographic characteristics tending to supersede in given contexts (e.g., age, gender, living arrangement, labor market participation) (Grönvik 2009).

In some contexts, the cause of the impairment matters greatly in individual- and group-level perception, as well as with the well-documented identity-group formation of veterans with disabilities in western societies (Gerber 2003) and with the differing policy treatment of workers compensation versus disability unemployment insurance in multiple national examples. In one surprising example, researchers demonstrated that socioeconomic status sometimes describes the degree to which individuals experience pain as disability (Dorner et al. 2011). Considering the challenges of formulating a legal definition of disability, the Court of Justice of the European Union considered this fluidity, noting that "it cannot be excluded that ... certain physical and mental shortcomings are in the nature of 'disability' in one social context, but not in another" (*Chacón Navas v. Eurest Colectividades SA* 2005, para. 58).

Meaning of Work in Industrialized Nations

The rise of capitalism, industrialization, and an attendant materialism led to new understandings of "the ways work, social relations, social attitudes, and family relationships were understood and experienced" (Abbas 2016: 136; Oliver 1990). Since the 18th century, the meaning of work in industrialized nations has evolved to prioritize profit maximization and individual competitiveness in the labor market. In many cases, this reformulation resulted in increased marginalization of individuals with disabilities, imposing "disablement upon those non-conforming bodies deemed less or not exploitable by the owners of the means of production" (Russell 2001: 87). The changes brought about by capitalist development, some argue, "resulted in an ideology of individualism, which, coupled with medicalization and the development of rehabilitation, brought about profound changes in the way that people with disabilities are seen and treated" (Riddell and Watson 2014: 6). Of course, the effects of the development of a medicalized disability *identity*, and its interactions with the capitalistic narrative of *individualism*, manifest themselves in unique ways that meld with community-level dynamics. Important community-level factors may include familial structure, gender roles, religious views, and reliance on physical labor (Smart and Smart 1991).

One analysis, focusing on stigma and attitudes toward disability in a single multicultural society, found significant differences in acceptance levels for 19 out of 20 disability groups among Anglo-Australian, Arabic, Chinese, German, Greek, and Italian communities, but remarkably similar "stigma hierarchies" (with HIV infection, intellectual disability, and psychiatric disabilities being more stigmatized) within those groups (Westbrook, Legge, and Pennay 1993). Studies of perceptions of autism and developmental disability in China show important unique contextual factors. These include efforts within families to hide disability, grounded in the belief that "disclosure of disability within a family (i.e., a child) can result in 'loss of face' and may negatively affect the perceived prestige of the entire family" and contextually relevant coping strategies such as positive reinterpretation and suppression of competing activities (Wang, Michaels, and Day 2011: 792). Overcoming bias is one of the fundamental challenges of improving employment outcomes for people with disabilities. For instance, a recent analysis of employment prospects for Jordanians with physical, visual, and hearing impairments cited widespread employer bias and prejudice, compounded by an over-reliance among governmental and community providers on institutional schemes (residential settings, sheltered workshops), and vocational training opportunities that provide a limited choice of trade (Turmusani 2018).

Cultural Context and Disability Definition

Disability is of course a fluid construct, taking on different connotations in different cultural contexts. As Bérubé (1998: vii–viii) puts it, "disability names thousands of human conditions and varieties of impairment, from slight to severe. … It is a category whose constituency is contingency itself." Efforts to create uniform theoretical constructs of disability, such as the World Health Organization's International Classification of Functioning, Disability and Health (ICF) (World Health Organization 2001), acknowledge the fact that "the functioning and disability of an individual occurs in context," alongside environmental and social factors. The ICF revised the previous health-based classification systems, which overlooked the "relativistic and multifactorial" nature of disability in favor of linear, progressive scales (Dahl 2002: 202). While the ICF potentially holds "considerable promise both as a nosological tool and as a heuristic" for guiding practitioner fields (rehabilitation, nursing, etc.) (Bruyère, VanLooy, and Peterson 2005: 114), and despite continued efforts to increase the conceptual clarity, the fact remains that there exists no universal international legal definition of disability with respect to income maintenance, employment measures, or social assistance with daily life activities (Degener 2006).

The CRPD does not explicitly define disability, and many nations retain their pre-existing definitions of disability in practice. For instance, a 2014 analysis of the Middle East and North African regions found that most countries still use "narrower, medical definitions in their laws as these have not yet been adapted to the CRPD. … These narrow definitions often refer to specific bodily limitations" (Swedish International Development Cooperation Agency [Sida] 2014). Some nations still have yet to implement an official legal definition of disability. Among Southeast Asian nations, for instance, Laos and Myanmar have no official definition, while Brunei lacks a common definition across agencies; many other nations, such as Vietnam and Thailand, have updated their legal definition of disability in the past decade to reflect different variations of a social model (Cogburn and Reuter 2017). An analysis of anti-discrimination legislation in 28 EU countries, four candidate countries, and three additional European Economic Area (EEA) countries found that, while "the majority of national legislation contains many examples of definitions of disability, … [t]hese often stem from the context of social security legislation rather than anti-discrimination law" (European Commission 2017: 21).

The commission determined that the definitions of disability in a number of countries failed to reference the interaction of impairment with environmental and cultural barriers, therefore adopting more of a deficit view inconsistent with CRPD Article 1 (these countries are Austria, Bulgaria, Cyprus, the Czech

Republic, Estonia, Ireland, Latvia, Liechtenstein, Norway, Romania, Sweden, and the United Kingdom)" (European Commission 2017). The CRPD describes people with disabilities as including "those who have long-term physical, mental, intellectual or sensory impairments which in interaction with various barriers may hinder their full and effective participation in society on an equal basis with others" (Article 1). This constitutes a "minimum list," and the Convention does not "exhaust the categories of the disabilities which fall within it nor intend to undermine or stand in the way of wider definition of disabilities under national law (such as persons with short-term disabilities)" (UN Enable, no date). Most countries that define disability in a legal sense do so in different ways, and some, like the United States, have multiple legal and regulatory definitions tailored to specific policy ends (e.g., anti-discrimination versus social security) and independent criteria for coverage (Quinn 2005).

Defining disability within a social model is indeed the threshold step to embedding a legal framework that facilitates and protects labor market access. Initial analysis of commentaries by the Committee on the Rights of Persons with Disabilities highlights a range of implementation concerns at the most basic levels. These include multiple concepts of disability across policies (Austria), use of the medical model (Austria, Azerbaijan, China, Costa Rica, Ecuador, South Korea), lack of coverage for certain disability types (Austria, Spain), unrepealed laws that contradict the Convention (Belgium), and insufficient participation of people with disabilities in legislative design (Hungary, Paraguay) (Hoffman, Sritharan, and Tejpar 2016). Despite the importance of defining disability in congruence with the CRPD—as this is the threshold legal step to availing such individuals—analysis by Nardodkar et al. (2016) found that laws in 27% of countries (52 Member States) did not explicitly define the term "disability." Next, we discuss global regulatory frameworks further.

GLOBAL REGULATORY FRAMEWORKS

The CRPD covers an array of human rights topics, including a right to work, and related rights to nondiscrimination, rehabilitation, awareness raising, education and training, accessibility, and quality of life. Prior to the CRPD, binding instruments of international human rights law neglected to recognize the equal rights of people with disabilities or fell into the common trope of defining such issues through the lenses of welfare, health, charity, and guardianship issues (Kayess and French 2008). The equality clauses of the International Bill of Rights (Universal Declaration of Human Rights 1948, International Covenant on Civil and Political Rights 1966, and International Covenant on Economic, Social and Cultural Rights 1966) did not explicitly mention disability. In the 1970s, several nonbinding instruments sought to address relevant policy themes but did so through clear appeal to the medical or deficit models. These included the Declaration on the Rights of Mentally Retarded Persons 1971, Declaration on the Rights of Disabled Persons 1975, and the Principles for the Protection of Persons with Mental Illness and the Improvement of Mental Health Care 1991. Of the major thematic conventions, only the Convention on the Rights of the Child 1989 referred to disability, creating obligations to provide "special care" in social integration and development of children with disabilities (Article 23), while the ILO Convention Concerning Vocational Rehabilitation and Employment (Disabled Persons) 1983 served as an important predecessor to the CRPD, acknowledging the importance of national vocational rehabilitation policies promoting employment opportunities for people with disabilities in the open labor market.

Prior to the CRPD, many international treaties tended to define the rights of people with disabilities in paternalistic terms, prioritizing "segregation through specialized services and institutions" (Kayess and French 2008: 14), although there were important exceptions, such as the ILO Convention Concerning Vocational Rehabilitation and Employment (1983), the Inter-American Convention on the Elimination of All Forms of Discrimination against Persons with Disabilities (1999), and the European Union Directive on Discrimination (2000).

Background of International Disability Human Rights Law

Initial efforts to develop a convention focusing on disability human rights failed in 1982, 1987, and 1989 (Kayess and French 2008). Still, one can identify progress toward a social model in examples such as the World Programme of Action Concerning Disabled Persons 1982 (WPA), which established a goal of providing equal opportunity for people with disabilities in society, culture, the physical environment, housing, transportation, health and social services, education, and work. The Standard Rules on the Equalization of Opportunities for Persons with Disabilities 1993 elaborated on the WPA, opining on the need for states to employ resources toward ensuring equal participation and opportunity for people with disabilities, incorporate a disability perspective into policy and planning, and make environments accessible.

Efforts to extend existing human rights instruments provided additional precedent. The Committee on Economic, Social and Cultural Rights (1994) noted, for instance, that the International Covenant on Economic, Social and Cultural Rights Article 2 anti-discrimination provision extended to people with disabilities by way of the "or other status" language. The Human Rights Committee (1989) drew an interpretive preference for substantive equality in the International Covenant on Civil and Political Rights, distinguishing equal treatment from identical treatment, extending protections toward eliminating conditions that perpetuate discrimination. Regional treaties also furthered social or rights-based models, such as the Council of Europe's Coherent Policy for the Rehabilitation of Persons with Disabilities 1992 and Inter-American

Convention on the Elimination of All Forms of Discrimination against Persons with Disabilities 1999.

Employment Topics in the UN Convention on the Rights of Persons with Disabilities

Work and training topics feature prominently in the CRPD. Article 26(1) requires that parties organize, strengthen, and/or extend comprehensive habilitation and rehabilitation programs and services in the areas of health, employment, education, and social services, including effective measures "to enable persons with disabilities to attain and maintain maximum independence, full physical, mental, social and vocational ability, and full inclusion and participation in all aspects of life." Article 27 outlines the right to work and employment "on an equal basis with others." This includes the "opportunity to gain a living by work freely chosen or accepted in a labor market and work environment that is open, inclusive and accessible." It also places a prohibition on employer discrimination (hiring, retention, and advancement) and provides rights to equal remuneration, reasonable accommodation, favorable and safe working conditions, systems for redress of grievances, union participation, and access to technical and vocational guidance and training. These requirements constitute a mix of traditional human rights edicts such as equal access and nondiscrimination as well as positive measures such as accommodations and vocational training.

The CRPD is a modern human rights instrument that distinguishes equal treatment from identical treatment and extends policies beyond negative policy measures, toward eliminating the conditions that perpetuate discrimination. Article 27 takes affirmative responsibilities a step further, calling for state parties to promote advancement and return-to-work efforts, as well as alternative pathways to employment such as self-employment, entrepreneurship, cooperatives, public sector employment, and affirmative action programs/incentives. Article 27(1)(h) requires states parties to "promote the employment of persons with disabilities in the private sector through appropriate policies and measures, which may include affirmative action programmes, incentives and other measures." 27(1)(j) requires that states parties "promote the acquisition … of work experience in the open labour market." Article 24 further contains language implicating not only a nexus between education and the right to work but also identifying the importance of vocational training, tertiary education, and lifelong learning as human rights. Article 8's Awareness Raising provision is also relevant to the employment context, owing to the fact that mistaken assumptions and negative attitudes make up a significant barrier to employment for people with disabilities.

Implementation Efforts

Ratification makes the terms of a treaty legally binding, but responsibility for enforcement falls on states parties, through domestic incorporation (Lord and

Stein 2008). As a result, substantive rights "often get their complexion from the local cultural environment within which they have to be given concrete, practical meaning" (Ncube 1998: 14–15). As discussed previously, many states have yet to incorporate some of the CRPD's fundamental provisions, including a social model definition of disability that is inclusive of the full spectrum of impairments while accounting for environmental barriers. Beyond finding that 52 countries had yet to define disability in their legal provisions, Nardodkar et al. (2016) also found that 51% of Member States (98 countries) had no explicit legal protections against dismissal, termination, or suspension of employment on health grounds. Looking specifically at legal protections for individuals with mental health conditions, the authors further found that 28 countries (14% of Member States) lacked explicit prohibitions of discrimination for this population, while 26% (53 Member States) did not have specific affirmative action provisions for employment of people with mental health conditions (Nardodkar et al. 2016). Dinerstein (2017) noted that many Southeast Asian countries implicitly perpetuated medical views of disability by choosing social welfare or health agencies as their CRPD implementation focal point, rather than justice-based agencies.

One initial step that a nation takes toward improving employment outcomes for people with disabilities is to pass legislation prohibiting discrimination by public and private employers. Historically, many national frameworks instituted hiring quota systems prior to adopting anti-discrimination law, but modern frameworks often start with a baseline of nondiscrimination and civil rights—similar to that created by the Americans with Disabilities Act (1990) in the US context—before implementing positive measures to increase employment outcomes. However, these nondiscrimination frameworks must be enforceable, through either governmental oversight, reporting requirements, or litigation. For instance, an analysis of Pacific Island states found that, while many had some type of nondiscrimination provision under the law, most lacked appropriately comprehensive frameworks for enforcement (Harpur and Bales 2010). The duty to provide reasonable accommodations is a fundamental component to such nondiscrimination frameworks, and while many countries have general anti-discrimination requirements, weak or incomplete accommodation duties can undermine efforts at equalization.

For example, a recent analysis of EU, candidate, and EEA countries found that about a quarter lacked a reasonable accommodations directive suitable for compliance with the CRPD or EU Employment Equality Directive, and some had no directive at all or an incomplete formulation of the duty that applied only to current, rather than prospective, employees (European Commission 2017). Moreover, those with a suitable provision varied considerably in the scope of that directive. Some states provided only "a basic duty with little elaboration on how this should be implemented (e.g., Lithuania) or how a disproportionate burden must be assessed (e.g., Croatia, the Former Yugoslav Republic of Macedonia, and Latvia)," while others had "more extensive guidance on the practical application of the reasonable accommodation duty (e.g., the United Kingdom)" (European Commission 2017: 23). Nardodkar et al. (2016) found that 30% of UN Member States (58 countries) had no explicit or implied legal provisions for providing reasonable accommodation to people with disabilities.

Examples of National Strategies for Increasing Labor Market Involvement

Beyond rights to nondiscrimination (sometimes referenced as a type of "negative" right—the right *not* to be subjected to adverse employment and hiring actions, although this is complicated somewhat by adjoining reasonable accommodations requirements), states parties have taken a range of different approaches to affirmatively influencing labor market conditions to render them more conducive to inclusive hiring practices. Efforts by nations include education, training, and rehabilitation initiatives; supported employment frameworks; employment services geared toward "targeted" employment; employer quotas and penalties; employer incentives such as subsidies and wage contribution; "flexicurity" programs; and more. As previously mentioned, a survey of UN Member States found affirmative action policies on disability employment in 59% of countries. These policies include tax exemptions, incentives to facilitate employment for people with disabilities, disability-related quotas in the public and/or private sector, and sanctions for failure to meet requirements such as mandatory contributions to disability welfare funds (Nardodkar et al. 2016).

In some countries, supported work policies focus on providing intensive, ongoing, and individualized job support (such as job coaching) to people with disabilities who have traditionally experienced exclusion from competitive work. For example, many EU countries (e.g., Sweden, Germany, and Norway) use government-sponsored supported employment opportunities, removing some of the onus from the employer while often *incentivizing* employer involvement (Waldschmidt, Sturm, Karačić, and Dins 2017). In Sweden, supported employment entails financial support for the purchase of assistive devices in the workplace by employers or individuals, as well as "special introduction and follow-up support" services before or during the introductory period of a job and up to a year after employment commences (Committee on the Rights of Persons with Disabilities 2012). Germany's social services subsystem supplements supported employment frameworks and an influential hiring quota scheme by offering training and retraining centers, and integration centers that help individuals with severe disabilities identify and maintain employment, move from training centers to work, and liaise with employers to moderate accommodations and special dismissal procedures (Sainsbury and Coleman-Fountain 2014). Norway promotes supported employment through subsidies, grants, assistive technology centers, vocational training and higher education opportunities, and incentives for the provision of accommodations (Sainsbury and Coleman-Fountain 2014). From 2000 through 2010, a 50% increase occurred in the population of Norwegians with disabilities working in supported employment (Official Norwegian Reports 2012).

Quota Systems

Quota systems have similarly been a common policy directive, with some nations opting to penalize, others to incentivize, and still others to treat quotas as explicitly or implicitly (owing to a lack of enforcement mechanism) aspirational. The size of the hiring quota (e.g., 6% in France, 1.5% in China), the mode of enforcement, and the size or type of company covered are important considerations here. Starting in 2008, the Chinese government, for instance, instituted a quota requiring that all public and private employers reserve a minimum 1.5% of job opportunities for people with disabilities in accordance with provincial regulatory requirements, and monitored by the taxation authority. Failure to meet the quota results in a fee to the Disabled Persons Employment Security Fund, thus cycling them back into vocational training and job-placement services. The Chinese system calculates penalties based on the average salary within an employer's global business, causing multinationals to face potentially higher penalties (Feng 2018). Japan uses a levy-grant scheme originally established in 1976, requiring private firms to achieve a quota for hiring people with disabilities or else pay a levy.

While the government has modified this system several times since, the general structure remains, requiring a 2% target level for private firms, or a monthly penalty of ¥50,000 per person. Since the system's inception, the "legal targeted level has never been satisfied, and the proportion of disabled people in the entire workforce has always been approximately 0.2% points below the targeted level. ... Some administrators and specialists criticize that the levy is too low to motivate employers" (Mori and Sakamoto 2018: 4). On the incentives side, Uganda, for instance, has provided tax cuts for private sector employers who employ people with disabilities at a rate of 5% of their total workforce (Persons with Disability Act 2006). However, 2009 amendments cut the available tax refund from 15% to 2% (Income Tax Amendment Act of 2009), a figure that commentators note is unlikely to provide the needed incentive to employers (Nyombi and Kibandama 2014).

Italy instituted measures for a targeted employment framework, graduated hiring quota, and regionally implemented assessment guidelines for work capacity, job-matching a candidate's skill set to employer needs, and training criteria (Agovino and Rapposelli 2011; Law 68/1999). Penalties exist for failing to meet quotas (companies of 15 through 35 employees must hire one person with a disability, 36 through 50 must hire two, and 50 or more have a quota of 7%), while conversely, employers may receive incentives for employing people with disabilities, such as tax subsidies, wage contributions, and reimbursement for workplace adaptations (Sainsbury and Coleman-Fountain 2014).

Other countries incorporate an element of choice. The Czech system allows employers to hire people with disabilities "directly," or "indirectly" by commissioning goods and services from organizations that do: For 2010, direct employment accounted for 56% of the obligations met (Committee on the Rights of Persons with Disabilities 2013; see also Employment Act of 2004). Governments often allow employers to miss the quota in exchange for payment of a penalty or additional taxation. Serbia's quota system outlines penalties and subsidies for missing, making, or exceeding targets (see Act on Professional Rehabilitation and Employment of Persons with Disabilities 2009; Prohibition of Discrimination Act of 2009). While many employers choose to pay the fine rather than comply, the government applies penalties to employment, education, and poverty reduction initiatives for people with disabilities (Sainsbury and Coleman-Fountain 2014).

Active Labor Market Policies

Active labor market policies (ALMPs) aim to improve the functioning of the labor market by first addressing unemployed and vulnerable populations (Waddington, Pedersen, and Ventegodt Liisberg 2016). Such efforts account for both the supply- and demand-side of labor by equipping unemployed individuals with demand-driven skills needed to enter the labor market while simultaneously offering incentives to employers and the means for employers to identify individuals within those talent pools who fit their needs (Auer, Berg, and Cazes 2007).

Certain policies attempt to alleviate some of the concerns about the potential negative consequences of "work-first" policies for benefits security, with Denmark's "flexicurity" labor market model providing a useful success case (Ventegodt Liisberg 2011). The flexicurity model prioritizes both high levels of income support during unemployment and quick reentry into the labor force, especially through upgrading of skills and "activation" obligations for unemployed individuals (Danish Government 2013). The percentage of Danish individuals with disabilities in supported employment conditions rose from less than 10% in 2002 to more than 25% in 2014 (Waddington, Pedersen, and Ventegodt Liisberg 2016). The Danish policy framework focuses on incentivizing rather than merely compelling employers (e.g., no quota, high degree of freedom in termination/hiring decisions). Denmark's system includes subsidies for "ice breaker" wages for recent graduates, flexjobs (subsidized wages for transitional work in special working conditions such as adapted environments or schedules), workplace alterations, mentor opportunities, job trials, and technical or personal assistance (Gupta, Larsen, and Thomsen 2015).

CONCLUSION AND RECOMMENDATIONS

This chapter has introduced some global perspectives on employment for people with disabilities, including contextual barriers and regulatory environments. Developments in disability employment policy represent opportunities to re-imagine labor problems and the employment relationship itself, including the ways that employers recruit, accommodate, and retain workers. Increasingly, policy efforts in this domain aim not only to improve job-seeker prospects (through nondiscrimination provisions, reasonable accommodation requirements, education, vocational training and services, pro-work benefits and programs, etc.) but also to positively compel or encourage employer behavior. For labor and employment relations specialists, this represents an opportunity wherein employers can improve and "future proof" their talent pools—and avoid government sanctions or liabilities—by reorienting their policies and practices toward prospective employees with disabilities. This stems from the fact that, setting aside any governmental desire to align disability policy with labor and poverty alleviation efforts, the critical initial step in getting and keeping people with disabilities in the workforce lies with the employer's recruitment, selection, hiring, and advancement processes, which take different forms in different regions and economies.

Research indicates that private employers who value workforce diversity desire additional government support in adapting their recruitment and hiring practices—perhaps even beyond legally prescribed levels—and are more open to collaborating with government agencies that "understand their needs" (Henry, Petkauskos, Stanislawzyk, and Vogt 2014). Many of the policy challenges and solutions discussed in this chapter aim to improve the quality of employer involvement in some of these facets. Often, governmental policy serves as a vital catalyst, but implementation and organizational change happen at the level of the employer. Employers therefore play a central role, both in incorporating and adhering to governmental regulations, but also exceeding them, and developing policies that account for the importance and potential upside of diverse hiring and advancement practices, both for society and for the organization itself.

In broad terms, national frameworks must take steps to incorporate the most basic elements of the CRPD framework. At present, many nations do not have an appropriate social model definition of disability outlined in their legal frameworks, or have conflicting definitions that still have roots in medical models. By extension, many countries need to renew their focus on the broad spectrum of disabilities rather than focusing legislation on physical or "visible" disabilities, considering the role of environmental factors and the fluidity of disability as an identity as well as its intersection with other identities and sociodemographic factors. Where possible, countries should assign CRPD "focal point" agencies that are more directly associated with employment, civil rights, and community integration, rather than localizing implementation and enforcement to social services agencies. Many countries still need to update their laws to incorporate progressive anti-discrimination, reasonable accommodation, and affirmative hiring requirements that are tethered to effective oversight and enforcement mechanisms and that situate reasonable accommodations requirements *within* nondiscrimination frameworks rather than as a separate requirement.

Nondiscrimination and affirmative action policies must be supplemented by appropriate training opportunities that are responsive to national, regional, and local economic factors. For this reason, basic demographic data collection and employment data are necessary for policy planning and evaluation. At present, many countries do not have effective data collection mechanisms. As nations develop more robust training, benefits, and vocational rehabilitation frameworks, it is important that policy recognize the complex relationship between income security or disability benefits and competitive integrated work. Without placing individuals in precarious situations where they must "choose" between income security and paid work, benefits and rehabilitation frameworks should be integrated and coordinated so as to offer both individuals and employers incentives and job-matching services that help connect skills to employer-side demand. Successful examples of this include (1) stipends or tickets that allow for work without loss of benefits, (2) governmental "ice breaker" wage contributions and job coaching offerings, (3) training investment that coincides with employer incentives, and (4) awareness-raising efforts regarding the importance of workforce diversity and the untapped talent pools that likely exist where hiring processes are made more inclusive.

A focus on interest convergence and nuanced governmental policies—responsive to both individual, family, and employer needs—can help late-CRPD adopters and countries with emerging rehabilitation and benefits systems avoid some of the thematic pitfalls that have existed in modernizing disability policy internationally. In short, best practices from the international literature provide exciting new directions for increasing equitable labor markets for people with disabilities around the world.

ACKNOWLEDGMENTS

The authors would like to thank Ariel Avgar, associate professor of labor relations, Cornell University ILR School; Barbara Murray, (retired) senior disability consultant, International Labour Organisation; and Sophia Mitra, professor of economics, Fordham University, for their reviews, feedback, and thoughtful commentary.

REFERENCES

Abbas, J. 2016. "Economy, Exploitation, and Intellectual Disability." In *Disability Politics in a Global Economy: Essays in Honour of Marta Russell*, edited by R. Malhotra. New York, NY: Routledge.

Act on Professional Rehabilitation and Employment of Persons with Disabilities [Serbia]. 2009. NATLEX Database of National Labour, Social Security and Related Human Rights Legislation. Geneva, Switzerland: International Labour Organization. http://bit.ly/2Kfqayl

Agovino, M., and A. Rapposelli. 2011. "Inclusion of Disabled People in the Italian Labour Market: An Efficiency Analysis of Law 68/1999 at Regional Level." *Quality & Quantity* 47 (3): 1577–1588. doi.10.1007/s11135-011-9610-2

Annable, G., Colleen Watters, Deborah Stienstra, Annette Symanzik, Brenda L. Tully, and Nadia Stuewer. 2003. *Students with Disabilities: Transition from Post-Secondary Education to Work: Phase One Report*. Winnipeg, Manitoba: Canadian Centre on Disability Studies.

Auer, P., J. Berg, and S. Cazes. 2007. "Balancing Flexibility and Security: The Role of Labour Market Policies and Institutions." *Tilburg Law Review* 14 (1): 4956.

Barnes, Colin, and Geof Mercer. 2010. *Exploring Disability* (2nd ed.). Hoboken, NJ: Wiley

Barsoum, Ghada. 2016. "Job Opportunities for the Youth: Competing and Overlapping Discourses on Youth Unemployment and Work Informality in Egypt." *Current Sociology* 64 (3): 430–446. doi.10.1177/0011392115593614

Bérubé, M. 1998. *Claiming Disability: Knowledge and Identity*. New York, NY: New York University Press.

Bruyère, Susanne M., Sara A. VanLooy, and David B. Peterson. 2005. "The International Classification of Functioning, Disability and Health: Contemporary Literature Overview." *Rehabilitation Psychology* 50 (2): 113–121.

Burkhauser, Richard V., Mary C. Daly, and Nicolas R. Ziebarth. 2016. "Protecting Working-Age People with Disabilities: Experiences of Four Industrialized Nations." *Journal of Labour Market Research* 49 (4): 367–386. doi.10.1007/s12651-016-0215-z

Chacón Navas v. Eurest Colectividades SA. 2006 (Mar. 16). Case C-13/05 (2005) ECR I-6476. Opinion of Advocate General Beelhoed. http://bit.ly/2MsZmsT

Cogburn, Derrick L., and Tina Kempin Reuter. 2017. *Making Disability Rights Real in Southeast Asia: Implementing the UN Convention on the Rights of Persons with Disabilities in ASEAN*. New York, NY: Lexington.

Committee on Economic, Social and Cultural Rights. 1994. General Comment No. 5, HRI/GEN/1/Rev 8, Add.1.

Committee on the Rights of Persons with Disabilities. 2012. Implementation of the Convention on the Rights of Persons with Disabilities. Initial Reports Submitted by States Parties Under Article 35 of the Convention: Sweden. CRPD/C/SWE/1.

Committee on the Rights of Persons with Disabilities. 2013. Implementation of the Convention on the Rights of Persons with Disabilities: Initial Reports Submitted by States Parties Under Article 35 of the Convention: Czech Republic. CRPD/C/CZE/1.

Council of the European Union. 2015 (May 10). Council Decision (EU) 2015/1848 of 5 October 2015 on Guidelines for the Employment Policies of the Member States for 2015. OJ L268/28.

Cotter, Anne-Marie Mooney. 2007. *This Ability: An International Legal Analysis of Disability Discrimination*. Burlington, VT: Ashgate.

Dahl, Tóra H. 2002. "International Classification of Functioning, Disability and Health: An Introduction and Discussion of Its Potential Impact on Rehabilitation Services and Research." *Journal of Rehabilitation Medicine* 34 (1): 201–204.

Danish Government. 2013. "Disability Policy Action Plan 2013: One Society for All." http://bit.ly/2sQo25f

Degener, Theresia. 2006. "The Definition of Disability in German and Foreign Discrimination Law." *Disability Studies Quarterly* 26 (2). http://bit.ly/31rDeVV

Dinerstein, R. 2017. "Norm Diffusion and CRPD Implementation and ASEAN." In *Making Disability Rights Real in Southeast Asia: Implementing the UN Convention on the Rights of Persons with Disabilities in ASEAN*, edited by Derrick L. Cogburn and Tina Kempin Reuter. Lanham, MD: Lexington.

Dorner, Thomas E., Johanna Muckenhuber, Willibald J. Stronegger, Éva Ràsky, Burkhard Gustorff, and Wolfgang Freidl. 2011. "The Impact of Socio-Economic Status on Pain and the Perception of Disability Due to Pain." *European Journal of Pain* 15 (1): 103–109. doi:10.1016/j.ejpain.2010.05.013

Eckert, Sophie, and Stefan Kohler. 2014. "Urbanization and Health in Developing Countries: A Systematic Review." *World Health and Population* 15 (1): 7–20.

Eide, Arne H., and Benedicte Ingstad. 2011. *Disability and Poverty: A Global Challenge.* Bristol, UK: Policy Press.

Employment Act of 2004 [Czech Republic]. 435/2004 Coll. http://bit.ly/2Mxjc66

Erickson, William, Camille Lee, and Sarah von Schrader. 2016. "2015 Disability Status Report: United States." Ithaca, NY: Cornell University Yang-Tan Institute on Employment and Disability. http://bit.ly/2MrCbPH

European Commission. 2017. "A Comparative Analysis of Non-Discrimination Law in Europe: 2017. The 28 EU Member States, the Former Yugoslav Republic of Macedonia, Iceland, Liechtenstein, Montenegro, Norway, Serbia and Turkey Compared." Brussels, Belgium: Publications Office of the European Union. http://bit.ly/2MxNYvL

Eurostat. 2014. "Disability Statistics–Employment Patterns." http://bit.ly/2sOQlkQ

Feng, Emily. 2018 (May 9). "Chinese Employers Choose Fines over Meeting Disability Quotas." *Financial Times*. https://on.ft.com/2sOQR2g

Fujiura, Glenn T., and Kiyoshi Yamaki. 2000. "Trends in Demography of Childhood Poverty and Disability." *Exceptional Children* 66 (2): 187–199. doi.10.1177/001440290006600204

Gerber, David A. 2003. "Disabled Veterans, the State, and the Experience of Disability in Western Societies, 1914–1950." *Journal of Social History* 36 (4): 899–916. doi.10.1353/jsh.2003.0095

Gething, Lindsay. 1997. "Sources of Double Disadvantage for People with Disabilities Living in Remote and Rural Areas of New South Wales, Australia." *Disability & Society* 12 (4): 513–531. doi.10.1080/09687599727100

Global Reporting Initiative. 2014. "Disability in Sustainability Reporting." http://bit.ly/2sL5Z0r

Goodley, Dan. 2017. *Disability Studies: An Interdisciplinary Introduction* (2nd ed.). London, UK: Sage.

Grönvik, Lars. 2009. "Defining Disability: Effects of Disability Concepts on Research Outcomes." *International Journal of Social Research Methodology* 12 (1): 1–18. doi.0.1080/13645570701621977

Grover, Chris, and Linda Piggott. 2010. "Social Security, Employment and Incapacity Benefit: Critical Reflections on *A New Deal for Welfare*." *Disability & Society* 22 (7): 733–746. doi.10 .1080/09687590701659584

Gunn, Christopher. 2004. *Third-Sector Development: Making Up for the Market*. Ithaca, NY: Cornell University Press.

Gupta, Nabanita Datta, Mona Larsen, and Lars Stage Thomsen. 2015. "Do Wage Subsidies for Disabled Workers Reduce Their Non-Employment? Evidence from the Danish Flexjob Scheme." *IZA Journal of Labor Policy* 4 (10): 1–5. doi.10.1186/s40173-015-0036-7

Harper, Sarah. 2013. *Ageing Societies: Myths, Challenges and Opportunities*. New York, NY: Routledge.

Harpur, Paul, and Richard Bales. 2010. "The Positive Impact of the Convention on the Rights of Persons with Disabilities: A Case Study on the South Pacific and Lessons from the US Experience." *Northern Kentucky Law Review* 37 (4): 363–388.

Henry, Alexis D., Kathleen Petkauskos, Jason Stanislawzyk, and Jay Vogt. 2014. "Employer-Recommended Strategies to Increase Opportunities for People with Disabilities." *Journal of Vocational Rehabilitation* 41 (3): 237–248. doi.10.3233/JVR-140716

Hoffman, Steven J., Lathika Sritharan, and Ali Tejpar. 2016. "Is the UN Convention on the Rights of Persons with Disabilities Impacting Mental Health Laws and Policies in High-Income Countries? A Case Study of Implementation in Canada." *BMC International Health and Human Rights* 16 (1): 28. doi.10.1186/s12914-016-0103-1

Hogstedt, Christer, David H. Wegman, and Tord Kjellstrom. 2006. "The Consequences of Economic Globalization on Working Conditions, Labor Relations and Workers' Health." In *Globalization and Health*, edited by Ichiro Kawachi and Sarah Wamala. Oxford, UK: Oxford University Press.

Hoogeveen, Johannes G. 2005. "Measuring Welfare for Small but Vulnerable Groups: Poverty and Disability in Uganda." *Journal of African Economies* 14 (4): 603–631. doi.10.1093/jae/eji020

Houtrow, Amy J., Kandyce Larson, Lynn M. Olson, Paul W. Newacheck, and Neal Halfon. 2014. "Changing Trends of Childhood Disability, 2001–2011." *Pediatrics* 134 (3): 530–538.

Humpage, Louise. 2007. "Models of Disability, Work and Welfare in Australia." *Social Policy and Administration* 41 (3): 215–231. doi.10.1111/j.1467-9515.2007.00549.x

ILO Global Business and Disability Network. 2013. "China Overview: Current Situation." Geneva, Switzerland: International Labour Organization

Income Tax Amendment Act of 2009 [Republic of Uganda], Act 15. 2009. http://bit.ly/2MzVQwH

International Labour Organization. 2010. "Disability in the Workplace: Company Practices." Geneva, Switzerland: International Labour Organization. http://bit.ly/2sNLAIc

Jolly, D. 2010. "Personal Assistance and Independent Living: Article 19 of the UN Convention on the Rights of Persons with Disabilities." Leeds, UK: University of Leeds, Disability Studies. http://bit.ly/2sKRVUR

Kayess, Rosemary, and Phillip French. 2008. "Out of Darkness into Light? Introducing the Convention on the Rights of Persons with Disabilities." *Human Rights Law Review* 8 (1): 1–34. doi.10.1093/hrlr/ngm044

Kulkarni, Mukta, and K.V. Gopakumar. 2014. "Career Management Strategies for People with Disabilities." *Human Resource Management* 53 (3): 445–466. doi.10.1002/hrm.21570

Lamichhane, Kamal, and Tomoo Okubo. 2014. "The Nexus Between Disability, Education, and Employment: Evidence from Nepal." *Oxford Development Studies* 42 (3): 439–453. doi.10.1080/13600818.2014.927843

Law No. 68/1999 on the Rights of Workers with Disabilities [Italy]. 1999 (Mar. 12).

Leonard Cheshire Disability. 2018. "Bridging the Gap: Examining Disability and Development in Four African Countries." London, UK: University College London. http://bit.ly/2sMsulC

Liu, Jufen, Iris Chi, Gong Chen, Xinming Song, and Xiaoying Zheng. 2009. "Prevalence and Correlates of Functional Disability in Chinese Older Adults." *Geriatric & Gerontology International* 9 (3): 253–261. doi.10.1111/j.1447-0594.2009.00529.x

Loeb, Mitchell, Arne H. Eide, Jennifer Jelsma, Mzolisi ka Toni, and Soraya Maart. 2008. "Poverty and Disability in Eastern and Western Cape Provinces, South Africa." *Disability and Society* 23 (4): 311–321. doi.10.1080/09687590802038803

Lord, Janet E., and Michael Ashley Stein. 2008. "The Domestic Incorporation of Human Rights Law and the United Nations Convention on the Rights of Persons with Disabilities." *Washington University Law Review* 8 (4): 449–479.

Loyalka, Prashant, Lan Liu, Gong Chen, and Xionying Zheng. 2014. "The Cost of Disability in China." *Demography* 51 (1): 97–118. http://bit.ly/2MA0ieJ

Marks, D. 1999. *Disability: Controversial Debates and Psychosocial Perspectives*. London, UK: Routledge.

Metts, Robert L. 2000. "Disability Issues, Trends and Recommendations for the World Bank." Washington, DC: World Bank. http://bit.ly/2MyCmIJ

Mitra, S. 2018. *Disability, Health and Human Development*. New York, NY: Palgrave.

Mitra, Sophie, and Usha Sambamoorthi. 2008. "Disability and the Rural Labor Market in India: Evidence for Males in Tamil Nadu." *World Development* 36 (5): 934–952.

Mizunoya, Suguru, and Sophie Mitra. 2013. "Is There a Disability Gap in Employment Rates in Developing Countries?" *World Development* 42 (1): 28–43.

Mizunoya, Suguru, Izumi Yamasaki, and Sophie Mitra. 2016. "The Disability Gap in Employment Rates in a Developing Country Context: New Evidence from Vietnam." *Economics Bulletin* 36 (2): 771–777. doi.10.2139/ssrn.2766103

Monshipouri, Mahmood, Claude Emerson Welch, and Evan T. Kennedy. 2003. "Multinational Corporations and the Ethics of Global Responsibility: Problems and Possibilities. *Human Rights Quarterly* 25 (4): 965–989. doi.10.1353/hrq.2003.0048

Mori, Yuko, and Norihito Sakamoto. 2018. "Economic Consequences of Employment Quota System for Disabled People: Evidence from a Regression Discontinuity Design in Japan." *Journal of the Japanese and International Economies* 48 (1): 1–14. doi.10.1016/j.jjie.2017.02.001

Nardodkar, Renuka, Soumitra Pathare, Antonio Ventriglio, João Castaldelli-Maia, Kenneth R. Javate, Julio Torales, and Dinesh Bhugra. 2016. "Legal Protection of the Right to Work and Employment for Persons with Mental Health Problems: A Review of Legislation Across the World." *International Review of Psychiatry* 28 (4): 375–384. doi.10.1080/09540261.2016.1210575

Ncube, W. 1998. "The African Cultural Footprint? The Changing Conception of Childhood." In *Law, Culture, Tradition and Children's Rights in Eastern and Southern Africa*, edited by W. Ncube. Farnham, UK: Ashgate.

Nguyen, Huu-Chi, Thanh Tam Nguyen-Huu, and Thi-Thuy-Linh Le. 2016. "Non-Standard Forms of Employment in Some Asian Countries: A Study of Wages and Working Conditions of Temporary Workers." Geneva, Switzerland: International Labour Organization. http://bit.ly/2MvDRHC

Nyombi, Chrispas, and Alexander Kibandama. 2014. "Access to Employment for Persons with Disabilities in Uganda." *Labor Law Journal* 65 (4): 248–258.

Official Norwegian Reports. 2012. "Labour Market Measures." Oslo, Norway: Office of the Prime Minister and Ministries.

Oliver, Michael. 1990. *The Politics of Disablement: A Sociological Approach*. Basingstoke, UK: Palgrave Macmillan.

Organisation for Economic Co-operation and Development (OECD). 2009. "Sickness, Disability and Work: Keeping on Track in the Economic Downturn." Paper Presented at the High-Level Forum, May 14–15, 2009, Stockholm, Sweden. http://bit.ly/2sMHNLd

Ozawa, Martha N., and Yeong Hun Yeo. 2006. "Work Status and Work Performance of People with Disabilities: An Empirical Study." *Journal of Disability Policy Studies* 17 (3): 180–190. doi.10.1177/10442073060170030601

Peng, Xiaoxia, Shige Song, Sheena Sullivan, Jingjun Qiu, and Wei Wang. 2010. "Ageing, the Urban–Rural Gap and Disability Trends: 19 Years of Experience in China–1987 to 2006." *PLoS ONE* 5 (8): e12129. doi.10.1371/journal.pone.0012129

Persons with Disabilities Act, 2006. [Republic of Uganda]. 2006 (May 24). http://bit.ly/2MvJlSX

Phillips, Michael R., Jingxuan Zhang, Qichang Shi, Zhiqiang Song, Zhijie Ding, Shutao Pang, Xianyun Li, Yali Zhang, and Zhiqing Wang. 2009. "Prevalence, Treatment, and Associated Disability of Mental Disorders in Four Provinces in China During 2001–05: An Epidemiological Survey." *The Lancet* 373 (9680): 2041–2053. doi.10.1016/S0140-6736(09)60660-7

Prohibition of Discrimination Act of 2009. Official Gazette of the Republic of Serbia No 22/2009. http://bit.ly/2MvFaGw

Quinlan, Michael, Claire Mayhew, and Philip Bohle. 2001. "The Global Expansion of Precarious Employment, Work Disorganization, and Consequences for Occupational Health: A Review of Recent Research." *International Journal of Health Services* 31 (2): 335–414. doi.10.2190/607H-TTV0-QCN6-YLT4

Quinn, Peggy. 2005. "Disability Policy (United States)." In *Encyclopedia of Social Welfare History in North America*, edited by John M. Herrick and Paul H. Stuart, pp. 84–86. Thousand Oaks, CA: Sage.

Riddell, Sheila, and Nick Watson. 2014. "Disability, Culture and Identity: Introduction." In *Disability, Culture and Identity*, edited by Sheila Riddell and Nick Watson. New York, NY: Routledge.

Russell, Martha. 2001. "Disablement, Oppression, and the Political Economy." *Journal of Disability Policy Studies* 12 (2): 87–95. doi.10.1177/104420730101200205

Sainsbury, Roy, and Edmund Coleman-Fountain. 2014. "Diversity and Change of the Employment Prospects of Persons with Disabilities: The Impact of Redistributive and Regulatory Provisions in a Multilevel Framework." DISCIT Deliverable 5.1. http://bit.ly/2sQvttb

Saleh, Matthew C., and Susanne M. Bruyère. 2018. "Leveraging Employer Practices in Global Regulatory Frameworks to Improve Employment Outcomes for People with Disabilities." *Social Inclusion* 6 (1): 18–28. doi:10.17645/si.v6i1.1201

Salehizadeh, Mehdi. 2007. "Emerging Economies' Multinationals: Current Status and Future Prospects." *Third World Quarterly* 28 (6): 1151–1166. doi.10.1080/01436590701507586

Scheer, Jessica, and Nora Groce. 1988. "Impairment as a Human Constant: Cross-Cultural and Historical Perspectives on Variation." *Journal of Social Issues* 44 (1): 23–37. doi.10.1111/j.1540-4560.1988.tb02046.x

Schneider, Friedrich. 2015. "Size and Development of the Shadow Economy of 31 European and 5 Other OECD Countries from 2003 to 2014: Different Developments." *Journal of Self-Governance and Management Economics* 3 (3): 7–9.

Shrestha, Laura B. 2000. "Population Aging in Developing Countries." *Health Affairs* 19 (3): 204–212. doi.10.1377/hlthaff.19.3.204

Smart, Julie F., and David W. Smart. 1991. "Acceptance of Disability and the Mexican American Culture." *Rehabilitation Counseling Bulletin* 34 (4): 357–367.

Stieb, David M., Marc Smith-Doiron, Jeffrey R. Brook, Richard T. Burnetta, Tom Dann, Alexandre Mamedov, and Yue Chen. 2002. "Air Pollution and Disability Days in Toronto: Results from the National Population Health Survey." *Environmental Research* 89 (3): 210–219. doi.10.1006/enrs.2002.4373

Swedish International Development Cooperation Agency (Sida). 2014. *Disability Rights in the Middle East & North Africa.* Stockholm, Sweden: Sida. http://bit.ly/2sLdvIH

Trani, Jean-Francois, and Mitchell Loeb. 2010. "Poverty and Disability: A Vicious Circle? Evidence from Afghanistan and Zambia." *Journal of International Development* 24 (S1): S19-S52. doi.10.1002/jid.1709

Turcotte, Martin. 2012. "Persons with Disabilities and Employment." Statistics Canada. http://bit.ly/2MClBg4

Turmusani, Majid. 2018. *Disabled People and Economic Needs in the Developing World: A Political Perspective from Jordan.* New York, NY: Routledge.

UN Economic and Social Commission for Asia and the Pacific. 2015. "Disability at a Glance 2015: Strengthening Employment Prospects for People with Disabilities in Asia and the Pacific." New York, NY: United Nations. http://bit.ly/2sMhCEl

UN Enable. No date. "Frequently Asked Questions." New York, NY: United Nations. http://bit.ly/2MOkXzL

United Nations. 2018. Realization of the Sustainable Development Goals by, for, and with Persons with Disabilities (Advanced Unedited Version). New York, NY: United Nations. http://bit.ly/2MwDRqU

US Bureau of Labor Statistics. 2015 (Jun. 18). "Largest Proportion of Workers with a Disability Work in Education and Health Services in 2014." Washington, DC: US Bureau of Labor Statistics. http://bit.ly/2sNn4XO

Vanek, Joann, Martha Alter Chen, Françoise Carré, James Heintz, and Ralf Hussmanns. 2014. "Statistics on the Informal Economy: Definitions, Regional Estimates & Challenges." WIEGO Working Paper (Statistics) No. 2. Manchester, UK: Women in Informal Employment Globalizing and Organizing. http://bit.ly/2sViYNn

Ventegodt Liisberg, Maria. 2011. "Disability and Employment: A Contemporary Disability Human Rights Approach Applied to Danish, Swedish and EU Law and Policy." Ph.D. Dissertation. Maastricht University, Netherlands.

Vos, Theo, R.M. Barber, B. Bell, A. Bertozzi-Villa, S. Biryukov, I. Bolliger, F. Charlson, et al. 2015. "Global, Regional, and National Incidence, Prevalence, and Years Lived with Disability for 301 Acute and Chronic Diseases and Injuries in 188 Countries, 1990–2013: A Systematic Analysis for the Global Burden of Disease Study 2013." *The Lancet* 386 (9995): 743–800. doi.10.1016/S0140-6736(15)60692-4

Vosko, Leah F. 2006. "What Is to Be Done? Harnessing Knowledge to Mitigate Precarious Employment." In *Precarious Employment: Understanding Labour Market Insecurity in Canada*, edited by Leah F. Vosko. Montréal, QC: McGill-Queen's University Press.

Waddington, Lisa, Mads Pedersen, and Maria Ventegodt Liisberg. 2016. "Get a Job! Active Labour Market Policies and Persons with Disabilities in Danish and European Union Policy." *Dublin University Law Journal* 39 (1): 1–24.

Waldschmidt, Anne, Andreas Sturm, Anemari Karačić, and Timo Dins. 2017. "Implementing the UN CRPD in European Countries: A Comparative Study on the Involvement of Organizations Representing Persons with Disabilities." In *The Changing Disability Policy System: Active Citizenship and Disability in Europe*, edited by R. Halvorsen, B. Hvinden, J. Bickenbach, D. Ferri, and A.M. Guillén Rodriguez. New York, NY: Routledge.

Wang, Peishi, Craig A. Michaels, and Mathew S. Day. 2011. "Stresses and Coping Strategies of Chinese Families with Children with Autism and Other Developmental Disabilities. *Journal of Autism and Developmental Disorders* 41 (6): 783–795. doi.10.1007/s10803-010-1099-3

Westbrook, Mary T., Varoe Legge, and Mark Pennay. 1993. "Attitudes Towards Disabilities in a Multicultural Society." *Social Sciences and Medicine* 36 (5): 615–623. doi.10.1016/0277-9536(93)90058-C

World Bank. 2014. "For Up to 800 Million Rural Poor, a Strong World Bank Commitment to Agriculture." Washington DC: World Bank. http://bit.ly/2MwFG7e

World Economic Forum. 2016. "The Future of Jobs: Employment Trends." Cologny, Switzerland: World Economic Forum. http://bit.ly/2MxwFea

World Health Organization. 2001 (May). "International Classification of Functioning, Disability and Health." Geneva, Switzerland: World Health Organization. http://bit.ly/2sMMapB

World Health Organization and World Bank. 2011. "World Report on Disability." Geneva, Switzerland: World Health Organization; Washington, DC: World Bank. http://bit.ly/2sOjgFA

Yap, Margaret, and Alison M. Konrad. 2009. "Gender and Racial Differentials in Promotions: Is There a Sticky Floor, a Mid-Level Bottleneck, or a Glass Ceiling?" *Industrial Relations* 64 (4): 593–619. doi:10.7202/038875ar

CHAPTER 12

Impact of Cash Transfers on Access to Employment of People with Disabilities

OLA ABU ALGHAIB
United Nations Partnership on the Rights of Persons with Disabilities

BACKGROUND: SOCIAL PROTECTION

The term "social protection" has evolved over recent decades as it has become increasingly popular. Social protection commonly refers to "public actions taken in response to levels of vulnerability, risk, and deprivation, which are deemed socially unacceptable within a given polity or society" (Conway, de Haan, and Norton 2000: 7). Owing to its ambiguity, the term remains confusing (Devereux and Sabates-Wheeler 2004: 5), presenting a danger of being used with different definitions in mind. As Conway, de Haan, and Norton explain, understanding of the term varies "between definitions which focus on the nature of the deprivations and problems addressed, and those which focus on the policy instruments used to address them; and between those which take a conceptual as opposed to a pragmatic approach to the task" (2000: 21).

There is no universal consensus on the precise definition and objectives of social protection. As a result, understanding the emergence of the social protection paradigm, as well as the conceptual frameworks and their philosophical underpinnings, has important implications in assessing social protection programs.

Norton, Conway, and Foster (2001) explain that social protection addresses the vulnerabilities and deprivation of the poorest citizens and, additionally, provides security to the nonpoor by protecting them from potential shocks in the future. Social protection may encompass governmental or nongovernmental action. The authors elucidate various rationales for developing social protection as a policy field, including social justice, equity, and protection from risks.

The International Labour Organization (ILO) and the World Bank, two key players in shaping international social protection policy, have distinct definitions of social protection. The ILO defines social protection as the "provision of benefits to households and individuals through public or collective arrangements to protect against low or declining living standards" (Devereux and Sabates-Wheeler 2004: 5). As Barrientos explains, this definition encapsulates the concept of social protection generally held by developed countries: social insurance (i.e., "contributory programs covering life-course and work-related contingencies") and social assistance ("consisting of tax-financed programs addressing poverty and vulnerability") (2014: 2–3). The World Bank defines social protection as "public measures intended to assist individuals, households, and communities in managing income risks in order to reduce vulnerability and downward fluctuations in incomes, improve consumption smoothing and enhancing equity" (Devereux and Sabates-Wheeler 2004: 5).

Critics such as Standing (2008) argue that social protection terminology has advanced in response to globalization and the restructuring of the labor market. Meanwhile, de Haan and Warmerdam (2014) warn of the aid industry becoming marked by fads, somewhat controlled by political changes in donor countries and changes in Europe in the early 2010s. Nonetheless, de Haan and Warmerdam maintain that social protection itself is no fad but an integral aspect of sustainable development, a position endorsed in this section.

Barrientos argues that a "proper understanding of social protection needs to go beyond an institutional approach and consider underlying development foundations" (2014: 9). However, the underlying theoretical basis for social protection is rarely discussed in the literature (Barrientos and Hulme 2009). To provide a sound basis for analysis in this research, it is contended that policy frameworks and their related programs (including cash transfer programs) "need to be grounded in theories of economic and social development" (Barrientos and Hulme 2009: 18). To this end, Munro (2008) identifies three traditional sources for justifications for social protection: human rights principles (mainly economic and social rights), market failure and unexpected risks, and needs-based principles.

In this chapter, we adopt Devereux and Sabates-Wheeler's (2004) understanding of social protection, which is grounded in a vision of policy provisions designed to target pro-poor growth; governance structures accountable and receptive to all citizens, rich and poor; and an approach to development based on social justice principles. Emerging from a broader conceptualization of vulnerability, which takes into consideration structural inequalities, this constitutes the Transformative Social Protection approach.

INTRODUCTION

The past few years have brought more attention to addressing disability in social protection programs (Schneider, Waliuya, Munsanjie, and Swartz 2011). It is, therefore, essential to assess and critically evaluate social protection policies and programs and evaluate the extent to which these provide just and effective remedies, particularly to persons people with disabilities (PWDs).

Though social protection has grown to include a variety of approaches—job training, job search and placement, microfinance, community driven development, and nonwork-related benefits—to support income generation, cash transfer remains a cornerstone of disability benefits (Grosh, del Ninno, Tesliuc, and Ouerghi 2008). If intended to empower people, social protection should generally be delivered based on the demands of citizens with entitlements rather than as charitable "handouts" to beneficiaries (Devereux and Sabates-Wheeler 2004).

In this chapter, we focus on cash transfers, a social protection program that has historically been used to support PWDs and can generate work disincentives. We present different modalities of disability benefit in high-income countries (HICs) in Europe and various low- and middle-income countries (LMICs). There are several debates about the advantages and disadvantages of different cash transfer modalities, including their equity and cost effectiveness. This chapter considers whether these pros and cons have particular salience for PWDs, as well as for disability benefits, and presents the findings of a literature review that examined the impact of cash transfers on the economic independence of PWDs living in LMICs.

Prior to the international adoption of the United Nations Convention on Persons with Disabilities (CRPD), the disability movement hesitated to advocate strongly for social protection, fearing that social protection programs targeting PWDs would generate work disincentives, undermining the capacity of PWDs to achieve economic independence and have a fair share in the labor market. However, the movement's views on social protection have significantly changed over the past decade, as evidenced by its strong endorsement of the International Disability Alliance (Swedish International Development Cooperation Agency 2014) in the report issued by the UN Special Rapporteur on the Rights of Persons with Disabilities (2015). The research argues that well-designed social protection programs are a crucial means of combating poverty and promoting independence, inclusion, and participation of PWDs in a sustainable manner (United Nations 2015). In many respects, this research has helped to shift perceptions on the potential of social protection programs, now recognized as an important means to support PWDs in becoming active participants in the economy and society.

In summary, although cash transfers play an important role in supporting PWDs, the majority of studies examined suggest that in isolation, they are not expected to solve the welfare problem for this population. The welfare of PWDs is equally affected by other disability-related policies and development interventions.

CASH TRANSFER PROGRAMS AND PEOPLE WITH DISABILITIES

A growing mass of research showing disproportionately higher poverty rates among PWDs (Banks, Kuper, and Pokack 2017; Braithwaite and Mont 2008; Mactaggart et al. 2018; Mitra et al. 2017; Mont and Cuong 2011; Palmer 2011; Tareque, Begum, and Saito 2014; Trani and Loeb 2012) has obliged countries to provide social protection to poor PWDs and their households (World Health Organization and World Bank 2011: 11). Article 28 of the CRPD clearly mandates the provision of social protection and cash transfers to ensure PWDs receive the basic support they need to meet at least the lowest acceptable standard of living. States have been asked to commit to social protection for PWDs rather than simply having it as a "policy option" (Barrientos and Hulme 2009). To date, social protection programs for PWDs in LMICs have largely been designed to respond to severe income poverty. However, the potential of these programs to empower PWDs in obtaining gainful employment to achieve economic independence is receiving increased attention (United Nations 2015).

The main design concerns for cash transfers include the frameworks for selecting recipients, payment modalities, and implementing bodies. Additional challenges include ensuring allocation of the right benefit levels and establishing suitable targeting mechanisms (World Food Programme 2011). When reviewing current social protection (mainly cash transfer) schemes regarding disability, five separate issues must be considered in relation to their design and implementation levels (Table 1).

As evident in Table 1, the main potential barriers for PWDs in taking up cash transfers are inaccessibility (of the environment and systems); negative attitudes; absence of protective legal frameworks; preconditions for receiving benefits, such as school attendance; and limited access to information about the availability of and eligibility for the program (Gooding and Marriott 2009). Additionally, applying a traditional means-testing assessment, with an income-based poverty line for eligibility, and allocating fixed benefits to all beneficiaries may not reflect the real levels of the needs of PWDs, particularly because most PWDs face additional disability-related costs and needs (Palmer et al. 2015). Mitra et al. (2017) estimate the additional costs to be as high as one third of the average wage.

Hence, for social protection to be more inclusive and effective in encouraging PWDs to participate in the labor force, the existing eligibility criteria and assessment mechanisms need to be revised (Gooding and Marriott 2009). A one-size-fits-all assessment and eligibility process may cause injustice by including only some PWDs. Moreover, determining eligibility for and the adequacy of cash benefits without considering the extra disability-related costs and needs, either in the means tests or the awarded benefit amounts, could create disparities in the level of impact for recipients with and without disabilities (Palmer 2011). What may be adequate for nondisabled persons will probably not be adequate for PWDs. Mitra et al. (2017) show that extra disability-related costs and needs further vary substantially by disability type and by country. Without adequate funds to cover additional disability-related costs and unmet needs, PWDs may not have the resources available for job search and associated costs. Furthermore, a traditional income-based poverty line for benefit eligibility can discourage labor market participation because a new source of income can cause PWDs to lose their means-tested benefits completely.

Approaches to Disability Benefits In OECD Countries

Almost all European countries provide a range of public assistance to PWDs. The main objectives of existing schemes are to ensure social inclusion and promote the economic prospects of PWDs, and/or compensate for the additional

TABLE 1
Policy Considerations Related to Cash Transfer Program Design for People with Disabilities

Issues	Considerations and Challenges
Targeting and eligibility in mainstream and disability-specific schemes	• Social protection programs for PWDs rely mainly on national definitions of disability, based mostly on impairment from a medical perspective. • PWDs are not a homogeneous group: They differ in disability types and the levels and nature of their needs; this makes targeting remarkably challenging in design and implementation. • In most LMICs, access of PWDs to cash transfers is restricted to those who meet the poverty criteria. The means-tested tools designed to determine household income levels tend to either overlook the extra cost of disability or only cursorily assess a PWD's personal and environmental factors influencing that cost. • Eligibility for covering expenses related to rehabilitation or assistive devices, often cited as the greatest need in this area, may also be subject to means testing, which deprives many PWDs and increases their risk of falling into poverty through having to bear those costs. • Conditional cash transfers linked to children's school attendance are not always accessible for families of PWDs; as such, children with disabilities have limited access to education.
Disability assessment	• In addition to the means-testing assessment, PWDs must prove their disability to be eligible for benefits. Many countries rely mainly on a medical assessment performed by doctors, with no consideration of the person's functioning. PWDs are considered eligible if diagnosed with a qualifying medical condition or if their determined percentage of disability meets a predetermined threshold. • Limited administrative and technical capacities and corruption in this process may often lead to targeting errors and high exclusion rates among applicants with disabilities.
Accessibility	• PWDs' access to social protection programs is highly influenced by the surrounding physical environment (public buildings, transportation, etc.), in addition to available, accessible means of communication and information. • Cash transfers are usually disbursed by bank transfer, and the accessibility of cash machines in many LMIC banks is very limited.
Adequacy of benefit levels	• The question of whether the allocated cash amounts are sufficiently large to meaningfully contribute to people's lives remains unresolved, yet this question has specific relevance for PWDs, given their additional disability-related costs. • In general, existing schemes for disability benefits are directed mainly toward securing minimum living standards, without consideration of the individual's current and future socioeconomic development and independence. • Disability benefits are usually designed based on a flat rate for all, with no consideration of the specific needs, such as the impairment level and disability type, of the eligible recipients with disabilities.
Promotion of work opportunities	• The design of many existing cash transfer schemes limits PWDs' chances to access the labor market because "inability to work" is a precondition for eligibility. This criterion generates disincentives to improve a person's economic well-being because benefits may be lost if an individual seeks employment or engages in any other livelihood initiative.

impairment-related costs or needs (Shima and Rodrigues 2009). Some benefits are contributory, based on a person's employment record linked to the country's social security system. However, several other benefits are noncontributory and do not require an employment record. Many European countries offer benefits such as social security disability pensions and social assistance disability allowances. Each scheme has its own eligibility and assessment system, based on the country's policy framework and regulations (Council of Europe 2003). In LMICs, PWDs face significant barriers to employment in the formal labor market, and they often resort to the informal sector or self-employment, therein barring them from benefiting from contributory social protection schemes.

Among the types of benefits, "general income replacement benefits" or "targeted benefits" supporting the costs of personal care and assistive devices are mainly paid in cash. Others, such as the Plan to Achieve Self-Support program in the United States, allow people to build up assets over the means test as a way of saving for assistive technology or other expenditures needed to enable work. Other benefits are provided in kind, such as covering personal assistant service hours at home or in the workplace. The final type is benefits that could provide a gateway to other benefits, such as receiving reduced rates for specific services (e.g., transportation), free access to certain public places (e.g., museums), and free parking (Shima and Rodrigues 2009).

In the United Kingdom, for example, the government has been engaged in a widespread program of "welfare reform" since 2010, aiming for "greater fairness to the welfare and pensions systems by making work pay and reinvigorating incentives to save for retirement … while protecting the most vulnerable—disabled people and pensioners" (UK Department for Work and Pensions 2013: 13). The ongoing reform of disability benefits aims to reduce the system's complications. In addition to substituting the disability living allowance with personal independence payments (PIPs), the reform combines many of the working-age allowances into one payment, termed universal credit, which began its staged implementation in 2016. According to the director of Disability Rights UK, managed migration to universal credit was set to take place in January 2019, affecting nearly 3 million people—a third (36%) of whom have a disability or long-term health condition (employment and support allowance [ESA] claimants). However, close to a million disabled people will still be worse off on universal credit by more than £200 a month despite the measures announced in the budget.

Burchardt (1999) classifies the UK's disability benefits into four categories: (1) compensatory benefits, such as industrial injury or war disablement benefits; (2) earnings replacement benefits, providing financial benefits, such as ESAs, to individuals unable to work because of a disability (Kuper et al. 2016); (3) extra costs benefits to support disability-related costs and needs; and (4) income to top up the means-tested mainstream benefits, such as income support and housing or council tax benefits to PWDs.

Table 2 summarizes the main disability-specific benefits available for adults with disabilities and/or their families in the United Kingdom.[1]

TABLE 2
Main Disability-Specific Benefits Supporting Independent Living of PWDs in the United Kingdom

Employment and Support Allowance (ESA) (Kuper et al. 2016)	Two types: • The contributory scheme, directed toward applicants who meet national insurance conditions* • The income-related scheme, available for applicants who fail to meet the contribution criteria but pass the means test;** applicants must undergo a work-capacity assessment to determine eligibility
Personal Independence Payment (PIP) (UK Department for Work and Pensions 2013)	This is a nonmeans-tested, noncontributory, and nontaxable benefit to support individuals of ages 16 through 64 in bearing the extra costs related to disability or health conditions. PIP is split into two schemes, one for daily life and the other for mobility. Applicants may be able to access one or both types. Applicants may be eligible for the daily life component if they need help with daily activities, such as eating or dressing, or with housekeeping, interaction, and communication with others, and making financial decisions. Claimants can also benefit from the mobility scheme if they need help with traveling or moving around. Each scheme is disbursed at two different rates—the standard rate and an enhanced rate—depending on the applicant's ability to perform activities of daily life and/or mobility level. Eligible applicants are classified as having "limited" or "severely limited" abilities, assessed by the person's ability to perform 12 key activities related to daily life and/or mobility needs during the day and at night. The accumulated score verifies access to either scheme and the prescribed rate. If accepted, beneficiaries are not obliged to reveal how they spend the money; however, approved applicants are regularly reassessed.
Universal Credit (UNISON)	This is a means-tested welfare benefit that the UK government introduced in 2013, aimed at gradually replacing the following means-tested benefits and tax credits: child tax credit, housing benefit, income-related ESA, income-based jobseeker's allowance, income support, parts of social funding, and working tax credit. Applicants are evaluated according to the work capability assessment to decide whether they are fit to work or have limited capacity to work. Based on this assessment, applicants are informed about the preconditions they must meet to receive universal credit.
Personal Budgets	These are means-tested direct payments, considered to be a central component of the UK's "personalization" agenda. The program is designed to give beneficiaries choice and control over the care services they need by directly managing their own support.
Access to Work	A self-directed support available for PWDs, the Access to Work program is a cash benefit designed to cover the additional impairment-related costs encountered by PWDs in employment, such as adaptations in the workplace, having a support worker, and traveling to work.

*To be eligible for a contributory ESA, the applicant must have made sufficient national insurance contributions in specific tax years.

**The applicant's needs (and those of her or his partner, if there is a partner) are compared with her or his available money (i.e., income and savings) to determine the income-related ESA rate. It can be paid on its own (if the claimant is not entitled to contributory ESA) or as a top up to contributory ESA (if the claimant is entitled). Income-related ESA can include amounts to help toward mortgage interest payments and other housing costs.

The variety of schemes provided for PWDs in the United Kingdom could serve their independent living needs in addition to securing a minimum income when they are unable to work. Eligibility for the non-means-tested PIP is not preconditioned on inability to work, unlike many cash transfer schemes in LMICs, which will be discussed in the next section.

The Academic Network of European Disability Experts' (ANED) 2009 report presented evidence on the policy design modalities of social protection in 21 European Union countries, developed between 2006 and 2008 (Shima and Rodrigues 2009). Its findings confirm that many European countries follow a twin-track approach to designing social protection policy, aiming to address the continuing risks of economic and social exclusion for PWDs.

The first track aims to ensure that PWDs are equally addressed in mainstream programs geared toward the entire population, such as contributory social pensions and means-tested social assistance programs. The second track comprises disability-specific benefits and services, aiming for economic empowerment of PWDs through gainful employment—for example, disability-related income support, deinstitutionalization, and direct payment schemes.

The ANED report indicates that many countries continue to focus mainly on poverty-related schemes, such as income support, with fewer programs aimed at labor force participation and social inclusion. However, some countries have achieved progress in enhancing empowerment of PWDs by shifting from the medical model to the social model in disability assessment systems, thereby paying more attention to functioning and work abilities than to physical limitations (Shima and Rodrigues 2009). In terms of supporting legislative frameworks, a significant number of anti-discrimination laws have been adopted in many European countries, with the intention of increasing PWDs' economic participation and social inclusion and supporting their equal access to care, education, employment, and financial support (Waddington and Lawson 2009).

ANED's report indicates that, despite the evident progress in focusing on disability in social protection policies, the specific needs of PWDs received the most emphasis rather than mainstreaming disability across all social protection programs and interventions. It also concludes that, despite all the implemented measures, many PWDs still suffer from poverty and inability to access needed services, owing to a lack of affordability, accessibility, and availability of supportive administrative and legal frameworks. Therefore, many PWDs in Europe continue to encounter a higher risk of economic dependence and social exclusion than nondisabled citizens (Shima and Rodrigues 2009).

Approaches to Disability Benefits and Transfers in LMICS

Disability grants are a form of targeted cash transfers in some LMICs. They are usually means-tested, noncontributory cash transfers provided for people of working age who are unable to work as a result of physical or mental disabilities

(Standing 2008). The payments are granted on a long- or short-term basis, depending on the eligibility criteria specified in each country.

The structure of disability benefits in LMICs differs from that in HICs, such as those in Europe. For example, while European countries typically combine contributory social protection schemes with complementary means-tested schemes for low-income people, only a few LMICs have contributory systems, and the operating structures of such systems have limited coverage, usually restricted to government employees and, more rarely, the private sector (Bastagli 2013). Contributory schemes are frequently inaccessible to PWDs in LMICs because a high percentage of them are likely to be unemployed, self-employed, or working in the informal sector (World Health Organization and World Bank 2011).

As indicated earlier, the available disability benefits are mainly directed toward poverty alleviation and are mostly restricted to PWDs assessed as unable to work. There are, however, some examples of benefits being directed to cover additional costs and needs of PWDs, such as rehabilitation, assistive devices, transportation, and personal caregiving. Linking such benefits to inability to work or poverty status varies among countries, but requiring a medical-based disability assessment is a predominant condition in most (Mitra, Posarac, and Vick 2013).

In the design of cash transfer programs in LMICs, considerable differences between targeted and mainstream programs were identified. Targeted programs mainly employ means-tested eligibility criteria. Most of the papers address targeted programs that focus on disability. Such programs are mostly limited to PWDs unable to work because they are poor (i.e., unable to afford the costs associated with job searching) or living with severe impairment. The programs provide monthly payments, with significant size variation identified among countries—for example, at the time of the respective studies, the transfers provided in Nepal (which currently scores 29.55 on Numbeo's Cost of Living Index) were US$1.20 per month, while those in South Africa and Brazil (which score 42.11 and 40.48, respectively, on the cost of living index) ranged from US$112 to US$154 per month.[2] However, some countries do have a targeted benefits that are not tied to the ability to work.

In Brazil, the Continuous Cash Benefit Program, which began in 1996, is the country's second largest noncontributory cash benefit program. It targets people ages 65 and over who are not working or are PWDs incapable of both working and living an independent life. Proof of family per capita income less than 25% of the minimum wage (below US$1 per day in December 2005) is also required. In 2005, around 2.1 million people were receiving benefits under this program, divided equally between PWDs and the elderly (Medeiros, Britto, and Soares 2008).

In contrast, mainstream programs target broader groups generally at risk of poverty. Some of the identified programs explicitly include PWDs among their targeted beneficiaries. There were fewer mainstream programs than targeted ones within the identified studies.

In Zambia, the District Cash Transfer Scheme, a mainstream program initiated by the government in 2003, includes disabled people. Its main goal is to decrease poverty levels in the poorest households. The scheme has adopted a unique participatory targeting system, applying three eligibility criteria to select recipients: being extremely needy, being incapacitated, and having no valuable assets (Schneider, Waliuya, Munsanje, and Swartz 2011).

From the existing data, there is weak evidence that mainstream programs systematically include PWDs among their targeted beneficiaries. This reinforces the four reasons advanced by Marriott and Gooding (2007: 29) to explain PWDs suffering barriers to access:

- low awareness and limited public information, physical inaccessibility, and bureaucracy
- means tests that may unfairly exclude disabled people who face high costs and unmet needs associated with disability
- conditions attached to transfers, such as school or health clinic attendance, that may exclude disabled people if these services are not accessible
- public works schemes that are likely to exclude disabled people unless special provisions are made

A study conducted by the ILO shows that access to and the coverage of existing schemes remain important concerns for PWDs, especially in remote areas.

The ILO investigated existing practices in relation to noncontributory cash transfer schemes in six LMICs: Argentina, Ethiopia, Ghana, Indonesia, Kyrgyzstan, and South Africa (Abu Alghaib and Wilm 2016). "Inability to work" was found to be the predominant eligibility criterion in Indonesia, Kyrgyzstan, and South Africa. Most of the existing schemes are means tested and involve some form of disability certificate and related assessment procedures. Available data indicate that the related complexity, or corruption, involved in such processes can limit PWDs' access to benefits.

IMPACT OF CASH TRANSFERS ON THE ECONOMIC INDEPENDENCE OF PWDS IN LMICS

Despite Article 28 of the CRPD confirming that PWDs in all countries have an equal right to social protection (Rohwerder 2014), access to social protection programs in LMICs falls far below PWDs' needs. Eight of the studies reviewed for this chapter related to barriers faced by PWDs in accessing social protection programs (Banks, Kuper, and Pokack 2017). In their 2016 systematic review, Banks, Kuper, and Pokack found that not all disability grants directed to PWDs were sufficient to protect or promote minimum living standards, let alone independent living. In Vietnam, for example, the cash transfers are insufficient to even cover the minimum daily food intakes of PWDs. Such evidence raises questions regarding the adequacy of social cash transfer amounts, whether household or targeted. Banks, Kuper, and Pokack (2017) highlight that social protection schemes often fail to cover the additional disability-related expenses—such as assistive devices, and medical and transport costs—which often impose a significant financial burden on households. Disability-associated costs can account for as much as 18% to 31% of total household income.

Hence, the main objective of our literature review was to assess evidence on how existing social protection programs affect access to services, economic independence, and social inclusion of PWDs in LMICs. Our review found moderate evidence that cash transfer programs in LMICs can improve PWDs' opportunities to access basic services, notably in healthcare. However, evidence on the impact of cash transfers on PWDs' education and employment opportunities is relatively weak. Additionally, coverage and benefit levels remain low, as most existing schemes are limited in resources and impact. Furthermore, none of the studies we identified presented evidence on the impact of cash transfers on PWDs' capacity to live independently.

The factors identified in the review as influencing impact can be summarized as follows:

- Most of the identified studies focus on targeted programs, where eligibility is limited to people with severe impairment who are unable to work or are living below a specified poverty threshold.
- The main indicated causes of limited coverage in existing schemes are limited funding, lack of awareness, failure to consider physical access, and bad administrative practices.
- In existing schemes, the complexity of disability assessment and basing it mainly on medical diagnosis creates an additional barrier to equal access for PWDs. There was little evidence of the adoption of homogeneous assessment criteria, which should consider the social context and properly balance the medical and social aspects affecting PWDs.
- In addition to disability assessment, means-tested entry requirements are seen by researchers as an exclusion factor because they mainly consider the potential recipient's income rather than her or his expenditures and unmet needs.

RECOMMENDATIONS

This chapter examined the need to consider specific issues of social protection policies when addressing economic empowerment of PWDs, focusing primarily on cash transfers. Based on the evidence presented, we offer the following recommendations for improving cash transfers:

- Recognize extra disability-related costs and needs when determining payment amounts.

- Adopt a more comprehensive assessment approach, including not restricting aid to PWDs based on medical assessments focusing on limitations rather than functioning.
- Recognize the heterogeneous nature of disability, allowing for flexibility in determining benefits and services based on a scale of options.

Holistic Policy Reform

Although cash transfers remain a cornerstone in supporting PWDs, this review suggests that such transfers, in isolation, are not expected to solve the welfare problem for PWDs. It is also important to consider other disability-related policies and development interventions that also affect the welfare of PWDs.

Noncontributory disability benefits play a central role in protecting PWDs who fail to earn a living because of age, severity of disability, or inaccessibility of the formal labor market, and in facilitating access to employment and other social services. Policy reforms should pay particular attention to finding the right balance between supporting engagement in employment and providing an adequate level of income security for PWDs. Future efforts to achieve more inclusive policies and programs should consider the following:

- *Legal frameworks.* There must be explicit obligations in terms of social protection for PWDs in national legislative and regulatory frameworks. The CRPD provides a clear direction for the scope of social protection for PWDs (Articles 16, 19, 23, 24, 27, and 28). Any social protection system should follow and be assessed against the principles of the CRPD, particularly with regard to nondiscrimination, participation, inclusion, equal opportunities, accessibility, and other criteria.
- *Coverage and design.* The design of social protection schemes for PWDs needs to respond to the heterogeneity (in terms of types of disabilities, location, age, gender, and other factors) of PWDs and the resultant diversity of their needs. Social protection for PWDs needs to extend beyond poverty alleviation or reduction: additional support through disability-specific schemes is required to effectively address additional disability-related costs and needs and promote greater participation, autonomy, and choice of PWDs. Though the scope of this chapter is limited to cash transfer schemes (just one of a variety of social protection programs that try to create greater participation for PWDs), inclusivity in social protection programs can still be improved on a holistic level. The design of social protection strategies for PWDs must consider environmental factors and challenges (e.g., lack of availability of services). Linkages need to be developed between social protection strategies and schemes and other relevant services (e.g., rehabilitation and assistive devices) to promote access.
- *Access and eligibility determination.* There is a specific need to review global knowledge and experience on the issue of eligibility determination for

social protection programs in LMICs. There is also a need for understanding the implications of the definition of disability used for determining eligibility (i.e., who is considered disabled in a country, which types of disabilities are included) for access to and use of social protection programs for PWDs. Resources, tools, and technical support are necessary to guide countries when they choose to adopt the disability determination mechanisms of the International Classification of Functioning, Disability, and Health framework. Additionally, there is a need for a deeper understanding of the differentiation between mainstream and disability-specific schemes in terms of eligibility and impact in the lives of PWDs.

- *Coordination and linkages between schemes and services*. The links between noncontributory and contributory disability-specific schemes must be established and strengthened, as must effective linkages between cash benefits, benefits in kind, access to services, and programs aimed at disability inclusion in employment, without creating negative disincentives.
- *Monitoring and evaluation (M&E)*. Global poverty monitoring programs continue to leave out disability in their tracking and reporting. There is a need for better disaggregation of data within programs, information management systems, and M&E to track the inclusion of PWDs in mainstream programs and measures to provide greater access to the labor market (e.g., public–private partnerships). A constant review of assessment tools and their compliance with the ILO Social Protection Floors Recommendation is required to ensure that PWDs receive adequate support. The participation of PWDs through their representative organizations in all processes of design, M&E, and policy reform of a social protection system is a basic prerequisite for ensuring inclusive design, practice, and impact. Additionally, adequate resources are required to ensure the provision of tools and measures for collecting and processing complaints in a way that is simple, effective, and accessible to PWDs.
- *Evidence and research*. More evidence is needed on how social protection in LMICs can be more inclusive of PWDs, including identifying what works in existing programs that are designed to be inclusive and piloting new interventions to test inclusive approaches. There is a need to identify ways of making better use of collected data on disability within social protection programs to promote more effective program and benefit design and to ensure that benefits and services better match the needs of PWDs. In addition, more evidence is needed on indicators of social inclusion and how they relate to social protection, and further research is required to enhance cost methodologies and to ensure adequate and sustainable financing of social protection benefits for PWDs.

CONCLUSION

The evidence presented in this chapter indicates that social protection strategies for PWDs in HICs are more pro-employment than in LMICs. For instance, the UK schemes neatly illustrate the range of benefits and services provided to PWDs within a twin-track social protection framework, offering "economic protection" and addressing "social vulnerability." Some schemes are responsive to economic risks and vulnerabilities and are either contributory or noncontributory but means tested, such as the ESA (Kuper et al. 2016). Meanwhile, many others address other forms of disability-specific vulnerabilities—"social vulnerability" under the Transformative Social Protection approach—including payments to cover disability-related services and additional costs and needs, such as the PIP and the personal budgets schemes.

Personal budget schemes recognize the essential need for complementing local-level services and PIP cash payments by supporting disability-related additional costs and needs (Disability Rights UK, no date). This is considered the route to achieving independent living based on the social model of disability. It assists PWDs in living an active life and participating in society, and it enables them to achieve their objectives by personalizing their care and providing support planning. Via the personal budget, PWDs are empowered to live the life they choose, and the whole process is centered on their personal aspirations and preferences.

Conversely, many LMICs retain the narrow safety-net conception of social protection for addressing disability. Though a few countries are moving toward a more comprehensive approach that looks beyond poverty alleviation, disability benefits are mostly still restricted to PWDs assessed as being unable to work.

For employment relations professionals in HICs and LMICs, it is important to understand the specific barriers and challenges that PWDs face in the country of operation and assess what gaps can be filled on a private, or nonstate, level to improve inclusivity and access for PWDs. Moreover, employment relations professionals with multi-country operations should consider how their policies and frameworks regarding PWDs can be adjusted for different countries rather applying the same policy globally.

ACKNOWLEDGMENTS

The author and editor would like to thank Daniel Mont, co-president and co-founder, Center for Inclusive Policy; Sophie Mitra, professor of economics, Fordham University; and Ariel Avgar, associate professor of labor relations, Cornell University ILR School, for their review of this manuscript.

ENDNOTES

[1] The main source of information is the homepage of the Department for Work and Pensions (http://bit.ly/2uCBpa5), and Disability Rights UK factsheets published in 2014.

[2] Numbeo's Cost of Living Index (excluding rent) is a relative indicator of consumer goods prices, including groceries, restaurants, transportation, and utilities. The index doesn't include accommodation expenses such as rent or mortgage. If a city has a Cost of Living Index of 120, it means Numbeo estimates it is 20% more expensive than New York, excluding rent (http://bit.ly/2HYN3E8).

REFERENCES

Abu Alghaib, O., and S. Wilm. 2016. "Building Social Protection Floors for Persons with Disabilities: Lessons Learned from Non-Contributory Programmes in Argentina, Ethiopia, Ghana, Indonesia, Kyrgyzstan and South Africa." Geneva, Switzerland: International Labour Organization.

Banks, M.L., H. Kuper, and S. Pokack. 2017. "Poverty and Disability in Low and Middle Income Countries: A Systematic Review." *PLoS One* 12(12): e0189996.

Barrientos, A. 2014. "Social Protection." In *International Development: Ideas, Experience, and Prospects*, edited by B. Currie-Alder, R. Kanbur, D.M. Malone, and R. Medhora, Chapter 11. Oxford, UK: Oxford University Press.

Barrientos, A., and D. Hulme. 2009. "Social Protection for the Poor and Poorest in Developing Countries: Reflections on a Quiet Revolution: Commentary." *Oxford Development Studies* 37 (4): 439–456.

Bastagli, F. 2013. "Feasibility of Social Protection Schemes in Developing Countries." Brussels, Belgium: European Union. doi:10.2861/11066. http://bit.ly/2uAEZl6

Braithwaite, J., and D. Mont. 2008. "Disability and Poverty: A Survey of World Bank Poverty Assessments and Implications." *Alter—European Journal of Disability Research/Revue Européenne de Recherche sur le Handicap* 3 (3): 219–232.

Burchardt, T. 1999 (Jun.). "The Evolution of Disability Benefits in the UK: Re-Weighting the Basket." LSE STICERD Research Paper No. CASE026. London, UK: London School of Economics. http://bit.ly/2xEPoOm

Conway, T., A. de Haan, and A. Norton, eds. 2000. "Social Protection: New Directions of Donor Agencies." Paper for the DFID-ODI Inter-Agency Seminar on Social Protection. http://bit.ly/2I2vpzt

Council of Europe. 2003. "Assessing Disability in Europe—Similarities and Differences." Report by the Working Group on the Assessment of Person-Related Criteria for Allowances and Personal Assistance for People with Disabilities. Strasbourg, France: Council of Europe Publishing.

de Haan, A., and W. Warmerdam. 2014. "The Politics of Aid Revisited: A Review of Evidence on State Capacity and Elite Commitment." In *The Politics of Inclusive Development: Interrogating the Evidence*, edited by S. Hickey, K. Sen, and B. Bukenya. Oxford, UK: Oxford University Press.

Devereux, S., and R. Sabates-Wheeler. 2004. "Transformative Social Protection." IDS Working Paper 232. Sussex, UK: Institute of Development Studies. https://uni.cf/2xCWJ0T

Disability Rights UK. No date. "Social Care and Personal Budgets." http://bit.ly/2LJk49j

Gooding, K., and A. Marriott. 2009. "Including Persons with Disabilities in Social Cash Transfer Programmes in Developing Countries." *Journal of International Development* 21 (5): 685–698.

Grosh, M., C. del Ninno, E. Tesliuc, and A. Ouerghi. 2008. "For Protection and Promotion: The Design and Implementation of Effective Safety Nets." Washington, DC: World Bank.

Kuper, H., M. Walsham, F. Myamba, S. Mesaki, I. Mactaggart, M. Banks, and K. Blanchet. 2016. "Social Protection for People with Disabilities in Tanzania: A Mixed Methods Study." *Oxford Development Studies* 44 (4): 441–457.

Mactaggart, I., L. Banks, H. Kuper, G.V.S. Murthy, J. Sagar, J. Oye, and S. Polack. 2018. "Livelihood Opportunities Amongst Adults With and Without Disabilities in Cameroon and India: A Case Control Study." *PloS One* 13 (4): e0194105.

Medeiros, M., T. Britto, and F. V. Soares. 2008. "Targeted Cash Transfer Programmes in Brazil: BPC and the Bolsa Familia." Working Paper 46. Brasilia, Brazil. International Policy Centre for Inclusive Growth.

Marriott, A., and K. Gooding. 2007 (Jul.). "Social Assistance and Disability in Developing Countries." London, UK: UK Department for International Development and Sightsavers International.

Mitra, S., M. Palmer, H. Kim, D. Mont, and N. Groce. 2017. "Extra Costs of Living with a Disability: A Review and Agenda for Research." *Disability and Health Journal* 10 (4): 475–484.

Mitra, S., A. Posarac, and B. Vick. 2013. "Disability and Poverty in Developing Countries: A Multidimensional Study." *World Development* 41: 1–18.

Mont, D., and N.V. Cuong. 2011. "Disability and Poverty in Vietnam." *The World Bank Economic Review* 25 (2): 323–359.

Munro, L.T. 2008. "Risks, Needs and Rights: Compatible or Contradictory Bases for Social Protection." In *Social Protection for the Poor and Poorest: Concepts, Policies and Politics,* edited by A. Barrientos and D. Hulme, pp. 27–46. London, UK: Palgrave Macmillan.

Norton, A., T. Conway, and M. Foster. 2001 (Feb.). "Social Protection Concepts and Approaches: Implications for Policy and Practice in International Development." Working Paper 143. London, UK: Centre for Aid and Public Expenditure. http://bit.ly/2HWuAbk

Palmer, M. 2011. "Disability and Poverty: A Conceptual Review." *Journal of Disability Policy Studies* 21 (4): 210–218.

Palmer M., N. Groce, D. Mont, O. Nguyen, and S. Mitra. 2015. "The Economic Lives of People with Disabilities in Vietnam." *PLoS One* 10 (7): 1–16.

Rohwerder, B. 2014 (Jan.). "Disability Inclusion in Social Protection." GSDRC Helpdesk Research Report 1069. Birmingham, UK: GSDRC. http://bit.ly/31vE18l

Schneider, M., W. Waliuya, J. Munsanje, and L. Swartz, L. 2011. "Reflections on Including Disability in Social Protection Programmes." *IDS Bulletin* 42 (6): 38–44.

Shima, I., and R. Rodrigues. 2009. "The Implementation of EU Social Inclusion and Social Protection Strategies in European Countries with Reference to Equality for Disabled People." Report Prepared for the Academic Network of European Disability Experts. http://bit.ly/2I0Z5wM

Standing, G. 2008. "How Cash Transfers Promote the Case for Basic Income." *Basic Income Studies* 3 (1): 1–30.

Swedish International Development Cooperation Agency. 2014. "Disability Rights in the Middle East and North Africa." Stockholm, Sweden: Swedish International Development Cooperation Agency.

Tareque, M.I., S. Begum, and Y. Saito. 2014. "Inequality in Disability in Bangladesh." *PLoS One* 9 (7): e103681.

Trani, J.F., and M. Loeb. 2012. "Poverty and Disability: A Vicious Circle? Evidence from Afghanistan and Zambia." *Journal of International Development* 24: S19–S52.

UK Department for Work and Pensions. 2013. "Department of Welfare and Pension Reform: DWP's Welfare Reform Agenda Explained." London, UK: UK Department for Work and Pensions.

UNISON. No date. "Universal Credit and Other Benefits." London, UK: UNISON. http://bit.ly/2LHDJGN

United Nations. 2015. "Special Rapporteur on the Rights of Persons with Disabilities, No. A/70/297*." Geneva, Switzerland: United Nations Human Rights Office of the High Commissioner. http://bit.ly/2HZIolB

Waddington, L., and A. Lawson. 2009. "Disability and Non-Discrimination Law in the European Union. An Analysis of Disability Discrimination Law Within and Beyond the Employment Field." Brussels, Belgium: Publications Office of the European Union. http://bit.ly/2I5HcwO

World Food Programme. 2011. "Cash Transfer Feasibility Study in Nusa Tenggara Timur and Nusa Tenggara Barat." Rome, Italy: United Nations World Food Programme and OXFAM. http://bit.ly/2uwDnJn

World Health Organization and World Bank. 2011. "World Report on Disability." Geneva, Switzerland: World Health Organization. http://bit.ly/2I6fr7J

Conclusion

The Way Forward: Implications for Labor and Employment Professionals and the Future Workplace

Susanne M. Bruyère
Sara VanLooy
Cornell University

Work is love made visible.
—Kahlil Gibran

Work brings economic security, financial independence, and most important, dignity and an opportunity to contribute to the greater society in a meaningful way. This Labor and Employment Relations Association 2019 research volume has focused on employment and people with disabilities, in the belief that each person has a right to work. This fundamental premise guides the regulatory environment surrounding equitable access to work, as well as access to education, voting, housing, transportation, and commercial establishments. The premise is further evident in human resources policies designed to ensure that employment nondiscrimination and affirmative action regulations permeate workplace practices in the daily work environment, including for people with disabilities.

KEY THEMES ACROSS THIS VOLUME

Across the 12 chapters of this volume, we have covered a wide array of topics relative to employment and disability. This concluding chapter summarizes some of the key findings, highlighting themes that have emerged through the distinct focus of each chapter. The cross-cutting themes that we will highlight here are the following:

- the impact of regulations on both workplace practice and employment outcomes for people with disabilities more broadly
- how workplace disability-inclusive policies and practices can contribute to improvements in the employment experience of people with disabilities
- how increased attention to target populations of people with disabilities who are currently significantly underrepresented in the US labor force can potentially improve access to a previously largely untapped labor pool and thereby also improve overall disability employment participation rates
- how regulatory requirements, as well as emerging workforce-development and employer-led initiatives, offer promise of long overdue improvements

in labor force participation and true workplace inclusion of individuals with disabilities, both in the United States and globally

Implications offered by our authors to employment and labor relations practitioners are also briefly summarized

Impact of Regulatory Frameworks

Several of the chapters in this volume focus on the importance and impact of regulatory frameworks on employment outcomes for individuals with disabilities, both at national and international levels. Employment disparities for people with disabilities is a worldwide issue, contributing to entrenched income and poverty inequities, and attendant imbalances in access to education, housing, and healthcare.

Two chapters in this volume focus on global disability policy. Although these chapters appear later in the volume, we are starting with this policy here, as the balance of the remaining discussion focuses largely on US employers and the American workplace experience.

In Chapter 11, "Global Perspectives on Employment for People with Disabilities," Matthew Saleh explores issues of employment for people with disabilities from a global perspective, providing an overview of thematic barriers, international regulatory frameworks, and contextual factors at regional and national levels that influence employment outcomes for people with disabilities. Looking across country-specific boundaries, this chapter assists the reader in gaining an appropriately broad perspective of how regulatory frameworks sit within national and regional contexts influenced by local economic conditions, as well as the number, size, and type of employers in the country. Saleh explores how these factors moderate the practical impact of regulatory efforts and how they may mediate employers' responses to their legal responsibilities toward current and prospective employees with disabilities. The author describes in detail the collective global benefit of attending to employment disparities for people with disabilities, from not only a human rights perspective but also from ameliorating the aggregate negative social and economic consequences of discriminatory hiring policies, which lead to lost labor access, high benefit levels, and health and social inequalities. Saleh offers some of the economic and workforce development provisions of the United Nations Convention on the Rights of Persons with Disabilities as appropriate guideposts to address needed country-level structural changes in regulations and employer practices.

Ola Abu Alghaib, in Chapter 12, "Impact of Cash Transfers on Access to Employment of People with Disabilities," provides a perspective complementary to Saleh's broader focus on global regulations across various types of employment legislation, with a laser emphasis on cash transfer programs across countries of different income levels. Abu Alghaib explores existing cash transfer programs and practices in high-income and low- and middle-income countries that allow people with disabilities to participate in gainful employment, using country-specific examples to trace how often, particularly in many low- and middle-income countries, disability benefits are still restricted to people with disabilities who are assessed as being unable to work. The chapter discusses the significant drawbacks of this continuing "safety net" perspective of social protection legislation and programs and contrasts this philosophy with policies in other (mostly higher-income) countries that are moving toward a more comprehensive approach that looks beyond poverty alleviation as the sole purpose for such programs. Abu Alghaib advocates for a broadened perspective of social protection legislation that looks beyond an exclusive focus on poverty alleviation toward a more comprehensive approach that addresses social vulnerability while also offering economic protections and incentives to move the needle toward improvements in employment participation.

This theme of unintended consequences and the sometimes shorted-sightedness of public policy resonates within Chapter 1. In "US Employment and Disability Policy Framework: Competing Legislative Priorities, Challenges, and Strategies," Matthew Saleh, Thomas Golden, and Ellice Switzer trace the 100-year trajectory of US disability policy around employment of people with disabilities. The authors discuss how the employment status of people with disabilities continues to lag woefully behind that of nondisabled Americans, even though there is extensive regulation in the United States to protect the employment rights of people with disabilities and provide employment supports. Saleh and his co-authors attribute this persistent disparity in part to the design of public policies meant to support individuals with disabilities and facilitate employment, which contradict and conflict with each other. The authors describe how these competing priorities might be partly responsible for incomplete efforts to end employment gaps and segregated/exclusionary employment practices, and they conclude that data-driven decisions should point the way toward policies and programs that definitively drive desired employment outcomes for people with disabilities. However, they also establish that, setting policy aside, the critical initial step in getting people with disabilities into the workplace lies with the employer. Public and private employers alike can take a more proactive role in better understanding their own responsibilities under the array of potentially applicable pieces of federal legislation.

This leads us to the second major theme that emerges from these chapters: workplace and human resources policies and practices, employment nondiscrimination, and workplace disability inclusion.

Workplace Policies and Practices

Several chapters focus on the relevance of employer policies and practices in improving employment outcomes and the employment experience of people with disabilities. The regulatory environment theme re-emerges as a common thread throughout these chapters, with many of the authors referencing the significant impact that the Americans with Disabilities Act of 1990 (ADA) Title I employment provisions have had on contemporary US employment policy and practices. These chapters cover specific topics such as the reasonable accommodation process, disability disclosure, the impact of a unionized workplace in employment outcomes for individuals with disabilities, and how federal agency employment disability nondiscrimination enforcement administrative data can inform our understanding of workplace climate—specifically, the harassment experiences of individuals with disabilities.

Protections offered by Title I of the ADA (and for federal sector employers, Section 501 of the Rehabilitation Act) have been the essential regulatory framework creating the opportunity for workers with disabilities to access accommodations when needed. In Chapter 4, "Creating an Accommodating Workplace: Encouraging Disability Disclosure and Managing Reasonable Accommodation Requests," Sarah von Schrader, LaWanda Cook, and Wendy Strobel Gower focus on the reasonable accommodation requirements of the ADA. The authors use discussion and observations taken from the case notes of US Equal Opportunity Commission employment discrimination charges to illustrate how accommodations are meant to allow people with disabilities to approach their work differently in order to overcome barriers presented by the functional limitations of a disability. They distill their findings to a few key critical workplace practices that facilitate effective workplace disability accommodations, and they discuss at length the importance of disability disclosure in the accommodation process. This is significant because when employers are aware of workers' disabilities and willing to provide needed accommodations, the individual, her or his colleagues, and the organization as a whole tend to benefit.

Mason Ameri, Mohammad Ali, Lisa Schur, and Douglas Kruse, in Chapter 3, "Disability and the Unionized Workplace," focus our attention on unionized workplaces, which are subject to the National Labor Relations Act as well as the ADA, and examine how related requirements around workplace policies and practices can impact individuals with disabilities. Their chapter addresses the dearth of related information in the literature, using new data to examine trends in unionization, union wage effects, and accommodation requests by disability status, and it explores how unionized workplaces may facilitate (or impede) employment of workers with disabilities. Results suggest that unions may indeed support employees with disabilities in exercising their rights to workplace accommodations under the ADA. The authors' exploratory data reveal that both union coverage and disability status increase the likelihood of requesting accommodations, supporting the idea that unions can amplify the voice of individuals to exercise their rights. However, the results also reveal that while unions appear to help workers with disabilities in the United States, unionized positions are becoming less available to workers with disabilities. The union rate for employees with disabilities in the United States declined more rapidly than for employees without disabilities over the period from 2009 through 2017. The authors speculate that the decline could be attributable to employer concerns following the ADA amendments in 2008, which may have made employers particularly anxious about hiring workers with disabilities in the early stages of the economic recovery because they may have perceived these workers as riskier.

In Chapter 5, "Unwelcoming Workplaces: Bullying and Harassment of Employees with Disabilities," LaWanda Cook, Sarah von Schrader, Valerie Malzer, and Jennifer Mimno assist the reader in looking beyond the regulatory environment's influence to explore the impact of workplace culture on the experience of employees with disabilities. The authors specifically focus on how bullying and other forms of harassment create negative work environments for individuals with disabilities, resulting in significant, damaging consequences for employees and organizations alike. The authors cite existing literature on disability-related workplace bullying and harassment, which suggests that employees with disabilities often feel that their employing organizations are not only unwelcoming but openly hostile toward them. Cook and her co-authors use data from the Equal Opportunity Employment Commission's Integrated Mission System to examine reported incidents of workplace harassment described in case notes from verified charges. Results of this analysis present a disturbing portrayal of the specific types of harassment that people with disabilities experience.

The overarching discussion on the theme of workplace policies and practices that support key regulatory requirements through policies impacting the day-to-day experiences of individuals with disabilities in the workplace is continued in the next broad theme: how these issues affect specific populations.

Access to Previously Underrepresented Populations

Although this volume focuses on areas in need of attention for improving employment outcomes for people with all kinds of disabilities, several targeted disability areas merited a heightened focus: veterans with disabilities, those with mental health disabilities, and youth with disabilities. An additional chapter focuses on hiring initiatives targeting individuals with autism, but we reserve a discussion of that for the section on innovations and initiatives that follows.

In Chapter 6, "Welcoming (All) Veterans into Our Workplaces: The Employment of Veterans with Disabilities," Hannah Rudstam, James Whitcomb, and Lorin Obler provide a compelling overview of the dilemma of re-integrating veterans into civilian society post service, along with a discussion of the significant employment challenges that confront returning veterans, especially those with disabilities. With a quarter of returning veterans who have served in conflicts since 1990 having acquired disabilities, it is a most critical area for focus. The statistics presented by the authors substantiate the disparities in employment and resulting poverty these veterans are facing. The authors provide a list of ten workplace practices that can facilitate success in the hiring, retention, advancement, and inclusion of veterans with disabilities, which are consistent with those identified in other chapters, more generally focused across disability types.

The National Institute of Mental Health estimates that almost one in five Americans experiences a mental health issue at some point in his or her life. In Chapter 8, "Mental Illness and Employment: Understanding a Major Disability Population in the US Workforce," Hannah Rudstam, Hsiao-Ying (Vicki) Chang, and Hassan Enayati bring in a focus on how the prevalence rates of mental health issues both in the United States and globally, as well as the continuing significant related stigma, make this a critical area of focus for employers. Both an organization's applicant pool and workforce can be impacted, and employers must proactively develop the resources and workplace educational awareness necessary to address the factors impacting worker well-being and overall organizational effectiveness. The authors offer an array of proven good practices that can assist in mitigating the stigma that may discourage people from disclosing their need for an intervention or an accommodation that can assist in getting into the job and being able to maintain employment and thrive.

The third underrepresented population highlighted is the focus of Chapter 7, "Youth with Disabilities: A Human Resource for the 21st-Century Workforce," by Thomas Golden, Kelly Clark, and Catherine Fowler. The authors focus on youth because this group represents a significant portion of the population of individuals with disabilities in the United States and worldwide, and to date this population has not been adequately prepared to enter the workforce. Preparing youth with disabilities to join the competitive workforce is not exclusively the responsibility of the education system or local educational institutions but rather, as the authors emphasize, requires partnerships across community stakeholders, especially employers. Employers can contribute to the better preparation of youth for employment by collaborating with schools, agencies, and other organizations to provide work-based learning opportunities for youth and young adults with disabilities. The authors point out that research confirms that early work experience, including job shadowing, internships, paid employment, apprenticeships, and job sampling, is one of the most frequently identified predictors of post-school employment for students with disabilities. To meaningfully contribute to the process of developing and integrating this workforce, employers will need to understand the contextual factors that impact employment-related training and employment for this young population.

Regulatory and Employer-Led Initiatives and Innovations

The last highlighted theme emerges across several chapters that discuss current regulatory, industry, and employer-led initiatives addressing historical employment disparities for individuals with disabilities. The specific chapters address how regulatory requirements for federal employer and federal contractor employers are providing data about the effectiveness of workplace disability inclusion policies and practices; employment opportunities in the fields of science, technology, engineering, and math (STEM) fields and the continuing challenges for individuals with disabilities; and employer-driven initiatives to explore pursuit of neurodiverse populations, particularly those with autism, as a source of talent to fill growing workforce needs, particularly in tech and tech-intensive industries.

In Chapter 2, "Minimizing Discrimination and Maximizing Inclusion: Lessons from the Federal Workforce and Federal Subcontractors," Hassan Enayati, Sarah von Schrader, William Erickson, and Susanne Bruyère take advantage of data collected on federal employees and federal contractors as required by federal regulations to examine how employer practices impact employment outcomes. Because these two sectors collectively represent approximately a quarter of all working Americans, the findings have significance for other employers as well. Both employer groups have target goals for the proportion of the workforce that should be composed of people with disabilities—currently 12% for federal sector agencies and 7% for federal contractors. The overarching conclusion from the data is that pursuing good policies and practices, as well as having targets and the ability to measure outcomes relative to the goals set, is advantageous both to the organization and to individual employees. Research results document that the federal government and federal contractors are more likely than private sector employers to have disability-inclusive policies and practices in place. The regulatory framework governing each sector has necessitated data collection that allows each employer sector to measure the effectiveness of its outreach and recruitment efforts and learn from efforts to improve practices and outcomes over time. Findings have also pointed to the importance of creating a climate of workplace disability inclusion that encourages and supports individuals with disabilities in disclosing their disability and need for accommodations, as well as being able to "bring their whole selves to the workplace."

In Chapter 9, "Employment in High-Tech Industries: What Does It Mean for People with Disabilities?," William Erickson, Sara VanLooy, and Wendy Strobel Gower discuss the possibilities for improved employment outcomes for individuals with disabilities afforded by high-growth "high tech" industries such as those in the STEM fields. High-tech firms play an important role in income, employment, and productivity growth overall and are often among the set of cutting-edge businesses that can drive economic growth. For example, as the authors point out, information technology jobs make up 14% of all open jobs across the United States and 10 of the 25 "best jobs in America." Post-secondary education has become increasingly vital for people to gain quality employment, and this is especially the case with STEM-related occupations. The authors discuss how access to these desirable jobs is often predicated on appropriate STEM-focused education at the bachelor's degree level or higher. However, even though young people with disabilities enter STEM education programs in similar proportions to their peers without disabilities, they are not making their way into STEM jobs in equitable numbers. To take advantage of the tremendous opportunities for employment that the high-tech sector offers young people with disabilities, more work is needed to understand whether lack of related work experience, self-confidence issues, employer bias, or something else is keeping STEM graduates with disabilities from successfully navigating to employment in comparable proportions to their nondisabled peers.

The last chapter relevant to the theme of industry-led innovations is Chapter 10, "Autism at Work: Targeted Hiring Initiatives and What We Can Learn for Other Groups," by Susanne Bruyère. Because individuals with autism are now the fastest-growing segment of the developmental disability population, and 85% of this population is unemployed or under-employed, it's a group very worthy of focus. This chapter calls attention to the way that high-tech and tech-intensive employers are now targeting this population as an untapped labor force because autistic individuals have characteristics that may advantage them in certain jobs, such as the ability to focus and to recognize patterns. It's a terrific example of how differences can be identified not as deviance that necessitates discard (from the employment process and therefore the labor force) but rather as potential advantages to business strategy. This shift of philosophy in perception of difference as a strategic business advantage—and how workplaces can accommodate such differences for mutual advantage—is the central message in this chapter. Employers pursuing "autism at work" initiatives are demonstrating a flexibility and creativity in recruiting, selection, interviewing, training, and retention strategies to heighten candidate success that many other previously marginalized and under-represented segments of the American population could benefit from. Such industry-led innovations deserve significant attention because they not only offer newfound opportunities for autistic individuals but may also contribute lessons learned that can present similar advantages for other largely untapped segments of the labor force.

The innovations and initiatives across these three examples illustrate the importance of regulations and attention to the multifaceted interventions needed for previously marginalized populations to take advantage of the employment afforded in high-growth industries. They also demonstrate how employers can lead the way in designing workplace systems that smooth the path for entry. We end this conclusion to the volume with a discussion of the relevance to labor and employment relations professionals of the themes that emerged across these chapters.

IMPLICATIONS FOR LABOR AND EMPLOYMENT RELATIONS PROFESSIONALS

The goal of this volume has been to raise visibility among labor and employment relations (LER) professionals about employment and disability issues so that they and other workplace professionals are aware of the continuing challenges in equitable employment participation for people with disabilities. By so doing, it is hoped that LER professionals can reflect on how they can best work to mitigate these continuing impediments to equity that may need to be addressed within the workplaces within which they practice. A number of specific takeaways for LER professionals have crystallized across these 12 chapters, including the importance of knowledge of regulatory environments; the value of having clearly articulated, effectively communicated, and enforced workplace disability-inclusive workplace policies and practices; the necessity of proactively building an internal organizational infrastructure for inclusion; the criticality of training supervisors, co-workers, and organizational leadership about organizational responsibilities and individual applicant and employee rights pertaining to employment equity; the need for leveraging relevant internal expertise and identifying community partnerships to fill needed skills and service gaps; and the merits of keeping related metrics and analytics to hold all stakeholders accountable for organizational progress across defined goals. Brief elaboration on each of these follows.

Knowledge of Employment and Disability Regulations

The nature of labor and employment relations practice means that LER professionals are well-versed in employment law. However, familiarity with the array of employment and disability-focused legislation and related regulations may be less common. With the demographics of an aging workforce, veterans with disabilities returning from conflict, an increase in mental health–related issues in the workplace, and the introduction of special hiring initiatives for targeted populations such as people with autism, this knowledge is becoming increasingly crucial. Vital implications of employment and disability regulations are laced throughout most chapters in this volume, with or without explicit emphasis. It is ever more important to have knowledge of the ADA, of regulations governing the federal sector workforce and private sector federal contractors, of occupational- and nonoccupational-related disability and health-related leave and benefits, and of laws regarding access to school-to-work transition and vocational training opportunities. Employers will want and need guidance on how to navigate these regulatory environments in order to reach their goals in innovative hiring initiatives and provide ongoing retention and equitable career progression of their ever-more diverse workforces. As multinational companies scale their disability-inclusive initiatives across national borders, knowledge of country-specific regulations governing disability and employment will also be imperative.

Workplace Disability Inclusive Policies and Practices

A significant number of the chapters of this book highlight the importance of embedding explicit attention to workplace disability inclusion within HR and workplace policies and practices. Additionally, a critical finding that accompanied these recommendations is the importance of communication about these policies.

It is not enough to merely have these policies in place; effective policies must designate point people or offices and explicit processes and clearly communicate them across the organization. This can be seen in the chapters that describe structures and procedures to support the accommodation process and disability self-disclosure. Other examples of this include descriptions of communicating a clear, consistent, and transparent process for the case-by-case provision of accommodation, creating a centralized accommodation fund, training managers and employees about rights and responsibilities under the ADA, and offering a grievance process that is fair and unbiased to encourage people to disclose their disabilities and request needed support before work performance is significantly impacted. Similarly, such clearly articulated processes are important in addressing concerns identified about disclosure, as well as in communicating appropriately about why disclosure data are being collected. Disability self-identification and disability disclosure, more generally, remain a complex issue for employers and employees alike: Known barriers to employee self-identification include a perceived risk of termination or loss of healthcare benefits, limitations on promotion opportunities, unsupportive management, and differential treatment by co-workers and supervisors (von Schrader, Malzer, and Bruyère 2014).

Building a Disability-Inclusive Organizational Infrastructure

The strongest base for disability inclusion policies in the workplace is a broader understanding of diversity and inclusion rooted in lessons learned working with other minority populations. Simply increasing the diversity of the workplace in terms of disability representation is not a sufficient goal or outcome. Rather, prior race and gender diversity studies have documented that true workplace disability inclusion needs to be managed and monitored across the entire employment process (Prieto, Phipps, and Osiri 2009, and discussed in this volume). It means creating a more inclusive environment from top to bottom by putting in place the necessary building blocks for true inclusion. Select elements for building a disability inclusive organizational infrastructure identified across the chapters in this volume are as follows:

- emphasizing the importance of top management commitment
- having processes in place for accommodations
- setting target diversity goals
- looking at where disparities might occur across the employment process
- communicating about expectations for inclusion and available resources to support delivery on desired outcomes
- using naturally occurring internal resources such as employee/business resource groups and employee assistance programs
- forming partnerships with external community service providers
- underscoring the responsibility that leadership, managers, and the general workforce have for building a climate for workplace inclusion, including for individuals with disabilities

LER professionals can assist organizational leadership in understanding the big picture on workplace disability inclusion, as well as the critical organizational infrastructure elements that must be in place to ensure that true inclusion will be possible over time.

Educating the Workforce

Providing effective education about differences in the workplace and broadening acceptance of and appreciation for diversity has been an ever-evolving challenge through gender, race/ethnicity, religion, generational, sexual orientation, and now disability considerations. Proactive communication by the company and education of the workforce as a whole is critical to mitigate potential issues before they arise and to facilitate longer-term inclusive behaviors. Training of supervisors and workplace professionals who are in the position to address these issues when they occur is a vital step in this process. Managers may not have the skills to assist with inclusive selection and interviewing, accommodations, and performance management of employees with disclosed disabilities; therefore, it is advisable that organizations develop training to raise awareness and skills, as well as cultivate expertise to address these issues at the central level. Because managers and supervisors may change roles or experience turnover in the organization, continued messaging and alternative training approaches such as online learning are critical in facilitating ongoing education for managers.

Equally important is education at all levels of the organization, not just for supervisors. Creating an appreciation of difference and true inclusion and providing basic training on civility and awareness of one's own biases are important elements. It is also vital that company leadership demonstrate good social intelligence and communication skills. When top leadership, along with mid-level managers, model positive, respectful behaviors that take into account the needs and diverse backgrounds of employees, they establish a fundamental expectation of the value of inclusion—of taking time to listen to and get to know workplace colleagues. This, in turn, opens the possibility of two-way communication in which employees are comfortable communicating to their supervisors and company leadership.

Leveraging Internal Expertise and Community Partnerships

An array of company internal resources and targeted community resources can significantly increase the effectiveness of disability-focused affirmative hiring initiatives, as well as retention of employees with disabilities and their career progression over time. Services such as workplace health and safety, employee assistance programs, and wellness programs, along with communication and training departments, can offer appropriate and targeted support if informed and aligned with the intent and activities of disability inclusion goals. For example, employee assistance programs could offer supports to individuals with disabilities and supervisors about conflict resolution pertaining to accommodation requests or issues in the performance management process, accommodation requests with a mental health focus, or issues that may surface in the aging with a disability process. If designed with accessibility in mind, organizational wellness programs can present a welcoming and inclusive climate to employees with disabilities and help to keep employees who are aging with a disability healthier over time. External community organizations are essential partners for a wide variety of other kinds of supportive services to maximize workplace disability inclusion. They can provide such services as sourcing qualified candidates with disabilities, assisting with design of inclusive selection and interviewing processes, job coaching on job entry or when job tasks or positions change, and providing consultation and training for supervisors. To be of assistance when issues arise, LER professionals will need to be aware of how existing internal organizational resources and targeted external community partnerships can support the building and sustainment of workplace disability inclusive initiatives and the necessary broader culture.

Metrics and Analytics to Assess Progress and Build Accountability

Finally, change in the employment status of people with disabilities will occur only if organizations and systems are holding themselves accountable by designing metrics and analytics to measure their progress against goals established. This requires first establishing an understanding of the current state of affairs, instituting measurable goals across the employment process, and assessing what existing or newly formulated measures can be put in place to hold the organization accountable to the desired outcomes. It is imperative that an organization tracks data, whether it is to ensure compliance with regulations and related workplace policies or to assess improvements in workplace climate over time. For example, the effectiveness of community-based partnerships in referring qualified candidates can be assessed by the annual number of referrals who make it to the interview stage and then to actual hiring. Accommodation data can assist in identifying which kinds of accommodations have been useful for specific types of disabilities in particular positions, locating vendors to provide particular accommodations, or recognizing recurring accommodation needs that can be proactively addressed by redesign of work stations or work spaces. In addition, areas where equity disparities commonly occur can be monitored when data kept for other under-represented populations are also kept for applicants and employees with disabilities. This includes data such as where people with disabilities are in particular job categories compared with their peers without disabilities, comparability of career progression and advancement opportunities, and compensation equity in particular job categories. LER professionals can play a role in assisting their organization in establishing such metrics and analytics, collecting the data, and regularly using this information to monitor progress over time.

FINAL THOUGHTS

The chapters included within this volume were specifically selected to be of interest and of use to labor and employment relations professionals. The themes that emerged across all the chapters highlight a final important point relevant to the field—that effective implementation of disability-inclusive policies, whether in response to disability nondiscrimination legislation or as part of a larger effort to create an inclusive workplace, relies heavily on *relations*. Successful inclusion of employees with disabilities comes out of the relationships between an organization and the community in which it is situated, and out of the relationships between employees, between manager and employee, between CEO and workforce. The practice recommendations summarized in this concluding chapter are, ultimately, a pathway to managing the network of interpersonal and interorganizational ties that affect the work experience of every individual and are the building blocks of every organization. When disability inclusion is addressed in this way, individuals and organizations both are the better for it.

REFERENCES

Prieto, L.C., S.T.A. Phipps, and J.K. Osiri. 2009. "Linking Workplace Diversity to Organizational Performance: A Conceptual Framework." *Journal of Diversity Management* 4 (4): 13–22. doi:10.19030/jdm.v4i4.4966

von Schrader, S., V. Malzer, and S.M. Bruyère. 2014. "Perspectives on Disability Disclosure: The Importance of Employer Practices and Workplace Climate." *Employee Responsibilities and Rights Journal* 26 (4): 237–255. doi:10.1007/s10672-013-9227-9

About the Contributors

Ola Abu Alghaib is manager of the United Nations Partnership on the Rights of Persons with Disabilities, part of the United Nations Development Programme (UNDP). She has over 20 years of experience working on issues relating to gender and disability in development, including in fragile and crisis-affected settings in the Arab states, Africa, and Asia. She joined UNDP from her position as a director for global influencing and research at Leonard Cheshire Disability, London. During the past 10 years, she has worked with global, regional, and country offices of several UN agencies (ILO, WHO, UNDP, UNESCO, UNESCWA, and UNICEF) as an expert to support their work in disability-inclusive policies and programs. Alghaib also served as vice chair of the international Disability and Development Consortium and as a board member of the Disability Rights Funds. She was recently featured in the Gender Equality Top 100 list of the most influential people in global policy in 2019. She has a Ph.D. in social protection from the University of East Anglia.

Mohammad Ali is an associate professor of management in the School of Business Administration at Pennsylvania State University–Harrisburg. Previously, he taught for the School of Management at the New York Institute of Technology. He earned his doctorate in management from Rutgers University. His dissertation addressed stakeholder management, and he continues to explore that topic and its benefits to businesses. Ali's research has been published in the *Journal of Workplace Rights*, *Advances in Industrial and Labor Relations*, *Journal of Occupational Rehabilitation*, *Monthly Labor Review*, and others.

Mason Ameri is an assistant professor of professional practice at Rutgers Business School and specializes in managing diversity by analyzing equal access opportunities for people with disabilities in the workplace and the sharing economy. This applied research has been profiled in more than 100 media outlets, including *The New York Times*, *Los Angeles Times*, *The Washington Post*, *Forbes*, *The Guardian*, and "PBS NewsHour." His published works can be found in *Academy of Management Discoveries*, *IZA Institute of Labor Economics*, *Industrial and Labor Relations Review*, and others, which has led him to earn the Excellence in Scholarly Contributions Award at Rutgers Business School. He teaches in the areas of management skills, organizational behavior, human resource management, and negotiations and has earned the prestigious Presidential Award for Excellence in Teaching at Rutgers University and the Dean's Meritorious Teaching Award at Rutgers Business School.

Susanne M. Bruyère is a professor of disability studies and the director of the Yang–Tan Institute on Employment and Disability at Cornell University's ILR School. She has served as the director or co-director of numerous federally sponsored research, dissemination, and technical assistance efforts focused on employment and disability policy and effective workplace practices for people with disabilities and served as the director of Cornell University's faculty–staff health program. She is a past president of the Division of Rehabilitation Psychology of the American Psychological Association, the American Rehabilitation Counseling Association, and the National Council on Rehabilitation Education. Bruyère holds a doctoral degree in rehabilitation counseling psychology from the University of Wisconsin–Madison, is a Fellow in the American Psychological Association, a member of the National Academy of Social Insurance, and currently serves as an executive board member of the Division of Rehabilitation Psychology of the American Psychological Association. She also is past chair of GLADNET (the Global Applied Disability Research and Information Network on Employment and Training), as well as past chair and a current board member of the Commission on Accreditation of Rehabilitation Facilities.

Hsiao-Ying (Vicki) Chang is a research associate at the Yang–Tan Institute at Cornell University. She is a certified rehabilitation counselor and has more than five years of experience in research and supporting people with disabilities. She received her Ph.D. in counselor education and supervision from Pennsylvania State University, a master's degree in rehabilitation and mental health counseling from the University of Iowa, and a bachelor's degree in psychology, also from the University of Iowa. Her work emphasizes mixed-methods research methodology and program evaluation in disability education. Chang's research interests aim to promote awareness of disability culture; improve rehabilitation services, education, and employment for people with a disability; and link research findings to counseling practices.

Kelly Clark is the director of transition and educational achievement at Cornell University's Yang–Tan Institute on Employment and Disability. Her research has primarily focused on the development of an intervention to teach soft skills for employment using components of self-determination and technology-aided instruction. Other work has focused on interventions that combine components of self-determination with academic skills, effective professional development practices, and international special education services. Clark has a master's in school administration from the University of North Carolina–Charlotte. During her doctoral work at that university, she served as a graduate research assistant for the National Technical Assistance Center on Transition. Before pursuing graduate studies, Clark was a secondary special education teacher.

LaWanda Cook is an extension faculty associate with the Yang–Tan Institute on Employment and Disability at Cornell University's ILR School. She designs and delivers training on the Americans with Disabilities Act and engages in research related to disability identity, the well-being of individuals with disabilities, and the inclusion of people with disabilities in work and leisure settings. Her work explores an array of issues that impact the lives of individuals with disabilities, including the intersection of disability with characteristics such as race, gender, and age, as well as concerns such as workplace bullying and harassment. Cook's research is supported by many years as a practitioner in vocational counseling and staff development. She holds a Ph.D. in recreation, sport, and tourism from the University of Illinois at Urbana-Champaign, with an emphasis on the work and life balance of employed people with disabilities.

Hassan Enayati is a research associate with the Yang–Tan Institute on Employment and Disability at Cornell University and with the Cornell ILR School Institute for Compensation Studies. His work specializes in methodological approaches to labor economics, and he is currently examining the outcomes of the New York State PROMISE (Promoting the Readiness of Minors in Supplemental Security Income) project. Enayati obtained his Ph.D. in labor economics from Michigan State University, funded by an Economics of Education Program Fellowship under the Institute for Education Sciences (IES). As part of his IES appointment, Enayati worked with the Michigan Consortium for Educational Research in the building and analysis of administrative education data for all Michigan public school students from their elementary through post-secondary education.

William Erickson is currently a research specialist with the Yang–Tan Institute on Employment and Disability in the ILR School's Extension Division at Cornell University. His current projects include public and private sector employer surveys on the implementation of disability regulations and legislation and the development of customized estimates of disability statistics using a variety of publicly available data sets. Erickson has a master's degree in human environment relations from the Department of Design and Environmental Analysis at Cornell University.

Catherine H. Fowler is a project coordinator for the National Technical Assistance Center on Transition at the University of North Carolina–Charlotte, a program funded by the Office of Special Education and Rehabilitative Services. In that role, she provides technical assistance to states on such topics as using data to make system-level decisions on secondary transition programs, using transition assessment information to develop transition-focused individualized education programs, and implementing evidence-based practices to improve student outcomes. Previously, Fowler worked for the National Secondary Transition Technical

Assistance Center, the Self-Determination Technical Assistance Center, and the Self-Advocacy Synthesis Project. She has also worked as a developmental disabilities specialist, providing service coordination and educational intervention services to families of young children with development disabilities and as a classroom teacher of middle-grade students with autism and elementary age students with intellectual disabilities in the Charlotte–Mecklenburg schools.

Thomas P. Golden is the executive director of the Yang–Tan Institute on Employment and Disability in the ILR School at Cornell University. Since joining the Cornell faculty in 1991, his learning, practice, research, and publications have focused in four primary areas as they relate to individuals with disabilities: social insurance policy and its relation to return to work and greater economic independence and self-sufficiency; transition planning for youth to live, learn, and earn in their communities as adults; organizational behavior and systems change, with an emphasis on facilitating inclusive communities and integrated service delivery options; and workforce development and vocational rehabilitation. As a faculty member, he teaches in the disability studies sequence in the ILR School and has managed over $250 million in federal and state-sponsored research, training, and organizational development initiatives focused on community participation and inclusion of people with disabilities. Golden received a master's degree in science in rehabilitation counseling from Syracuse University and has a doctorate in education from George Washington University.

Wendy Strobel Gower is a project director at the Yang–Tan Institute on Employment and Disability in the ILR School at Cornell University. She leads the Northeast ADA Center, the Diversity Partners Project, and fee-for-service work to educate managers and supervisors about including people with disabilities. She holds a master's degree in rehabilitation counseling from the Medical College of Virginia at Virginia Commonwealth University. She has worked extensively in the application and training of issues around employment and reasonable accommodation in the workplace for people with disabilities, gaining valuable experience in project management and project direction over the past ten years. Other areas of interest include person-centered planning philosophy and tools, disability legislation and its impact on services, and the identification and accommodation of the functional limitations of disabilities across the lifespan.

Douglas Kruse is a Distinguished Professor in the School of Management and Labor Relations at Rutgers University and a research associate at the National Bureau of Economic Research. He served as senior economist on the Council of Economic Advisers in 2013–2014. He received a master's degree in economics from the University of Nebraska–Lincoln and a Ph.D. in economics from

Harvard University. His research has focused on the employment and earnings effects of disability and the causes, consequences, and implications of employee ownership and profit sharing. His most recent co-authored books are *The Citizen's Share: Reducing Inequality in the 21st Century, People with Disabilities: Sidelined or Mainstreamed?* and *Shared Capitalism at Work*. He has published widely in peer-reviewed journals and is an editor of the *British Journal of Industrial Relations*. He has testified four times before the US Congress on his economic research, authored or co-authored three US Department of Labor Studies, and served on the President's Committee on Employment of People with Disabilities.

Valerie Malzer is a research specialist at Cornell University's Yang–Tan Institute on Employment and Disability. In that role, she provides technical assistance to research sites and designs and implements program evaluation and research activities using qualitative, quantitative, and mixed-method designs. Her primary areas of focus are transition to adulthood for youth, workplace experiences, and employer-focused programming to increase and improve workforce participation for individuals with disabilities.

Jennifer Mimno joined Cornell University's Yang–Tan Institute in April 2014. She is the project coordinator for the New York State Consortium for Advancing and Supporting Employment and provides project support for the New York State PROMISE (Promoting the Readiness of Minors in Supplemental Security Income) project, Work–Life Balance project, and various other projects at the Yang–Tan Institute. Mimno previously worked for the Peabody Museum at Harvard University as a curatorial assistant, where she assisted the director of collections with research projects and helped inventory the museum collections. She also has prior experience as a freelance editor.

Lorin Obler is a senior analyst with the US Government Accountability Office (GAO), a nonpartisan research arm of the US Congress. He has been with GAO's Education, Workforce, and Income Security team throughout his 18-year tenure with the agency. Much of his work has involved reviews of federal programs serving people with disabilities or promoting workforce development, including those administered by the Social Security Administration, Department of Veterans Affairs, and Department of Labor. Obler holds a bachelor's degree from Swarthmore College and a master's in public policy from the Harvard Kennedy School.

Hannah Rudstam completed her Ph.D. at the University of Wisconsin–Madison, Following that, she worked as a program planner and evaluator at the Royal Adult Learning Academy in Stockholm. Back in the United States, she became a senior research scientist at the University of Wisconsin, researching a statewide health risk prevention program. After relocating to the upstate New York area, she took a position as a senior organizational development consultant at United

Technologies and then at Eagle Consultants in Syracuse. In that capacity, she designed tools for hiring, performance management, and employee development systems. Also, she developed a turnover prevention program that has been adopted by a number of national and global organizations. In 2004, she took her current position as senior extension faculty with the Yang–Tan Institute at Cornell University. In that role, she conducts research and creates programming on a range of topics related to disability and employment and presents at state, national, and international conferences. More recently, she has focused her research and program development on three key issues. First, how can employers create effective workplace policies for the significant number of employees who are working with a mental illness? Second, what are the employment barriers faced by veterans with disabilities and how can employers create workplace practices that are responsive to their needs? Third, how can knowledge translation approaches be applied to disability and employment issues?

Matthew C. Saleh is a member of the research faculty at Cornell University's Yang–Tan Institute on Employment and Disability. He received his J.D. from Syracuse University and his Ph.D. from Columbia University. Saleh was a 2015–2016 US Fulbright Scholar in Barbados, where he studied the impact of social networks and service coordination in school-to-work transition for youth with disabilities. At Cornell, his responsibilities include project leadership for the program fidelity and collaborative network study for New York State PROMISE (Promoting the Readiness of Minors in Supplemental Security Income), a federal initiative providing case management, service coordination, and transition-based services to youth (ages 14–16) and families receiving supplemental security income in New York.

Lisa Schur is a professor and chair of the Department of Labor Studies and Employment Relations at Rutgers University. Her focus is on disability issues in employment and labor law, particularly the Americans with Disabilities Act and its relationship to other laws and social policies. She also studies alternative work arrangements such as contingent work and the connections between workplace experiences and political participation. Her work has appeared in *Industrial and Labor Relations Review*, *Social Science Quarterly*, *Political Research Quarterly*, *Industrial Relations*, and other journals. Schur is co-author of the 2013 book *People with Disabilities: Sidelined or Mainstreamed*, part of the Cambridge Disability Law and Policy Series.

Ellice Switzer joined Cornell University's Yang–Tan Institute in 2012. She has nearly 20 years of university and nonprofit experience in the field of disability. She develops content across multiple modalities and provides national-level technical assistance and training on topics related to disability and employment and US disability policy under grants from the US Department of Health and Human

Services, Administration for Community Living. Switzer is also a project associate with the New York State Transition Services Professional Development Support Center and provides consultation and content development expertise on topics related to the intersection of special education transition services and disability policy to support regional transition specialists throughout the state.

Sara VanLooy is a publications and administrative assistant at the Yang–Tan Institute on Employment and Disability at Cornell University, providing administrative, research, editing, and writing support on numerous projects. She currently provides research and editorial support to the Yang–Tan Institute research team and to the New York State PROMISE (Promoting the Readiness of Minors in Supplemental Security Income) project. She previously worked at the University of Missouri journalism library.

Sarah von Schrader is assistant director of research in the Yang–Tan Institute on Employment and Disability at Cornell University. Her research focuses on employer practices related to success in recruiting, hiring, and advancing individuals with disabilities. She continues to work on a long-term project using discrimination charge data from the US Equal Employment Opportunity Commission. She received her doctorate in education measurement and statistics from the University of Iowa in 2006 and bachelor's degree in mathematics from Colorado College in 1994. von Schrader previously worked in the fields of health policy and management, educational testing, and evaluation.

James Whitcomb is an assistant director for the Education, Workforce, and Income Security team at the US Government Accountability Office, focusing on federal disability programs. He previously served as a senior analyst, where his work focused on disability issues at the Department of Veterans Affairs and the Social Security Administration, as well as on polling place accessibility for people with disabilities. Whitcomb has also worked on performance budgeting, education, and workforce issues. He holds a master's in public administration from George Washington University and a bachelor's degree in history from Moravian College.

LERA Executive Board Members 2019–20